PANTHEISM

PANTHEISM

A non-theistic concept of
deity

Michael P. Levine

London and New York

First published 1994
by Routledge
11 New Fetter Lane, London EC4P 4EE

Simultaneously published in the USA and Canada
by Routledge
29 West 35th Street, New York, NY 10001

Phototypeset in Baskerville by
Intype, London

Printed and bound in Great Britain by
TJ Press Ltd, Padstow, Cornwall

British Library Cataloguing in Publication Data

A catalogue record for this book is available from the British Library

Library of Congress Cataloging in Publication Data
Levine, Michael P. (Michael Philip)
Pantheism : a non-theistic concept of deity / Michael P. Levine.
p. cm.
Includes bibliographical references and index.
1. Pantheism. I. Title
BL220.L48 1994
211'.2–dc20   93–34726

ISBN 0–415–07064–3

Buddha in Glory

Center of all centers, core of cores,
almond self-enclosed and growing sweet -
all this universe, to the furthest stars
and beyond them, is your flesh, your fruit.

Now you feel how nothing clings to you;
your vast shell reaches into endless space,
and there the rich, thick fluids rise and flow.
Illuminated in your infinite peace,

a billion stars go spinning through the night,
blazing high above your head.
But *in* you is the presence that
will be, when all the stars are dead.

Rilke
(translated by Stephen Mitchell)

Stephen Mitchell, editor and translator, *The Selected Poetry of Rainer Maria Rilke* (New York: Random House, 1982)

CONTENTS

Part III Method

PREFACE

The book recognised as containing the most complete attempt at explaining and defending pantheism from a philosophical perspective is Spinoza's *Ethics*, finished in 1675 two years before his death. In 1720 John Toland wrote the *Pantheisticon: or The Form of Celebrating the Socratic-Society* in Latin. He (possibly) coined the term "pantheist" and used it as a synonym for "Spinozist." However, aside from some interesting pantheistic sounding slogans like "Every Thing is to All, as All is to Every Thing", and despite promising "A Short Dissertation upon a Twofold Philosophy of the Pantheists" Toland's work has little to do with pantheism. As far as I know, aside from Thomas McFarland's excellent study *Coleridge and the Pantheist Tradition* (Oxford: Oxford University Press, 1969) there has been no other full-length work on pantheism since Spinoza's *Ethics*. McFarland's book is not intended as a philosophical investigation of pantheism although it contains much useful philosophical material.

Of course there have been many studies of Spinoza's *Ethics* and so indirectly many studies of pantheism. Historically, however, pantheism has numerous forms and Spinoza's version is best considered as one among many variations, albeit a particularly philosophical variation, on pantheistic themes. In short – and surprisingly in my view – not only is there no recent book-length philosophical examination of the concept itself, there seems to be no such study at any time. No extended analysis of the concept itself exists apart from discussion of particular pantheists such as Spinoza, Hegel (?), Plotinus (?), Eriugena, or the study of pantheistic aspects of religious and philosophical traditions such as those found in some of the Presocratics.

This book is intended to fill what I see as a surprisingly broad

– and somewhat mysterious – lacuna. Given the interest in pantheism, and given that it is the classic religious alternative to theism, I do not understand why there has been no philosophical investigation of it.

I should remark that as far as I can tell I am not a pantheist. It is a regrettable sign of the times that an intellectual endeavour of this sort appears to place one in a camp of some kind. Unlike much – not all – of the mainstream philosophy of religion currently being published, this work is neither a profession of faith nor an outline of an evangelical agenda. It is simply a work in natural theology. Contemporary analytic philosophy of religion (mostly "christian") has become a task undertaken by the brethren, for the brethren – and it is often startlingly parochial.

I am at home, philosophically speaking, in less wide open spaces. Yet, given my interest in the philosophy of religion, and a deepening dissatisfaction with some of the provincialism and idle expertise belabouring traditional theism, I find myself with little choice but to answer – like a shabby wild-eyed desert dwelling but unprophetic character, or an overly intellectual indoor-loving Jack London protagonist – the call of the wild. I hope, then, that this book will appear as a howl – not a hoot.

Michael P. Levine

ACKNOWLEDGMENTS

I have been working on this project for a long time and I completed sections of it while holding various research and teaching positions. I gratefully acknowledge the support of the following: the University of Western Australia; the Australian Academy of Humanities and Social Sciences and the Chinese Academy of Social Sciences, for a research grant to the People's Republic of China (1987); La Trobe University Research Fellowship, Melbourne, Australia (1986–7); Andrew W. Mellon Postdoctoral Fellowship in the Humanities, University of Pennsylvania (1985–6); Andrew W. Mellon Postdoctoral Fellowship in the Humanities, Center for Advanced Studies, University of Virginia (1983–5).

Earlier versions of some of the chapters first appeared in journals. "Unity" appeared as "Divine Unity and Superfluous Synonymity," *Journal of Speculative Philosophy*, 4 (1990), pp. 211–36; "Monism" appeared as "Pantheism, Substance and Unity," *International Journal for Philosophy of Religion*, 32 (1992), pp. 1–23; "Monism and Pantheism" appeared in the *Southern Journal of Philosophy*, 30 (1992), pp. 95–110; "Transcendence" appeared as "Transcendence in Theism and Pantheism," *Sophia*, 31 (1992), pp. 89–123; "Ethics and Ecology" appeared as "Pantheism, Ethics and Ecology," *Journal of Environmental Values* (1994). My thanks to the editors of these journals for permission to use this material; and to Random House Publishers for permission to reprint Rainer Maria Rilke's poem "Buddha in Glory" in Stephen Mitchell, editor and translator, *The Selected Poetry of Rainer Maria Rilke* (New York: Random House, 1982).

Mary Ellen Trahan bore the brunt of the early bibliographical research necessary to this work and I thank her. I am especially grateful to Kim Grant for her editing and comments. I am indebted to the following people (among others) for discussion and interest: Lorna Aikman, Ira Auerbach, Lee Carter; Marie-Louise Carroll; Wendell Dietrich; Sue Dodds; Robyn Ferrell; Colleen Henry; Jeff Malpas; Behan McCullough; Dov Midalia; Page Nelson-Saginor; Jocelyn Rappaport; John P. Reeder Jr; Ted Roberts; Robert Scharlemann; Stewart Sutherland – in whose series the book was long ago to be published; Alan Tapper; Robert Young and Susan Williamson.

My mother still on occasion asks me what I do, but thankfully she has stopped suggesting accountancy as a suitable career – despite the fact that, "they do very well you know." Judi, Madeline, Susan and Debbie are my sisters, and I am their brother, and there is something so marvellously familial about it that it is to them I not only dedicate this book but promise to send a copy. The book is also in memory of my father Charles C. Levine.

1

INTRODUCTION

There are two and only two systems of philosophy that can
be offered. The one posits God as the transcendent cause
of things; the other makes God the immanent cause. The
former carefully distinguishes and separates God from the
world; the latter shamefully confounds God with the
universe . . . The former establishes a foundation for every
religious devotion and for all piety, and this the latter fundamentally overturns and takes away.[1]

Christoph. Wittich

There is a great deal of confusion as to what pantheism is, and
so I begin by defining pantheism and distinguishing it from
theism. I then argue that pantheism is not atheism. The remain-
der of the introduction describes the general scope and outline
of the book, and some of its principal contentions.

Pantheism is a metaphysical and religious position. Broadly
defined it is the view that (1) "God is everything and everything
is God . . . the world is either identical with God or in some way
a self-expression of his nature" (H.P. Owen). Similarly, it is the
view that (2) everything that exists constitutes a "unity" and this
all-inclusive unity is in some sense divine (A. MacIntyre).[2] A
slightly more specific definition is given by Owen who says (3)
"'Pantheism' . . . signifies the belief that every existing entity is,
only one Being; and that all other forms of reality are either
modes (or appearances) of it or identical with it" (p. 65).[3]

What is the relevant sense of "unity" in pantheism's "all-inclusive divine unity"? What is meant by "all-inclusive"? What is meant
by calling it "divine"? These issues are taken up in Part I where

1

the meaning of pantheism is examined. Prominent misunder-
standings of pantheism are discussed in section 2.1.

Theism is the belief in a "personal" God which in some sense
is separate from (i.e. transcends) the world. (Theists just about
always believe God to be a "person." But few theists hold that
God is completely transcendent.) Where pantheism is considered
as an *alternative* to theism and atheism, rather than compatible
with either, it involves a denial of at least one, and possibly both,
central theistic claims. Pantheists usually deny the existence of a
"personal" God. They deny the existence of a "minded" Being
that possesses the characteristic properties of a "person," such as
having "intentional" states, and the associated capacities like the
ability to make decisions. Taken as an alternative to, and denial
of, theism and atheism, pantheists deny that what they mean by
God (i.e. an all-inclusive divine Unity) is completely transcendent.
They deny that God is "totally other" than the world. As Owen
says, "although pantheists differ among themselves at many
points, they all agree in denying the basic theistic claim that God
and the world are ontologically distinct" (p. 65).

What does it means to say that pantheists believe that God and
the world are not "ontologically distinct" – and is this really
a requirement? This requirement is based on the pantheistic
identification (in some sense) of God and the world. But the
idea that the all-inclusive divine Unity must be ontologically identical to the world is questionable. The relevance of ontology, the
question of ontological identification or distinctness, is something
of a red herring as we shall see. For now, it suffices to know
that pantheism denies that the divine Unity and the world are
"ontologically distinct" if this is taken to mean that the Unity is
"totally other" than the world. It does not mean that finite entities
and the pantheistic God (i.e. the divine Unity) may not be distinct. The totality that is a divine Unity may allow for the existence
of ontologically real and separate entities. In terms of the theism/
pantheism contrast, where theism claims God is transcendent,
pantheism claims God is radically immanent. But pantheists need
not claim that there are no transcendent aspects to the divine
Unity. Pantheists may maintain the divine Unity's immanence
without denying (1) that the divine Unity and finite entities are
ontologically distinct or (2) that there are transcendent aspects
to the pantheistic Unity.

With some exceptions, pantheism is non-theistic, but it is not atheistic. It is a form of non-theistic monotheism, or non-personal theism. It is the belief in one God, a God identical to the all-inclusive unity, but it does not believe God is a person or anything like a person.[4] The fact that pantheism *clearly* is not atheistic, and is an explicit denial of atheism, is rather astonishingly overlooked or disputed by its critics. In his non-pantheistic phase, Coleridge claimed that "every thing God, and no God, are identical positions."[5] Owen says, "if 'God' (theos) is identical with the Universe (to pan) it is merely another name for the Universe. It is therefore bereft of any distinctive meaning; so that pantheism is equivalent to atheism ... [pp. 69–70] ... taken strictly it [pantheism] is equivalent to atheism" (p. 74). Similarly, Schopenhauer said that "to call the world 'God' is not to explain it; it is only to enrich our language with a superfluous synonym for the word 'world.' "[6] Schopenhauer's view is discussed in the section on Unity.

The primary reason for equating pantheism with atheism pertains to non-personalistic types of pantheism (i.e. most types). The critic simply presupposes that there can be no such thing as non-personal theism. It is assumed that belief in any kind of "God" must be belief in a personalistic God, because God must be a person. Though not explicitly referring to pantheism here, Rudolf Otto says:

> We need not dispute that the denial of personality to God is simply a disguised form of atheism, or betokens a desperate attempt to equate faith with belief in natural law and with naturalism. But it would be a huge error to suppose that anything of this kind is in the mind of the mystics when they set themselves to oppose the idea of personality in deity.[7]

Otto is discussing the "origin of that tendency to let the conception of personality and the personal ... be submerged in ... 'nothingness', a tendency which is in appearance so irreligious." However, since Otto allows that in the case of mysticism the denial of personality to God is merely irreligious in appearance, then surely the same can be said of pantheists who, as non-personal theists, *never* equate their God (i.e. the divine unity) with the world *simpliciter*, simply with belief in natural law, or with mere naturalism.

If non-personal theism is assumed incoherent, then there can be no intelligible forms of pantheism that deny the application of personalistic concepts to a pantheistic unity (God). But what reason is there, even *prima facie*, to make this assumption? It is question begging to assume that pantheism, or any kind of belief in "God," must conceive of God as a person if it is to count as belief in "God." It is a refusal to take pantheism, and other non-theistic types of belief in God, to be types of belief in God because they deny God is personal. The limitation is stipulative and unduly restricts the extent to which alternative theories of deity can be formulated. Pantheism cannot even be taken as a theory of deity on such a· view. If, contrary to what most pantheists believe, pantheism has to conceive of God as a "person," then it must be a kind of personal theism. And if there are problems, as there surely are, inherent in conceptions of God as a person, then these would exist for pantheism as well. There is little reason, however, to accept the theistic restriction on what can count as God – even for a theist.

The charge that pantheism is atheistic is as old as pantheism itself. Christopher Rowe says,

> When Cicero's Velleius describes Speusippus' pantheism as an attempt to "root out the notion of gods from our minds", he is echoing a charge which was commonly made against the pantheism of the earlier Greek natural philosophers . . . like Anaximander or Heraclitus. These tended to be identi-fied as atheists in the popular mind; and indeed Plato him-self implies a similar view . . . the opponents who classify them as atheists are in reality attacking them for under-mining traditional beliefs about the gods – or, to borrow a phrase from the indictment against Socrates, "for not believ-ing in the gods the city believes in". (In Plato's *Apology*, one of the prosecutors, Meleteus, is portrayed as feeling no embarrassment about accusing Socrates of being an atheist, at the same time as formally charging him with "introducing new divinities") . . . The puzzling statement attributed to Thales . . . that "everything is full of gods" [Aristotle, *Physics* 203 b 10ff.] . . . may well imply a deliberate criticism of conventional religion; the gods, Thales may be saying, are not to be found, or merely to be found . . . where they are placed by traditional belief, but are much more widely present in nature.
>
> (Rowe, pp. 54–5)

The claim of Schopenhauer, Coleridge (who at one time was a pantheist), and others who charge that pantheism is atheistic is either an oblique way of saying that pantheists do not believe in a theistic God, which is both true and trivial; or it is based on their assessment of what the central claim of pantheism finally amounts to – that belief in a divine Unity is equivalent to atheism. Of course, pantheists do not deny that they do not believe in a theistic God, but they do deny that their position is atheistic. Clearly the assertion of a divine unity is meant to be a denial of atheism. Rowe says "it may very well be that from the philosophical point of view, pantheism and atheism may be very close together. But the Presocratics are certainly not atheistic by intention" (p. 54). Rowe's point is applicable to other pantheists as well. Pantheism is not meant to be atheism – and it cannot be atheism if atheism is the denial of both a theistic and a nontheistic God. Furthermore, there is no reason to suppose that "from the philosophical point of view, pantheism and atheism may be very close together."

Since atheism is an unacceptable interpretation of what pantheists intend to assert, the view that pantheism is atheistic must be defended in terms of an analysis of what the position amounts to (i.e. entails). But, no such analysis could be successful given that pantheism involves, as part of its meaning, the denial of atheism. Any reductionist account of pantheism that eliminates God is no longer an account of pantheism. Of course, the pantheistic view concerning the nature of God may be incoherent. When implications of pantheistic claims about the divine unity are examined, it may turn out that their notion of God cannot be what they would have liked or thought it to be. Nevertheless, no analysis can show that pantheism is atheistic since the denial of atheism is intrinsic to the position. At most, what Schopenhauer, Coleridge, Owen etc. can show, and probably all they intend, is either that the pantheistic Unity can be explained in terms that would eliminate the notion of deity from pantheism altogether, or that it is incoherent. They want to show that believing in a pantheistic God is a convoluted and confused way of believing in something that can adequately be described apart from any notion of deity – and in this they are mistaken.

Showing that a particular pantheistic concept of deity is incoherent is different from showing that pantheism is atheistic. If the theistic notion of deity were shown to be incoherent, it would follow that such a deity could not be instantiated. However, it would not mean that theists were really atheists. If "God" as conceived of by theists is incoherent, then some suitable revision of the concept of a theistic God would be required that would retain as many of the essential features of that concept as possible. The object of the theist's belief may be incoherent without their being atheists. Similarly, showing that a pantheistic notion of deity is incoherent does not indicate that pantheism is atheism. It shows that the pantheistic concept of deity needs to be reformulated so as to resolve the incoherency without giving up (if possible) what is regarded as essential to the concept. In short, pantheists cannot be atheists since belief in God (i.e. in a divine Unity) is essential to pantheism.

The claim that "pantheists are atheists" may also be another way of saying that pantheists do not believe in the existence of a theistic deity, which is true, but uninteresting. (Even pantheists who believe the divine unity is personal or a person do not believe in the theistic God.) I do not think this is what Schopenhauer etc. have in mind. Rather, they want to show that the pantheistic God cannot plausibly be termed "God." If their term for God (the all-inclusive divine Unity) does refer to anything it cannot be God. It must be something like the "world." The claim is that when pantheists purport to talk about God they are really talking about the world. I have argued that this is not possible. They may be talking about the world as in fact they claim to be; but pantheists cannot plausibly be interpreted as talking about the world apart from God.

Pantheists deny God's ontological transcendence. The divine Unity is radically immanent in the world. H.D. Lewis describes transcendence as referring to "the peculiar 'beyondness' or 'otherness' of God implied in the perfection ... of His nature ... as distinguishing Him altogether from any of His creatures."[8] The idea of God's transcendence is so central to religion in general and theism in particular that religion is sometimes defined as the belief in "another dimension," or in God(s) that are "separate" from the world. God is conceived of as transcending the spatio-temporal world; and depending on what one takes this to imply, various metaphysical, logical and epistemological issues arise. For example, if God (due to his "otherness") is transcendent in a radically epistemic sense, then how is any knowledge of God possible? And if such knowledge is impossible, how can one conceptualise or talk about God? If one cannot conceive of God because he is "other," then how can one know anything about God?[9] Or, if God is conceived of as ontologically and metaphysically distinct, how is it possible to have anything to do with God, or for God to have anything to do with the world?

Given this partial account of transcendence and religion it is not difficult to see why the "problem of transcendence" is the central philosophical problem for theism and philosophy of religion in general. There are tensions between the concept of a transcendent God on the one hand and the primary goal of religion as a "relation" to God, an overcoming of transcendence, on the other. The deistic idea that God is completely transcendent sees the pursuit of a relationship to God as essentially misdirected. If God is completely transcendent, religion may perhaps still be seen as a foundation of morality, and a basis for happiness – though it is unlikely. But its explicitly stated goal of "salvation" as a relation to God must be regarded as a chimera.

Issues in theism involving the concept of transcendence include theories concerning God's nature; creation; revelation; incarnation; salvation; knowledge of God (including mystical knowledge); and the problem of evil – where the "distinctness" between God and the world is stressed by way of establishing God's lack of responsibility for evil.[10] An analysis of transcendence is an important element in addressing these, but so is the notion of divine immanence. Pantheism, as a doctrine of divine immanence, offers distinct formulations of these issues, and distinct solutions. The dichotomy between transcendence and immanence has been a principal source of philosophical and religious concern in Western and non-Western traditions; and all major traditions have at times turned to pantheism as a way of resolving difficulties associated with the theistic notion of a transcendent deity or reality.[11]

Since most types of pantheism deny that the divine Unity is transcendent in what theism regards as a significant sense (e.g. ontological or epistemological), pantheism can be seen as a radical solution to the theistically generated "problem(s) of transcendence." Not only does the pantheist sometimes conceive of the divine Unity as the immanent as opposed to transcendent cause of the universe; it is also conceived of as all-inclusive;

7

something one is part of and can relate to; and both a possible and a desirable object of knowledge. The divine Unity is not a "creator" in the theistic sense, though it may be an immanent "cause" of the universe – as for Spinoza. Whether pantheism requires a doctrine of creation is discussed in section 4.1.

Not all of the problems generated by the theistic notion of God are also problems for pantheism. But given a suitable reformulation, some of them will be. And, as expected, pantheism will also generate some difficulties peculiar to itself. Thus, although evil and creation do not present identical problems for pantheism and theism, and may even be inherent to theism, it *may* also be possible to reformulate them in a way that makes them applicable to pantheism. There may be pantheistic counterparts to the problem of evil and other classical theistic problems, and perhaps they can be resolved by pantheism.[12]

In comparing the cogency and plausibility of theism versus pantheism, it is necessary to determine (1) which theistic problems are applicable to pantheism; (2) whether pantheistic versions of traditional theistic problems (e.g. evil) can be more plausibly resolved by pantheism than by theism; and (3) whether pantheism introduces problems that do not have any theistic counterpart and that affect its cogency compared with theism. Some of these issues are taken up in Part II. I give an account of how some philosophical/theological problems associated with theism can be recast in pantheism, and how they might be resolved.

Rāmānujua with his "qualified non-dualism" (the world as the body of God), and recently Robert Oakes and Grace Jantzen, are among those who claim that pantheism is not merely compatible with theism, but essential to it. I discuss some alleged relations between theism and pantheism in Chapter 3 and other places in Part II, and deny some of the connections between them that have been posited.

The type of pantheism I am concerned with is non-theistic – the kind, as I have said, that denies God is a "person" and transcendent. The reason for this is that I want to consider pantheism as an alternative to theism, especially in terms of religious practice, rather than as an extension of it. The limitation is justified because pantheism and theism are generally regarded as mutually exclusive. Furthermore, if one finds theism implausible, it is doubtful that grafting aspects of pantheism onto theism, or arguing that they are intrinsically connected, will make either position more plausible.

Of course, this is not necessarily the case. Grace Jantzen claims that it is correct to regard theism as pantheistic in some respects, and doing so makes theism more plausible. Nevertheless, I think that Jantzen's theistic pantheism, and Rāmānuja's, retain many of the problems of theism. Jantzen admits as much when she notes, for example, that "the problem of evil is not *more* of a problem to one [i.e. the pantheist] who believes that the universe is God's body than it is to one who believes that an immaterial God created everything out of nothing and sustains it by his will."[13] Evil is not a greater problem for the pantheist than for the theist according to Jantzen, but it is just as much of a problem. However, this assessment of the problem that evil presents for the pantheist assumes that pantheism and theism are integrally related. It supposes that the universe is God's "body" where God is theistically conceived. If God is not so conceived, the problem of evil for the pantheist must be reconceived. This is discussed in section 4.2.

In an effort to resolve difficulties associated with theism, Jantzen reinterprets theistically conceived divine properties like omnipresence somewhat pantheistically.[14] For example, she claims not only that omnipresence does not conflict with spatial locatability, but that it makes more sense to speak of God as omnipresent if God is spatially located. If the world is God's body – that is, if God's relation to the world is analogous to the relation ordinary persons have to their bodies – then contrary to the theistic idea that God is non-spatial, God should be thought of as spatially located *everywhere*. In keeping with classical theism, a spatially locatable God would be accessible everywhere and, theoretically, to everyone and everything. Jantzen sees this immanent God as preserving the theistic notion of God's omnipresence, while resolving conceptual difficulties related to the idea of a non-spatial but omnipresent God or person. (The idea that God is present everywhere may be far more disconcerting than the idea of a transcendent God. Jantzen does not consider this.)

Seeing "the world as God's body" also has implications for omniscience and omnipotence according to Jantzen. Just as people perceive things from their bodily location, so God perceives (senses, knows) from God's bodily location which is the entire world. Spatial location is a limitation upon, as well as a necessary condition of, the perceptual capacities of ordinary persons. However, because God and the world are spatially coextensive (i.e. God is everywhere) God meets the necessary condition for perception without being limited by any particular location. Since there are no other limitations, God can perceive everything. Also, God does not act in the world indirectly or non-basically by first moving something else, as we must in cases other than those of moving our own bodies. Instead, God's action in the world (God's body) is direct or basic in the way we usually move our own bodies. In terms of the mode of action employed, God stands in relation to the world as we do to our own bodies.

Jantzen argues that her reinterpretation of God's properties based on the hypothesis of the world as God's body is not without theological and philosophical support. And she succeeds in showing that the hypothesis has important implications for the nature of God. However, its significance for belief and practice is less clear. What practical (or practicable) difference does it make for the believer if God's omnipotence is explained in terms of God's performing basic actions upon his body (the world), rather than in terms of God's ability to do anything that it is logically possible to do – by acting through efficient causes on bodies other than his own, at places where he is not and cannot be located? What practicable difference does it make whether God's omniscience is explained (in part) as knowledge that is omni-perspectivally based as Jantzen explains it, rather than as knowledge of everything that it is logically possible to know apart from any spatial location or perspective?[15]

According to Jantzen, an adequate analysis of God's attributes implies that theism is compatible with pantheism. But it is the fact that theists conceive of God as a person, rather than alternative analyses of God's attributes, that is religiously significant. The practices elicited are those suitable for establishing a personal relationship with God – i.e. prayer etc. In terms of practice, it is the theistic rather than the pantheistic element that overwhelmingly counts. If this is right, then since God remains a person on Jantzen's account, even if her pantheistic interpretation of God's attributes is correct, the ensuing pantheism, if it is pantheism, has little impact on what believers will do. It is not that the ways in which divine attributes are understood is insignificant. But relative to the practicable consequences of conceiving of God as a person, Jantzen's pantheistic reinterpretation of the divine attributes, even if correct, is nil. I discuss some of these issues further in section 3.2.

To reiterate: Most versions of pantheism reject the idea that God is a person (Lao Tzu, the Presocratics, Spinoza, Plotinus, Bruno).[16] Indeed, I know of no prominent versions of pantheism that conceive of God as a person. Pantheists may, at times, conceive of God as a person. But if pantheism is to be a practicable alternative to theism, it must reject such a conception. The theistic core of theism/pantheism hybrids like Jantzen's makes it implausible to suppose that they can be genuine religious alternatives to theism, rather than significant philosophical variations on the familiar theistic theme.

The view that "the world is God's body" is sometimes seen as pantheistic, but others regard it as panentheistic. Panentheism claims that "the world is a self-expression of God . . . [and] there is an aspect of God's life which is entirely separate from and independent of the world."[17] It is a variant of both pantheism and theism, and although distinct from both it is best taken as a theistic variant. Like Jantzen's theistic pantheism, panentheism is essentially theistic. (Jantzen's theistic pantheism may itself be a type of panentheism.) Panentheists conceive of God and aspects of the divine nature in terms applicable only to a person.[18] As in the case of Jantzen, the practices associated with panentheism will largely be a function of its theistic elements. Since pantheism usually contains no such elements, the practice of pantheism, whatever it is, will have no intrinsic connection to theistic practice.

Theistic versions of pantheism (or vice versa), like panentheism, may compound rather than resolve the difficulties found in theism and pantheism individually. For such accounts of God to be at all plausible, what needs to be shown is (1) that any *prima facie* inconsistent elements in such hybrids are not really inconsistent; and also (2) that difficulties inherent in each are overcome. Jantzen undertakes this task, as do panentheists generally. Panentheists like Hartshorne claim to eliminate the problems associated with theism and pantheism individually, while preserving what is best *and true* of each into a comprehensive account of God and reality.

Without examining specific panentheistic accounts (e.g. Whitehead's) it is not possible to say whether panentheism offers a more coherent account of God than theism or pantheism. And even if it did, the question of whether it offers a more plausible or, better yet, a true account remains. The plausibility of any account of God (i.e. the likelihood of its being true) is of course not simply a function of its coherence. Consistency is hardly reason to assume an account true. Theism might be more plausible than pantheism, or panentheism than atheism etc., even if it contains incoherencies. These might be resolved or unimportant, and overall there might be better reason to believe theism true rather than pantheism etc. Consistency among propositions describing coherent essential aspects of a divine nature implies that such a divine nature could exist; but by itself this is no reason to believe that it does exist. Although the overall coherency of pantheism, especially compared with theism, is a concern in this book, I shall not be concerned with whether pantheism is true. I am concerned with its plausibility only in so far as questions of coherence and internal consistency are relevant.

I have suggested that Hartshorne's Process theology, and other types of panentheism, may be regarded as types of theism.[19]Leaving the question of whether they should be interpreted theistically aside, Process and Neoplatonic theories of deity are part of contemporary philosophy of religion, and are currently discussed. However, some clearly *non-theistic* concepts of deity have also received limited attention from Western philosophers this century. Tillich's God as "ultimate concern," God as the impersonal ground of Being, and aspects of Heideigger's *Dasein* are prominent examples. These have been discussed and used in some contemporary, for example "existential," theologies. Yet despite the ever growing rejection of classical (and all other types) of theism, and associated theistic practices, the classical non-theistic concept of deity – pantheism – remains ignored. The overwhelming focus of analytic philosophy of religion continues to be the classical theistic concept of God (e.g. Swinburne and Plantinga). And the focus of the relatively recent interest in comparative philosophy of religion is also on theism. Except for studies of Spinoza or the Presocratics, pantheism in its non-theistic, non-panentheistic forms is neglected. Furthermore, studies in Spinoza or the Presocratics are, at best, only oblique treatments of pantheism.

As with theistic pantheism, further consideration of panentheism would blur the focus on pantheism proper. As already intimated, unlike theism or panentheism, pantheism is not discussed in terms of its contemporary philosophical viability – or equally important, its religious viability. Instead, if it is treated at all it is as an issue in the history of philosophical theology. I shall forgo most of the historical treatment that can be done concerning individual pantheists in order to concentrate first on explaining pantheism and then on its philosophical viability – especially in relation to theism.

Also, given that part of my concern in Part III is to determine what the practicable religious implications of pantheism are, only non-theistic versions of pantheism need be considered; not hybrids such as panentheism where associated practice will basically be theistic practice (e.g. prayer). Thus, for present purposes, it is not necessary to examine pantheistic or panentheistic reformulations of classical theism. Because pantheists do not believe in a theistic God, they will not do what theists do – or at least they should not.

The book proceeds as follows. After analysing the meaning of pantheism (Part I: Meaning), I discuss the relationship between theism and pantheism. I then examine how problems associated with theism may also present problems for pantheism – albeit in a different form (Part II: Philosophy of Pantheism). Is evil a problem for pantheism, and if so, what form does the problem take and how might it be resolved? The classical theistic problem of evil cannot even arise for the pantheist unless parallels are found for the theistic attributes of omniscience, omnipotence and perfect goodness that generate the problem. Theistically conceived, the "free will defence" or theodicy is likewise inapplicable to pantheism.

In Part III: Method, I ask how one might pursue pantheistic beliefs "religiously." Speculation is in order here, and my conclusions are tentative. What might it mean to "practise" pantheism? Are traditional modes of practice such as prayer and worship unavailable to pantheists? In sections 5.1 and 5.2 I argue that they are. How can pantheistic practice cohere with the beliefs that inform pantheism and those it allegedly expresses? Comparisons between the practices such beliefs elicit with those they appear to entail should say something about both pantheism and the relation between belief and practice in general. How does belief influence, or fail to influence, religious practice? (Philosophical anthropology and the philosophy of social science has been more concerned with this than has the philosophy of religion, which merely enhances the irrelevancy of aspects of the latter.)

The analysis of pantheism I offer should be judged partly in terms of its material adequacy. It should not flagrantly conflict with whatever descriptive accounts of the beliefs and practices of pantheists can be given. For the most part, I leave this descriptive task for others. It is not an easy one since pantheists are not found in groups worshipping – as I discuss in section 6.2. Considerations of material adequacy should not preclude the conclusion that the practices of some pantheists may not cohere with their beliefs where those beliefs can be carefully articulated. Conceptually speaking, alternative practices may be in order. On the one hand, my concern is in examining ways in which practice follows belief. But belief may sometimes follow practice and have to be explained in terms of it. The suitability and coherence of beliefs may be questioned given the practices they are associated with – and vice versa.

I intend to offer more of a normative account of pantheism than a descriptive one. And this normative account (i.e. what pantheists *should* maintain and do even if they do not) should follow to some extent from descriptive accounts. The analysis in Part III is meant to suggest what pantheists should do given the beliefs they express. Although the primary purpose of this section is analytic, it involves some first-order "theologising" as well. It is a prolegomena to a philosophy of pantheism.

There are probably more (grass-root) pantheists than Protestants, or theists in general, and pantheism continues to be the traditional religious alternative to theism for those who reject the classical theistic notion of God. This inquiry may interest some of those non-theistic believers.[20] Not only is pantheism not antithetical to religion, but certain religions are better understood as pantheistic rather than theistic when their doctrines are examined. Philosophical Taoism is the most pantheistic, but Advaita Vedānta, certain forms of Buddhism and some mystical strands in monotheistic traditions are also pantheistic. But even apart from any religious tradition many people profess pantheistic beliefs – though somewhat obscurely.

The conservatism among contemporary philosophers of religion belies the fact that many believers, as well as nonbelievers, find the theistic concept of God seriously wanting. Conservatives like Alvin Plantinga and Richard Swinburne are far to the "right" of most contemporary (non-fundamentalist) theistic theologians in terms of their concept of God and related issues. Neither their concepts nor concerns are representative. It is not just official churches that have lost touch with current belief and practice, but philosophers and theologians as well. The focus of contemporary philosophical theology remains classical theism, but such theism has become peripheral not only for the nonbeliever but in terms of religious belief generally. As was the case earlier in this century, though for different reasons, philosophy of religion is woefully out of touch with the religious. By "religious" here I mean both the person in the pew and the more numerous religious people who, regarding the pew as irrelevant, do not bother with it. It is no longer the case that simple piety and the religiosity of the "common believer" can be equated with the "person in the pew." Such persons have left the pews in "flocks" to take up other Sunday pursuits.

Pantheism remains a much neglected topic of inquiry for both natural theologians and comparativists. Given their prevalence, non-theistic notions of deity have not received the kind of careful philosophical attention they deserve. Attention is warranted not only because of the prevalence of non-theistic concepts of deity, but also because of their philosophical merit, their ability to cope with critical theistic problems and their "religious" adequacy. Certainly the central claims of pantheism are *prima facie* no more fantastic or unbelievable than the central claims of theism – and probably a great deal less so.

Dissatisfaction with the traditional notion of deity is evidenced by secularisation. No doubt there are many contributing factors to secularisation. However, the most straightforward and obvious factor is that the traditional theistic concept of God has increasingly come to be regarded as mistaken on evidential, intellectual and – perhaps most surprisingly – spiritual grounds. People do not believe in God because they do not think there is good enough reason to do so. Indeed, they believe there is positive reason not to believe in God; and they could not believe if they wanted to. Is there reason to believe that pantheism offers an alternative?

I shall neither critique nor defend either the theistic or pantheistic hypothesis *per se* – or do so only in passing. This is an inquiry in the tradition of natural theology, but as applied to a nontheistic concept of deity. It may be that the pantheist is in no better position evidentially speaking than the theist – that pantheism is as "hopeless" as theism. The purpose of this investigation is not to prove pantheism true, or even more plausible than theism. The purpose is to examine pantheism – along with its problems and advantages – as an alternative philosophical and religious view.

The relegation of pantheism to the pile of outlandish philosophical theses may be warranted. But in the absence of a thorough-going analysis its dismissal has been premature. There has been no book-length treatment of pantheism in contemporary philosophy – *or ever* – and very little discussion of it in essays. This neglect is odd if for no other reason than that there are so many pantheists.[21] Philosophically speaking, unlike panentheism and dipolar theism, pantheism is a "household" word; yet it is the former instead of the latter that are attended to. Pantheism remains the classic religious alternative to theism, and as ever increasing numbers reject theism and embrace pantheism, the viability of pantheism needs to be examined.

NOTES

1 *Christoph. Wittichii, Anti-Spinoza sive Examen Ethices Benedicti de Spinoza* (Amstelaedami, 1690), Praefatio. The quotation is taken from Thomas McFarland, *Coleridge and the Pantheist Tradition* (Oxford: Oxford University Press, 1969), pp. 53–4. McFarland notes, "The author of the preface if not identified, but is clearly not Wittich himself" (p. 54n.). "The system here termed the 'latter', in which God is *causa immanens*, is the system represented by Spinoza ... God is the immanent, not the transcendent cause of all things. That is to say, he is not the creator of things but rather the things themselves" (p. 54).

2 H. P. Owen, *Concepts of Deity* (London: Macmillan, 1971), p. 74. See pp. 65–75. Alasdair MacIntyre, "Pantheism," *Encyclopedia of Philosophy* (New York: Macmillan and Free Press, 1967), vol. 5, p. 34. Also see John Macquarrie, *In Search of Deity* (London: SCM, 1984), "everything

is God or God is everything" (pp. 51–2).

Nels Ferré describes pantheism as follows:

Pantheism is the position that God is the spirit of the whole universe. He is no separate being, creating or coming into the world. He is the soul of the world. He is the world bethinking itself. He is the process directing itself. The pronoun "he", to be sure, in spite of common usage, is meaningless, for in pantheism God is not a personal being distinct from the world or the process, but the inner directedness of the world or the process itself... Whitehead and Tillich have both told me at times that they would prefer, in contradistinction from theism, to be called pantheists.

Nels F. S. Ferré, *Living God of Nowhere and Nothing* (Philadelphia: Westminster, 1966), p. 9.

The term "pantheism" was possibly first coined by John Toland in 1705. He wrote *Pantheisticon* (first published in 1720; reprint of 1751 edition, New York and London: Garland, 1976). However, Thomas McFarland says "I am not entirely convinced... that Toland did coin the term" (McFarland, "Toland and the Origin of the Word 'Pantheism,'" in *Coleridge and the Pantheist Tradition*, pp. 266–7, at p. 266).

Toland uses the word "pantheist" as an exact synonym for "Spinozist"... Toland is specific about the identification of God and nature, of the one and the many: "all things in the world are one, and one is all in all things" intones the mystic moderator; and the response of the others in the [pantheist] society then equates divinity with this primary equation of the one and the many: "what is all in all things is God, eternal and immense, neither born nor ever to die" (*Pantheisticon*, p. 54).

(McFarland, p. 267)

Like "atheism" the term "pantheism" was used in the eighteenth century as a term of "theological abuse," and it often still is. See Alan Tapper, *Priestley's Metaphysics*, Ph.D. Dissertation, University of Western Australia, 1987. Armstrong says the term "pantheistic" is a "large, vague term of theological abuse" (A. H. Armstrong, "The Apprehension of Divinity in the Self and Cosmos in Plotinus," in R. Baine Harris (ed.), *The Significance of Neoplatonism* (Norfolk: International Society for Neoplatonic Studies, 1976), pp. 187–98, at p. 187.

3 Owen's definition (3) appears to be contradictory. The first sentence suggests that pantheists believe in a plurality of entities (i.e. "every existing entity..."), while the second sentence says they believe there is only one "real" entity or "Being," and that "all other forms of reality are either modes (or appearances) of it or identical with it." To resolve this conflict one would have to assume one of the following alternatives: (a) that the modes or appearances of the one Being are real entities (and divine) in their own right even though they are modes of the one Being, and that this all-inclusive divine plurality of entities constituted of the one Being and its modes suffices for

17

pantheism; or (b) that the modes and appearances do not exist as ontological entities in their own right (i.e. they are *not* entities in the ontologically significant sense of existing, or of being capable of existing, apart from the Being they are a mode of), but exist only as modes of the one Being. In context it is clear that Owen thinks the pantheist is committed to alternative (b). So even if pantheists believe that finite entities are modes of God they still believe that there is no real plurality of entities. According to Owen, pantheists are monists at least in so far as they believe that the only one real entity exists.

Owen's definition can be subsumed under MacIntyre's and they are similar in crucial respects. They share the view that according to pantheism everything is "in some sense divine," and that this divine everything, whether made up of one or more ontologically real entities, constitutes a "unity." If we adopt (b), then one form the unity will take (not necessarily the only form) is the unity of the only (ontologically) existing Being itself. And if we adopt (a) one form the unity will take is whatever type of unity is attributed to the one Being, other than that of being the only ontological entity. This Being may be made up of, or identical with, its modes and appearances. Depending on one's ontology, these modes and appearances may be existing entities in their own right. MacIntyre's broader definition allows for either (a) or (b) since he does not specify the type of unity involved (i.e. whether ontological, logical etc.).

4 Cf. Christopher Rowe, "One and Many in Greek Religion," in Adolf Portman and Rudolf Ritsema (eds) *Oneness and Variety* (Leiden: E. J. Brill, 1980), p. 53. Rowe notes that monotheism is sometimes used (e.g. by Guthrie) to mean "theism." W. K. C. Guthrie, *A History of Greek Philosophy* (Cambridge: Cambridge University Press, 1962) vol. I, pp. 247–9. Although Rowe regards pantheism as a type of monotheism he also thinks that it is compatible with Greek polytheism for the Presocratics since recognition of a plurality of Gods is not meant to undermine the idea of a single greatest God (p. 57). For example, Anaximenes, " 'attributed all the causes of things to infinite air, and did not deny that there were gods . . . yet he believed not that air was made by them, but that they arose from air' . . . the result is a universe which is divine, or god, and which is also peopled by gods" (p. 58). Rowe goes on to say "Werner Jaeger rightly points out that the Greek Gods are usually conceived of as being within the universe . . . 'they are descended from Heaven and Earth . . . they are generated by the mighty power of Eros, who likewise belongs within the world as an all-engendering primitive force' " (p. 58). See Werner Jaeger, *The Theology of the Early Greek Philosophers* (Oxford: Oxford University Press, 1947), pp. 43–4.

5 McFarland, p. 228. Also see I. M. Crombie, *An Examination of Plato's Doctrines* (London: Routledge & Kegan Paul, 1962), vol. I, p. 370. He described the "Spinozistic atheism of many of the philosophers who used the words and sentiments of religion to dignify what were little more than physical forces." See Rowe, p. 54.

6 Arthur Schopenhauer, "A Few Words On Pantheism," in *Essays From*

The Parerga and Paralipomena, trans. T. Bailey Saunders (London: George Allen & Unwin, 1951), p. 40. I will discuss Schopenhauer's claim at length, but as an account of what pantheists mean to be asserting it is clearly false. As Macquarrie says, "In pantheism, the world is not mere world which may also be called God ..." (*In Search of Deity*, p. 52). Gregory Vlastos notes that the early Greeks "could call nature god without indulging in an empty figure of speech." "Theology and Philosophy in Greek Thought," *Philosophical Quarterly*, 2 (1952), p. 100. This reference is cited by Rowe who also cites D. Babut, *La réligion des philosophes grecs*, Paris 1974, pp. 6ff. Babut also claims that the pantheism of the Presocratics is really equivalent to atheism.

David Berman interprets Spinoza as an atheist. David Berman, *A History of Atheism in Britain: From Hobbes to Russell* (London: Croom Helm, 1988). This is an odd claim for Berman to make since he eschews those who claim that there really are no atheists (see Chapter 1). If Berman is willing to take speculative atheists at their word concerning their adherence to atheism, why does he reject the idea of pantheism (Spinoza's in particular) as belief in another kind of deity, and a genuine religious position? Either Berman is incorrectly psychologising (i.e Spinoza does not really believe in God) or else he is mistakenly assuming (1) that theism and atheism are mutually exhaustive categories and (2) that pantheism is atheism because it is not theism.

7 Rudolf Otto, *The Idea of the Holy*, 2nd edn (Oxford: Oxford University Press, 1950), p. 197. But Otto also says,

> *all* Gods are more than mere (personal) gods ... the greater representations of deity show from time to time features which reveal their ancient character as "*numina*" and burst the bounds of the personal and theistic. This is obviously the case where the experienced relation of the worshipper to his god does not exclusively take the form of contact with a "beyond" and transendent being, but comes somehow as the experience of seizure and possession by the god, as being filled by him ... or assimilates him to his own divine nature ... becoming very part of him; or, again, where the god becomes the sphere in which "we live and move and have our being." And what god has not in some sense had this character?
>
> (p. 199)

Yet, Otto claims that only in seeking "an answer to the question as to the general place of 'Personalism' and 'Supra-personalism' in religious history ... are we likely to avoid confounding this question with the question of Theism and Pantheism, with which it has nothing in common" (p. 202). I take it that Otto is mistaken in this categorical claim. The issue of personalism has a great deal to do with pantheism.

8 H. D. Lewis, *Our Experience of God* (New York: Macmillan, 1959), p. 66.
9 See Michael P. Levine, " 'Can We Speak Literally of God?,' " *Religious Studies*, 21 (1) (1985), pp. 53–9.
10 Though pantheistic and mystical components within traditions often

overlap and intertwine, they are distinguishable, and it is pantheism rather than mysticism that is my concern. Thus, though pantheism is most readily found in mystical strands of religious traditions, they should not be equated. The mystic may stress the epistemic relation that one bears to God rather than unity in any sense that may be required by pantheism. Cf. Nathan Rotenstreich, "Symbolism and Transcendence: On Some Philosophical Aspects of Gershom Scholem's Opus," *Review of Metaphysics*, 31 (1978), p. 612.

11 Rather than seeing pantheism as a proposed solution to the problem of transcendence it can be seen as an "opposing tendency." See A. J. Festugière, *La Révélation Hermès Trismégiste*, esp. vol. ii, *Le Dieu Cosmique* (Paris, 1949). Referring to Festugière, D. A. Rees says

> A distinguished French scholar has recently set himself to delineate the history of Greek thought, from the time of Plato through the formation of the Hellenistic systems to the days of the empire, distinguishing two opposing tendencies, one towards pantheism and the other towards a philosophy of transcendence. But that distinction can be traced also in earlier periods . . .

D. A. Rees, "Greek Views of Nature and Mind," *Philosophy*, 29 (1954), p. 99.

12 I use "classic" and "classical" interchangeably throughout. The term "classical" as applied to theism is imprecise, but I take it to refer to the standard Christian doctrines of Aquinas, Augustine etc. and the problems they address.

13 Grace Jantzen, *God's World, God's Body* (Philadelphia: Westminster, 1984), p. 137. See J. J. Lipner, "The World As God's 'Body': In Pursuit of Dialogue With Rāmānuja," *Religious Studies*, 20 (1984), pp. 145–61. Lipner says "it would be theologically fertile, both conceptually and devotionally, for Christians to regard the world, and its individual components, as God's body" (p. 159). Jantzen's book is an original and sustained treatment of this suggestion, especially as it concerns the conceptual rather than devotional issues.

14 Jantzen's analysis of omnipresence follows a suggestion by Jonathan Harrison. Jonathan Harrison, "The Embodiment of Mind or What Use is Having A Body?," *Proceedings of the Aristotelian Society*, 74 (1973–4), pp. 35–55. See pp. 54–5.

15 If omniscience entails that God perceives everything from all perspectives, and one must be spatially located at or near a particular location in order to have a particular perspective, then this requirement of spatial location presents no problem for a God who is omnipresent in the sense of being spatially coextensive with the world and so in possession of all perspectives at once.

16 See Ludwig Feuerbach, *Principles of the Philosophy of the Future*, tr. Manfred Vogel (Indianapolis: Hackett, 1986), p. 20. "That which separates theism from pantheism is only the conception or the imagining of God as a personal being."

17 Owen, *Concepts of Deity*, p. 94. Owen is referring to Pringle-Pattison's version of panentheism. Owen notes that for the panentheist "the

world is divine because it is the self-expression of God" (p. 92). What then makes God divine? Owen also cites the following definition of panentheism from the *Oxford Dictionary of the Christian Church*: "the belief that the Being of God includes and penetrates the whole universe, so that every part of it exists in him, but (against pantheism) that his being is more than, and is not exhausted by the universe" (Owen, pp. 74–5). "It was a contemporary of his [Hegel's] in the same idealist tradition, Karl Krause, who invented the term 'panentheism' for a philosophy which seeks to find a path between theism and pantheism, so doing justice to both divine transcendence and divine immanence" (Macquarrie, *In Search of Deity*, p. 15).

18 "Panentheism's assumption, when viewed in the light of substance philosophy, that God could be a distinct being and yet worked from within the world, is . . . simply theism" (Ferré, *Living God of Nowhere and Nothing*, p. 10). Panentheism is not theism, but it is closer to theism than pantheism. This is why it is favoured by those who, like John Macquarrie, are troubled with the classical theistic concept of deity, but find it more congenial that the more radical (because non-personal) pantheism. See Macquarrie, *In Search of Deity*, p. 54. Macquarrie calls his own position "dialectical theism," and describes it as being "roughly synonymous" with panentheism (p. 15).

Whitehead's "Process theology" and Hartshorne's dipolar theism are both types of panentheism. Although they differ from classical theism in important ways, they are not non-theistic. Hartshorne's "dipolar" concept of deity is s synthesis of theistic and non-theistic elements. But it is not a non-theistic view, as the name "dipolar theism" indicates. Hartshorne agrees that panentheism is closer to theism than to pantheism.

19 The extent to which Process philosophers, Neoplatonists, and Heideggerians regard their concepts of deity as theistic or antithetical to theism and its associated practices varies. Theism must be more or less dramatically reinterpreted in their view. In this respect they are unlike other "radical" twentieth-century theologians (e.g. *some* feminist and liberation theologians) whose concepts of deity coincide far more with the classical theistic notion of God.

20 John Leslie, *Value and Existence* (Oxford: Blackwell, 1979), p. vi. He says:

> Recent social research has shown that in Great Britain, for example, two in every five people share a faith in some universal purpose acting to produce good, though they reject belief in a divine Person. It is worth asking what sense there is in their position, which is in fact that of traditional Platonist theology as represented by Paul Tillich, for instance – though it might also be defended independently of any traditional religious movement.

Ninian Smart told me at a conference that he did not know anyone who was a pantheist. Granted that we travel in different circles, it still cannot be the case that he does not know any pantheists. He knows many – though he may not know he knows any. Pantheists are not as difficult to recognise as Kierkegaardian "knights of faith" – though they too may look like tax collectors. See Soren Kierkegaard, *Fear and Trembling*, tr. W. Lowrie (Princeton: Princeton University Press, 1969), p. 49.

21 It is a mistake to think of this neglect as benign. The reason for it is an issue for the sociology of knowledge.

Part I
MEANING

2

WHAT IS PANTHEISM?

2.1 UNITY

Is the unity, men have asked themselves, a oneness of stuff, matter, substance, or a oneness of form, principle, plan etc.? Does it consist in a singleness of origin or of present nature or of ultimate destination? Is it conscious (or even self-conscious) or, on the other hand, is it blind to itself, or again, does it subsist in some intermediate condition?[1]

J. A. Smith

It is not a matter of saying that the world is one, or the world is many; for it is possible that the world may be one in a given sense, and many in another sense . . . there are various meanings, respects and even degrees of unity.[2]

Raphael Demos

should he [Virgil] insist . . . that earth, sea, and moon really are the limbs of God, then he has lapsed into pantheism.[3]

Grace Jantzen

Pantheism is the view that "everything that exists constitutes a unity [in some sense] and . . . this all-inclusive unity is divine [in some sense]."[4] Different versions of pantheism offer different accounts of the meaning of "unity" and "divinity." There is no one meaning in all forms of pantheism, and within some forms several types are found. Often, the meaning of unity present is vague and indeterminate. Because of this, the central problem of pantheism, unlike theism, is to determine just what pantheism means. For example, philosophical Taoism is one of the best articulated and thoroughly pantheistic positions there is. The Tao is the central unifying feature. But what exactly is the Tao? It is

25

a unifying metaphysical and naturalistic principle of sorts. But of what sort, and how is it to be understood?[5] Only after a determination is made as to what is meant by the central pantheistic claim that "everything that exists constitutes a divine Unity" can one raise the kinds of substantive issues in regard to pantheism that are central for theism – the problem of evil for example. What kind of unity is (or should be) claimed by pantheists and which, if any, is plausible? After dealing with these fundamental questions, the philosophical and religious consequences of analysing unity in some particular way can be examined.

For some versions of pantheism the *relevant sense of unity* (hereafter "Unity") can be explained in terms of the identity of the "person" that allegedly constitutes or is constitutive of the whole. A principle of individuation that employs personalistic criteria could be applied. However, since I am considering only non-theistic, non-personal varieties of pantheism – what I term "non-personal theism" – ascriptions of unity that are based upon personal identity, or other essentially personalistic criteria, need not be considered.

I examine several historically prominent senses of Unity in which general points concerning conditions for an adequate criterion of Unity will be discussed. Rather than detailed analysis of particular kinds of Unity, conditions of adequacy for a criterion of Unity is a main concern. To some extent this is a "negative" task. I argue how Unity should not be understood in an effort to determine possible ways in which it can be understood. There may be acceptable alternative criteria, and so several acceptable notions of Unity. But even if there are alternatively acceptable criteria, some may be more acceptable to the pantheist than others – given criteria of adequacy in addition to those necessary. Among those that are acceptable, they need not be equally acceptable. However, just as there are alternative theisms, one would expect that there are alternative pantheisms. Pantheism need not be, any more than theism needs to be, a univocal view.

2.1.1 Misunderstandings

Schopenhauer criticised pantheism's identification of "the world" with "God" on the basis of what he took to be the meanings of both for the pantheist. He said calling the world "God," or God "the world," is "superfluous," and redundant. He also ridiculed the idea that the world could be called God given our general notions of what God and the world are like. Schopenhauer's criticism fails because he equivocates on the terms central to his argument. The meanings of both Unity and divinity involved in the pantheistic claim that there exists an all-inclusive divine Unity are different from the senses Schopenhauer attributes to the world and God in his criticism. The pantheist does not mean what Schopenhauer means by God, and the "all-inclusive Unity" in pantheism is not another word for the "world" as he uses it (i.e. everything). The interpretation of "world" Schopenhauer attributes to pantheists is not what they mean when they describe it as a Unity. He says,

> The chief objection I have to pantheism is that it says nothing. To call the world "God" is not to explain it; it is only to enrich our language with a superfluous synonym for the word "world." It comes to the same thing whether you say "the world is God," or "God is the world." . . . if you start from "God" as something that is given in experience, and has to be explained, and then say, "God is the world," you are affording what is to some extent an explanation . . . but it is only a verbal explanation. If however, you start from what is really given, that is to say, from the world, and say, "the world is God," it is clear that you say nothing, or at least you are explaining what is unknown by what is more unknown . . . Hence Pantheism presupposes Theism; only in so far as you start from a god . . . can you end by identifying him with the world; and your purpose in doing so is to put him out of the way in a decent fashion. In other words you do not start clear from the world as something that requires explanation; you start from God as something that is given, and not knowing what to do with him, you make the world take over his role. This is the origin of Pantheism. Taking an unprejudiced view of the world as it is, no one would dream of regarding it as a god. It must be a very ill-advised god who knows no better way of diverting himself than by turning into such a world as ours, such a mean, shabby world . . . [6]

Schopenhauer's account and criticism of pantheism is not just uncharitable, it is inaccurate. Pantheism does not presuppose theism, it denies it. More importantly, pantheism never has been a simple identification of the world with God. Spinoza's distinction, for example, between *natura naturans* and *natura naturata* (*Ethics* I, Proposition XXIX, note) is meant to be an explicit denial of such an identity.[7] Pantheists may not be giving an adequate explanation of the world in calling it God, or vice versa – though I doubt this is meant to be an explanation. Perhaps all that Schopenhauer wants to claim is that in calling the world "God" nothing is explained. Nevertheless, as an account of what the pantheist means (e.g. Lao Tzu, Spinoza, Plotinus, Bruno) it is mistaken. Few pantheists, *if any*, ever do call the world "God." And if they do, it is not meant as a simple identification.

"World" and "God" are not synonyms nor are they logically equivalent terms for the pantheist. To call the world "God" is not to utter a synonymous expression, but to say something significant, even if not true, about both the world and God. Similarly, for the pantheist, describing the world as an "all-inclusive Unity" is to say something significant about the world rather than to superfluously redescribe it with an alternative referring term.[8] For the pantheist, God and the world generally are not and should not be taken as intentionally equivalent. Something about the world – namely the fact that it is taken to be an all-inclusive divine Unity – is the reason for calling the world "God." If both God and the world are taken in the sense of "all-inclusive divine Unity," then they will be extensionally equivalent, referring in fact to the same thing, according to the pantheist. But apart from using them in this sense the pantheist, like anyone else, need not take them as extensionally equivalent, or as meaning the same thing.

In general, then, God and the world do not mean the same thing, nor do they necessarily refer to the same thing for the pantheist. However, pantheists do take the world and God to have identical sense and reference on a certain interpretation of each. God, the world and the all-inclusive divine Unity all allegedly refer to the same thing. So they believe things to be true of God and the world that non-pantheists do not. It is not just a question of disagreement over the properties of God and the world, but over their meanings. When pantheists claim that the world, or God, is an all-inclusive divine Unity, they mean something different by God and the world than in the non-pantheistic usage of these terms.

Historically, few, if any, pantheists made the identification of

God and the world complete or synonymous in the way claimed by Schopenhauer, Owen, and Pringle-Pattison. It is often difficult to determine the senses of Unity and divinity operative in particular versions of pantheism, and sometimes whether a position is pantheistic at all. Who are the pantheists? Nevertheless, pantheism must not be interpreted in a way that makes the identification of God with the world, and sees "God" as an all-inclusive divine Unity, redundant. Even if Schopenhauer is right in claiming this is the view of some pantheists, it is a mistaken caricature to treat this view, especially *only* this view, as "pure pantheism."

For the pantheist, however Unity is interpreted, the world is not simply an all-inclusive Unity in the sense that the world, understood to be everything, is the "unity" composed of everything. This would be to interpret it as asserting that everything that exists simply *is* everything that exists; or to put it another way, everything is (of course) all-inclusively everything. This is true but vacuous, and it trivialises pantheism at the outset.

Attributing Unity simply on the basis of all-inclusiveness is irrelevant to pantheism. Formal unity can always be attributed to the world on this basis alone. To understand the world as "everything" is to attribute a sense of unity to the world, but there is no reason to suppose this sense of all-inclusiveness is the pantheistically relevant Unity. Similarly, unity as mere numerical, class or categorical unity is irrelevant, since just about anything (and everything) can be "one" or a "unity" in these senses. Suppose "formal unity" to be "the sense in which things are only in virtue of the fact that they are members of one and the same class . . . the same universal."[9] Then clearly formal unity is not pantheistic Unity. Furthermore, formal unity neither entails or is entailed by types of unity (e.g. substantial unity) sometimes taken to be Unity. Hegel's *Geist*, Lao Tzu's Tao, Plotinus' "One," and arguably Spinoza's "substance," are independent of this kind of formal unity.

> Thus it could well be that a universe which is substantially many, in that it consists of several entities, may be formally one in that the several entities are exemplifications of one and the same form or category. Yet the bare statement that all things come under one highest genus would not carry us very far; for all things could not help being under one particular class, namely, the class of things that exist . . .

formal unity (or diversity) and substantial unity (or plurality) are logically independent of each other . . . if it be true that the universe is formally one, it does not follow that the universe is substantially one; and if the latter is true, it does not follow that the former is true.[10]

MacIntyre similarly says,

It is first and most clearly not a unity derived from membership of the same class, the view that seems to have been taken by Boehme. "There is no class of all that is," wrote Aristotle. Why not? Because existence is not a genus. To say that something exists is not to classify it at all . . . The notion of *a* unity that includes all that exists – or even all that exists and all that does not exist – is a notion devoid of content. What could be unitary in such an ostensible collection?[11]

I do not see why MacIntyre thinks it is "a notion devoid of content," rather than just a notion not pertinent to Unity, but the basic idea is the same. Formal unity will not do. Even if some pantheists like Boehme did think of it this way, and it is not clear that he did, this is not generally a correct descriptive – let alone normative – account of Unity.

The important point, of course, is that the pantheist believes things to be true of the all-inclusive Unity that is the world that non-pantheists do not. Even if they both believe the world is a formal unity, the pantheist means something more. Unity needs to be explained in terms of what distinguishes "all-inclusive Unity" from the world or all-inclusiveness *per se*, as Schopenhauer interprets it. And it needs to be distinguished from various senses of unity or "oneness" that are predicable of all things in all sorts of ways.

The world is God?

Schopenhauer ridiculed the idea that the world should be called God. "Taking an unprejudiced view of the world as it is, no one would dream of regarding it as a god. It must be a very ill-advised god who knows no better way of diverting himself than by turning into such a world as ours, such a mean, shabby world." Is he right? It is not clear what he means by calling the world "shabby."

The world as the totality of all that exists is not itself an item in the world like my coat or your care of the cat. Ordinarily it is the latter sorts of things we may take to be shabby, rather than the world itself. Perhaps if we were able (*per impossibile*) to compare the world (as totality) with another world it would make sense to describe this world as shabby by comparison. Similarly it is not entirely clear what it means to say that the world, rather than things in it, are evil.

But what it means to say that there are shabby things in the world is clear, and this is sufficient to make Schopenhauer's claim sensible. He doesn't think the whole world is shabby either – just some things in it. He is saying that if the world is God, if it is divine, then it should not contain shabby (or evil) things. But he may mean that the world as a whole is shabby, and this too is meaningful – even apart from our inability actually to compare it with other worlds. One can imagine a criterion of shabbiness applicable to worlds as wholes. Given such a criterion, other imaginable worlds may be more or less shabby than our own. Schopenhauer thinks that there are so many things in and about the world that are "ungodly" that the world as a whole should be regarded as such – even if there are lovely things in it.

It may seem that for shabbiness or evil in the world to present even a *prima facie* conflict for an "identification" of the world as God, the world and God must be understood personalistically. This is the way Schopenhauer understands pantheism. Just as in the theistic problem of evil where there is a difficulty in reconciling God's perfect goodness, power and knowledge with the presence of evil, so in pantheism there is difficulty in reconciling the world as it appears, evil and all, with the idea that it is a personal God. Since I have indicated why I do not want to consider personalistic versions of pantheism, it may seem that the conflict need not arise for the types that concern us.

However, the Unity need not be thought of personalistically for this difficulty to arise. If the Unity is divine, then whether or not it is personal, its containing mean things may be seen to conflict with its divinity or its Unity. Like Schopenhauer one might argue that these things should not, indeed *could not*, be part of the Unity – given the very concept, personalistic or not, of God or the divine. So the question arises as to whether the divine Unity can be ugly and evil, in part, and still be all-inclusively divine. Maybe the claim that there exists a divine Unity is not irreconcilable with the fact that aspects of the world are shabby or evil, just as in theism there may be a resolution to the problem of evil. If so it must be shown how and why. Thus, even if his first criticism of pantheism as superfluous is misguided, Schopenhauer raises an important question – one analogous to the theistic problem of evil – concerning the propriety of attributing divinity to the Unity.

In fact, pantheists do not deny the existence of evil or "meanness." Not even Spinoza denies this, though he interprets evil as a function of our lack of understanding. For Spinoza, evil is defeated through knowledge. In general, pantheists regard evil as not consonant with Unity and as something one should strive to overcome. Understanding the nature of the Unity is a feature of pantheistic solutions to evil. Thus, according to Lao Tzu, in so far as the metaphysical Tao can be understood through its manifestations, we are presented with a model for human relations and a standard for human behaviour that if followed will minimise evil, "discord" etc.[12] These issues are further discussed in the section on evil.

MacIntyre

Unlike Schopenhauer, Alasdair MacIntyre denies that Unity is unity in the logically all-inclusive sense. Yet he appears to ignore this when he implies that Marcus Aurelius is not a pantheist because "when he addressed the Universe itself as a deity [he] did not clearly address it in the sense of all that is rather than in the sense of some principle of order that informs all that is." Despite MacIntyre's denial that Unity means "everything that exists," he seems to require it of pantheism. He also unduly limits the sense in which Unity must be taken as divine to qualify as pantheism. Because "early Greek thinkers, did not distinguish clearly between asserting that an object [in the sense of all that is] was divine and asserting that a divine power informed the object's movement"[13] he questions if they are pantheists.

A failure by commentators themselves to observe this distinction makes it misleadingly easy to present both earlier Presocratic and later Stoic philosophers as recruits to the ranks of pantheism. But even Marcus Aurelius, the only notable thinker among them who can plausibly be represented as a pantheist, when he addressed the Universe itself as a deity did not clearly address it in the sense of all that is rather than in the sense of some principle of order that informs all that is.[14]

The distinction, though clear, may not be significant – which is why it may not have been observed. It misplaces the relevant pantheistic sense of unity for these early Greeks (i.e. Unity based on a principle or power informing the whole) by substituting unity as all-inclusiveness *per se*. "Asserting that a divine power informed the object's [i.e. 'all that is'] movement" may suffice for pantheism. This is because (1) the "unitive" aspect of "all that is" may be attributable to the informing principle and (2) the object may be divine in virtue of the informing principle.

So if Marcus Aurelius addresses the Universe as a deity because it is informed by a principle of order, rather than because it is (merely) "all that is," this is indicative of what he takes to be the relevant unitive feature of all that is. It does not show that he is not a pantheist. Why *would* one address the universe as a deity "in the sense of all that is" rather than because a divine principle informs it? To require that it be addressed as a deity solely on the grounds MacIntyre deems relevant is to see the only sense of unity relevant to pantheism that of all-inclusiveness *per se*. Yet, no pantheist need ever take this sense to be relevant, and there is no evidence that this is what has been meant by Unity. Remarkably, Unity has often been interpreted in this way by those critical of pantheism. Historically and normatively this is a mistake.

That a principle or power informs the object may not only be sufficient for Unity, but also for its divinity. Why assume, as MacIntyre does, that the object must be divine apart from some divinely informing power? Pantheism requires that the Unity be divine, but it does not stipulate that what makes it so cannot be a divinely informing power – perhaps inherent in the object. What difference would it then make if it was said that the object itself was divine or that a divine power informed its movement and for that reason it was divine? In the pantheism of Giordano Bruno "the contrast between God and Nature, between the divine and natural, is valid only with reservations . . . God penetrates nature, and matter itself 'is divine.' "[15]

Of course, MacIntyre's point is that the object may *not* be divine, but only informed by a power that is divine. But there is no reason to assume that to qualify as pantheists the Greeks had to observe this distinction. Like Aurelius, others thought that if an ordering principle informed the object, this sufficed for the object's divinity as well its Unity. (Compare Lao Tzu with Aurelius: Lao Tzu thought that apart from the Tao informing the "myriad things" they could neither exist nor flourish. The Tao, as principle or power, is essentially part of the nature of things.) To suppose that the world is informed by a divine principle or one that makes it divine is to suppose that the all-inclusive Unity is divine. This is all that is required for pantheism under MacIntyre's own definition.

MacIntyre implies that if the world (i.e. "all that is") is taken to be divine, rather than merely informed by a principle that makes it divine, this would suffice for pantheism. But this is not the case. The world's being divine, in a sense yet to be determined, is not necessarily sufficient for its Unity. It depends on how Unity is interpreted. The divinity of the whole does not ensure Unity any more than Unity of the whole ensures its divinity. In most versions of pantheism, including that of Marcus Aurelius, they are related. But pantheism *per se* does not require this. The Universe may be divine, and yet be quite un-Unified.[16]

In interpreting Unity as mere all-inclusiveness, Schopenhauer and MacIntyre give a fictitious account of what has been, and should be, meant by Unity and, more generally, by pantheism. MacIntyre also unduly restricts the conditions under which divinity can be attributed to the Unity. Schopenhauer interprets divinity (God) personalistically, but he points out at least *prima facie* difficulties in taking the all-inclusive Unity to be divine even on the pantheist's non-personalistic account.

Everything is God?

"Pantheism . . . means strictly, the view that God is everything and everything God."[17] The existence of an all-inclusive divine Unity does mean, in a sense, that everything is God. But what does this mean? It means that God is the all-inclusive whole, the "everything" that is *appropriately* unified. Apart from a unifying element (e.g. substance, Tao, *Geist* etc.) the all-inclusive whole would not be God. Before further examining grounds for attributing Unity, a final confusion concerning what is meant by "god is everything" should be dispelled.

The view that since God is everything God therefore is each thing – the ocean, the toaster etc. – is not pantheism. Although Hegel thinks an ambiguity in the meaning of pantheism allows for this peculiar interpretation, he says (correctly) that this interpretation is mistaken and that this sort of pantheism is found in religion. G.H.R. Parkinson explains Hegel's view as follows.

> The term "pantheism," he [Hegel] says, is ambiguous... One associates with pantheism the doctrine that God is "hen kai pan" (literally, "one and all")... this may mean that God is the one-all (*das eine* All), the all that remains simply one. But "pan" can also mean "everything" (*alles*), and to speak of pantheism in this sense is to speak of the view that everything is God. This, says Hegel, is the doctrine of the "everything-God," not of the "God who is all" (*die Allesgotterei, nicht Allegotterei*) ... "everything-God" is the view that God is all things, where "things" are regarded as individual and contingent. It is the view that "God is everything – he is this paper, and so on" ... Hegel asserts that pantheism of this kind is not to be found in any religion, far less in any philosophy. In this sense, then, Spinoza is not a pantheist.[18]

Hegel is right in pointing out the ambiguity, but he is mistaken in claiming that the ambiguity extends to pantheism. Since, as he says, pantheism of this sort (i.e. God is this paper etc.) is not found in any religion, far less in any philosophy, why assume it should count as pantheism at all?

Note that in describing a more appropriate way of interpreting the pantheistic God as "the all that remains simply one," Hegel does not interpret it as all-inclusiveness *per se*. It remains "one" because something unifies the "all" to keep it "one." For Hegel, that "something" is (arguably) *Geist*. It informs, indeed is constitutive of, all history and all of reality.

Hegel says that "God is everything" in the sense of "this paper" etc. has never been found in any religion or philosophy. Similarly, "God is everything" in the sense of all-inclusiveness *per se* has never been found. However, commentators have probably not always been mistaken in finding them. But the point is that no well-developed, philosophically respectable, version of pantheism allows these views. No plausible analysis of pantheism allows for either interpretation.

2.1.2 Pantheistic Unity: a topology

Rather than as synonymy of world and God, or all-inclusiveness *per se*, the pantheist's central claim must be understood in terms of what is meant by Unity and divinity. Belief in an all-inclusive divine Unity is the reason for the identification of the world with God and *not* vice versa.

Unity is explained in various ways that are often interrelated. These connections range from mutual entailment to different types of causal and contingent relations. Roughly, Unity is interpreted (1) ontologically; (2) naturalistically – in terms of ordering principle(s), force(s) or plans; (3) substantively – where this is distinguished from "ontologically"; and (4) genealogically – in terms of origin. Christopher Rowe calls (4) a "genealogical model of explanation" of unity. "Thales, Anaximander, and Anaximenes, the Milesian monists appear to have claimed that what unifies the world is that it sprang from a single undifferentiated substance."[19] Similarly, we can describe (1) as the ontological model of explanation of Unity etc.

For the Milesian monists, explanations of unity in terms of origin and in terms of substance are related, though not necessarily equated. Similarly, different kinds of unity may be thought to involve one another in various ways. (1) and (2) are related especially often. Unity in terms of substance is regarded as significant because it is taken as a type of ontological unity which in turn is allegedly significant. Nevertheless, these models of explanation of unity are distinguishable. Substance might not even be part of one's ontology, so one could speak of ontological unity apart from substance. Alternatively, one might talk of substantial unity apart from ontology.[20] To take another example, unity can be based on origin without extending it to ontology, substance or principles of order. Whatever the relations among types of unity may be, it is useful first to consider them individually. This way the operative senses of "all-inclusive" can be kept as distinct as possible.

These types of unity are not merely different ways, alternative foci, of explaining the all-inclusive Unity. If they were, then a complete analysis of any one of them would essentially refer to the others. But, there is no reason to suppose that any of the above models entails any other. In fact, with the exception of the ontological and substance models, particular versions of pantheism describe Unity employing one model and relate the others to it tangentially. If Unity is primarily explained in terms of an ordering principle, as it most often is, then although genealogical and other models may be related (e.g. as in Taoism) they are of less consequence.

Particular accounts of Unity should explain connections among the various models, and examine the wider philosophical implications of the type of Unity thought to be most relevant. This involves consideration of metaphysical and other (e.g. ethical) issues undertaken by only a few philosophical pantheists such as Spinoza and Lao Tzu. Pantheists may have a theory about Unity, but it cannot be a well-developed theory unless it addresses the fundamental metaphysical and practical questions (i.e. religious ones) that pantheists have traditionally examined. Still, the pantheist's primary task is to give an account of Unity, since discussion of its broader implications presupposes this. In explaining Unity the relevance of a particular model and sense of the term must be shown.

The ontological model

Unity on the ontological model can mean almost anything, and vagueness is the model's greatest deficiency. Pantheists who employ this model also interpret Unity in terms of one or more of the other models as well. Unity is partly ontologically based in Spinoza, Plotinus, Bruno, Hegel and Lao Tzu; but all explain their respective senses of it using other models. Thus, the metaphysical Tao can be characterised partly on the ontological model, but its operations and manifestations in the phenomenal world, and its use as a standard for behaviour (i.e. its *Te*), are best explained under the naturalistic model. Hegel's *Geist* is characterised ontologically. But an understanding of its movement and operations involves reference to all the other models.

Ontologically, Unity can be taken monistically as a single entity, kind of entity or substance. Or, it may be taken as a single entity that can be ontologically differentiated from others like parts from wholes. Those who think of Unity as a single entity of organic and inorganic matter in symbiotic relation do not deny that entities constitutive of the whole exist in their own right. Things may be regarded as ontologically distinct from one another and from the Unity – even if part of it. Some versions of (ontological) pantheism may deny this, but they need not. Even when, ontologically speaking, the Unity is not taken to be an individual entity it can still be ontologically based – e.g. grounded in "Being." Paul Tillich may exemplify this approach.

Where Unity is regarded as an entity (e.g. the "One") it can be taken to include any of the following: (i) its proper parts, if it has any; (ii) entities that are independent of it in the sense that they could exist on their own; (iii) entities that cannot exist apart from it. If it is supposed that other entities cannot be independent of the Unity, this should not be taken to follow trivially from its all-inclusive character.

Although Unity can be ontologically based in countless ways, and usually is partly so based, by itself the ontological model is obscure. It is too broad to explain Unity unless it is elaborated upon in terms of other models. The type of ontologically grounded Unity that is of most concern is best treated under the substance model. Examples are Spinoza and Bruno.[21] This is taken up in section 2.3.1.

The naturalistic model

Laws of nature, and other principles or forces, are used to explain Unity when taken as informing or ordering the whole in some "significant" way. What counts as "significant" or relevant is indicative of a sense of Unity that is partly presupposed.

On the naturalistic model of Unity, the description of principles, forces etc. as "natural" does not imply that they, or the Unity, cannot also be interpreted metaphysically, or that they are not divine. For instance, the Tao has both metaphysical and naturalistic senses. It is a metaphysical reality (i.e. a single entity that actually exists), "natural law" and a system of self-regulated principles. The Tao creates things and is responsible for and controls their development. It informs the entire phenomenal world. While the Tao is not a deity, it may be taken as divine. On this model, pantheists take Unity to be divine either because the ordering principles are so regarded or for independent reasons.

It is clear that the naturalistic model does not rule out seeing the Unity as divine if one considers the Presocratics, the Tao, or Spinoza – where his sense of Unity is interpreted primarily on this model instead of substance.[22] Consider what Vlastos says about "the unique achievement of the Presocratics as *religious* thinkers."

> This, in a word, lies in the fact that they . . . dared transpose the name and function of divinity into a realm conceived as a rigorously natural order and, therefore, completely purged of miracle and magic . . . To present the deity as wholly immanent in the order of nature and therefore absolutely law-abiding was the peculiar and distinctive religious contribution of the Presocratics . . . They took a word which in common speech was the hallmark of the irrational, unnatural, and unaccountable and made it the name of a power which manifest itself in the operation, not in the disturbance, of intelligible law. The transposition opened new religious possibilities.[23]

Unifying powers and principles may be metaphysically distinct from natural laws and forces, or they may be identical to them. But such principles or powers, whether or not divine, come under the naturalistic model, since they are immanent and operative in the all-inclusive whole. They are a part of the Unity in which there is no longer a distinction between the natural and supernatural, and they govern intrinsically rather than extrinsically.

In the final analysis it seems that no completely natural fact alone can be the basis of Unity. This is a contentious claim – especially in view of the fact that monism has often been taken to be central to pantheism (e.g. Spinoza). However, on the naturalistic model as well as the others, pantheists generally do not, and should not, explain Unity in simply factual terms. Instead, they resort to an explanation that is at least partly given in terms of value.

Suppose everything was created by, and now depends for existence on, the theistic God. Why is this significant? Why, for example, should such a God be worthy of our worship? This kind of question must be put to the pantheist concerning factual bases of Unity. Just as the theist cannot explain the relevance of God's attributes or actions by citing additional facts, the pantheist cannot even fully explain Unity, or the relevance of facts about the world for Unity, in factual terms alone. Questions about the significance of factual matters require extra-factual explanation.

The view that there is a conceptual connection between, for

example, God's goodness and God's "worthiness of worship" is indicative of the difficulty in trying to show, either necessarily or factually, why God should be worshipped. If arguments citing conceptual connections or mere matters of fact are rejected, then explanations citing extra-factual reasons must be given. Such reasons are required if one accepts the fact/value distinction (i.e. if "is" does not entail "ought") and agrees that there cannot be a successful argument simply from what is the case (alone) to what ought to be. If the distinction between fact and value is accepted, then the *significance* of God's nature for the practice of worship must be explained. Why is worship the appropriate response – though not a response that one is logically compelled to take up?

Statements of (1) the relevance of matter of facts for Unity and (2) the practical significance of Unity for how people should live must refer to something extra-factual or a vicious regress results. Facts can be cited endlessly with no explanation of their relevance for Unity, or the significance of Unity – in short, with no explanation of Unity. Even if facts about the world suffice to ensure Unity, any explanation of the conditions of sufficiency must be partly evaluative. Thus, without resorting to evaluative resources the pantheist cannot formulate an account of pantheism, since she cannot explain Unity. This can be overlooked if one is mystified by the ontological or empirical, and mistakenly thinks that by themselves these entail substantive answers to questions of relevance.

Not all reasoning from "is" to "ought" is confusion involving the naturalistic fallacy. If one can non-fallaciously argue from matters of fact to those of value, as pantheists like Spinoza and Lao Tzu try to do, then the way the world is could be the basis of an explanation of Unity and the importance of that Unity for our lives – as the naturalistic model claims. Yet, facts by themselves cannot self-evidently show what Unity is, or how it is to be explained.

2.1.3 Unity as force, principle or plan

Consider again the idea of Unity interpreted in terms of force, principle or plan. Historically *this* is the most prevalent version of pantheism, despite the high profile of the substance model among some of the best known pantheists (e.g. Spinoza). In versions of pantheism where other models are apparent, and in religious traditions – including theistic ones – with pantheistic elements, there are significant elements of this type of unity as well. Lao Tzu, Spinoza, Plotinus, Bruno etc. are all best interpreted on this model – even though, as for Spinoza, other models may be more readily (and misleadingly) apparent. This is the type most prevalent among the early Greeks. Christopher Rowe describes the "typical Greek 'pantheistic' view" as that of

> a certain force . . . by which all things are governed and which is endowed with life . . . All the Presocratics seem to have believed that they could identify a basic order and unity underlying the apparent chaos of the phenomenal world. Nature could somehow be reduced to some kind of rational system.[24]

Rowe notes that, in some interpretations of the *Timaeus*, Plato's Demiurge (Divine Craftsman) is "a symbol of the essential intelligibility and rationality of the cosmos . . ." (p. 62).

The Presocratics relied on the concept of an ordering principle or force to explain the operations of nature, and its Unity and divinity. The principle(s), and nature as a whole, are seen as having moral and other valuational (not necessarily non-natural) properties associated with them. This is radically different from post-enlightenment ideas of nature, laws and naturalistic principles where no values are taken as inherent, and where associating moral judgements with nature makes no sense.

According to Vlastos, most of the Presocratics criticised or ignored the religious cults of their time. Instead,

> their theme is nature, and their object to explain the how and why of its unfailing order. When they find in this a moral meaning – and they all do before the atomists – they may express the trust and reverence they feel for it by calling it "god" . . . Not only is it true that properties and functions traditionally reserved to the gods are now transferred to an utterly different sort of entity . . . the properties and functions themselves have changed. . . . Traditionally the justice of Zeus is "ordained unto men" . . . the forces of nature, uncertainly personified as earthborn deities, are subdued by Zeus . . . But there is no notion of natural laws issued and maintained by Zeus. So far from maintaining

natural regularities, Zeus himself override[s] them left and right ... what could be further from the Justice of the *Apeiron* whose laws, fixed in the physical structure of the world, are cosmic in their scope and natural in their execution? When Jaeger tells us that Anaximander's cosmology offers "the first philosophical theodicy" ... it is essential to remember that their "justice" and "reparation" ... operate simply through the self-regulative periodicities of a physical equilibrium. This is certainly more, as Jaeger observes, than "a mere explanation of nature" in *our* sense of these words ... [25]

This illustrates the way in which the Presocratic view of nature is connected to their evaluative and other religious concerns. In criticising the religious cults the Presocratics were nevertheless addressing many of the cults' central concerns. Their "theme" may be nature, but their concerns are the usual religious ones – order as opposed to anomie in both the natural and moral spheres. For the Presocratics – as for Lao Tzu and Spinoza – the natural and the moral are intrinsically connected.

Anaximander used *apeiron* to "denote the endless, inexhaustible reservoir or stock from which all Becoming draws its nourishment ... the word *apeiron* points unequivocally to boundlessness as the real meaning" (Jaeger).[26] It is not only an originative principle, but also a governing one, an example of how, as Vlastos says, "the properties and functions traditionally reserved to the gods are now transferred ..." This is evident in Aristotle (*Physics* iii). "As a beginning, it must also be something that has not become and cannot pass away ... the beginning of everything else. And it encompasses all things and governs all things ... And this, they say, is the Divine. For it is immortal and indestructible ..."[27]

The *apeiron* is all-inclusive because it encompasses and governs everything; and it is regarded as divine, at least partly because it is immortal. Where it is taken as inherent in the world, then the world may be taken as an all-inclusive divine Unity informed by this principle. Earlier I discussed MacIntyre's view that because the early Greeks did not distinguish between (a) the world being informed by a divine principle and (b) the world itself being a divine Unity, some of those taken to be pantheists are not really pantheists. (a) is not a pantheistic view according to MacIntyre, while (b) is. Given the interpretation of *apeiron* above, it is clear why the distinction may be irrelevant. Unity is based upon and so explained in terms of this principle. From what has been said thus far about the Tao, it is clear that useful comparisons can be drawn between it and the *apeiron*. The grounds for comparison are deeper than that they both rely on a naturalistic model to explain Unity.

When I stated that pantheism has always been the most sought after religious/philosophical alternative to theism, this is the type I had in mind. Whereas Unity explained in terms of substance, ontology etc. is too abstract a basis for religious belief, an account in terms of a unifying principle is not. There are of course varying interpretations of such principles. But often it is in terms of explicitly moral and evaluative categories such as goodness, justice, beauty or love – vague as these may be. Unifying principles or forces are themselves taken to be good etc., or evaluative judgements are seen as following from them.[28]

The notion of force, or better yet "principle," is ambiguous between principle as fact and principle of value. It can be seen as unifying on either interpretation. But, even if the principle is taken factually, its relevance to Unity must be explained in terms of value – and this is *always* done no matter if the pantheist is Presocratic or Chinese. The evaluative aspect of "principle" is necessary to an account of Unity.

Whatever values are associated with unifying principles, they must not violate general canons of evaluative discourse – for example, the fact/value distinction. If value supervenes upon certain facts about the world, or if some other relation between fact and value warrants a judgement concerning the relevance of a unifying principle, Unity can, plausibly or implausibly, be explained on the naturalistic model. Of course, whether or not a particular account is true depends upon the way the world is (given a realist, non-epistemic, account of truth).

The idea that unifying principles or forces exist or do not exist finds frequent expression in modern and contemporary (i.e. non-theistically informed) arts. If there is a single most important hermeneutic applicable to the greatest number of significant (and insignificant) works of art, this is it. It is an existential theme. And this is why there is the kind of "intrinsic" connection between a range of art and religion that is widely recognised and rarely explained. The idea of unifying principles is also present in nature mysticism, which is really what Wordsworth's and the other Romantics' pantheism is; and it is in classical literature and music (e.g. "pantheistic overtones" in Beethoven's music). The idea that Unity that is rooted in nature is what types of nature mysticism (e.g. Wordsworth and Robinson Jeffers, Gary Snyder) have in common with more philosophically robust versions of pantheism. It is why nature mysticism and philosophical pantheism are often conflated and confused for one another. They are distinguishable in theory, even though they both talk about unity and are partly the result of the same intimations and feelings.

It is not surprising that a naturalistic explanation of Unity is the most prevalent one. Not only is it unquestionably the most accessible; it may *prima facie* be the most plausible, since it is not readily committed to theories about substance, origins of existence, appearance and reality etc. – though naturalistic accounts do have concomitants. Unlike some of the other models, naturalistic accounts have been seen to have more apparent consequences, religiously speaking, in terms of world-view, ethos, and the practices these generate and reflect. For that reason, it is and has been the most religiously accessible type of pantheism as well. For various reasons, it is the type that both affectively and intellectually most readily suggests itself.

On the naturalistic model, Unity sometimes includes the idea of a plan or purpose. For Fichte and Hegel it does, but not for Spinoza or Lao Tzu. MacIntyre says, "In Fichte and Hegel the unity ascribed to the universe is one of an over-all purpose manifest in the pattern of events ... in Fichte's case ... about moral development ... in Hegel's case ... about historical development."[29] For the type of non-theistic pantheism (i.e. non-personal theism) that I am discussing, plan or purpose cannot be interpreted as the intentional result of an agent. On that interpretation pantheism reduces to a type of theism, since theists believe in an agent responsible for a divine plan (i.e. "providence"). Pantheistic Unity based on plan or purpose must be distinguished from the plan or purpose theists posit in terms of divine providence. It is usual to talk of a plan as the result of intentional acts, but it is not necessary to do so. What is a plan apart from intentional action? I think it reduces to what occurs in accordance with an ordering principle or force. To say it is not the result of intentional action does not mean that agents and their actions are not part of any such plan. It means that the purpose or plan is not formulated by a personal agent. However, agents' actions may promote the overall purpose and presumably must accord with it.

Hegel can be used to illustrate. For Hegel, the overall purpose manifest in history is the self-realisation of Absolute Spirit. History is the process through which this takes place – a process in which persons have their part. Intentional action and consciousness are involved in the process, but the purpose that progressively manifests itself is not the result of Spirit self-consciously formulating and following a plan. It is not the intentional result of an agent (Spirit) for Hegel. Yet, the overall purpose that does manifest itself is not just the result of chance. There is an intrinsic logic, and so order, to the process of self-realisation that results from the dialectical movement constitutive of history. The process that is history is not thoroughly deterministic, but the unifying overall purpose, which in this case is the Absolute coming to know itself as the Absolute, is inviolable. Spirit is not some self-conscious individual out to fulfil a goal, and it is not the total of finite consciousnesses and their goals.

On the naturalistic model, Unity is not equated merely with the unity of a teleological system. For example, it is not unity resulting from evolution and natural forces, nor is it these principles and forces themselves. To interpret Unity this way would be to misinterpret the naturalistic model reductionistically in a Schopenhauerian mode. (Schopenhauer gave a ludicrously reductionistic account of Unity, and then criticised pantheism for not being able to see through the reduction.) Reductionistic accounts of Unity, whether in terms of naturalistic or other models, are resisted by pantheists. Unity is not evolution or nature and its laws. Rather, the pantheist sees evolution, laws of nature etc. as themselves part of the Unity subject to higher order (i.e. pantheistically more fundamental) principles. The situation is similar in theism where evolution and laws are not taken as God's powers or plans themselves, but as the means by which those powers are instantiated and plans are achieved.

The relevance that evolution and laws of nature have for Unity must be partly explained evaluatively; but Unity is not just nature and laws taken evaluatively instead of descriptively. On the naturalistic model, Unity is not reducible to nature and nature is not explainable except in terms of Unity, and with reference to more fundamental principles. Thus, the Tao as natural law and a system of self-regulating principles, and the Tao as a standard for behaviour, are understood partly in terms of the Tao as a metaphysical reality.

Unity and divinity

Thus far the operative notions of Unity and divinity have been kept relatively distinct. However, for reasons given in the discussion of the naturalistic model and the Presocratics, this is artificial. Unity may have to be explained partly in terms of divinity. The all-inclusive whole may be a Unity because it is divine – either in itself (Spinoza's substance) or because of a divine power informing the whole, as with the Presocratics. The Presocratics give an account of why they think the unifying principle is divine. It is immortal and indestructible. But this does not satisfactorily explain the relation between Unity and divinity, or why divinity might be seen as a basis of Unity. Similarly, though less naturally, the question arises as to whether the all-inclusive whole is divine because it is a Unity. Can Unity be a basis for attributing divinity to the whole?

If divinity is the basis for Unity, as it may be for the Presocratics, or alternatively if Unity is the basis for divinity, then there is something of a redundancy in the definition of pantheism as the belief that everything that exists constitutes a divine Unity. A simpler non-redundant definition would be that pantheism holds that "everything is divine." If divinity is the basis of Unity, or vice versa, this does not mean that either aspect is less important than the other, but that the one must be interpreted in terms of the other. Both features remain necessary for pantheism, but one might be conceptually prior or more basic. It is more likely, however, that two aspects mutually involve one another with neither being more central.

The existence of all-inclusive unity apart from its being divine would no more be pantheistic than would the existence of a divine unity that was not relevantly unified. Attributing "divinity" to the whole without making it, or some other property, a ground for attributing a significant sense of unity to the whole, would not suffice for pantheism. It would no more suffice than would the existence of an all-inclusive, but non-divine, unity. But for various reasons, unity of a certain type may be seen as ensuring divinity – and/or vice versa. This is the view of the Presocratics, Spinoza, and probably Hegel as well. There are clearly important connections between the unitive and divine aspects of the all-inclusive whole for pantheists. The connection may have an affective as well as a cognitive base – as it clearly does for Wordsworth and Jeffers.

Before the problematic relationship between the divine and unitive aspects of Unity can be addressed, a concept of divinity relevant to pantheism must be given. An idea of "divinity" is also needed before pantheism's treatment of issues like creation, evil, and salvation can be examined in Part II.

2.2 DIVINITY

In pantheism, the world is not mere world which may also be called God; it is the presence of spirit that divinizes the world.[1]

John Macquarrie

I define a divine being as a backwardly eternal being who is perfectly free, omnipotent, and omniscient.[2]

Richard Swinburne

This whole is in all its parts so beautiful, and is felt by me to be so intensely in earnest, that I am compelled to love it, and to think of it as divine. It seems to me that this whole alone is worthy of the deeper sort of love; and that there is peace, freedom, I might say a kind of salvation, in turning one's affections outward toward this one God, rather than inwards on one's self, or on humanity . . . [3]

Robinson Jeffers

I use the terms "divinity" and "holiness" interchangeably. "Divine" is defined as pertaining to God ("of, from, or like a god"), but also as "sacred" or "holy." Either definition suits the present purpose, since determining why pantheists regard the Unity as divine, or god, is equivalent to determining why they regard the Unity to be sacred or holy. The idea of "divinity" in pantheism is similar in some respects to its theistic meaning and use.

Why do pantheists ascribe divinity to the Unity? The reason is similar to why theists describe God as holy. They experience it as such. In Otto's experiential account, what is divine is what evokes the numinous experience. This can be a theistic god, but it can also be a pantheistic Unity. And, when looked at from socio-scientific perspectives in terms of how the concept of divinity *functions* intellectually and affectively (e.g. its ethical, soteriological and explanatory roles), its application in theism and pantheism is much the same.

Religions give conflicting accounts of what is meant by God – and what it means to say something is divine or holy varies accordingly. Divinity is often interpreted with a tradition-specific Being in mind. In Christianity the category of the holy is sometimes conceived in terms of God as a perfect being.[4] It is in virtue of possessing the "divine" perfections that God is divine and worthy of worship – indeed, that God is "God." Otto's analysis of the holy is an alternative to accounts dependent upon particular traditions. The category of the holy encompasses more than God and more than one kind of god – though even he took the Christian (Lutheran) God as the apotheosis of the holy. He claims the holy is a *sui generis* category. In terms of experience it is logically primitive. It is not reducible to other kinds of experience and cannot be adequately expressed in terms of other concepts. The holy has an objective correlate in the object (i.e. the numinous) that evokes the experience. Otto's analysis can be applied across formidable boundaries; boundaries that include very different notions of deity, and vastly different cultures and historical epochs.[5]

Experiential/expressive models of religion like Otto's and socio-scientific ones like Clifford Geertz's agree that there are accounts of holiness, and more significantly, of the nature of religion in general, that are applicable to the entire range of traditions and interpretations of God. They disagree, however, as to what the correct account is. Analyses like those of Otto's or Geertz's are formulated with no essential reference to any particular religion, and are meant to be applicable to all traditions. It is in analyses such as these, rather than in tradition-specific accounts, that one must look for an account of divinity applicable to pantheism.

The issue raised at the close of section 2.1 concerning the relation between Unity and divinity is considered at the end of this section. I claim that the senses of Unity and divinity relevant to pantheism are best kept distinct. Pantheism is best understood as the view that there exists an all-inclusive divine Unity, where Unity and divinity are regarded as distinct properties which are nevertheless inextricably connected in various ways. The two notions essential to pantheism cannot be properly understood without direct reference to one another, and neither is more fundamental or less necessary than the other. Still, it is not possible to establish that the terms mutually entail one another. This is not because they are not conceptually linked for the pantheist. Rather it is because showing entailment requires the kind of explicit account of pantheism, "unity" and "divinity" that does not exist, or, despite pantheism's attraction as a religion, exists in only one or two philosophical versions of pantheism. Historically and normatively, the pantheist does not conceptually segregate Unity and divinity. But neither is reducible to, or entails, the other.

I shall consider Otto's account of the "holy" as an example of the experiential/expressive approach to "divinity," and apply it to pantheism. An influential example of a cultural/linguistic account will then be examined. However, it is useful first to consider some narrower accounts of divinity.[6]

John Macquarrie claims that it is "the presence of spirit that divinizes the world," but what does this mean? Suppose it is taken as analytically true. Divinity is defined as the presence of [indwelling] spirit. This does not tell us much about what is meant by "divine." It can forestall the question "What is it about spirit that makes the world divine?," since "spirit" is taken to mean "that which divinizes." The postponement, however, is temporary. The issue concerning the nature of divinity is simply pushed back, and the question becomes "what is 'spirit' or 'divinity'?" Of course, Macquarrie is right in claiming that "In pantheism, the world is not mere world which may also be called God." More is needed – namely that the world is, in some ultimately evaluative sense, both a unity and divine. But saying that "it is the presence of spirit that divinizes the world" does not get us very far. One suspects that if spirit is what divinizes the world, this is only because spirit is already divine, or has divine making properties – and so we are back to asking about "divine" *per se*. In context, it is unlikely that Macquarrie means to define divinity in terms of spirit.

Macquarrie's assertion is most naturally taken as an explanation of what pantheists mean by saying the world is divine, rather than as a definition. Yet, it is wrong on either account. Pantheists do not generally attribute divinity to the world because they think there is an "indwelling spirit" in it. No pantheists that refer to that idea are mentioned by Macquarrie. Hegel and Plotinus come to mind. But Hegel denies he is a pantheist and, at any rate, means something different by *Geist* than "indwelling spirit" as Macquarrie understands it. And Plotinus does not mention anything like "indwelling spirit" in his mystical theology. Depending on how it is understood, the presence of "spirit" is one among several conditions sometimes taken as necessary and/or sufficient for divinity. The presence of a world-soul, whether distinguished from spirit or similar to it, is another. But neither of these explain divinity. In explaining pantheism, Macquarrie gives a theistic interpretation of the Unity's "divinity." What could make the world, or pantheistic Unity, holy? Macquarrie models his answer on a specifically Judaeo-Christian conception of the divine. It is "spirit" in a theistic sense that Macquarrie has in mind when he claims its presence divinizes the world. To reiterate, however, this explanation is not satisfactory. If we grant the world is divine because of spirit, the question arises: "What is it about spirit that makes the world divine?"

More importantly, there is little reason to suppose the idea of "divinity" relevant to pantheism should be modelled after a specific tradition's concept of spirit or divinity – in this case Christianity. At best, this tradition-dependent concept would be relevant to Christian/pantheist and other theist/pantheist hybrids (e.g. panentheism). It is too specific for any general analysis of pantheism, and it refers primarily to the theistic variants of pantheism which, for reasons already given, are the most inconsequential for pantheistic practice. Macquarrie's account is problematic partly because theism and pantheism are usually taken on religious and philosophical grounds to be incompatible. There are theories in which aspects of each are combined (e.g. Plotinus).[7] But to put the matter bluntly: whatever the pantheist's reason is for attributing divinity to the world, it certainly is not the presence of something like a theistic spirit – the non-existence of which is presupposed by the typical pantheist.

Macquarrie is not alone in modelling his answer as to why the world is "divine" according to pantheism, or more generally what "divinity" is, on a Christian conception of spirit. Richard Swinburne, in *The Coherence of Theism*, does not attempt to define "holiness," preferring instead to adopt *what he takes to be* Otto's analysis. However, he does define "divine being" (i.e. God) from a theistic perspective "as a backwardly eternal being who is perfectly free, omnipotent, and omniscient." Of course, Swinburne is not concerned with a notion of divinity broad enough to apply to both pantheism and theism since divinity for him is linked exclusively with theism. For Swinburne, unlike Otto, "holiness" is a property that God necessarily has along with his other properties. Divinity is either entailed by these other properties or is nothing distinct from the co-presence of God's properties. Swinburne's understanding of divinity is so bound up with the Christian God that the predication of holiness to anything else must be understood in relation to that God.[8]

As applied to God, the notion of holiness for Macquarrie and Swinburne is tied to that of a personal god.[9] This is true of Swinburne even though he allegedly adopts Otto's concept of holiness – a concept that is not originally connected with the personal, let alone Christianity. It is not just a question of conceiving of the theistic god as paradigmatically holy. Rather what Macquarrie and Swinburne do is make personhood a necessary condition of divinity for god. Other things or persons may be holy, but for god to be holy, god must be a person. On this view it is not possible to attribute divinity to the pantheistic Unity, or to the god of any other type of non-personal theism.

The notion of divinity as applied to God has virtually become connected to that of "person" in theistic traditions. To be a god, or God, something must be a person; and only a god who is a person can possess the property "divinity." For example, Macquarrie says

> Of all the modes of creaturely existence, personality is the highest and so the fittest to serve as an analogy of divine being ... No merely impersonal force could merit to be called "God", but perhaps he is best called "suprapersonal", and this is obscured in much classical theism, which speaks of him in exclusively personal terms ... [I]n classical theism ... God has been represented as personal, even to the point of anthropomorphism. This is entirely appropriate.[10]

It is not evident what Macquarrie means by "supra-personal" (better than personal?); but being supra-personal entails being personal, or something analogous. On this account the world or Unity, not being a person, can no more be divine than can a stone.

Whatever criteria are decided upon as necessary for attributing divinity to something, one cannot decide *a priori* that the possession of divinity requires personhood without ruling out the possibility of the most typical types of pantheism (i.e. non-personal types). After all, theism is what pantheism is most of all trying to distance itself from. I am not sure the reverse is true – but theism does ordinarily strongly oppose itself to pantheism. In any case, Spinoza's God and Lao Tzu's Tao, for example, are distinctly non-personal, as are the governing principles of the Presocratics. It seems unwarranted, therefore, to suppose that a necessary condition of something's being divine is that it be personal on the grounds that "Of all the modes of creaturely existence, personality is the highest and so the fittest to serve as an analogy of divine being." At least to do so begs the question against Spinoza, some of the Presocratics, Lao Tzu, probably Plotinus, as well as against experiential and socio-scientific accounts of divinity. Macquarrie and Swinburne take theism as not simply paradigmatic of the divine but as essential to it.

In fact, in Otto's account of "the holy," its distinctive aspect is non-rational and non-personal. He coined the word "numinous" to describe "that aspect of deity which transcends or eludes comprehension in rational or ethical terms" (p. xv). It is the "extra in the meaning of 'holy' above and beyond the meaning of goodness" (p. 6).[11] The "numen" has a supra- personal aspect, but is neither "super-personal" nor a "person." The rational and ethical connotations of the holy are accretions according to Otto. Although "no distinction of the non-rational and the rational aspects of God should imply that the latter is less essential than the former" (p. 99), the rational and ethical aspect is something deity shares with other thinking things, and is not present in the original idea. The distinctive non-rational factor in the idea of the holy is the non-personal *numinous*. Swinburne's adaptation of Otto's analysis leaves out this essential feature of the account.

Macquarrie claims that personality is the highest "mode of creaturely existence" and so "the fittest to serve as an analogy of divine being ... No merely impersonal force could merit to be called 'God.' " He says this emphasis on the personal has a tendency to miss those incomprehensible aspects of deity "obscured in much classical theism, which speaks of him [God] in exclusively personal terms." If Otto's analysis of the divine is correct, then Macquarrie's qualification is crucial. Emphasis on the personalistic aspect of deity must not exclude the non-rational factor in the holy. It is this exclusion that Otto is at pains to redress.

In order to make Otto's analysis appear compatible with his own, Swinburne distorts it by neglecting the non-rational factor Otto stresses. Swinburne defines a "personal ground of being" as

> a person who is eternally perfectly free, omnipotent, and omniscient . . . [an] omnipresent spirit, creator of the universe, perfectly good, and a source of moral obligation.
>
> (p. 224)

> a personal ground of being . . . would not merely be worthy of men's worship; he would have most, and probably all, of the properties which make up holiness, classically described by Rudolf Otto.
>
> (p. 292)

Leaving aside the question of why such a being would be worthy of worship let us examine the claim about holiness.

Swinburne thinks there is a connection between "holiness," in Otto's sense, and "personal ground of being," such that a personal ground of being must be holy.[12] Yet in Otto's account there is no such connection. If moral perfection (etc.) has become a necessary feature of anything "holy," it is an accrued feature. In its original usage there is no connection whatsoever between the numinous and goodness or moral obligation. Furthermore, "holiness" *per se* had nothing to do with being omnipotent etc., and nothing to do with being a "Being."[13] Swinburne claims that "a holy being is a perfectly good being who is also something else, which Otto calls 'numinous' " (Swinburne, p. 293), but Otto says something different.

> we have come to use the words "holy" . . . in an entirely derivative sense . . . We generally take "holy" as meaning "completely good"; it is the absolute moral attribute . . . But this . . . is inaccurate . . . moral significance is contained in

53

the word "holy", but it includes ... a clear overplus of meaning ... Nor is this merely a later or acquired meaning; rather "holy" ... denoted first and foremost *only* this overplus; if the ethical element was present ... it was not original and never constituted the whole meaning of the word ... in our inquiry into that element which is separate and peculiar to the idea of the holy it will be useful ... to invent a special term [the numinous] to stand for "the holy" *minus* its moral factor ... and, as we can now add, minus its "rational" aspect altogether ...

(pp. 5–6)

Swinburne's claim is therefore misleading. We have come to equate the holy with the perfectly good, but perfect goodness has nothing to do with a Being's holiness where "holiness" is taken as denoting, as it originally did, the "overplus" of meaning in the concept. As Otto sees it, the defining characteristic of holiness, before it accrued the moral elements that it is now mistakenly defined in terms of, was that it was distinct from *any* rational categories or omni-predicates, including moral perfection.

If Swinburne is correct in claiming that "a personal ground of being ... has most, and probably all, the marks of holiness" (p. 294), even if such a being has them in virtue of having the properties essential to such a being, this is not the only way of being holy. On Otto's account, being a personal ground of being is neither necessary nor sufficient for being holy. Swinburne has not shown that the properties of (a) being holy and (b) being a personal ground entail one another; and his claim that a personal ground of being will have the marks of holiness is unsubstantiated. Even if being a personal ground of being did entail holiness, holiness does not, on Otto's account, entail being a personal ground of being.

It may not always be personhood *per se* that is regarded as necessary for divinity in theism. Sometimes it may be the property of mind or rationality associated with persons. We are made in the image of God where this *imago dei* has to do with rationality. Perhaps pantheists may claim that the Unity is divine, in part, because it is rational or minded, but deny the Unity is a person. Is the notion of a rational or minded Unity intelligible apart from conceiving it as a person? Minimally, even if the Unity is not itself conceived in personal terms, it may have a rational aspect to it by containing minded entities – though something more than this is usually meant. Something more is meant by Hegel, for example, although *Geist* is not a person. But to be "rational" the Unity need not be rational throughout, any more than to be rational a person needs to be so at all times and places. Even if rationality is required for divinity, the Unity need not be rational in *just* the way persons are. It cannot be unless it is a person. It need not be rational (or "minded") in a manner identical to persons, *if* sense can be made of predicating rationality to things other than persons and animals. Yet if one is to avoid equivocating on the meaning of rationality, then as applied to Unity it must be analogous to its ordinary applications. John Stuart Mill made a similar point concerning the predication of "good" to God.[14]

Perhaps the pantheist can claim the Unity is impersonally rational and use this as a partial reason for asserting its divinity. It is more significant, however, that pantheists can deny the Unity is minded, or conscious (let alone a person), and still claim it divine. If pantheists are right in this, as they are on Otto's analysis, it is possible to explain why the Unity is divine without also claiming it is rational or a person. However, the Unity may still have personal properties associated with it in ways that are independent of divinity. The Unity's divinity may have nothing to do with its being rational, or some type of rationality may be a necessary but insufficient condition for divinity as it is for some of the Presocratics.

Before returning to Otto's analysis, and finally to a socio-scientific one, it will be useful to examine a Presocratic notion of divinity that is not reliant on personality.

There is greater unanimity and clarity among the Presocratics about what makes something divine than about what constitutes a Unity. What would make the Unity divine? Christopher Rowe says,

> When Anaximander called his originative substance "the divine" . . . that substance is evidently to be regarded as "god" . . . and as possessing the essential attributes of the traditional gods – in particular, it is "immortal and imperishable", and it has a governing function. (Aristotle says that it "surrounds all things and steers all things," and this could

be a direct quotation from Anaximander) ... The Milesian monists, appear to have claimed that what unifies the world is that it sprang from a single undifferentiated substance. This substance was called "divine" for the reasons given us in Aristotle's report about Anaximander's originative substance; or, in a paraphrase ... because "it lived forever and was the author of its own movement and change, and of all the ordered world."[15]

The originative substance, or god, is divine because it is " 'immortal and imperishable', and it has a governing function ... because 'it lived forever and was the author of its own movement and change, and of all the ordered world'." But why associate these properties with "divinity"? Why suppose that because something is "immortal and indestructible" it is also, as Aristotle says, divine? Is divinity entailed by these properties? Does it supervene upon them?

Consider infinity and eternity. (Neither are explicitly mentioned by Rowe, but both are implied.) MacIntyre says "The infinity and eternity of the universe have often been the predicates which seemed to entail its divinity, but the sense in which the universe is infinite and eternal is surely not that in which the traditional religions have ascribed these predicates to a god."[16] MacIntyre may be right, but it is difficult to say since the meaning of "infinite" and "eternal" as applied to either the universe or a god is not explained. Even if the terms carry different connotations relative to the objects to which they are ascribed, why suppose equivocation is involved? If we think of "eternal" and "infinite" in somewhat different ways when ascribed to gods and the universe, it does not follow that these terms have a radically different sense when applied to the universe (e.g. a pantheistic universe), instead of to traditional gods. This is especially so when the universe is regarded as a god.

Even if MacIntyre's point concerning "eternal" and "infinite" is accepted, the same is not obviously true of another property cited by Rowe as constitutive of divinity – the "governing function." One of the reasons given for calling the Unity (i.e. the single undifferentiated substance from which the world originated) divine is that it "was the author of its own movement and change, and of all the ordered world." Why this property, along with "living forever" is taken to entail divinity is unclear.

But it seems to be ascribed to god by traditional religions in a sense similar to the one in which it is predicated of Unity by the Presocratics. At least it is not clear that it is being used differently. Note too that the above ideas of unity and divinity are not entirely discreet. Even if there is no entailment, the notion of divinity is integrally related to the concept of unity.

The difficulty in determining the properties associated with divinity as applied to Unity (i.e. why call the Unity "divine"?) has little to do with the possibility of equivocation as MacIntyre suggests. It has to do with the basic question concerning the nature of divinity. Why associate any of the above properties with "divinity" as applied either to the gods or Unity? If god or the Unity is "immortal and indestructible," why also take it to be divine? Both experiential and socio-scientific accounts of religion suggest reasons for this. (In Berger's and Geertz's account, associating immortality and indestructibility with the divine indicates cosmic insecurity. It reflects a fear of anomie and a corresponding need for stability and order.) Analyses of divinity in terms of either its function or the experiences associated with it (i.e. the numinous experience) give accounts of why gods are regarded as divine that can be extended to Unity. These types of analyses are suggestive of reasons why properties such as infinity and eternity are grounds for ascribing divinity.

Experiential accounts of the holy like Otto's are based on an examination of the phenomenological content of a kind of basic religious experience taken to be historically and culturally pervasive. On this view a thing is divine in the first instance, not because it is eternal, infinite, or has a governing function; but because it evokes the experience of the holy (e.g. the numinous experience). Upon subsequent intellectualisation, properties like "infinite" and "eternal" accrue to this experientially based interpretation of divinity. But nothing is divine merely in virtue of being eternal, infinite etc.

Otto describes rather than defines the numinous because he regards any verbal definition of it as inadequate. He aims at a description of the phenomenologically unique experience of the numinous that is as close to an ostensive definition as possible. It is a quality of the object, an objective property, and not a subjective feeling or psychological state, though the "numinous feeling" is what one gets when "apprehending" a numinous object (i.e. the "Holy"). The "emphasis is always upon the objective reference, and upon subjective feelings only as indispensable clues to this" (p. xvii). " 'Holiness' – 'the holy' – is a category of interpretation and valuation peculiar to the sphere of religion" (p. 5).

The complete title of Otto's book is *The Idea of The Holy: An Inquiry into the Non-rational Factor in the Idea of the Divine and Its Relation to the Rational.* As we have seen, Otto claims the idea of the divine consists of both non-rational and rational and ethical properties, but "holy" refers first and foremost to the non-rational, non- personal aspect of the divine. (He sometimes uses "holy" and "divine" interchangeably.)

> The non-rational ... in the idea of the divine was found in the numinous ... [R]ationalistic speculation tends to conceal the divine in God[17] ... before God becomes for us rationality, absolute reason, a personality, a moral will, He is the wholly non-rational and "other", the being of sheer mystery and marvel.
>
> (pp. 193–4)

Otto's account can help in a general way to explain the pantheistic predication of divinity to the all-inclusive Unity, though it needs to be supplemented, and probably subsumed, by the socioscientific accounts of divinity – what it means and what the whole idea of it is about. It may also help explain the grounds for ascription of Unity since the divine is explained partly in terms relevant to some accounts of Unity.

Not all pantheists mean by "divine" what Otto means. However, it is plausible to suppose that, for many, the pantheistic intuition and ground for attributing divinity to the Unity (i.e. the pantheist's intimations of divinity) rests on numinous experience or something like it. It is affectively and experientially grounded. The Unity is experienced as numinous – i.e. as "divine." The basis for calling the Unity divine is experiential and affective. There is better reason to suppose experience is the basis for ascribing divinity than to take properties like infinity and eternity as reasons. This supposition can be supported partly by reading pantheists like Whitman or Jeffers, and also by noting affinities between pantheists and some mystics. This experientially based concept of divinity offers a reasonable, though partial, account of what pantheists have meant by calling the Unity "divine." Divinity is not predicated of Unity because it is associated with properties like "eternal" unless, as is often the case, "eternal" is itself attributed to the Unity on experiential grounds. (See the quotation from Jeffers at the beginning of section 4.4.) Non-experientially based accretions in meaning are later attributed to Unity or other gods on rationalistic grounds. (Socio-scientific models of religion like those of Geertz and Berger indirectly offer more comprehensive accounts of why properties like "eternal" and "immutable" are ascribed to Unity, though experience and emotion are necessary in their accounts as well. If ever there were anti-anomic (i.e. anti-chaos) ordering terms projected onto the universe at large, "eternal" and "immutable" are two of them.)[18]

If the numinous is a basis of the pantheistic ascription of divinity, then pantheism is importantly similar to theism in Otto's account. Theists and pantheists have the non-rational aspect of their different ideas of deity, and the experiential basis of their respective religions, in common. Experience of the numinous, and response to it, is similar if determined only by non-rational elements. Revisionary conceptualisation of the numinous experience is what distances religion – detrimentally in some ways according to Otto – from this largely univocal experiential basis of deity.

John Harvey, the translator of *The Idea of the Holy* (*Das Heilige*), warns against the following distortion of Otto's view of the holy: "that of so far humanising our conception of the divine and the sacred that a severance is brought about between the divine as immanent and as transcendent, between God as rational and moral Person and God (if indeed in this view the name could also be applied here) as Majesty and Mystery and superhuman Otherness" (p. xv).[19] But Harvey's warning is itself misleading since the severance between the rational ("personal") aspect of God and the "wholly other" aspect is precisely what Otto calls attention to. Holiness originally and primarily resides in the latter aspect. Severing the rational and non-rational elements of the divine is merely a way of isolating the element Otto regards as overlooked and more fundamental. He repeatedly argues against an anthropomorphic reduction of the divine in ethical or other personalistic terms. The two elements are related, but the basic aspect of the "holy" is non-rational. It is "the real innermost core" of religion (p. 6).[20] Otto's analysis is meant as a corrective to the distortion of the idea of the holy that has occurred – a distortion in both intellectual and religious terms. In changing the meaning of "holy," traditions have undermined the foundations of religion, and religiously speaking this is a danger. Otto thinks it is important to attend to the numinous and uncover its original meaning, because failing to do so puts us religiously (and so "humanly") at risk.

Furthermore, being "wholly other" does not so much imply transcendence in any strong ontological sense as it does a kind of epistemic transcendence. The "wholly other" is "beyond our apprehension and comprehension . . . because our knowledge has certain irremovable limits" (p. 28). Yet this transcendence is not absolute. It is meant primarily to reflect the partially incomprehensible nature of the "wholly other" when approached by rational means alone. Affectively, in terms of "feeling-content," the situation is different, and it is capable of being partially apprehended.[21] Transcendence is bridged via our affective natures.

Conceptually, the terms "supernatural" and "transcendent" applied to the "wholly other" are "merely negative and exclusive attributes with reference to 'nature' and the world or cosmos respectively" (p. 30). The "wholly other" is supernatural (i.e. not natural) and transcendent to anything in the natural world. These are purely "negative" terms in so far as they describe the "wholly other" as that which this "natural" world is not.[22] Admittedly this sounds contrary to pantheism. But whatever the precise meaning of transcendence Otto has in mind, it need not be interpreted so as to undermine the pantheist's claim of Unity.[23] After all, the Tao is taken to be transcendent in some respects, as is Plotinus' One and Hegel's *Geist*.

Otto says "It is essential to every theistic conception of God, and most of all to the Christian, that it designates and precisely characterises deity by the attributes spirit, reason, purpose, good will, supreme power, unity, selfhood. The nature of God is thus thought of by analogy with our human nature of reason and personality . . ." (p. 1). Yet where divinity is distinguished from the theistic or specifically Christian concept of God, it has no intrinsic properties of reason and personality. And even in the Christian sense "the view that the essence of deity can be given completely and exhaustively in such 'rational' attributions . . . is not an unnatural misconception" (p. 2). However, deity always has an "essential" *supra*-personal, *supra*-rational aspect, which implies a qualitative rather than quantitative distinction.[24]

Otto describes "the object to which the numinous consciousness is directed" (p. 25) as the "*mysterium tremendum.*" The feelings associated with this experience are complex and diverse. It is

> the deepest and most fundamental element in all strong and sincerely felt religious emotion ... The feeling of it [*mysterium tremendum*] may at times come sweeping like a gentle tide ... It may pass over into a more set and lasting attitude of the soul ... thrillingly vibrant and resonant ... lead to strange excitements ... and ecstasy. It has its wild and demonic forms and can sink to an almost grisly horror ... it may be developed into something beautiful and pure and glorious.
>
> (pp. 12–13)

Experience of the *tremendum* includes an element of "fear that is more than fear proper" and "religious dread" – an aspect of "awefulness." He notes that some feelings associated with the *mysterium tremendum* (e.g. "creature-consciousness") are at times also found in mysticism. This is not surprising since mysticism also stresses non-rational apprehension of the divine.[25]

The "identification" of self with "transcendent Reality" that Otto sees as common to numinous experience and mysticism is relevant to both the unitive and divine aspects of pantheism.

> a characteristic common to all types of mysticism ... the *identification*, in different degrees of completeness, of the personal self with the transcendent Reality ... it must be Identification with the Something that is at once absolutely supreme in power and reality and wholly non-rational.
>
> (p. 22)

The basis for this identification is religious experience, and the "Something" that one identifies with is the *mysterium tremendum* or *numen*. It is divine but "wholly non-rational."

If there is, as Otto suggests, an experiential basis for the concept of divinity, then his analysis suggests why no "clear conceptual expression can be given to it" (p. 30). The idea of the divine is grounded in "positive feeling content" that eludes conceptualisation. Extrapolating from this we can ask: why is the pantheistic notion of divinity less precise than the theistic account? It is because theism, but not pantheism, over-conceptualises this feeling content. The pantheistic notion of divinity is affectively based in a way that the theistic notion is not – or is no longer. The fact that we are conceptually vague about the numinous is compensated for by its being affectively powerful. Otto sees numinous experience, this "peculiar moment of consciousness," as the foundation of all religion, and as affectively grounding latter day rationalisations of religion.[26]

There is an aspect of the divine, says Otto, "which cannot be reduced to idea, world-order, moral order, principle of being, or purposive will" (p. 96). To conceive of the divine exclusively in these terms is not only reductionistic, but raises irresolvable theistic difficulties. Thus, it is impossible to understand the story of Job in purely rational and moral (i.e. non-numinous) terms. The category of the numinous is necessary to making the story of Job comprehensible.[27] This suggests reasons both why pantheism avoids some difficulties associated with theism, and also why theism fails to resolve them. This is discussed in connection with the problem of evil (section 4.2).

I want to discuss one final feature of Otto's account: his claim that the numinous is an *a priori* category. This claim is not directly related to the applicability of his concept of the divine to pantheism, but it is allegedly central to his theory. I argue that the claim is unnecessary and does nothing to jeopardise his account overall. Otto claims that holiness is

> a *purely a priori* category ... seeking to account for the ideas in question [the rational ideas of absoluteness, completion, necessity, the good etc.] we are referred away from all sense-experience back to an original and underivable capacity of the mind implanted in the "pure reason" ... But in the case of the non-rational elements of our category of the Holy we are referred back to something still deeper ... referring to empirical knowledge, he [Kant] distinguishes that part which we receive through impressions and that which our own faculty of cognition supplies from itself ... The numinous is of the latter kind[28] ... The proof that in the numinous we have to deal with purely *a priori* cognitive elements is to be reached by introspection and a critical examination of reason ... We find ... in the numinous

experience, beliefs and feelings qualitatively different from anything that "natural" sense-perception is capable of giving us . . .

(pp. 112–13)

Because of its *a priori* character the numinous consciousness "predisposes" certain kinds of historical and psychological reactions that would otherwise be difficult to explain. He claims that other theories attempting to explain these things, such as "primitive monotheism" or "naturalistic" explanations of religion, fail (pp. 129–31). He sees these theories as obscuring the *a priori* character of the numinous because, in associating the numinous with allegedly naturalistic foundations, its character remains unrecognised. In naturalistic theories the numinous is seen as qualitatively no different from ordinary feelings and emotions, and perceivable in ordinary sense experience. But according to Otto, the numinous is itself the *a priori* – and thus non-naturalistic – foundation of religion.[29]

The claim that the numinous is an *a priori* category appears, for Otto, to be entailed by his claim that "We find . . . in the numinous experience, beliefs and feelings qualitatively different from anything that 'natural' sense-perception is capable of giving us" (p. 113). It is unclear what is meant by "qualitative difference" in this context, or why this should be taken as evidence of the *a priori* character of the numinous. Mystical experience is taken to be qualitatively different from sense experience. But this is not accompanied by the claim that mystical consciousness is *a priori*. To the extent that kinds of mystical experience can be equated with numinous experience, Otto is alone in claiming that the numinous is an *a priori* category, and that an *a priori* cognitive element in our minds is required for its apprehension. Perhaps Otto regards "*a priori*" as honorific, just as mystics sometimes regard "ineffable" in that way. If the numinous were an *a priori* category perhaps it would be exempt from everyday exigencies, and religion would be grounded in the structure of consciousness and Being.

Furthermore, it is difficult to see why Otto thinks the *a priori* character of the numinous makes it incompatible with naturalistic explanations of religion. Could it not be a basis for such explanations? Naturalistic explanations are not necessarily incompatible with religious truth claims – albeit they endanger them. Why

63

introduce the contentious claim concerning the *a priori* character of the numinous when nothing of importance seems to hinge on it? Whether or not the numinous is an *a priori* category, or experience of it is merely qualitatively distinguishable from ordinary sense experience, it could be seen as an essential part of various theories, including naturalistic ones, concerning the foundations of religion. The only thing it would not be is what Otto wants it to be: the sole foundation – one that is constitutive of human consciousness. It seems that, for Otto, human beings are essentially *homo religiosus*, and this follows from the fact that he takes the faculty for the apprehension of the numinous as constitutive of human consciousness.

Whether one regards the numinous as an *a priori* category or, more straightforwardly, as empirical in character, Otto has given a generic account of an experientially based concept of the divine. It is as appropriate to the idea of the divine in pantheism as it is to the idea in theism. Indeed, I have suggested why it is more appropriate. Given Otto's analysis, the concept of the divine employed by pantheists is no less cogent or more mysterious than that employed by theists; it cannot be since it is the same, except that in theism it has been rationalised and personalised. Given Otto's account, the reason pantheists ascribe divinity to the Unity is because they experience it as such.

Despite the intricacy of Otto's descriptive account and his alleged reliance on the phenomenological character of the numinous experience I believe his account is largely fictitious. It is drawn not so much from analyses of traditions and experience as it is by extrapolating from accounts of mystical experience. He succeeds in describing some aspects of a particular, largely mystical, kind of religious experience. But, there is little reason to accept this as a generic account of such experience, or of holiness. There is no more reason to accept Otto's account than there is to suppose that mystical experience is the foundation of religion and of all conceptions of the divine.

To say that Otto's account is largely fiction is not to deny that religious experience contributes to the foundation of religion, and to conceptions of divinity. It is not to deny that the reason pantheists ascribe divinity to the Unity is because they experience it as such. It only means that the nature and character of the experience is not as Otto describes it. (Undoubtedly some experiences do resemble numinous experiences in some ways – but

Otto's thesis involves much more than this.) If experience is a basis for a concept of divinity, then the extent to which the theist and pantheist share such a concept will partly depend on the character and object of their respective experiences. Whatever the character and object of their respective experiences, they may both ascribe divinity to something (the same or more likely different things), because they experience it as divine. But even if the character and object of their experiences and their concepts of the divine are different – perhaps because they are informed by different beliefs – their respective experiences and ideas of the divine may function similarly. In denying the accuracy of Otto's account, I am not disputing the idea that experience is an important ground for religion; that religion is to some extent an expressive objectification of such experience; or that experience is partly a basis for various conceptions of divinity.

Lindbeck says

> there are many and significantly different ways of describing the basic religious experience, as is illustrated by a succession of influential theories of religion stretching from Schleiermacher through Rudolf Otto to Mircea Eliade and beyond. Nevertheless, whatever the variations, thinkers of this tradition all locate ultimately significant contact with whatever is finally important to religion in the prereflective experiential depths of the self and regard the public and outer features of religion as expressive and evocative objectifications (i.e. nondiscursive symbols) of internal experience.
>
> (p. 21)[30]

Socio-scientific analyses of religion, including those of Freud, Durkheim, Weber, Malinowski, Geertz and Berger, acknowledge the importance of experience, affectivity and intellect in their accounts of the nature and function of religion.[31] The view that certain kinds of experience may partly be a basis for conceptions of divinity, and a reason for ascribing divinity, is affirmed in these accounts.

I turn now to a discussion of divinity from a cultural/linguistic view. The focus is on the "divine," but more specifically on the relevant functional aspects of religion itself. A concept of divinity is located in a religious world-view, and as with Otto's analysis the idea of divinity and a broader understanding of religion are connected. Pantheism should be seen as one type of religion among others.

The functionalist analyses I examine are not meant to be reductionistic. Although once the various functions of religion have been accounted for, so has much of religion, it cannot be understood exclusively in terms of its various functions. Many psychological, social anthropological (etc.) theorists of religion believe that it is impossible to understand significant aspects of religion non-functionally. But such analyses do not necessarily deny, for instance, that religious truth claims are important.[32]

In "Religion as a Cultural System" Clifford Geertz defines religion as "a system of symbols which acts to establish powerful, pervasive, and long-lasting moods and motivations in men by formulating conceptions of a general order of existence and clothing these conceptions with such an aura of factuality that the moods and motivations seem uniquely realistic" (p. 90).[33] He says,

> sacred symbols function to synthesize a people's ethos – the tone, character, and quality of their life, its moral and aes-thetic style and mood – and their world-view – the picture they have of the way things in sheer actuality are, their most comprehensive idea of order. In religious belief and practice a group's ethos is rendered intellectually reasonable by being shown to represent a way of life ideally adapted to the actual state of affairs the world-view describes, while the world-view is rendered emotionally convincing by being pre-sented as an image of an actual state of affairs peculiarly well-arranged to accommodate such a way of life.[34] This confrontation and mutual confirmation has two fundamen-tal effects. On the one hand, it objectivizes moral and aes-thetic preferences, by depicting them as the imposed conditions of life implicit in a world with a particular structure ... On the other, it supports these received beliefs about the world's body by invoking deeply felt moral and aesthetic sentiments as experiential evidence for their truth. Religious symbols formulate a basic congruence between a particular style of life and a specific (if, most often, implicit) metaphysic ...
>
> (pp. 89–90)[35]

What are the implications of this influential analysis of religion for pantheism and divinity?[36]

First, it helps to explain the nature and function of pantheism in so far as it is a religion. As with other religions, pantheism will be distinctive in many respects. And even among pantheists there will be vast differences – in their world-view for example – that depend upon their historical and cultural settings. Nevertheless, as a religion, pantheism will function similarly to other religions in the manner Geertz describes. Second, the above analysis suggests ways of interpreting a pantheistic notion of divinity. It is to be interpreted as a "sacred symbol" or system of symbols, similar in ways to the idea (or symbol) of divinity in theism. Third, Geertz's account supports the view that the relevant pantheistic notion of Unity should be explained evaluatively. I discuss these points in turn.

If it is difficult to regard pantheism as a religion much like any other then this is because there have been few, if any, historically concrete examples of it as a cultural system (and one wonders why?), though there have been and continue to be individuals with a pantheistic view and ethos.[37] For some reason, pantheism finds expression not through a unified church, but either (a) philosophically (e.g. Spinoza etc.); (b) within strains – usually mystical – of other religious traditions; or (c) among individuals who reject both theism and atheism as equally unviable for making sense of the cosmic status quo. By "making sense of the cosmic status quo" I mean interpreting ordinary life against a background of existential issues like the fact of existence, death, moral evil, meaning, suffering, love etc.

However, even if pantheism has not been manifest in any tradition in a sustained manner, it does not follow that it does not function religiously for those who are pantheists. Indeed, it must. (Since the religion among various American Indian tribes is largely pantheistic, it is not true that pantheism has not been practised in a sustained manner.) The pantheist has a unified picture of "the way things in sheer actuality are ... a comprehensive idea of order" (i.e. there exists a divine Unity). Even apart from being able to fully articulate the nature of a pantheistic ethos, it is as plausible to suppose that it is identifiable as it is to suppose a theistic one is. (At any rate, Whitman does a good job articulating the pantheistic ethos.) If there was not a recognisable ethos and world-view we would not be able to identify paintings, dances etc. as being pantheistic.[38] The "tone, character, and quality of their life, [their] . . . moral and aesthetic style and mood" is identifiable – even if vague. To understand it one must have conceptual recourse to their world-view. But this is no different from trying to come to grips with a theistic ethos.

As in the case of theism, or deism, or atheism, or agnosticism, or just plain not caring at all about the issues,

[the pantheist's] ethos is rendered intellectually reasonable by being shown to represent a way of life ideally adapted to the actual state of affairs the world-view describes, while the world-view is rendered emotionally convincing by being presented as an image of an actual state of affairs peculiarly well-arranged to accommodate such a way of life.

(Geertz, p. 89)

Pantheism may present a case in which, because of its world-view, there is a more direct and radical melding of world-view and ethos than in many religions. It could be argued that in pantheism ethos and world-view are brought as close together as possible, that they do not just reflect one another, but instead are in some ways indistinguishable. Lao Tzu's explanation of the metaphysical Tao is directly related to the character and standards of human behaviour. In Taoism, ontology and ethics are related, the fact/value distinction is ultimately dissipated, and moral realism results. This has a Spinozistic, Hegelian, quasi-mystical, pantheistic air about it.

This is not to suggest that pantheism is a functionally superior religion because of the relative closeness of ethos and world-view. In fact, on both Geertz's and Berger's view a religion's ability to function depends on a tension and dialectic between the immanent and transcendent, between ethos and world-view. This functional capacity depends – one might say – on a robust sense of the transcendent.[39] A sacred symbol system functions as both a "model of reality" and a "model for reality" according to Geertz, and these are dialectically related. In so far as pantheism denies any meaningful role to the transcendent, and envisions Berger's "sacred canopy" as immanent rather than transcendent, its ability to cope with the "problem of meaning" may be impaired. However, pantheism does not deny the role to the transcendent that is necessary for its symbol system to function as both a model of and model for reality. Pantheism entails the denial of certain kinds of ontological transcendence that are supposedly essential to theism, but it still operates with a "healthy" notion of transcendence.

Given Geertz's analysis, how is a pantheistic notion of divinity to be interpreted? Divinity is a symbol and it functions as such. It is not ascribed to a theistic God, distinct from the world and transcendent, who is a moral guarantor and supreme judge. The predication of divinity to the Unity follows from an analysis of Unity, or from appraising the world as a Unity. If Unity is evaluatively based, then the predication of divinity relates to the Unity's intrinsic value or whatever it is that is taken evaluatively as that which makes the world a pantheistic Unity. As in the experiential model, divinity is ascribed to the Unity by the pantheist because it is experienced as divine. What it means to experience it as divine is complex and must be put in the context of a world-view and ethos. But experiencing the Unity as divine partly means that it is experienced as having value. This has important consequences for the pantheist.

Divinity for the pantheist functions symbolically in a manner not unlike the way "God" does for the theist. It is part of a system of symbols, one of which is Unity, that enables those for whom the symbols are operative to do what all sacred symbol systems (i.e. religions) do; that is, to get about the business of "ordering" and "making sense of," of making moral judgments, working, relating to others – in short – living in a world which no matter how grand is fundamentally difficult. Thus, theistic and pantheistic concepts of divinity are functionally equivalent.

What has been said concerning Geertz's analysis and the function of divinity supports the contention, albeit obliquely, that Unity must be explained evaluatively. It is, after all, experienced as valuable. This is worth elaborating upon.

In discussing the relation between fact and value in the context of his theory of religion Geertz says,

> The concepts used here, ethos and world view, are vague and imprecise ... [but] One almost certain result of such an empirically oriented, theoretically sophisticated, symbol-stressing approach to the study of values is the decline of analyses which attempt to describe moral, aesthetic, and other normative activities in terms of theories based not on the observation of such activities but on logical consider-

ations alone ... the overwhelming majority of mankind are continually drawing normative conclusions from factual premises (and factual conclusions from normative premises, for the relation between ethos and world-view is circular) despite refined ... reflections by professional philosophers on the "naturalistic fallacy." An approach to a theory of value which looks toward the behaviour of actual people in actual societies living in terms of actual cultures for both its stimulus and its validation will turn us ... to a process of ever-increasing insight into both what values are and how they work.[40]

The claim is that a radical fact/value distinction is descriptively false. People draw evaluative conclusions from factual premises and vice versa – and Geertz's suggestion is that they are justified in doing so. Ethos and world-view are partially determinative of one another.

Given that Unity is central to a pantheistic world-view it is implausible to suppose that it could be categorised and explained apart from terms which refer to evaluative considerations partly constitutive of ethos. The reverse is also true. A pantheistic ethos, like any other, is determined by its world-view. No matter of fact alone, no reference to how the world is, can by itself suggest a basis for Unity. If Geertz is right concerning the relation between fact and value, then the pantheist's understanding of Unity and divinity are inextricably linked. The actual connection between ethos and world-view in each religion is distinctive, but the nature of the relation is the same in pantheism as it is in any other religion.

In explaining Unity at the end of section 2.1, I suggested that separating the question of what constitutes Unity from what constitutes divinity might not be possible. The whole (i.e. everything) might be a Unity because it is divine, or the whole might be divine because it is unified in a relevant pantheistic sense. If this were so – and we have seen reasons for supposing it is so to some extent – there would be something of a redundancy in the definition of pantheism as the belief in a divine Unity. One would expect to find close connections of various types between account of divinity and Unity in different versions of pantheism. This is the case among Presocratics, Spinoza, Hegel, and in non-Western traditions such as Taoism. Furthermore, both the experiential/expressive and the cultural/linguistic analyses of divinity I have presented support the view that there must be close connections between a particular pantheistic understanding of Unity and its correspondent concept of divinity. But however the relation is to be explained, given the analyses of Unity and divinity presented, there is no reason to suppose it is one of entailment.

Some versions of pantheism are clearer than others about their sense of Unity and divinity (e.g. Taoism and Spinoza). In some versions a vagueness about these concepts makes it difficult to determine what the relation between them is. Even in philosophy vagueness is not always a bad thing. But it should be noted that in this context vagueness is transitive. One can be no clearer as to what is meant by Unity than one can be as to what is meant by divinity, and vice versa. And one can be no more explicit as to what pantheism means than one can be as to what is meant by both of these.

The affective basis for regarding a thing as divine may be the same as that for regarding the whole a Unity. There are grounds in pantheism, as well as in Otto's and Geertz's analyses, for thinking so. Yet apart from a further explanation of the relation between Unity and divinity, one that would only come with a specific account of pantheism, the two should be kept separate. To be divine is one thing, to be a Unity another – though one and the same thing may be both for similar reasons. The definition of pantheism as the belief in a divine Unity is not redundant.

2.3 MONISM

Pantheists are "monists" . . . they believe that there is only one Being, and that all other forms of reality are either modes (or appearances) of it or identical with it.[1]

H. P. Owen

pantheistic pathos. That it should afford so many people a peculiar satisfaction to say that All is One is, as William James once remarked, a rather puzzling thing. What is there more beautiful or more venerable about the numeral one than about any other number? . . . [W]hen a monistic philosophy declares, or suggests, that one is oneself a part of the universal Oneness, a whole complex of obscure emotional responses is released.[2]

Arthur Lovejoy

the problem of the One and the Many . . . is so ancient that I am glad to be able to quote unchallengeable evidence that it is still modern, still alive, still troubling and urgent . . . if a man's decided Monism or decided Pluralism is the sincere and genuine expression of his life . . . it is the best evidence not only of what the rest of his *opinions* are, but also of what are his interests, his concerns, his feelings, sentiments, emotions, his desires and aspirations, his aims, purposes and volitions.[3]

J. A. Smith

Although, like Spinoza, some pantheists may also be monists, and monism may even be essential to some versions of pantheism (like Spinoza's), pantheist's are not monists. Like most people they are pluralists. They believe, quite plausibly, that there are many things and kinds of things and many different kinds of value. Even in Spinoza's case, explaining his pantheism in terms of his substance monism glosses the far more significant, pantheistically speaking, evaluative implications he sees as entailed by that monism for his pantheistic metaphysic and his concept of Unity. The *Ethics* is not about monism, but about what it entails. Why Spinoza sees things as a Unity cannot be explained wholly or even primarily in terms of his monism.

Before discussing some general features of the alleged relation between monism and pantheism I return to the question of whether substance monism is relevant to pantheism. I have claimed that Unity can be ontologically based in various ways, and must be so based in some way. Given my typology of the most central pantheistic concept – Unity – the type of ontologically grounded Unity that has been of most concern since Spinoza, but also among some Presocratics, is best treated under the substance model. Can substance be a plausible basis of Unity? The question is bound up with the viability of "monism" – the view that there exists only one thing or kind of thing.[4]

2.3.1 Substance and Unity

Regarded as a primary type of ontological division, substance is an obvious candidate for Unity. Historically it has been taken as the most basic ontological category. Unity as "unity of substance" is the usual meaning of the *very few* monistic pantheists who are explicit about their monism or sense of Unity (i.e. Spinoza is the exception not the rule).[5] In fact, although Spinoza's monistic view that there can be only one infinite substance (i.e. God) is clear, its relevance to Unity is not – at least not in *Ethics* I. The implications of substance monism, and its significance particularly for human happiness, is the subject of the *Ethics* in its entirety. The substance model for the explanation of Unity, however, is an important one.

By those who believe there is such a thing, substance(s) is sometimes taken to be what basically exists. Among these may be metaphysical realists and anti-realists who think ontology is not completely subjective. For one to regard substance as that which basically exists in any absolute sense one must reject theses of "ontological relativity" such as Quine's which holds that any onto-logical scheme necessarily lacks absoluteness. However, even in a Quinean or anti-realist framework it is possible to speak of sub-stance as "ontologically primary," while acknowledging the possi-bility of alternative categories of ontological primacy. A Quinean ontological framework allows for the ontological respectability of substance – as well as just about anything else. It is not clear that an ontology that regards substance as basic is at odds with the current scientific theory that Quine, for example, thinks an ontology should be formulated in terms of.[6] But substance is a slippery term, and although it is often regarded as having a univocal meaning, it has been understood in various ways.[7]

Aristotle claimed that substance, considered as a kind, is one of the categories, one of the ultimate kinds of being.[8] Paradigm cases of "primary" substances were (sometimes) particular things. "Substance in the truest and primary and most definite sense of the word is that which is neither predicable of a subject nor present in a subject; for instance, the individual man or horse" (Aristotle, *Categories* 2_A11). Particular things are "subjects." "They are basically what is there to be talked about; for these purposes they are what basically exists" (Hamlyn, p. 39).[9] Aristotle thought that "the world must contain substances and it is only because of that fact that there can be other kinds of thing – qualities, quantities and the other so-called categories" (Hamlyn, p. 6). He stressed two characteristics of substance. They are ontologically primary and they are particular.

> entities in other categories apart from substance are dependent on substances for their existence ... they are inherent in substances ... general things, like species and genera, depend on particular substances as their instances ... Aristotle's belief in the ontological primacy of substances is obvious. It is meant to be evident in the way that subject—predicate language relates to the world, so that Aristotle can come to assert ... that particular substances are never predicated of anything else but everything else is predicated of them. They thus constitute ... "basic logical subjects".
>
> (Hamlyn, p. 61)

Aristotle considered God to be something that is a substance in a "primary" way and also the primary kind of substance. Noting that this is a controversial interpretation of Aristotle's view on God, Hamlyn says,

> one kind of substance – that which is exemplified in God and perhaps only in God, since it provides in some sense its own rationale – is said to be substance primarily. If this is his [Aristotle's] view, it follows that there is a sense in which by studying God one studies the primary kind of substance, and by studying substance one studies the primary kind of entity – so that in God one finds the best view of what it is to be an entity. Aristotle could thus say (*Metaphysics* E (6).1) that theology and the science of being-*qua*-being can be identified with each other.
>
> (p. 38)

Given this view of God and substance there is a rationale for attempting to interpret Unity in terms of substance. God is seen as the primary substance and kind of entity; the only one that provides its own reason for existence, and is capable of independent existence in an absolute sense (i.e. depends on nothing else for existence). So God, as a substance, is ontologically basic. (Descartes and Spinoza hold views similar to these.) If, like Spinoza, one also believes that there is, or can be, only one substance or God, then interpreting Unity in terms of substance may be

74

attractive. Given such monistic beliefs, along with Aristotle's idea of God as the primary substance, grounding Unity in these onto-logical features suggests itself – even though the question of why these features are relevant to Unity remains. The reason they appear relevant in this case is not primarily because there is only one substance, but because that substance is identified as God. Yet this suggests that in such cases Unity is not finally explained in terms of substance monism, but in terms of the nature of that one substance which is God.

Aristotle had at least six different notions of substance. The word he used most often for "substance" is *ousia.*

> The word *ousia* also occurs in philosophical writings before Aristotle as a synonym for the Greek word *physis,* a term which can mean either the origin of a thing, its natural constitution or structure, the stuff of which things are made, or a natural kind or species... [The six notions of sub-stance are] (1) the concrete individual, (2) a core of essen-tial properties, (3) what is capable of independent existence, (4) a center of change, (5) a substratum, and (6) a logical subject.
>
> (O'Connor, pp. 36–7)

The list is not exhaustive, but all of these meanings are prominent senses in which Unity can be explained in a substance model of Unity. If any of these notions of substance are a basis for ascrib-ing Unity, then a more general explanation of its relevance is required (e.g. in terms of its nature).

To say that substance is ontologically primary means that it is a basic, or most basic, existent. But many things have been meant by "most basic kind of existent." It has meant (i) temporally first; (ii) ontologically independent or self-subsistent; (iii) that which other things are dependent upon, contingently or necessarily, for their own existence; and (iv) that which is constitutive, in part or whole, of other things. These overlap or can be added to the above list of six.

If substance, in any of the above meanings, is going to be the basis for ascribing Unity, then principles of individuating substances must not imply pluralism. How are substances indi-viduated, and is it reasonable to suppose that there are criteria of individuation that make monism, in the sense of there existing only one substance in any of the above meanings, plausible? For each of the above meanings of substance for which it is plausible to suppose there is *more* than one substance, predicating Unity on the basis of everything being one substance, or a mode of it, will not be possible. Thus, for example, if "substance" means "the concrete individual," "what is capable of independent existence" etc., then normal principles of individuation which suggest a plurality of substances (e.g. more than one individual) rule out Unity based on that notion of substance.

However, substance monism might still be taken as relevant since Unity could be attributed on the ground that everything was *one kind* of substance rather than one single substance (i.e. individual thing). Indeed, where monism is interpreted in terms of substance as, for example, "the concrete individual," the claim that there is one substance is ambiguous between the claim that there is "one single substance" (i.e. numerically individual thing) and the claim that there is "one kind of substance" of which different things are constituted. A similar ambiguity would apply to substance as origin of a thing, centre of change, logical subject etc.

Individuating criteria that apply to (i) kinds of substances and (ii) substances as individual things may be different. They will be different unless one is a radical monist maintaining that there is and can be only one substance (or thing) and only one kind of substance. Let "substance" as "concrete individual thing" be substance$_1$ and as "kind" be substance$_2$. Depending upon criteria of individuation and the meaning attributed to substance, it is possible that there be one or many substances$_2$. So even if there are many substances$_1$ there may be only one kind of thing (i.e. one substance$_2$) and Unity may be posited as a result. The pantheistic claim would then be that all things are made of one kind of thing, and are therefore unified in virtue of their identity of substance$_2$. Where "substance" is not taken exclusively in any one of its senses, one can suppose there is more than one substance or kind of substance in one sense and still maintain the relevance of substance to Unity by showing that in another sense there is only one substance $_1$ or $_2$. But whatever substance is taken to mean, there is no apparent equation between monism and pantheism; and the relevance of any alleged monism for Unity needs to be addressed by those very few pantheists who see substance monism as a basis for pantheism.

Barring adherence to a radical "appearance/reality distinction"

(A/R), a reliance on the monistic one/one kind distinction to claim Unity in virtue of substance$_2$ instead of substance$_1$ is not useful. If we are inclined to admit a plurality of substances$_1$, then we are similarly inclined to admit a plurality of substances$_2$. Not everything appears to be made of the same thing any more than everything appears to be one thing. One must accept A/R to claim that the things we ordinarily regard as distinct substances, or kinds of substances, are not really distinct.

There is no reason to dismiss all versions of A/R out of hand. For one thing, mind/body dualism may rest upon such a distinction, and not all dualisms are vestiges of an unacceptable cartesianism. In fact, it is materialist analyses of mind, rather than dualist ones, that usually rely upon A/R. Surely our thoughts *appear* to be something different from brain states. Yet reductive materialists have claimed that thoughts are strictly identical to brain states. Nevertheless, the particular type of A/R that must be accepted to maintain that what we regard as substances $_1$ or $_2$ are not what we take them to be is a deep and pervasive application of the distinction. Ordinary phenomenological criteria of individuation would have to be taken as completely different from, and in conflict with, criteria of individuation based upon metaphysical ontological rationale. The acceptance of this pervasive type of A/R rests on a criterion of individuation that is part of prior metaphysical presuppositions. Therefore, unless one is prepared to argue independently for the applicability of this radical kind of A/R as applied to substance, one should not rely upon it as a basis for Unity in terms of substance – "despite appearances." Apart from a formidable argument for A/R the price is too great in terms of commitment to what is at least *prima facie* an implausible metaphysical theory. Few pantheists have ever argued for or presupposed A/R. The distinction is so "philosophical" that it is available to few pantheists and as a matter of commonsense, is, rejected by most. One need not be overly intellectual to be a pantheist. The fact that however "substance" is understood there seems to be a plurality of them suggests that ascribing Unity on the basis of substance monism is best avoided.

Some idealist monists, and non-Western versions of pantheism, are committed to A/R. Their arguments are usually embedded in complex metaphysical systems (e.g. Rāmānuja's). In these cases substance cannot be rejected as a basis for Unity unless A/R itself is discredited. To do so one must consider the metaphysical scheme in which the distinction is found.

Those who maintain A/R do not generally deny the reality of the phenomenal world and experience in a limited sense. It is rather that the existence of such a phenomenal realm should not be confused with ultimate reality. Thus, Śankara, Nagarjuna and the advaita Vedānta school do not categorically deny the reality of the phenomenal world. It exists as a kind of cosmic illusion. In the senses in which they affirm the phenomenal world's existence there is no point for those who adhere to A/R to deny its existence. In their most plausible forms, theories such as Berkeley's idealism that rely on A/R do not conflict with ordinary accounts of the phenomenological content of experience. (I take it Berkeley mistakenly denies that his idealism involves A/R.) Experience of the phenomenal world cannot, in any straightforward way, count as evidence against these theories. Because such theories maintain, correctly in my view, that they accord with ordinary views concerning the phenomenological content of experience, they can suppose that whatever occurs in terms of that experience cannot count against their theories. This is *why* these theories, though they include A/R, are *prima facie* the most plausible.

Thus, Berkeley maintains that his immaterialism accords with the facts of experience. If the views of Berkeley, Śankara etc. on the material world do conflict with experience, why they do must be explained in terms of an account of experience and not the phenomenological content of experience. Mere reference to "experience" will not refute A/R in Plato, Berkeley, Bradley or advaita Vedānta, because if A/R does conflict with experience it is not supposed to do so in terms of the phenomenological content of experience. Therefore, if there is a conflict it is not phenomenologically obvious. Indeed, the point of invoking A/R is to show how, *appearances notwithstanding*, reality is not what it appears to be.

Thus far I have argued that adherence to a strong version of A/R that is *prima facie* unacceptable makes it *possible* to use substance as a basis for Unity. But I have also noted that most theories employing A/R could not be regarded as unacceptable on the grounds that they conflict with ordinary experience since such theories do not entail such a conflict. So if one does adhere to an A/R distinction, then unless such a distinction is rejected on some theoretical, non-experiential ground, substance monism of some kind could perhaps be a basis for pantheistic Unity. But, why substance monism should be regarded as relevant to Unity is not evident and would still require explanation. I have argued in sections 2.1 and 2.2 that no such explanation is likely to be forthcoming. Unity is ascribed on evaluative grounds, not on the basis of an obtuse monism that pantheists generally neither care about nor understand.

There are other perhaps more significant ways in which one could try to base Unity on substance – though they too cannot succeed. The only thing that could really make it possible to posit Unity based on substance is an analysis of the concept of substance. Such an analysis could be a reason for accepting A/R as applied to substance. Alternatively, an account could claim that substance has no phenomenal properties at all, or at least none that are individuating. Since substance has no phenomenologically individuating characteristics whatsoever in such an analysis, there is, never *a fortiori*, a question of any commitment to A/R.

Suppose one admits a plurality of things and kinds of things in the world. An analysis of substance rather than adherence to A/R may lead one to claim that, although there are many things and/or kinds of things (e.g. infinite attributes and modes), there is only one substance. This view could rest on an analysis of substance as it did for Spinoza, rather than adherence to a doctrine of appearances. Whereas appearances are significant criteria for individuating objects phenomenally understood, they may be irrelevant criteria for the individuation of substances. In this case substance could not be taken in some Aristotelian senses of the term (e.g. concrete individual thing) where criteria for the individuation of substance are taken to be identical with criteria for the individuation of ordinary phenomenally perceived objects. However, it could still be taken in some of its other Aristotelian senses such as "substratum" and (possibly) "what is capable of independent existence." Whatever the criteria for identity of particulars may be, the criteria for substance may be different; they will be different if substances are not taken as phenomenologically identifiable.

Whereas we have a pre-analytic notion concerning criteria for individuating things, we have none for the identity of the philosophical concept of substance. Therefore ontological pluralism need not, even informally, commit one to substance pluralism.

This means that it is possible to maintain a substance model of Unity apart from any commitment to A/R. Alternatively, one's analysis of the concept of substance could be the basis for positing A/R in the first place. In this case the strategy of positing Unity based on substance might be abandoned for reasons already given (e.g. the relevance of substance monism for Unity requires an explanation that is unavailable). At the very least this strategy would need to be defended in terms of some broader metaphysical theory in which it was embedded.

Taking into account what has been said thus far about substance as a possible basis for Unity, an important objection to pantheism can be refuted. Owen objects to pantheism partly because it "fails to explain our awareness of distinctness and autonomy in things and persons . . . Our total experience of both personal and sub-personal entities is pervaded by the conviction that each is an independent form of existence."[10] He claims that, contrary to experience, pantheism denies there are independently existing entities. But I have shown that "awareness of distinctness and autonomy" is compatible with metaphysical theories that include A/R. Generally integral to A/R is the assumption, set in a broader metaphysical context, that such an awareness cannot provide reasons for making certain claims about reality. Therefore, by invoking such a distinction (A/R) one need not deny the *awareness* Owen points to. One need only deny the reality, in some metaphysical or ontological sense, of the alleged referents; that is, one need only deny that the objects of awareness are "real" or fully real entities. Given the account of reality that A/R views offer, our experiential "awareness of distinctness and autonomy" of entities must sometimes be differentiated from "the conviction that each is [ultimately] an independent form of existence." The latter is a view about the referents of experience and not about the phenomenological content of experience. The phenomenological content of the experiences is compatible with there being no real referents given accounts of reality of which A/R is a part.

Moreover, on certain understandings of "substance" in which criteria for their individuation are not the same as those for things and persons (i.e. where substances are not taken to be "things and persons"), it could not be true that our "awareness of distinctness and autonomy in things and persons" conflicted with pantheism based on substance monism. So even without invoking A/R there is no reason to suppose that pantheism based on substance monism necessarily denies "our awareness of distinctness and autonomy." Indeed, not only need pantheism not deny our awareness of such distinctness, it need not deny that such things really are distinct and autonomous in important ways. The Unity that the pantheist claims for the whole, depending on what it is, will not conflict with the view that things are distinct in a variety of ways. It need not even conflict with ontological schemes that maintain that things are distinct, so long as Unity is not ontologically based in a way that conflicts with such a scheme – as it surely will not be.

Just as important with regard to Owen's criticism, however, is that neither the awareness in experience of an apparent plurality of things or substances, nor their acceptance as real, implies a rejection of those versions of pantheism that rely on models of explanation of Unity other than the substance model. For example, Unity may be attributed not on the basis of a monism of substance *per se*, but on the basis of something about substance – or of something other than substance altogether. These other accounts of Unity need not rely upon A/R or any analysis of substance. Given that Owen's criticism is directed wholly to the substance model of Unity, and that that model is unacceptable for reasons already given, his criticism is spurious. It has no force whatsoever against, for example, Unity that is evaluatively based – which, I have argued, is how Unity generally is and should be grounded.

Before arguing that monism and pantheism must be sharply distinguished, I shall examine some other meanings of substance to see if they can be a basis for Unity. The claim that Unity cannot adequately be explained in terms of substance or ontology is reiterated.

To generalise from two logical senses of unity, (1) all-inclusiveness *per se* and (2) the bare logical sense of "capable of independent existence" (i.e. one prominent meaning of substance) that follows from all-inclusiveness *per se*, no merely logical account of unity will be relevant to pantheism, since the claim that there exists an all-inclusive divine Unity is not an analytic truth.[11] This was argued in the section on Unity. Pantheism rejects (or should

81

reject) this type of *a priori* argument for the existence of the all-inclusive divine Unity. This does not mean that pantheists must reject all forms of ontological argument. Perhaps the all-inclusive divine Unity exists necessarily. If so, the Unity shown to exist necessarily will not be one of the logical types rejected as trivial (e.g. "everything").

Consider the application of "substance as essence" for Unity; the idea that the world's essence is Unity. Does the concept of substance as essence hold more promise for Unity than that of substance as "capable of independent existence"? Whereas the latter account trivialises the idea of Unity, the former is idle. An essence for Aristotle is "a set of qualities that conjointly embody the nature of the thing they qualify, are grasped by intellectual intuition, and are expressed in the definition of the thing" (O'Connor, p. 39). Suppose then that the world (i.e. all that exists) is a Unity in virtue of its essence. The question then arises: "What is the essence of the world (i.e. "the set of qualities . . .") that makes it a Unity?" or "Why is the essence of the world a Unity?" – and we are back where we started from. Unity is specified in terms of essence and vice versa, but the question "What is the nature of the divine Unity (i.e. its essence)?" or "What is the essence of the divine substance?" involves a vicious regress. The essence of the divine substance is Unity and the nature of Unity is the essence of the divine substance. An explanation of Unity in terms of essence is sought, but *why* the essence of the world is Unity requires a non-regressive explanation. So to try to explain Unity just in terms of essence is not useful. In asking instead simply about the nature of Unity one avoids commitment to essentialism, or to any account of substance. The question of Unity can and must be raised apart from notions of substance and essence.

It is not always possible to describe Unity apart from substance and essence, but why essence is a basis of Unity always requires an explanation. Spinoza's account is inextricably linked to substance monism. "All things . . . are in God, and everything which takes place takes place by the laws alone of the infinite nature of God, and follows . . . from the necessity of His essence" (*Ethics* I, Proposition XV, demonstration). Unlike substance whose "essence necessarily involves existence, or, in other words, it pertains to its nature to exist" (*Ethics* I, Proposition VII, demonstration), "the essence of things produced by God does not involve existence" (*Ethics* I, Proposition XXIV). Unity consists of, or is based upon, one infinite substance whose essence is existence and from which everything follows necessarily. Although it is not possible to explain Spinozistic Unity apart from substance and its essence (i.e. existence), Unity is not accounted for by simply asserting substance monism but by examining the implications of his monism – as Spinoza does.

Turning to a consideration of origin as the basis of Unity: even if a unique origin can be traced to an originative substance, origin alone is not sufficient for Unity. If the genealogical model of explanation of Unity is to be plausible, whether in terms of an originative substance or simple (e.g. temporal) identity of origin, then the reason must be something about the nature or value of the origin. Pantheists assert not just past but present Unity. If an originative substance or origin sufficed for Unity, then since most people who think the world has an origin think it has a unique origin, the people could be pantheists. Whether they were pantheists would depend on whether they also took the Unity based on origin, perhaps the origin or originative substance itself, to be divine (e.g. the Presocratics). But what about origin makes it relevant to Unity? So what if everything originates from an undifferentiated substance? For origin to matter to pantheism it must be seen as having evaluative implications, or as having to do with the divinity of the all-inclusive Unity. "All-inclusiveness" might be explained in terms of origin, but apart from further explanation, Unity cannot be.

Whether or not substance monism is ontologically necessary for Unity, an explanation of its relevance requires something extra-ontological to be cited. The same is true of any factual ground for Unity. Delineating metaphysical or modal properties of a substance, or anything else, does not make their relevance to Unity obvious. So what if everything is made from one self-subsistent immutable substance? So what if everything is really a single organism when considered macrocosmically? Why would this be pantheistically, rather than merely metaphysically, significant? What is the evaluative or religious significance of natural features of the totality that pantheism claims is central to Unity? Because value must be partly constitutive of Unity, it must be explained in partly evaluative terms. This is a necessary condition for an adequate criterion of Unity. Without it one is left only with this or that fact as a basis for positing Unity, but no adequate account of the relevance of the basis, and so no account of Unity itself.

I have argued that depending upon one's metaphysics and ontology it is possible, though not plausible, to posit Unity in terms of some concepts of substance. Reasons have been given as to why a substance model of Unity is unacceptable. These reaffirm the claim in section 2.1 that Unity is not and cannot be solely based on some non-evaluative feature of the natural world, but must partly be explained evaluatively.

This has implications for theism with its insistence on the radical ontological differentiation between God and the world. If my remarks about unity in the logical and ontological senses as they relate to pantheism are correct, then similarly, the differentiation between God and the world insisted upon by theism should be inconsequential in and of itself. Its significance must be explained in terms that show why the differentiation is of consequence, and not by citing further facts (e.g. about how things are constituted). Theism attempts to do just this in terms of doctrines of creation, sin, and salvation. Perhaps the relevance of substance to Unity can be explained analogously. If so, Unity will not be accounted for by substance or any other ontological or logical notion. It will be explained partly by what there is, but also relationally in terms of various connections among things and their value.

2.3.2 Monism and pantheism

Peter Forrest describes the "initial, pre-reflective understanding" of monism as the denial "that (in reality) there are any differences, and/or to assert that (in reality) all is one."[12] While some speculative types of pantheism may entail non-trivial versions of monism, pantheism does not generally entail monism any more than monism entails pantheism. Even if they happen to be pantheists, monists may hold that the relevant sense of "One" referred to in their monism is not the "One" relevant to pantheism. It is of course possible to be a monist in one sense and a pluralist in others, so that monists can deny any alleged equivalence between what it is they are monistic or "unitive" about (e.g. substance) and the Unity necessary for pantheism. Even if they exist only as modes or aspects of the divine Unity in a Spinozistic type of pantheism, finite entities may be regarded as real existents rather than "mere appearance" in, for example, a Bradlean[13] monistic sense. And even if some versions of monism maintain that there is only one Really (i.e. non- illusional) existing thing, there will be no equivalence between the monistic One and the pantheistic Unity – even if the Unity is somehow based on that monism by the monistic pantheist.

Śankara's absolute monism denies reality to finite entities. They do not "*really*" exist since everything that does is strictly identical with Brahman who alone exists. To the not inconsiderable extent that Śankara can be taken to be a pantheist, and that his pantheism is taken as linked to his monism, these two aspects are distinguishable. Once Śankara is interpreted pantheistically the connection between his monism and pantheism must be regarded as intrinsic. However, even in this case, monism is not equivalent to pantheism and it will take a detailed account of Śankara's metaphysical monism to account for its connection to his pantheism. If this is so in the case of Śankara, it is also to be expected in other more generic types of pantheism that may be related to monism.

Where monists hold that finite entities do exist, perhaps as aspects of a single substance, pantheists do not regard the existence of real (i.e. not merely apparent) finite entities as inimical to Unity.[14] Whether such entities are regarded as ontologically derivative of a single substance is not necessarily relevant to the classification of such a monism as pantheistic. Consider a form of monism less radical than that of Śankara's. Rāmānuja's "qualified non-dualism" recognises the existence of finite entities while claiming that they are modes of (i.e. exist as) "the body of God." They are ontologically derivative of God in the sense that although they exist in their own right as finite entities they are also aspects of Brahman.[15] Neither form of their existence is more significant, though perhaps the fact that they are modes of Brahman is ontologically more basic. They can only exist as finite entities because they, like everything else, can exist only as modes of Brahman. Rāmānuja may also be regarded as pantheistic at times, though any doctrine of "the world God's body" is ultimately incompatible both with the non-theistic kinds of pantheism I am considering and with classical theism. Nevertheless, pantheists need not regard the dualist aspect (i.e. the qualification) of Rāmānuja's qualified non-dualism as incompatible with Unity.

Any simple equation of monism to pantheism can also be ruled out on the grounds that monists may deny that divinity should be attributed to whatever "One" their monism refers to. Whether one's monism is ontological in the sense that it refers to the number or kind of entities that exist, or evaluative in the sense (for example) "that only the sum total of things has intrinsic value,"[16] such monism does not entail pantheism if it denies divinity to the "One."

There may also be ways of conceiving of the monistic "One" such that it is taken both as a unity and as "divine" – yet still not as a pantheistic Unity. The monistic unity (the "One") may not be regarded as a "Unity" (i.e. unity in some relevant pantheistic sense). Not just any monistic unity (e.g. mere substance monism) suffices for pantheism, whether or not it is also regarded as divine. Thus, although Hegel conceived of Reality as unified and rational in terms of the Absolute (*Geist*), and in a manner that I take it would qualify *Geist* as divine, he denies, mistakenly in my view, that he was a pantheist.[17] Similarly, Śankara's Brahman is ontologically all-inclusive and is part of a metaphysical account of the nature of Reality that is religiously significant (i.e. "Reality" is divine in some sense). However, it may be denied that advaita Vedānta, although monistic, is pantheistic.[18] "Unity" is seen as absent from, or even antithetical to, essential aspects of advaita Vedānta such as its monism.

Monists, like pantheists, believe that Reality, or an aspect of it, is "One" or unified. Of course they also deny it is "One" or a "unity" in most other senses. Whatever similarities there are in this regard, there is insufficient reason for attributing pantheism to monists, because the oneness of Reality is neither a necessary nor a sufficient condition of pantheism. It is at most a necessary condition if monistic "oneness" is construed in a unitive sense that is constitutive of some particular pantheistic account of the divine Unity. An alleged entailment between pantheism and monism is even less likely since pantheists, like everyone else, are generally pluralistic. Any appearance to the contrary has been fostered by simply conflating Unity with monism, or by considering the few pantheists who were also monists and taking them as the norm. In fact, though it can only be reiterated here, the connection between Spinoza's monism and his pantheism does not rest on an identification of the two positions, but is instead the result of the wider metaphysical position constructed in his *Ethics.*

Before more closely examining Owen's claim that "pantheists are monists," I want to discuss Peter Forrest's account of Primitive Unity Monism and its relation to pantheism.

Forrest describes "Primitive Unity Monism" as

> the claim that there is a special *unity* in things . . . [it] is based on the distinction between a unity which is *natural* and one which is not . . . The intuitive idea here is that the unity is artificial if it is *just* a sum with no *further* claim to being a single item . . . To say that various different things form a primitive unity is to say that they form a single thing, that the unity or oneness of the thing they form is not artificial, and yet there is no further account of *why* they form a unity. They just do . . . Its [Primitive Unity Monism's] disadvantage is that a primitive unity is mysterious . . . One advantage is that it, like Spinozistic Monism, is a Conservative Monism. For ordinary experience does not contain an experience of the lack of primitive unity.
>
> (pp. 87–8)[19]

Forrest's examples of a "primitive unity" are the unity of a person and the unity in an object of art – aesthetic unity. "Natural Unity Monism" may seem conducive to a pantheist position, but the two positions cannot be equated.

The unity on which Natural Unity Monism is based may have little or nothing to do with Unity predicated by the pantheist. Furthermore, Primitive Unity Monism, a "strong" type of natural unity monism, is incompatible with pantheism. Whatever Unity is for the pantheist it cannot be a primitive unity in Forrest's sense. This is because in pantheism there must be an explanation of *why* Unity is predicated of the all- inclusive whole. The explanation defines the position. Without the explanation there can be no predication of Unity and so no position. If pantheists relied on a primitive unanalysable natural unity as the relevant sense of unity, pantheism would be based on a mystery. It would be virtually indistinguishable from Primitive Unity Monism – depending on how divinity was applied. So far as pantheists seek to explain the Unity they ascribe to the totality – and elucidating the meaning of Unity is a large part of being a (reflective) pantheist – they will reject Primitive Unity Monism.

I do not, however, think that pantheism is necessarily incompatible with Forrest's "Ultraradical Monism."

> we may extend Madhyamika Monism to cover *all* intellectual distinctions including those of evaluations. I call this Ultraradical Monism . . . the difference between the good, the bad and the indifferent would be due to our understanding, and so either ideal or illusory. This position can be expressed by saying that Reality is "beyond good and evil". I suspect it is more appropriate for the Ultraradical Monist to call the values assigned ideal, than to call them illusory. For surely they are still action-guiding even for the Ultraradical Monist. But illusory values should not be action-guiding.
>
> (Forrest, p. 89)

Both Spinoza and Lao Tzu (Taoism) at times appear to be "ultraradical monists." But to say that for the pantheist reality is "beyond good and evil" might be seen as conflicting with the view that Unity is fundamentally predicated on the basis of value.

Whether or not ultraradical monism is compatible with pantheism, it is certain that pantheism does not entail ultraradical monism. Pantheists may hold that "the difference between the good, the bad and the indifferent [is] . . . due to our understanding, and so either ideal or illusory," without believing the same to be true of all intellectual distinctions. Indeed, they may hold that view without being monists – and so without being ultraradical monists. However, they may also reject the view that reality is beyond good and evil. There is nothing in pantheism *per se* that seems to require such a view, and as I have said, there may be reason to reject it. Pantheists often do ascribe "goodness" to the Unity (e.g. Robinson Jeffers and even Spinoza) and mean it in what appears to be an objective sense.

Although Owen claims that "pantheists are monists" he recognises that monism is more inclusive that pantheism. However, the reason he gives for distinguishing monists who are pantheists from those who are not is objectionable. He says, "All these thinkers [e.g. the Stoics, Spinoza, Hegel, Śankara] hold that there is only one Reality and, therefore, that finite things and persons exist only in so far as they express its nature" (Owen, p. 67).

Furthermore, it is obvious that their respective monisms are not religiously neutral (e.g. merely ontological) accounts of Reality. Yet although they are all monists, Owen says they are not necessarily all pantheists. This is because,

> The One is not always called God. The Hindus call it Brahman. F. H. Bradley called it the Absolute and opposed it to the personal God of Christianity. Hence "monism" is more accurate than "pantheism" as an all-inclusive description. The justification for "pantheism" is that the One, by whatever name it is called, is the metaphysical equivalent to the God of theism.

(p. 67)

What does Owen mean in saying that for the monist to be a pantheist the "One" must be the "metaphysical equivalent to the God of theism?" The "One" is to be identified with the theistic God in crucial respects. But in what respects? Given what is most essential to the theistic conception of God, Owen probably means that the One must be identified with the ultimate cause or ground of being, and with the theistic conception of God as a person. If this is what he roughly means there are grounds for rejecting his view. Indeed, given Owen's requirement, and my view that pantheism is primarily a non-theistic view concerning the nature of a non-personal God (or divine Unity), there could be no pantheists. Pantheists reject the notion that the divine Unity is "the metaphysical equivalent to the God of theism," because there is too great a gap between them. To the extent that the theistic God is conceived in essentially personalistic terms, while the pantheistic God is conceived of in essentially non-personalistic terms, the two cannot be "metaphysically equivalent."

Thus, pantheism is not necessarily a kind of theistic monism, nor is theistic monism necessarily a type of pantheism, as Owen would have it. In fact, it is more likely that pantheism is necessarily not theistic monism and theistic monism is necessarily not pantheism. It is only possible to regard theistic monism as a kind of pantheism if the pantheistic Unity is not essentially conceived of in non-personal terms. Since there is little or no theistic element in pantheistic positions that are identifiable as monistic (e.g. Spinoza), it is implausible to suppose that pantheism should be taken as a form of theistic monism. What would it mean to say in such cases that the divine Unity is the metaphysical equivalent of a theistic God? They might be *functionally* equivalent – but why metaphysically equivalent? The "all-inclusive divine Unity" must, of course, be "divine," but it need not be identified with "God." Most pantheists do not – *clearly do not* – identify Unity with God in the theistic sense.

There are few instances in which pantheists do identify their divine Unity with God in the theistic sense (Giordano Bruno?) – and arguably such pantheists are theists first or theists only.[20] On Owen's account only these few "metaphysically theistically equivalent" monists are pantheists. But contrary to Owen, it is clear that the monistic "One" does not have to be identified with God to be pantheistic. In most accounts such an identification makes the monism more theistic than pantheistic.

Consider the possibility of the kind of philosophical/theological hybrid Owen thinks is the norm for pantheism. Is belief in a personal theistic God incompatible with pantheistic belief as I have claimed? The two are not compatible in the most representative cases of pantheism (e.g. Spinoza, Taoism). But there is no way to answer the question in regard to further particular cases apart from an account of their essential beliefs. Stipulative solutions are not going to be wholly satisfactory. The question of incompatibility can be discussed conceptually in terms of an essential aspect of theism, for example, being allegedly incompatible with an essential aspect of pantheism. The issue here is not so much, or only, if a particular theory is coherent, but whether the theory or tradition in question is better understood overall to be theistic, pantheistic or a hybrid. However, empirically it makes little sense to speak of the "incompatibility" of theism and pantheism if, as is the case, there are theistic traditions and theologies that have pantheistic elements and vice versa. The only question here is the descriptive one: which aspects are theistic and which are pantheistic. The presence of both pantheistic and theistic elements in a tradition may result in practices inappropriate to any pure version of either theism or pantheism.

I have given an account of some of the ways in which monists are to be distinguished from, or identified with, pantheists. Not all pantheists are monists, and in the end monism is rather incidental to pantheism. Monism is never sufficient for pantheism and is necessary for it only in those cases where the monism is itself explicated in terms of a wider pantheistic view. Various other reasons have been given why Owen's method of distinguishing monists who are pantheists from those who are not, in terms of whether the Reality they describe is to be identified with the theistic God, is mistaken. In no instance can non-pantheistic monists be distinguished from pantheistic monists on the basis of whether or not they identify their monistic "One" with the "metaphysical equivalent to the God of theism." Identifying the divine Unity as a monistic "ultimate Reality" or "One" is not even necessary for pantheism – let alone is metaphysically equating the divine Unity with the theistic God. Indeed, depending on what one takes the relation between theism and pantheism to be, such an equation might render pantheism incoherent.

Owen's account of the relation between monism and pantheism rests in part on his understanding of the "oneness" aspect of monism and the "unitive" aspect of pantheism as explicable exclusively in terms of substance. It also rests on his apparent denial that monists can be theists. They cannot be theists because they allegedly deny that "creatures are substantially distinct from the creature" (p. 68).

> Monists differ in the status which they accord to finite entities. They are all bound to deny that these entities are substantially independent of God (or therefore of each other) . . . All monists, then, can be called pantheists in so far as they hold that everything is either unreal or real to the extent that it is the self-expression of the Absolute.
>
> (Owen, p. 68)

Where monism is the position that there is only one thing or kind of thing (i.e. substance), the monist is committed to the view that finite entities are not "substantially independent of God" – where this simply means everything is one substance.[21] Nothing can be substantially independent of God because there is nothing else but God and God is that One substance. However, since pantheists do not identify Unity with substance or with a metaphysical equivalent of a theistic God, they will reject the equation between monism and pantheism. This of course is not to deny that monists who maintain that "everything is either unreal or real to the extent that it is the self-expression of the Absolute" may be pantheists.

According to Owen, monists cannot be theists but they can be pantheists. He says, "The differences between the various forms of monism are negligible when compared with the difference

91

between all of these forms and theism, which rests on the affirmation that all creatures are substantially distinct from the Creator" (p. 68). In Owen's account the theist, but not the monist or the pantheist, maintains that "all creatures are substantially distinct from the Creator" (p. 68). Yet given that there are monists who claim to be theists, asserting that monists deny that God and creation are substantially distinct and theists believe that they are does little to establish the incompatibility. A theistic monist need not maintain any substantial unity between God and finite entities since their "one thing or one type of thing" need not be substantively understood. "One thing" taken monistically in an ontological sense may be "many things" substantively understood.

So given that theism does hold that the creator and creation are substantively distinct, monists need not maintain that there is no such substantial distinction unless their monism is one of substance. Thus, monists can be theists as well as atheists or pantheists. Alternatively, one might hold that although theism does demand some kind of radical separation between creator and creatures, the distinction need not be explicated in terms of substance, or in any other way that makes it incompatible with monism. To assume otherwise is to unnecessarily make some obtuse metaphysical doctrine about the nature of substance essential to theism. It is just not clear that theism demands that "all creatures are substantially distinct from the creator." On some interpretations of the doctrine of divine conservation such a demand might be rejected. (I discuss this further in Part II.) At any rate, some theists do deny that God and creation are substantially distinct. Perhaps because the "distinction requirement" is more philosophical/theological than religious, it is not nearly as essential to theism as is the view that God is a person.

Substance monism need not have any implications concerning God or an Absolute in either a theistic or a pantheistic sense. Differences among substance monists may be greater than differences between monists who deny and theists who affirm that God and creation are substantially distinct. For example, a substance monist (e.g. Śankara – interpreted atheistically) need not identify substance with God, or recognise any God at all. In this case it is plausible to hold that the difference between such an atheistic monist and a theistic or pantheistic monist is far greater than that between the theistic monist who perhaps holds that creatures and creator are co-substantial (though the theistic monist need not hold this view) and the theistic non-monist (i.e. Owen's "theist") who believes that all creatures are substantially distinct from the creator. The latter two have their theism in common, while the former two have their monism in common. The latter two are "closer" in kind than the former, *if* (and so far as) one assumes that theism is a more significant common denominator than monism.

Therefore, Owen is mistaken in claiming that "the differences between the various [substance] forms of monism are negligible when compared with the differences between all of these forms and theism, which rests on the affirmation that all creatures are substantially distinct from the Creator" (p. 68). Owen's could be correct only if monism and theism are taken to be, as he takes them to be, mutually exclusive. But even granting Owen his use of (i) "monism" to refer only to unity of substance and (ii) "theism" to refer only to non-monistic theism, some types of "God" monism (e.g. some of those who identify the "One" with "God" or the "Absolute") have more in common with non-monistic theism than with other types of monism.

2.4 TRANSCENDENCE

Although pantheists differ among themselves at many points, they all agree in denying the basic theistic claim that God and the world are ontologically distinct.[1]

H. P. Owen

Why is there this horror of pantheism in traditional Western theology? And what *is* pantheism? The horror stems from the thought that there must be a gulf between God and creatures, and this in turn is because in the theistic traditions God is the sole object of worship, from whom all power and holiness flow. Merging with God is not possible for a worshipper, and pantheism – if it means somehow an identity between nature and God and between humans and God – has the flavour of blasphemy.[2]

Ninian Smart

Like the notions of "Unity" and "Divinity," understanding transcendence and immanence is essential to any account of pantheism. A defining feature of pantheism is allegedly that God is wholly immanent. However, what is actually (or mostly) involved in this claim is that pantheism denies the theistic view that God transcends the world.[3] Pantheism clearly does not claim that God in the theistic sense is immanent in the world since it denies that such a God – transcendent or immanent – exists. According to pantheism it is (of course) the pantheistic "God" (i.e. the all-inclusive divine Unity) that is immanent, not the theistic one. Theists and pantheists do not differ as to whether the theistic God is immanent or transcendent, but as to whether the theistic God exists. So to differentiate between them on the basis of one's affirming and the other denying immanence is utterly confused.

In Chapter 1 I said pantheism can be seen as the most radical solution to a complex set of interrelated issues broadly defined as "the problem of transcendence." It is seen as a solution because it is taken to deny that "God" is transcendent, for example, "ontologically" transcendent where this is taken as philosophically or religiously significant. Despite pantheism's denial that the all-inclusive divine Unity is ontologically distinct from or transcendent to the world, I shall argue that given a relevant conception of "transcendence" the view that pantheism overcomes all problems associated with transcendence is mistaken. It resolves some difficulties, but it is not an easy solution (e.g. a solution by definition) to them all. It is only when one regards problems generated by God's transcendence as solely a function of God's ontological distinctness from the world that pantheism is seen as a solution to such problems. And, even in the theistic view, few problems associated with transcendence are *really* a function of God's alleged ontological transcendence.

Many of the difficulties associated with theistic transcendence are not dissipated for the pantheist when relevantly adjusted. For example, theistic transcendence presents *prima facie* difficulties concerning knowledge of and relations with God. The pantheist is part of the Unity, but both the nature of Unity and its practical implications must be determined. In the *Meditations* of Marcus Aurelius this appears as much a problem for pantheists (if Aurelius is one) as knowing and relating to God is for theists.[4]

In a sense, the Unity in pantheism is wholly immanent, but this is bare ontological immanence that follows from the Unity's all-inclusiveness (i.e. there is nothing else). Yet even this overstates the pantheistic commitment to immanence. Aspects of the Unity or the unifying principle often have a transcendent aspect to them. Unity is "all-inclusive" but, with the possible exception of

Spinoza, pantheists generally deny complete immanence. Thus, the metaphysical Tao informs everything and is part of the all-inclusive Unity, but it does have a transcendent aspect to it. It does transcend the phenomenal world of "myriad things." The same is true of Hegel's *Geist*, the Plotinian "One" and Presocratic unifying principles as well. So the claim that pantheists deny "God's" transcendence is altogether misleading on several counts unless taken to mean what it usually does mean when asserted by theists – which is that pantheists deny the transcendence of a theistic God.

For the theist, God's transcendence is allegedly implied by the perfection or completeness of His nature. Pantheism's denial of ontological transcendence is more important to theism than to pantheism since theism distinguishes itself from pantheism on at least this basis. However, this is hardly the most significant factor that sets theism off from pantheism. Instead, it must be the idea that God is personal. Note that those who interpret the view that "the world is God's body" as compatible with theism, and so claim God is immanent, abandon one of the traditional criteria – some (*mistakenly*) say the most significant one – that allegedly distinguishes theism from pantheism.[5]

This section proceeds as follows. First, what are the problems associated with God's transcendence? Two analyses that critically examine the classical theistic notion of transcendence are then discussed. The view that pantheism is in a better position to resolve the concept's most intractable difficulties is disputed. The implications of pantheism's alleged denial of transcendence – what is and what is not being denied, and why – are further examined in this context. I have already suggested that what the theistic interpretation of pantheism's denial of transcendence usually amounts to is the denial of the theistic claim that God and the world are ontologically distinct. And if this is all that is being denied it is no surprise that transcendence remains problematic for pantheism.

Some theists claim God is completely transcendent to the created universe, but the usual claim is that God is transcendent in some respects and immanent in others. Thus, God might be conceived of as ontologically distinct from the created universe (e.g. as a Cartesian or Aristotelian substance); as logically transcendent (i.e. defying the laws of logic as God allegedly can according to Descartes); and/or epistemologically transcendent (i.e. impossible to conceive of in any adequate fashion), as is the case in part for Aquinas. Thus, transcendence has ontological, epistemological, logical and conceptual dimensions, and transcendence in one sense need not imply it in another. However, Aquinas's claim that God is ontologically transcendent *is* related to his assertion that in many ways God is also unknowable in some respects. There are things we do not and cannot know about God. If God is partly conceptually transcendent, if we cannot even conceive of certain things concerning God's nature, this implies a degree of epistemological transcendence since we cannot know what we cannot conceive of. For Aquinas, these kinds of transcendence are related, but it is important to distinguish among different senses of transcendence as Aquinas himself does.

The claim that there exists an all-inclusive Unity is in part a denial of the kinds of separation between God and the world claimed by theism. But this need not entail the denial of epistemological transcendence. Pantheism's denial of ontological transcendence in the theistic sense does not imply that there are answers to fundamental philosophical questions such as why there is something rather than nothing. There may be answers, but the claim that there are will not follow from a denial of ontological transcendence, but instead from an acceptance of a "Principle of Sufficient Reason." For theism the fact that certain things, especially about God, cannot be known is a consequence of God's nature (e.g. how can God exist necessarily, and why does God allow apparently gratuitous evil?). The pantheist need not deny that there are things about the Unity that may be unknowable. What is of course denied is that lack of knowledge results from something intrinsic to the nature of the Unity having to do with its ontological separation from everything else – since such separation is denied. For Spinoza there is a lot that persons, all of which are modes of God, will not know.[6]

For the theist, God is usually taken to be non-spatial and "timeless" (i.e. "transcendent" to space and time). Thus, questions arise concerning how God interacts with the world, or even if God is able to do so. These must be answered in terms of an account of divine immanence – an account that must be compatible with God's alleged transcendence. Transcendence is a central problem for theism because its goal is the establishment of a relation with God, and *prima facie* God's transcendence inhibits the task. How is one to relate to a God that is to some extent unknowable, transcends space and time, mysteriously tolerates certain kinds of evil etc.? The theistic answer, in general terms, is that the pursuit of such a goal is possible on the basis of what one does know, partly because of what God reveals or does. How a non-temporal (or atemporal) and non-spatial Being allegedly acts in the material world is more complicated, though solutions are offered here as well.

In pantheism, the conditions giving rise to these problems, and hence the problems themselves, are either denied or taken to be moot. There is no non-spatial or non-temporal God. If the goal of pantheism is to establish a non-personal relationship of a kind with the divine Unity, then the kinds of problems the theist must overcome which relate directly to God's ontological character, his non-spatiality etc. could not arise. In Part III I shall argue that the goal of pantheism is not to establish a relationship with the divine Unity in anything more than an attenuated sense. The pantheistic goal could be described as a relationship, but is best described as a way of life and a "state."

The problem of transcendence and the theistic concern of a personal relationship to God are inextricably linked. Given that God is transcendent, what are the implications for the religious life of theists? How does one relate to such a God? Since pantheism denies most of the suppositions generating perplexities surrounding God's alleged transcendence, one would expect the purpose and approach to religious life to shift dramatically in pantheism – and so it does. A religious life which seeks to establish a relationship between the divine Unity and the individual is misdirected according to pantheism, and the goal of salvation in the form of such a relationship, now and after death, is a false one.

How is transcendence to be understood? The following discussion focuses on accounts by W. D. Hudson and Ninian Smart.

Hudson claims that the concept of divine transcendence is grounded in the experience of the "wholly other" as described by Otto. He says, "the concept of divine transcendence ... [is] the form which the idea of the otherness of the holy has assumed within theism ... [T]his otherness can be conceived of ... as a

97

kind of separation that can be put into words or as one which cannot."[7]

How can "something elude apprehension in terms of concepts"? Hudson says it can be empirically impossible to describe something – when as a matter of fact we do not know enough (i.e. it is *beyond knowledge*); or it can be logically impossible because any description is bound to be incoherent. "[T]he meaning rules of the language . . . being what they are, no coherent description of it could be given" (p. 198).

> "Beyond knowledge" does *not* mean beyond *all* knowledge. It is really short for *beyond man's limited knowledge.* "Beyond description", on the other hand, *does* mean beyond *all* description of a certain kind. It is short for *beyond all coherent description in human language as ordinarily used.*
>
> (p. 199)[8]

On the "beyond knowledge" concept of transcendence, "Coherent descriptions of God's nature and activity can be framed in our language as ordinarily used but our knowledge of such descriptions which are true is limited" (p. 206). God is indescribable and so transcendent not because there is a logical barrier preventing description, but because we are too ignorant to comprehend and so describe God. However, the "beyond description" conception of transcendence denies the logical possibility of giving a coherent description of God.

Hudson argues that the "beyond knowledge" account of transcendence is preferable to the "beyond description" account. He examines and rejects "empirical, semantic, and theological grounds" in support of the latter. On the "beyond description" view it is not possible to describe God coherently as transcendent and so it is a self-defeating position. Like the mystics' claim that their experiences are literally ineffable, it attempts to describe what by its own account is indescribable. Reasons for rejecting the "beyond description" account are not applicable to the "beyond knowledge" account.

According to Hudson, his distinction raises the "central problem concerning divine transcendence." "Can God be coherently described in human language as ordinarily used?" (p. 198). This issue is important since it involves what we can say and know about God, and this has implications for practice. But it is not the central problem concerning transcendence; nor is there a single central problem. The central issues are about the relationship between God and the world.

Accepting the "beyond description" conception of transcendence either ends discussion of God since such talk would be incoherent, or forces one to extraordinary language – one "in which religious belief can be coherently expressed" (p. 203). Such language must not "rupture into unintelligibility." As John Stuart Mill argued, language can have a somewhat different meaning when applied to God. However, where properties allegedly have a completely different meaning as applied to God they completely lose their meaning.[9] If one equivocates absolutely on predicating "goodness" to God (i.e. if goodness means something completely different as applied to God) then we cannot know what it means to say God is good. Similarly, if one supposes religious belief is not asserting anything factual but is instead emotive or an expression of attitude or intent, one thereby discounts what believers want to assert and abandons the ordinary meaning of such beliefs.[10]

What limits knowledge of God in the "beyond knowledge" account is "at least . . . inadequate experience and confused conceptualisation" (p. 207). Given that this is the preferred account of transcendence, what becomes of problems associated with transcendence? What is the problem of transcendence? Hudson asks "If God is 'beyond knowledge' what is the appropriate aim of philosophical reflection? The answer is clear: to surmount the limitations on our knowledge of him so far as it lies in our power to do so" (p. 207). The problem of transcendence is thus conceived as primarily an epistemic one. The scope of God's transcendence can be reduced through philosophical reflection, and perhaps ideally can even be eliminated. In Hudson's "beyond knowledge" account, transcendence is partly a function of God's nature, but it is also a function of our inadequate experience and confused conceptualisations.[11] Nothing in principle rules out an ever increasing comprehension of God's nature. To suggest that there is some intrinsic or logical reason that ruled out knowledge of God (e.g. an irreversible constitutional lack on our part, or God's intrinsically unknowable nature) implies the "beyond description" account that Hudson rejects. The "beyond description" account would apply to the degree it was impossible to overcome lack of knowledge of God through additional experience and conceptualisation.

Hudson's view is not the classical theistic one in which God's transcendence is not interpreted primarily as epistemic and is not taken to be reducible. There may be things we do not know about God and can come to know through increased experience and more adequate conceptualisation, but this has little to do with God's transcendence. Transcendence is first and foremost an ontological property of God which has significant epistemological consequences. This includes the fact that what we can know of God is limited both by God's nature and by our own limited cognitive capacities. To know more about God then we can come to know either God must be different or we must be different. Theism's view of transcendence does not deny there are things about God that are temporarily "beyond knowledge." But if we can come to know these things they are not related to God's essential transcendence.

The "beyond knowledge" account of transcendence cannot be as easily separated from a "beyond description" account as Hudson suggests, because it follows from the latter. It follows if the "beyond knowledge" account is adjusted so as not to allow God's transcendence to be diminished through additional human experience and conceptualisation. Theists agree that we can learn previously unknown things about God, but this does not support the "beyond knowledge" account of transcendence. The crucial theistic claim is that we cannot know certain things about God because of his nature and our own. The limitation is extrinsic to us in that it is a function of God's nature and intrinsic in that it results from limitations of our own cognitive capacities. According to theism it is not the case that if one was more intelligent etc. then one could know everything about God – although some can know more than others. Aquinas allows that some people can know certain things about God through reason that others can only know through revelation. However, some things (e.g. that the world has not always existed) can only be known through revelation. Certain cognitive restrictions are intrinsic to all humans.

Hudson fails to capture the theistic understanding of the "beyond description" analysis because he has interpreted it (i.e. defined it) as being "beyond all description." He mistakenly equates it with the implausible claim of literal ineffability. What the account means to capture (e.g. Aquinas's account rather than Tertullian's) is not that God is beyond all description, thus transcending all experience and conceptualisation. Rather, the "beyond description" account more modestly maintains that there are things about God we cannot know because of the nature of God. The classical theistic account is a combination of Hudson's "beyond knowledge" and "beyond description" accounts. It does not accept one and reject the other.

Hudson says,

> we can never *know* that we could know more than we do know; but we can believe it and have good grounds for doing so. In the past, man's experience has enlarged and his conceptualisation has sometimes been clarified... There may be, however, some limitations upon our knowledge which are *ir*removable because their removal would require powers of perception or ratiocination of which our minds or bodies are simply not capable.
>
> (p. 208)

But if this limitation is a basis for God's transcendence, then surely such transcendence is being explained in terms of aspects of God's nature as being "beyond description" for us. The conceptual transcendence of God need not be absolute. The "beyond description" analysis of transcendence conceived of by Hudson requires complete transcendence (i.e. it is logically impossible for any concepts to apply to God), and entails the untoward consequences he delineates. But the "beyond knowledge" analysis also requires that God be "beyond description" in a limited sense. God's transcendence cannot be described as merely due to our limited resources. God is "beyond description" because of the way both we and God are constituted.

What then does Hudson's distinction come to? All he denies is that a "beyond description" analysis of God's transcendence is unacceptable if such an analysis is taken to mean that God is logically speaking beyond any description whatsoever. Such accounts of transcendence are generally repudiated within traditions (i.e. God is described). But a correct understanding of a "beyond knowledge" account entails a "beyond description" account, as long as the latter is not construed as "beyond any logically possible description." The theistic analysis of transcendence involves both accounts and does not regard them as two "distinct conceptions" (p. 209).

Given what has been said about transcendence thus far, there is no reason to think that pantheism is a solution to the problem. Of course, it dispenses with the theistic version of the problem since it denies the existence of the ontologically transcendent God that generates it. But the "problem of transcendence" (unlike the "problem of evil") need not be conceived of as inherently a theistic one. Pantheism does not claim that in principle one can know all there is to know about the divine Unity. Opacity may be due to the nature of the Unity or to the restrictions on individuals' cognitive capacities. Thus, for example, the pantheist may believe that one cannot know why there is something rather than nothing, and see this as following from the nature of oneself or that of the Unity. So for pantheism, the epistemic dimension of the problem of transcendence remains.

Morality, creation, meaning and purpose in life; all of these may have something to do with transcendence. It is naive to suppose that questions relating to these do not arise for pantheism because it denies that a theistic God exists or that the Unity is ontologically transcendent. Pantheism is no panacea, and to see it as resolving various difficulties relating to transcendence simply in virtue of its denial of theism is no different from seeing atheism as a solution. The ways in which issues relating to transcendence are addressed vary in accordance with the concepts and beliefs of a particular tradition. Some issues may only be relevant to theism. In general, however, no matter how distinct the proposed solutions are, the issues associated with transcendence arise not only for theism but for pantheism and atheism. This reflects the fact that the problem of transcendence is a function of the serious commonplaces that are the "human condition." Religions must have a strategy for dealing with those problems. From the epistemic point of view transcendence remains a problem for pantheism, even if ontologically speaking a certain category of problem associated with ontological "otherness" vanishes.

Ninian Smart's analysis of transcendence is very different from Hudson's almost exclusively epistemological account.[12] He discusses several types of transcendence, concentrating on what is meant by "God transcends the world." He claims that the sense in which god can be said to transcend the world is more important than the sense in which God can be said to "transcend human experience." By "transcends human experience" Smart means what Hudson does by "beyond description" (i.e. that God cannot be conceptualised). He rejects an analysis of transcendence in terms of transcending human experience.

> If we say that God transcends human experience ... we cannot mean that he is beyond all possible human experience. It is axiomatic that the believer thinks that he has or can have some experience of God ... A God who could never enter into human experience would *a fortiori* have no interpersonal relations with men. This would be flatly contrary to both the Christian revelation and to the beliefs of other theistic faiths ... Similar remarks apply to the notion that God is beyond comprehension.

> (pp. 477–8)

Like Hudson, Smart rightly claims that "God transcends human experience" should not be taken to mean that God transcends all possible human experience. To do so is no more plausible then supposing that God must elude all comprehension.

As Smart notes, without any experience and comprehension of God the relationship with God that theists claim desirable would be impossible. Analyses which claim impossibility of this kind must be rejected. But this does not affect the more common claim that God "transcends human experience" in some ways. It is because God is regarded as separate from the world and partly "beyond knowledge" that difficulties in knowing and relating to God (i.e. problems of transcendence) are generated. When the "*completely* beyond description or knowledge" account of transcendence is suitably weakened to a "*partly* beyond description or knowledge" account, it need not be abandoned because it no longer conflicts with God's alleged "interpersonal relations."

In rejecting the Tertullian "beyond description" account of transcendence Smart appears to also reject the "beyond knowledge" account. At least he does not distinguish the latter weaker and more prevalent account from the former. In so doing he omits consideration of what Hudson and classical theism generally take to be an indispensable aspect of God's transcendence: our inability to know certain things about God, and attendant difficulties in relating to a God who is transcendent in this way. Contrary to Smart, transcendence *is* to be explained partly in terms of "God transcends human experience." I have claimed that it is this "beyond knowledge" aspect of transcendence, the aspect that Smart appears to deny is significant, that makes the problem of transcendence applicable to both theism and pantheism.

Having rejected the idea that transcendence is to be explained even partly in terms of "God transcends human experience," Smart discusses what is meant by (i) "God transcends existence"; (ii) "God transcends space and time"; and (iii) "God transcends the world." He regards the last two locutions as more important than the first. They are the focus of his analysis and I shall examine their implications for pantheism's alleged denial of transcendence.

Consider first what Smart says about "God transcends existence."

> to say this is a way of showing that God is not a finite being, like a star. Yet it is a paradoxical thing to say. What it can scarcely mean is that, by transcending existence, God does not exist. To assert this is ... atheism ... [T]he analysis of transcendence here presented [below] should make it clear that God is *not* something like a star. Nor is he, for the believer, an entity additional to the furniture of the world; for the believer's universe already includes God.
>
> (pp. 478–9)

The above could be applicable to pantheism if one wanted to say that "Unity transcends existence." Whatever it might mean to say that "Unity transcends existence" it will not mean that the Unity does not exist. And if Paul Tillich is right in claiming there are difficulties in meaningfully asking "Does God exist?," then there may be similar difficulties for similar reasons in asking "Does the divine Unity exist?" According to Tillich, the question is not meaningful because it wrongly assumes God is a spatio-temporal object that may or may not exist.[13] Perhaps Unity cannot properly be regarded as an existent among other existents either – and so in this sense "Unity transcends existence." Unity is conceived of as "all-inclusive" but should it also be conceived of as a spatio-temporal object that may or may not exist? This question is especially appropriate in the context of Tillich's thought since his conception of God as "ultimate concern" (an evaluative concept) and "the ground of all Being" is often taken as being more pantheistic than theistic.[14] Although the Unity includes or extends to spatio-temporal objects it seems a mistake to regard it as itself a spatio-temporal object; especially since it is ascribed on the basis of value. Despite this there seems no reason to suppose it meaningless to ask if the Unity exists.

What does it mean to say that God transcends space? Smart says that if this is taken to mean that "God is outside or beyond space" it is paradoxical since " 'outside' and 'beyond' are themselves spatial words" (p. 479). It may mean "that God does not take spatial predicates like 'is a thousand feet long' " (p. 479). But something more is needed since numbers do not take spatial predicates either and yet it is assumed, as Smart says, that if God exists he exists in a way that numbers do not. If God transcends space, what is one to make of the fact that the Bible is full of spatial descriptions of an allegedly non-spatial God (e.g. "God was on the holy mountain").

> The reply . . . has two phases. First, the Bible also speaks of God as creator of the whole world. This implies the existence of God is either temporally or logically prior to the existence of spatio-temporal objects. Second, the Bible . . . speak[s] as though God is specially present or active at particular places and times. Without this particularity there would, it seems, be no revelatory events or experiences, and God would be a mere nonspatial First Cause. But the idea of special presence . . . does not necessarily conflict with that of God's nonspatiality, and does account for the spatial language used of God.
>
> (p. 480)

Smart notes that temporal predicates are also applied to a non-temporal God. But more importantly he claims that spatial predicates are used of God in the sense of "special presence"; and this supposedly accounts for the Bible's spatial descriptions of God without conflicting with God's non-spatiality.

Given that "special presence" accounts for the "spatial language used of God," it is not clear why "special presence" does not conflict with God's non-spatiality. How can God be specially present in revelation if he is spatially and/or temporally transcendent? This is part of the problem of transcendence and Smart disingenuously dismisses it. What is it about "special presence" that makes it possible for God to be present (e.g. "on the mountain") while at the same time not spatially present? How then is God present? "Special" in "special presence" changes the meaning of "present."[15] Is Smart suggesting that God both is and is not spatially present at the same place at the same time? If not, how can special presence account for spatio-temporal language ascribed to a non-spatio-temporal Being? Pantheism avoids this conundrum. The all-inclusive Unity is not *on* the mountain, but constitutive of it. It includes the mountain.

Smart says,

> To understand what it means to say that God is "beyond" or "behind" the cosmos, we must note the other elements included in, or closely related to, the idea of transcendence... [e.g. God's "invisible presence everywhere"]. This element of concealment, or "secret omnipresence"... accounts in part for God's being thought to be "behind the cosmos" and... behind the things and events which we encounter... [but] not within things in the way in which particles are.
>
> (pp. 480–1)

Does "omnipresence" mean what Smart claims it means – that God is "behind" the cosmos and events we encounter? More importantly, is the notion of God's invisible or "secret omnipresence" an aspect of the idea of his transcendence? Omnipresence seems to conflict with the notion of transcendence. In saying that God is transcendent does the theist mean that God is everywhere (i.e. "behind" everything)? God may be everywhere according to the theist – but is this explained *in terms of* his transcendence, rather than in spite of it?

In Smart's account God's secret omnipresence does not conflict with special presence. "[T]ranscendence [which includes the element of "secret omnipresence"] is everywhere *in religion* associated with that of a being or state accessible to human experience through particular events or experiences... God is specially present in certain events... he reveals himself through particular circumstances [e.g. Christ]" (pp. 482, 481). If it is true that the idea of transcendence is associated with special presence, it could also be true of transcendence in pantheism. Unity might be particularly manifest in some things rather than others. Such special presence might be an ontological or epistemological feature of some event or experience. But why accept the claim that "transcendence is everywhere *in religion* associated with that of a being or state accessible to human experience." Smart appears to suggest that what makes God accessible is his transcendence.

This turns the problem of transcendence as traditionally conceived on its head. Transcendence is a problem for accessibility not a solution to it. Of course, even if Smart is right he has not shown that such a concept of transcendence along with the "other elements included in it" is coherent. Why not say instead that transcendence conflicts with the idea of a being or state that is accessible?

Smart claims that the theistic "notion of transcendence goes with the belief that God is Creator" and so "outside" the cosmos. God and the cosmos are "different," which suggests that God can exist without the world, but not the world without God. Furthermore, according to theism the world depends continuously upon God's creative and sustaining activity. Smart therefore claims that "creativity and independence" (i.e. the "independence" of God from the world) are "two further aspects of transcendence" (p. 482).

Theism maintains that God is "independent," where this means that God can exist without the world. But "independence" does not obviously belong to the concept of transcendence. "Independence" may imply "creativity" (though I do not see why) but while the former notion *may* be, if suitably interpreted, an aspect of the concept of transcendence in locutions such as "God transcends the world," the latter is not. Perhaps "independence" does suggest something about God's conserving the world through creative power. This does not show that creativity is part of the concept of transcendence. Also, to say that "the idea of transcendence is everywhere *in religion* associated with that of a being or state accessible to human experience through particular events or experiences" (p. 482) does not show that "special presence" is to be included in the analysis of transcendence (even if not in the concept itself), rather than as presenting a fundamental problem for that analysis.

Summing up his account Smart says:

> Transcendence then comprises . . . five elements: nonspatiality, secret omnipresence, special presence, independence and creativity. The abandonment of this notion makes nonsense of traditional Christian belief . . . What the theist means can . . . be put as follows: "There is a holy Power working within and behind the cosmos, present to us

secretly everywhere, and specially present and active in such-and-such events and/or experiences".

(pp. 483, 487)

He claims these elements are all compatible, and that some may entail or at least "suggest one another" (e.g. creativity entails independence) (p. 484).

Given his analysis Smart is able to claim that the contrast between immanence and transcendence is misconceived. If immanence means "special presence" it can be contrasted with the other four elements essential to transcendence.

> But equally, we can mean by immanence God's working within all things. In this case the concept becomes identical with that of transcendence, for "within" is an analogy like "beyond" – not to be taken literally ... God's dynamic working within all things is surely equivalent to his continuous, omnipresent creativity. One thus has two choices about immanence: immanence$_1$ is just ... [special presence]; immanence$_2$ is just transcendence.

(p. 487)

Given Smart's analysis of transcendence as including secret omnipresence etc. it is obvious why he sees transcendence and immanence$_2$ as equivalent.

He denies a contrast between transcendence and immanence because he explains transcendence in a way that includes immanence. Smart claims that if " 'within' is an analogy like 'beyond'," then to talk about God's working "within" all things will be the same as talking about God's "omnipresent creativity." It will be the same if, contrary to classical theism (or ordinary understanding), "omnipresent creativity" or God's working "within" all things is *defined* as a transcendent rather than immanent property. The terms "beyond" and "within" are similar for Smart not only because they are both meant to be non-literal analogies, but because as applied to God they are synonymous in his account.

Smart does not consider questions which make the opposition between transcendence and immanence problematic. How can God be non-spatial and distinct from the world and yet at the same time sustain it and be specially present? The explanation Smart offers is an analogy with allegedly non-spatial mental

108

properties and their causal relations with our bodies (p. 484). But how good is the analogy? Does it make an essentially non-spatial God's interaction with the spatial world less problematic – especially if mental properties are taken to supervene upon (if not reduce to) physical properties as they usually are in contemporary philosophy of mind? If non-spatiality is an aspect of transcendence, and spatiality an aspect of immanence, the two conflict. In claiming that God's special presence, secret omnipresence, and continuous creative power are aspects of transcendence, Smart assures that transcendence cannot conflict with immanence. He has built the notion of immanence into transcendence and claims it is the theistic view. Theism, however, does not take transcendence and immanence as identical. Smart's view is therefore unorthodox. It is not consonant with the theistic account – let alone does it explain that account.

Smart's analysis of transcendence in theism is largely mistaken, but suppose it is not. What are the implications of his account for pantheism's alleged denial of transcendence? Problems generally associated with God's transcendence are either not acknowledged by Smart, or he thinks they do not follow from the concept itself, but from metaphysical and theological speculation about transcendence. In effect, then, given Smart's account there are no difficulties with the concept of transcendence, and no problems that it generates, for pantheism to resolve. Moreover, since pantheism's alleged solution to the problem of transcendence rests on pantheism's claim that the Unity is not transcendent but immanent, Smart's account not only renders the problem of transcendence innocuous or moot, but also renders superfluous the basis of any solution pantheism may offer. The theistic notion of transcendence *is* immanence according to Smart. If, after all, theism too claims that God is immanent, one need not resort to pantheism to avoid problems of transcendence.

Whether or not they are proper aspects of transcendence, it is worth considering how the five concepts that Smart thinks are part of the concept of transcendence are applicable to pantheism.

First, there is non-spatiality. If Unity is conceived of as material then it cannot be non-spatial. But given that Unity is not to be identified with the cosmos *per se*, it need not be taken to be spatial in any straightforward way. If the Unity is predicated on the basis of some kind of principle, plan or force as the naturalistic model of the explanation of Unity suggests, and if this in turn has some valuational basis, then one may suppose that the Unity is non-spatial though it extends to all things (or most things) that are spatial. Principles and plans are not spatially located, and forces need not be either when interpreted after the manner Smart interprets God as being "behind" those things that "form part of the fabric of the cosmos."

Second, there is omnipresence. Smart calls it "secret omnipresence." "God is invisibly present everywhere . . . [which] accounts in part for God's being thought to be 'behind the cosmos' and . . . the things and events which we encounter" (p. 481). This corresponds to the "all-inclusive" aspect of Unity. Unity can be present everywhere without being perceived. The idea of secret omnipresence seems more applicable to pantheism's Unity than to the theistic God. When this notion of secret omnipresence becomes dominant in theism it represents a move towards pantheism and is often recognised as such.

Third, there is "special presence." Theism maintains that God not only is invisibly present everywhere, but also "specially present in certain events and experiences." Smart acknowledges that special presence "may not strictly be part of the notion of transcendence; but [claims] it is impossible to divorce it from transcendence without distorting the meaning of the latter" (p. 481). Contrary to Smart's contention, however, special presence is not seen as linked to transcendence from the theistic perspective. Instead, it is seen as highlighting difficulties the idea of transcendence presents for immanence. For example, God allegedly becomes, or is specially present in, Christ. How can the non-spatial transcendent divine creator become the spatio-temporal human? One is not asking for the mechanics of an incarnation. But given that such a notion is logically inconsistent one is asking, as did Kierkegaard, how to understand it.

The present concern is not to further question the relation of special presence to transcendence, but to query its applicability to pantheism. Although the pantheistic Unity is all-inclusive, it can be conceived of as being specially present in some places at particular times. It depends on how Unity is interpreted, but on a naturalistic model of Unity "special presence" may be possible. Certain kinds of order or value might suggest a special presence while disorder or chaos (e.g. nihilism of various types) might indicate a lack of Unity – i.e. a "special absence."

Unity has an ontological dimension, but it also has an epistemic one. "Unity" can partly be a function of what people know, or fail to know, and how they live. For Spinoza, our happiness is proportional to what we know about how things are and how they must be. Although Spinozistic Unity is predicated on the basis of a single substance, it is also a function of what we know about it and what we do. The theistic notion of special presence is sometimes applied to individuals who are especially "holy." There could be a corresponding idea in pantheism. An individual who grasps Unity and lives in accord with it may be someone to whom Unity is specially present.

The final elements in Smart's analysis are "independence" and creativity. The Unity is not independent of (i.e. cannot exist apart from) the cosmos, and it cannot create the cosmos since it is not independent of it. This is a basic distinction between theistic transcendence and pantheistic immanence. If Unity is not interpreted on an ontological model (e.g. equated with substance monism), it may be independent of parts of the universe while encompassing it. But pantheism denies that there is any theistic type of ontological distinction between the cosmos and Unity such that Unity can exist apart from the cosmos. It is not even clear what this would mean. A more interesting question is whether the cosmos is seen by pantheists as capable of existing apart from Unity. I take it most do not think so.

Smart sees God's creativity as following from the independence of God from the world. Pantheism must take a very different view of creation since Unity is not distinct from the universe. It may play a creative role in the world, but it cannot be understood in terms of a theistic model where an ontologically independent entity is supposed to create the world.

I have argued that in various ways transcendence is as applicable to pantheism as to theism. The most important of these has to do with epistemic transcendence, and the least important or relevant is the essentially theistic notion of God's ontological transcendence. However, the concepts of transcendence and immanence most relevant to pantheism are found in non-theistic and non-Western religious traditions such as Taoism and Confucianism.

The following account, for example, is an elaboration by Shu-

Hsien Liu on a central Confucian theme in *Chung Yung* or *The Doctrine of the Mean*.[16]

> Heaven is the only ever creating metaphysical principle that works unceasingly in the universe . . . [and] the first manifestation of this metaphysical principle . . . Heaven creates and Earth sustains. These are the two main forces that keep the creative process in the universe going.
>
> (Liu, p. 46)

By "Heaven and Earth" *Chung Yung* does not mean the physical heaven and earth. In discussing the significance of this view Liu says "Not only is man capable of knowing this metaphysical principle, but also he can follow it as his model, which provides guiding lines for his behaviour" (p. 47). (Out of context this view sounds more Taoist than Confucian.) Thus, knowledge of the metaphysical principle has implications for religious practice and more generally for how to live. The metaphysical principle is a standard, and in following it one lives in accord with the nature of reality. Liu says,

> Now the Confucian approach to the problem of transcendence becomes clear. Heaven is transcendent in the sense that it is an all-encompassing creative power which works incessantly in the universe. It is not a thing, but is the origin of all things. And it cannot be detected by sense perceptions, because its "operations have neither sound nor smell." But heaven is also immanent in the sense that it penetrates deep in every detail of the natural order, in general, and the moral order of man, in particular. But Heaven in no sense should be regarded as something completely beyond nature; on the contrary, it is that which constitutes the warp and woof of nature. As for man, he is beyond any doubt a creature in the world and hence a part of the natural order . . . He can work along with the Way or he can work against the Way . . . transcendence and immanence are a pair of interdependent concepts for the Confucian philosophers. They are not contradictory to one another . . . the realisation of the Way of Heaven in human life is none other than the realisation of the way of man . . . it is by no means the case that all men will appreciate the work of Heaven. In fact, most people are not even conscious

of the existence of Heaven. One needs great insight to read
the message of the transcendent.

(pp. 49–50)

I have cited this as an example of how the concept of transcendence is applicable to pantheism. Confucianism is arguably a pantheistic tradition, or at least has such elements in it.[17]
Furthermore, transcendence and immanence are interpreted
above in a way that could be useful in elaborating the concept
of Unity on the naturalistic model. Here too pantheism cannot
be conceived of as either a denial of transcendence or an easy
resolution to the concept's attendant difficulties. This is a case
of a religious tradition in which transcendence is essential to
pantheism.

I began the introduction with a quotation claiming that the
view of God as the immanent cause of things "shamefully confounds God with the universe ... [and] fundamentally overturns
and takes away ... a foundation for every religious devotion and
for all piety." Although the idea of God (i.e. the divine Unity) as
immanent rather than transcendent does have implications for
religious practice (as seen above), they are not the ones claimed
by the quotation's author. In the end seeing Unity, or even the
theistic God, as the immanent rather than transcendent cause of
things is rather inconsequential.

2.4.1 Panpsychism; animism; macrocosm and microcosm

[I]n pantheism, God is supposed to be equally present in
every part of the physical universe ... In practice, however,
some things are accepted as more fully manifesting the
presence of God than others. But God would be present to
some degree in everything, so that pantheism often combines with a doctrine of panpsychism, the view that there
is some presence ... of mind or spirit in everything that
exists.[18]

John Macquarrie

[The] pre-Greek [Presocratic] view of the world drew no
sharp line between the human and non-human, between
the animate and inanimate. Everything was alive, was
ensouled and was in a way divine. So it was that Thales said
that all things were full of gods, and that Aristotle com-

113

plained that he and his immediate successors introduced into their systems no efficient cause of motion over and above the material cause . . . things were alive, and moved of their own nature . . . soul was within nature; soul and nature were inseparable.[19]

D. A. Rees

If pantheism is seen as the quintessential expression of divine immanence, then it is not difficult to see why it might be combined with panpsychism or animism. Like pantheism, both of these express a kind of pervasive immanence – "mind" in the former case and "living soul," "spirit" or "animal life" in the latter. But however consonant or combined with pantheism these may be, they should be distinguished both from each other and from pantheism. None of these three views entail one another, and the suggestion that pantheism and panpsychism naturally go together is vague apart from specific accounts of the two positions. Similarly, the fact that animism is sometimes conceived of as a naive precursor to panpsychism does not mean the two positions are identical or even very close. Panpsychism does not entail animism. The view that everything has mental properties is not the same as holding that all things (e.g. rocks etc.) are alive and have souls.

Animism is the attribution of "living soul to inanimate objects and natural phenomena."[20] It is probably closer to pantheism than panpsychism is. If so this is because animism itself has pantheistic elements in it. For instance it rejects a qualitative bifurcation of the inanimate and animate, or as Rees puts it in the above quotation, the separation of nature and soul. (Panpsychism is different in that it rejects any fundamental or intrinsic bifurcation of the physical and mental.) In itself this is not pantheism, but it may be conducive to a pantheistic position since it denies a kind of distinction that may be regarded as antithetical to Unity. It would not count as pantheism, however, unless "living soul" was taken as the basis of Unity. Although "living soul" is not itself a basis for Unity anymore than certain kinds of monism (e.g. materialism), it is perhaps more naturally combined with what is a suitable basis. At any rate, animists do not generally predicate living soul to all inanimate objects and natural phenomena but only to some.

Consider panpsychism's possible relation to pantheism more

closely. Panpsychism is the view that all things, both animate and inanimate, have mental or proto-mental properties.[21] Panpsychists do not generally maintain that their position can be proved. Instead they claim it is a more complete world-view – better than materialism for instance. Aside from arguments which combine psychological and emotional satisfaction with alleged overall explanatory coherence as a ground for accepting panpsychism, the principle argument offered in its favour is its denial of the possibility of the radical emergence of the mental from the physical (i.e. the "genetic" argument) and the reduction of the former to the latter. Panpsychists hold it implausible to suppose, as materialists do, that mental properties could have arisen out of inorganic matter which contained no inherent mental properties.[22]

Some panpsychists claim that their view has religious implications. Thus, Paul Edwards explains that G.T. Fechner thought "It is only by accepting panpsychism that a modern man (who finds it impossible to believe in the claims of traditional religion) can escape the distressing implications of materialism" (p. 23). Others, however, combined panpsychism with traditional theism. Pantheism, interpreted as the doctrine that divine consciousness is in everything, could be interpreted as a kind of panpsychism. But such a view goes far beyond panpsychism as ordinarily understood since it attributes not just mental properties but consciousness to things, and "divine" consciousness at that. The sense of "divine" predicated of all things is not specified, but it is theistic if taken to entail consciousness. Most panpsychists do not attribute consciousness to inanimate things, but only mental or protomental properties. Generally they do not maintain that trees and stones "feel" as animists or hylozoists do. And under the present interpretation of pantheism the divine Unity is not itself conscious – let alone must everything else be divinely conscious. The Unity encompasses the conscious and unconscious, the mental and the physical, without itself being conscious.

What immediately sets panpsychism apart from pantheism is its belief that mental activity, usually of a kind we can only at times be mildly aware of, is all-pervasive. Although such a supposition is not necessarily inconsistent with pantheism, it is not part of pantheism. Pantheism does not imply that the material/immaterial or organic/inorganic dichotomies must be rejected. It does not reject these distinctions, but implies that Unity ranges over such divisions.[23] Of course there are other major differences between the two positions as well. Pantheism is a much broader theory. It has implications beyond the scope of panpsychism where the latter is seen as an account of the origin of mind and the relation between mind and matter.

An additional position that is closer to pantheism than the others must be mentioned. This is that of the macrocosm/microcosm distinction – especially where this is combined with a doctrine of a world-soul.[24] Some part of the world, usually man, is taken to be a microcosm of the universe as a whole. Donald Levy describes it as follows.

> man and the universe are constructed according to the same harmonious proportions, each sympathetically attuned to the other . . . By an imaginative leap, the universe itself was thought to be, like man, living and conscious, a divine creature whose nature is reflected in human existence. Animism and panpsychism also regard the world as alive throughout, but the microcosm idea is distinct in emphasizing the unity or kinship of all life and thought in the world. If man is the microcosm of the universe, then not only is everything animated by *some* soul or other, but there is *one* world soul by which everything is animated. Thus, the followers of Pythagoras and Empedocles held, according to Sextus Empiricus, that "there is a certain community uniting us not only with each other and with the gods but even with the brute creation. There is in fact one breath pervading the whole cosmos like soul, and uniting us with them" (W. K. C. Guthrie, *A History of Greek Philosophy*, Vol. 1, p. 278).[25]

This is a kind of pantheism. Note that the "breath pervading the whole cosmos" is not equated with consciousness.

The similarities and relations between the various positions outlined are evident in Levy's account of the macrocosm/microcosm distinction in Presocratic philosophy.

> Taking all of nature to derive ultimately from a single common substance, they supposed it to have inherent in it a principle of motion and change (which they identified with life, soul). Since some of the resulting entities possess

consciousness, so too must their source. And if the universal soul is eternal and divine, then the human soul, which is a "fragment" of the One, as the Pythagoreans held, must also be eternal and divine.

(p. 122)

Levy's claim that the "source" of conscious entities was itself regarded as conscious is questionable and I think mistaken. Nevertheless, implications of the above view for religious practice and purpose follow.

The return of the individual soul to its divine origin could be realised by philosophical understanding of the cosmos; since like is known by like, as the cosmos becomes known the knower is assimilated to it. Thus, man is, and discovers himself to be, the part that most perfectly reveals the nature of the whole ... That man is the microcosm was, in the Renaissance, widely taken to mean that cosmic knowledge and influence might be achieved through contemplation of the powers and tendencies men find in their own imaginations. Such knowledge would be based not on mere inference from resemblance but rather on the kinship or identity of human life and consciousness with the forces governing nature as a whole.

(p. 122)

This is certainly pantheistic, and the naturalistic model of pantheistic Unity is clearly present.[26] However, pantheists with less of an anthropomorphic leaning could reject both the idea that persons are "the part that most perfectly reveals the nature of the whole" and the prominence of the role of reason. The macrocosm/microcosm distinction rejects a theistic ontological type of divine transcendence, and accepts the idea of immanent principles or forces governing the world.

The conclusion is as follows. Animism, panpsychism, and especially the doctrine of a world-soul as embodied in the macrocosm/microcosm distinction, have at times been equated with pantheism. These positions may be intrinsic to particular versions of pantheism, but pantheism as such is broader than these and distinct from them.

NOTES

2.1 Unity

1 J. A. Smith, "The Issue Between Monism and Pluralism," *Proceedings of the Aristotelian Society,* 26 (1925–6), p. 5. "Unity" and "oneness" are not equivalent and it is unity that is central to pantheism. Nevertheless, I use them to mean more or less the same thing. For a discussion of some distinctions, especially in Aristotle's *Metaphysics,* see Michael C. Stokes, *One and Many in Presocratic Philosophy* (Washington, D.C.: Center for Hellenic Studies, 1971), pp. 13–21. Aristotle (*Physics* 185bff.) asks "in which of its many sense the Eleatics applied the term 'one' to what is" (Stokes, p. 1). "Aristotle ... maintains that the early monists had believed in the unity of things in the sense that their one substance remained the same through change, without coming-to-be or passing-away" (p. 34).

2 Raphael Demos, "Types of Unity According to Plato and Aristotle," *Philosophy and Phenomenological Research,* 6 (1945–6), p. 534. Cf. Marvin Farber, "Types of Unity and the Problem of Monism," *Philosophy and Phenomenological Research,* 4 (1943–4), pp. 37–58. Hamlyn says, "it is arguable ... that simplicity is always a relative matter (as Plato in effect saw when he said in *Republic* 7 that 'one' is a relative term ... something can be called 'one' only if there is already available an answer to the question 'One what?' " D. W. Hamlyn, *Metaphysics* (Cambridge: Cambridge University Press, 1984), p. 63.

3 Grace Jantzen, *God's World, God's Body* (Philadelphia: Westminster, 1984), p. 145. Cf. Virgil, *Aeneid* VI.724. Jantzen nevertheless ends up endorsing a kind of pantheism, but one which maintains that God is essentially a person. See pp. 145–54.

4 Alasdair MacIntyre, "Pantheism," in Paul Edwards (ed.) *Encyclopedia of Philosophy* (New York: Macmillan and Free Press, 1967), vol. 5, p. 34.

5 Below, I discuss the Tao as a prime example of pantheistic Unity interpreted naturalistically as a principle or force. For an interpretation of the Tao see the introduction of Young and Ames in Ch'en Ku-ying, *Lao Tzu, Text, Notes, and Comments,* translated and adapted by Rhett Y. W. Young and Roger T. Ames (Republic of China: Chinese Materials Center, 1981).

6 Arthur Schopenhauer, "A Few Words on Pantheism," in *Essays from the Parerga and Paralipomena,* tr. T. Bailey Saunders (London: George Allen & Unwin, 1951), pp. 40–1. This passage is briefly discussed by F. C. Copleston, "Pantheism in Spinoza and the German Idealists," *Philosphy,* 21 (1946), p. 42, who appears to agree with Schopenhauer.

John Macquarrie echoes the latter part of Schopenhauer's criticism of equating the world with God. He says "If the world is God, it must be not only awesome and mysterious but also adorable; and this, surely, our ambiguous universe is not. The world is not itself divine ... there can be no simple pantheistic identification of God with the world-process" (pp. 110, 119). Macquarrie, *Thinking About God* (London: SCM, 1975).

Cf. Nils Bjorn Kvastad, "Pantheism and Mysticism." Part I: *Sophia*, 14 (2) (1975), pp. 1–15; Part II: *Sophia*, 14 (3) (1975), pp. 19–30. Kvastad discusses various types of pantheism. He rejects the idea that pantheism is using the term "God" as a synonym for "world."

7   by *natura naturans* we are to understand that which is in itself and is conceived through itself, or those attributes of substance which express eternal and infinite essence ... But by *natura naturata* I understand everything which follows from the necessity of the nature of God, or any one of God's attributes, that is to say, all the modes of God's attributes in so far as they are considered as things which are in God, and which without God can neither be nor can be conceived.

(*Ethics* I, Proposition XXIX, note)

Spinoza, *Ethics*, ed. James Gutmann (New York: Hafner, 1949), pp. 65–6. References to the *Ethics* are to this edition. Also see the translator's note. He says, "These are two expressions derived from a scholastic philosophy which strove to signify by the same verb the oneness of God and the world, and yet at the same time to mark by a difference of inflexion that there was not absolute identity" (p. 65).

8   For a contemporary reiteration of Schopenhauer's view that pantheism is a superfluous name for the world see H. P. Owen, *Concepts of Deity* (London: Macmillan, 1971), pp. 69–70. For the opposing view see Gregory Vlastos, "Theology and Philosophy in Early Greek Thought," *Philosophical Quarterly*, 2 (1952); reprinted in D. Furley and R. Allen, *Studies in Presocratic Philosophy*, (London: RKP, 1970), vol. I, pp. 92–129. Vlastos says the Presocratics "could call nature god without indulging in an empty figure of speech" (p. 97).

Pringle-Pattison's view is similar to that of Schopenhauer, but only with regard to what he called the "lower pantheism." Owen says,

Pringle-Pattison rejects what he calls the "lower Pantheism" which regards God as completely and equally revealed in everything. His grounds for rejection are two. First, pure pantheism (according to which God and the world are identical) reduces "God" to a mere class-name and so is equivalent to atheism. "The doctrine of immanence becomes on these terms a perfectly empty affirmation; for the operative principle supposed to be revealed is simply the characterless unity of 'Being' in which the sum-total of phenomena is indiscriminately housed. The unity reached is the unity of a mere collection ... Such a pantheism is indistinguishable from the barest Naturalism ..." [Owen is quoting from Pringle-Pattison's Gifford lectures.] Secondly, pure pantheism obliterates distinctions of value.

(Owen, p. 93)

Pringle-Pattison's account of "pure pantheism" is fictitious and his criticism of pantheistic unity is mistaken for the same reasons as

Schopenhauer's. Also, far from "obliterating distinctions of value," I shall argue that such distinctions are essential and that not everything is equally valuable for the pantheist.

9 Demos, p. 538.

10 Demos, pp. 538–9.

11 MacIntyre, p. 34. MacIntyre says, "In Spinoza the unity of the universe is a logical unity, with every particular item deducible from the general nature of things" (p. 35). As a description of what Unity is for Spinoza this is vague and incomplete – even if true. MacIntyre finds no notion of Unity plausible. He thinks of positing Unity, and of pantheism in general, as a pre-analytic and basically primitive intuition and reaction grounded in natural reactions to natural phenomena. He says (p. 35),

> pantheism as a theology has a source, independent of its metaphysics, in a widespread capacity for awe and wonder in the face both of natural phenomena and of the apparent totality of things. It is at least in part because pantheist metaphysics provides a vocabulary which appears more adequate than any other for the expression of these emotions that pantheism has shown such historical capacity for survival.

But can there be a rational basis for the emotional satisfaction that pantheism, like theism, can provide?

12 See Ch'en Ku-ying, pp. 14–15ff.

13 MacIntyre, p. 32.

14 MacIntyre, p. 32. Like MacIntyre, my primary concern here is not to offer an acount of what the Greeks did believe, but to explain what constitutes pantheism – what beliefs are required.

15 Paul Henri Michel , *The Cosmology of Giordano Bruno*, tr. R.E.W. Maddison (Paris: Hermann; London: Methuen; Ithaca: Cornell University Press, 1973), p. 60. Michel continues,

> Yet, if God be everywhere, His presence does not manifest itself everywhere likewise. It is necessary to distinguish between God who is implicating and God who is explicated. "Is implicating", He enfolds everything in his unfathomable unity; "explicated", He is nothing else but nature . . . Nature is the art of God; God in the semblance of a material universe offered to tangible experience, or a universe propounded . . . if that which is propounded is avaible for our investigation, then that which is not propounded is inaccessible: it is the domain of the Supreme One . . . Forbidden to the intellect, it can only be the object of love.

(pp. 60–1)

For a discussion of what Bruno means by Unity, and his references to Presocratic and neo-platonic sources, see Michel, pp. 77–95. In likening Bruno to Nicholas of Cusa (p. 78), Michel tends to interpret Bruno as a panentheist rather than a pantheist. Bruno's understanding of Unity remains obscure given Michel's account, though this may well be because Bruno's views are eclectic and complex. Michel says,

He has a deep-seated feeling, a taste for unity, which constrains him to place Unity at the heart of existence, if not even to confuse one with the other... "He who has found this oneness, I mean the reason for this unity, has found the key without which it is impossible to enter into true contemplation of nature" [Bruno]. This sentence... reflects the intention of the whole dialogue... "this unity is simple, it is stable and permanent... outside of this oneness all is as naught"... Bruno's references, sometimes neo-Platonic, sometimes pre-Socratic, seem to betray a wavering between two manners of conceiving unity and the relation of oneness to the manifold... between the Monist oneness of Parmenides and the transcendental oneness of Plotinus... As for the identification of the Unity with God... that goes without saying.

(pp. 77–8)

16 MacIntyre's interpretation of pantheism's requirement that the world ("all that is") must be divine misunderstands the nature of pantheism's "all-inclusive divine Unity" on two counts. First, it interprets Unity in the sense of all that is. Of all the senses of unity that may be relevant to pantheism, this is not one of them. Yes – the object, in the sense of all that is, is a Unity and it is divine; but Unity has nothing to do with its being "all that is." Unity encompasses "all that is," but is not constituted by it. Second, his interpretation claims that for the world to be divine it must not be divine because a principle informs it. This requirement is arbitrary. The Unity and "all that is" could be divine because a principle so informs it. And perhaps a divine power may inform the world withot thereby making it divine.

Nevertheless, not distinguishing between the object being divine and the object being informed by a divine power may just be a way of understanding the object to be divine in virtue of its being so informed. Alternatively, if the object is already considered divine, then the principle informing the object may also be considered divine. Therefore, the Greeks and commentators may not have failed to make the distinction MacIntyre says they failed to make. They may instead have regarded it as superfluous. Perhaps the "divinity" of a power is intransitive as apparently MacIntyre thinks it is. Apart from an argument for this it is not implausible to suppose that the presence of such a principle or power in the world may make it divine.

17 Owen, p. 74.

18 G. H. R. Parkinson, "Hegel, Pantheism, and Spinoza," *Journal of the History of Ideas*, 38 (1977), p. 450. In one of his denials that Spinoza was an atheist Hegel said " '*bei ihm ist zu viel Gott*' – with Spinoza there is too much God." Quoted from Thomas McFarland, *Coleridge and The Pantheist Tradition* (Oxford: Oxford University Press, 1969), p. 85. Nevertheless, Hegel did think that there was another sense in which Spinoza was a pantheist. See Parkinson, pp. 450–2. Hegel vigorously denied that he was himself a pantheist. See his *Lectures on the Philosophy of Religion* (Berkeley: University of California Press, 1984) vol. I, p. 344 n. 163, pp. 346–7, 374–8, 432. Apparently, he thought that

the Absolute, the whole, was to be importantly distinguished from anything that pantheism could possibly mean by 'all-inclusive divine unity," or whatever he took the central claim of pantheism to be. Hegel's Absolute bears little resemblance to the Spinozistic type of all-inclusive divine unity. But it is a unity, no matter how differentiated – and it is divine. Unless it could be shown why Hegel's Absolute could not be taken to be a unity in some relevantly pantheistic sense, or why his attribution of divinity to the Absolute is inappropriate to pantheism, then Hegel is a pantheist. His "Absolute" is a least a *prima facie* instance of an all-inclusive divine unity, and his denial that he is a pantheist is dependent upon his very particular understanding of what pantheism is. In denying that he was a pantheist he may in part have simply been trying to avoid some of the negative (i.e. non-theistic) connotations.

For additional discussion of Hegel and pantheism see F. C. Copleston, "Pantheism in Spinoza and the German Idealists," pp. 53–5. Copleston says,

> the Hegelian system . . . is neither unambiguous theism [nor] unambiguous pantheism . . . God must be more than finite consciousness taken together . . . as God . . . manifests Himself or itself, not only in and through the finite consciousness but also to the finite consciousness, there must be some real distinction between them . . . while the finite consciousness exists, it cannot, as a particular consciousness be called God: it is in God but it is not God. Hegel's notion thus seem to me to be rather one of panentheism than rigorous pantheism.
>
> (pp. 54–5)

Also see David MacGregor, *The Communist Ideal in Hegel and Marx* (Toronto: University of Toronto Press, 1984), pp. 84–5; Ludwig Feuerbach, *Principles of the Philosophya of the Future*, tr. Manfred Vogel (Indianapolis: Hackett, 1986); Charles Taylor, *Hegel* (Cambridge: Cambridge University Press, 1975), p. 349.

19 Christopher Rowe, "One and Many in Greek Religion," in Adolf Portman and Rudolf Ritsema (eds) *Oneness and Variety* (Leiden: E. J. Brill, 1980), p. 57. Contrary to Rowe, H. F. Cherniss denies that Anaximander thought that the world sprang from a single undifferentiated substance. H. F. Cherniss, "The Characteristics and Effects of Presocratic Philosophy," in D. Furley and R. Allen, *Studies in Presocratic Philosophy*, vol. I, p. 7.

Stokes (*One and Many in Presocratic Philosophy*, p. 40), citing Vlastos says

> the Greeks were accustomed to speak of an "originative substance" as if it were also the stuff of which things are made in their finished state . . . If this were so . . . it would be dangerous to distinguish too sharply between "originative stuff" and "constituent stuff." The early Greeks would talk naturally in terms of both when they talked of either.

Stokes argues that the Milesians did *not* believe in the unity of all things (p. 64), nor in

> one single stuff of which the many things in the world were made.
>
> (p. 244)

> It was only after Parmenides, and probably in acceptance, so far as possible, of his argument against differentiation, that the doctrine arose of the world's unity in one stuff... Nor did Xenophanes [an Eleatic] certainly believe in one God coextensive witht he world's plurality.
>
> (p. 249)

20 Lao Tzu's (Taoism's) and Hegel's pantheism are, in part, ontologically but not substantively based. The pantheism of Spinoza and some of the Presocratics is (partly) both substantival and ontological.

21 See Spinoza's *Ethics*. In fact, interpreting either Spinoza or Bruno as pantheists merely on the basis of their monism is simplistic. There are more significant aspects of their thought that lends itself to pantheistic interpretation.

Cf. Paul Henri Michel, *The Cosmology of Giordano Bruno*:

> In *De causa* ... we have: Unity is infinite, it contains all, "it contains no parts" ... where, however, all that we see of diversity and difference is only a distinct and different aspect of the same substance ... However, if Unity be everything, then the manifold none the less remains the subject of our experience ... From the manifold implicated in the Unity to the manifold explicated in the universe, there is at least a change of aspect...
>
> (p. 78)

Bruno's pantheism, if he is a pantheist, may involve substance monism. But this only begins to explain his pantheism. The larger part of the story lies in how and why "the manifold implicated in the Unity" becomes "the manifold explicated in the universe."

22 For Spinoza, Unity is based upon substance monism. Although he rejects the idea of any divine teleology interpreted as a theistic plan; a naturalistic model, non-theistically construed, may be useful in explaining his idea of Unity, his identification of God with nature, and his thorough-going determinism. Unity results from substance monism for Spinoza, but it involves much more than this.

23 Gregory Vlastos, in Furley and Allen, *Studies in Presocratic Philosophy*, vol. I, pp. 119–20. Other examples of the naturalistic model's compatibility with the attribution of divinity can be taken from Vlastos.

> In Ionian philosophy the divine is nature itself, its basic stuff and ruling principle. To say that the soul is divine is then to naturalize it; it is to say that it is subject to the same sequence of law and effect which are manifest throughout the whole of nature.
>
> (p. 123)

[The Presocratics] assumed from the start that they could apply to the soul the same categories of understanding which formed the framework of their natural inquiry. They thought of it as a part of nature, with a natural origin and a natural ending, but no less divine for being just that, since it shared the powers or wisdom and justice writ large throughout the universe and could therefore realize within the human microcosm some measure of the order which ruled the infinite worlds . . .

(p. 128)

24 Rowe, pp. 53, 57.
25 Vlastos, pp. 111–16. Vlastos (pp. 114–16) cautions that not all Pre-Socratics called their cosmogonic ordering principle "god."

> they may not go so far. Thus there is no good conclusive evidence that either Anaximander or Anaxagoras called their cosmogonic principle "god" or even "divine" . . . [The evidence] does not tell us that Anaximander called the *Apeiron* "god", but that he so called the "infinite worlds" . . . Reserving "agelessness" to the *Apeiron*, he was taking away from the gods their most characteristic prerogative . . . If the gods have a birth, they cannot be deathless; only the beginningless *Apeiron* can be truly ageless and immortal.

Still, Anaximander did attribute what he took to be an essential characteristic of divinity (i.e. immortality) to his cosmogonic principle.

Although the justice associated with the cosmogenic principle is a theodicy of sorts Vlastos says, "No theodicy could satisfy the cult which did not include a doctrine of individual providence, and no such doctrine could be squeezed out of Anaximander, or even Xenophanes, Heraclitus and others who did call nature 'god' " (p. 117). A doctrine of individual providence does not come about until "probably the Pythagoreans, and after them certainly Plato and the Stoics" (p. 118).

26 Werner Jaeger, *The Theology of the Early Greek Philosophers* (Oxford: Oxford University Press, 1947), p. 24. "According to Simplicius . . . Anaximander was the first man to say that the *aperion* was *arche* or principle" (p. 24). See Jaeger, pp. 24–37, for a discussion of various interpretations concerning the meaning and origin of *apeiron*. Also see Cherniss, "The Characteristics and Effects of Presocratic Philosophy." He says (in Jaeger, p. 7).

> This "unlimited", *to apeiron*, that from which all the worlds and all that is in them are separated out and into which they are again absorbed, is not a single unqualified substance . . . For Anaximander the *apeiron* was simply a boundless expanse of infinitely different ingredients.

According to Cherniss (p. 7), Anaximander did not take *apeiron* to mean "principle." That is Aristotle's sense of the term.

27 Cf. Jaeger, p. 25.
28 Some of the appeal of the movie "Star Wars" can be explained in

that it portrayed an easily identifiable religious perspective – the triumph of an omnipresent unifying good principle (i.e. the "Force") over evil. It was mythic on one level and like some other myths indicative of certain truths, and revelatory, on another. Of course, the idea of an omnipresent and unifying principle (e.g. goodness) is present in theism as well, but with important differences. The naturalistic model is abandoned for explanation in terms of God who is not part of the unity.

29 MacIntyre, p. 35. He says, "Neither hypothesis appears to be vindicated by the facts" (p. 35).

2.2 Divinity

1 John Macquarrie, *In Search of Deity* (London: SCM, 1984), p. 52. Cf. Macquarrie, *Thinking About God*, p. 110. "If the world is God, it must be not only awesome . . . but also adorable; and this, surely, our ambiguous universe is not. The world is not itself divine." Schopenhauer's view is similar.

2 Richard Swinburne, *The Coherence of Theism* (Oxford: Oxford University Press, 1977), p. 257.

3 Robinson Jeffers in a letter to Sister Power in 1934; quoted in George Sessions, "Spinoza and Jeffers on Man in Nature," *Inquiry*, 20 (1977), p. 512. This is nature mysticism, but Jeffers was a pantheist and the sense of divinity alluded to is pantheistic. His concept of divinity is experientially based, but can also be accounted for in socio-scientific analyses of religion that interpret "divinity," and religion generally, in functional terms. Note that Jeffers's understanding of the "divine" is linked to his perception of "the whole" (Unity). Unity and divinity are related for Jeffers.

4 See, for example, Thomas Morris's "christopocentric" preface and introduction to Thomas Morris (ed.) *Philosophy and the Christian Faith* (Notre Dame: University of Notre Dame Press, 1988); and his "Perfect Being Theology," *Nous*, 21 (1987), pp. 19–30. Morris extols the virtue of christian "Perfect Being" analyses of God as a philosophical virtue.

5 Like Schleiermacher's, Otto's analysis is an example of what George Lindbeck calls the "experiential/expressive" model of religion. These "picture religions in expressivist fashion as products of those deep experiences of the divine." He contrasts this with the "cultural-linguistic" model which sees religions "as producers of experience [a] . . . cultural and/or linguistic framework or medium that shapes the entirety of life and thought." Lindbeck notes that religions "have many aspects" including "legel, moral, ritual, institutional, and psychological ones . . . each of [which] can be a source of models in terms of which one seeks to organise one's understanding of all aspects of religion for particular purposes." George Lindbeck, *The Nature of Doctrine* (Philadelphia: Westminster, 1984), pp. 30–3. In claiming that pantheistic and theistic notions of divinity are similar,

I am claiming that on either of Lindbeck's primary models their concepts of divinity are functionally equivalent. For classic examples of the cultural/linguistic model see Clifford Geertz, "Religion as a Cultural System," in his *The Interpretation of Cultures* (New York: Basic Books, 1973), ch. 4, pp. 87–125; also chapter 5, "Ethos, World View, and the Analysis of Sacred Symbols," pp. 126–41; Peter Berger, *The Sacred Canopy: Elements of a Sociological Theory of Religion* (New York: Doubleday, 1967); Freud, *The Future of an Illusion* (New York: Norton, 1961). For examples of the experiential/expressive model see Rudolf Otto, *The Idea of the Holy*, 2nd edn (Oxford: Oxford University Press, 1950) (references to Otto refer to this edition); Friedrich Schleiermacher, *The Christian Faith* (Edinburgh: Clark, 1928). Lindbeck (p. 20) claims that Berger's theory is "basically experiential-expressivist." But this is certainly not the case in *The Sacred Canopy*.

I sometimes use "socio-scientific" to describe Lindbeck's "cultural/linguistic" model, but his term is narrower. It refers to a model which sees religions "as idioms for the construction of reality and the living of life" (p. 18).

6 For a very different analysis of "holiness" see Quentin Smith, "An Analysis of Holiness," *Religious Studies*, 24 (1988), pp. 511–28.

Plotinus' idea of the divine is related to that of Unity:

> in the thought of Plotinus we . . . have a single apprehension or awareness of divinity in self and cosmos taken together . . . we do not in fact leave the cosmos altogether behind until our awareness of divinity becomes so intense that we go "alone to the alone". . . the One or Good, which corresponds to what most of us who still use the word mean by "God", is absolutely unknowable. . . . Damascius insists that the One from which all things proceed can not only, in a way, be defined and understood in relation to the all but must in some sense be all things which proceed from it.
>
> (pp. 188–90)

A.H. Armstrong, "The Apprehension of Divinity in the Self and Cosmos in Plotinus," in R. Baine Harris (ed.) *The Significance of Neoplatonism* (Norfolk: International Society for Neoplatonic Studies, 1976), pp. 187–98. This quotation conflicts, *prima facie*, with Armstrong's view that "it is impossible to call Plotinus a pantheist."

7 Armstrong says "it is impossible to call Plotinus a pantheist" because of "the very marked separation of the material universe from even the lowest of the great hypostases." But what does Armstrong mean by pantheism? There are significant affinities between neoplatonism and some versions of pantheism. See Macquarrie, *In Search of Deity*, pp. 65ff.; A.H. Armstrong, *The Architecture of the Intelligible Universe in the Philosophy of Plotinus* (Cambridge: Cambridge University Press, 1940), p. 43. Macquarrie quotes Plotinus (*Enneads* IV, 9, 1) "If the soul in me is a unity, why need that in the universe be otherwise? And if that, too, is one Soul, and yours and mine belong to it, then yours and mine must also be one" (p. 68). That is arguably pantheistic. Yet Macquarrie approvingly cites Armstrong and says "I think it

is a mistake to suppose that his [Plotinus'] doctrine of emanationism leads to pantheism" (p. 65). Macquarrie sees Plotinus as a kind of idealist. See W.R. Inge, *The Philosophy of Plotinus* (London: Longman, 1928), vol. II, pp. 39–40. On the quotation from the *Enneads* Macquarrie remarks: "From this the conclusion is drawn that when one soul suffers, other souls must suffer with it, even the World-soul must suffer too. But this unity does not abolish the distinctness of souls."

8 Cf. Swinburne, *The Coherence of Theism*, p. 293. "[A] personal ground of being . . . would not merely be worthy of men's worship; he would have . . . the properties which make up holiness . . . A holy being is a perfectly good being who is also . . . 'numinous.' "

9 Macquarrie rejects classical theism for what he calls "dialectical theism" – a term "roughly synonymous" with panentheism. On Macquarrie's version of panentheism, like others, connections to the Christian God are especially clear. See Macquarrie, *In Search of Deity*, p. 15.

10 Macquarrie, *In Search of Deity*, p. 42.

11 Otto, *The Idea of the Holy*.

12 Swinburne says the term "personal ground of being" is "based on that of Tillich" (Paul Tillich, *Systematic Theology* (Chicago: University of Chicago Press, 1963), vol. 1, ch. 10. Why he adopts Tillich's terminology is not apparent, since he equivocates on Tillich's usage. Tillich is not a theist, and for Tillich a "personal ground of being" is not a person.

Swinburne uses " 'God' as the proper name of the individual . . . who is the personal ground of being" (p. 226), and argues that "there can only be one" (p. 225). He distinguishes between God as a "personal ground of being" and God as a "divine being." See pp. 257, 242.

13 William Wainwright, like Swinburne, conflates the numinous with the personal and ignores Otto's description of the numinous as non-personal. Wainwright says "those who enjoy numinous experiences tend to speak as if the object of those experiences is personal, whereas even those mystics who are theists tend to describe the object of their experience impersonally." William L. Wainwright and William J. Rowe (eds) *Philosophy of Religion: Selected Readings* (New York: Harcourt Brace Jovanovich, 1973), p. 252. The distinction Wainwright draws between the numinous and mystical is consistent with Otto's analysis, though Otto sees a closer connection between the two than Wainwright. But Wainwright's claim is as suspect as a claim about mystical experience as it is about numinous experience. Otto's view does not support Wainwright's unless Wainwright is referring to the numinous experienced in conjunction with the rational aspect of the divine.

14 John Stuart Mill, "Mr. Mansel on the Limits of Religious Thought," in Nelson Pike (ed.) *God and Evil: Readings on the Theological Problem of Evil* (Englewood Cliffs: Prentice Hall, 1964), pp. 37–45.

15 Christopher Rowe, "One and Many in Greek Religion," pp. 55, 57. The paraphrase is from W.K.C. Guthrie, *A History of Greek Philosophy* (Cambridge: Cambridge University Press, 1962), vol. I, p. 4.

16 MacIntyre, "Pantheism," p. 35.

17 Swinburne ignores this, and with it things in Otto's account contrary to the letter and spirit of his own account of divinity.

18 Geertz and Berger recognise the necessity for a strong affective component in religion. Religious symbol systems must be intellectually and emotionally satisfying to function and survive. Intellectual aspects of the system make the affective aspects acceptable and vice versa. Stasis and change in traditions are governed by dynamic tensions between these aspects. Otto is at odds with Geertz and Berger in claiming that the numinous is objective rather than a human projection. Sacred symbols must be thought of as objective for them to function as they do, but they are projections nonetheless. (Berger claims – unconvincingly – that his argument in *The Sacred Canopy* "rigidly bracket[s] . . . any questions of the ultimate truth or illusion of religious propositions about the world," p. v.)

19 Harvey, reiterating Otto, says, "the rational and moral is an essential part of the content of what we mean by holy or sacred: only it is not the whole of it. There is an overplus of meaning which is non-rational . . . The two elements . . . have to be regarded (in his [Otto's] favorite simile) as the warp and woof of the complete fabric, neither of which can dispense with the other" (p. xvii).

20 It is temporally, metaphysically, epistemologically and *religiously* antecedent to the rational. Otto talks about "the contrast between rationalism and the profounder religion" and says "orthodox Christianity manifestly failed to recognise its [the non-rational element's] value, and by this failure gave to the idea of God a one-sidedly intellectualistic and rationalistic interpretation" (p. 3). It is the non-rationalistic numinous element that is "quite unique in the religious experience, even in its primitive manifestations" (p. 4). Otto insists that this aspect of the divine is the more fundamental – partly because of its affective influence. He sees the numinous experience as the source of all religion.

21 As an example of the consciousness associated with the "wholly other" Otto cites Augustine's *Confessions* (ii.9.I): "What is that which gleams through me and smites my heart without wounding it? I am both a-shudder and a-glow. A-shudder, in so far as I am unlike it, a-glow in so far as I am like it" (p. 28).

22 Otto says,

> the "void" of the eastern, like the "nothing" of the western, mystic is a numinous ideogram of the "wholly other". These terms "supernatural" and "transcendent" give the appearance of positive attributes . . . On the side of conceptual thought this is nothing more than appearance . . . But on the side of the feeling-content it is otherwise; that *is* in very truth positive in the highest degree, though . . . it cannot be rendered explicit in conceptual terms. It is through this positive feeling-content that the concepts of "transcendent" and "supernatural" become forthwith designations for a unique "wholly other" reality and quality, something of whose

special character we can *feel*, without being able to give it clear conceptual expression.

(p. 30)

23 "Transcendent" is opposite to "immanent," but not to Unity. Otto says " 'transcendent' is a purely ontological attribute and not an attribute of *value*" (p. 52). Otto's point is about experience rather than ontology. He distinguishes experience of the "wholly other" from that of the natural world. "[M]usical feeling is rather (like numinous feeling) something 'wholly other', which, while it affords analogies and here and there will run parallel to the ordinary emotions of life, cannot be made to coincide with them" (p. 49).

24 The rational attributes of the divine are stressed because those are the ones most easily conceived of, and so conveyed in language; and, as Hume, Feuerbach, Freud and others have pointed out, deity is usually conceived of anthropomorphically.

25 "[M]ysticism is the stressing to a very high degree, indeed the over-stressing, of the non-rational or supra-rational elements in religion; and it is only intelligible when so understood" (Otto, p. 22). Cf. pp. 85n, 194.

26 Consciousness of the "wholly other" can be aroused by just about anything. "[T]his feeling ... will attach itself to, or sometimes be indirectly aroused by means of, objects which are already puzzling upon the 'natural' plane ... or things in inanimate nature, in the animal world, or among men" (p. 27).

27 Otto says,

here is indeed the point of the whole passage, comprising alike the theodicy and the appeasement and calming of Job's soul. The *mysterium*, simply as such, would merely ... be a part of the "absolute inconceivability" of the numen, and that, though it might strike Job utterly dumb, could not convict him inwardly. That of which we are conscious is rather an *intrinsic value* in the incomprehensible ... This is incommensurable with thoughts of rational human teleology and is not assimilated to them: it remains in all its mystery. But it is as it becomes felt in consciousness that Elohim is justified and at the same time Job's soul is brought to peace.

(p. 80)

28 Otto thinks this makes the numinous more significant. But the status Otto assigns the numinous introduces a question raised in regard to mystical experience. In one justified on the basis of such experience alone in believing it pertains to anything objective? (Otto's application of Kant is dubious.)

29 Otto takes pantheism, like animism, to be one of the mistakenly alleged "naturalistic foundations of religions" (p. 129), but does not explain this. Pantheism, and probably animism, are more plausibly construed as themselves having naturalistic foundations. They *are* religions – not the foundation for it. Pantheism can be described as

a naturalistic foundation for religion only if, as for Otto, a hierarchy of "better" religion is supposed.

30 Lindbeck asks if "it is conceptually and empirically better to picture religions in expressivist fashion as products of those deep experiences of the divine . . . or whether one should opt for the converse [cultural/linguistic] thesis that religions are producers of experience" (p. 30). He chooses the latter and acknowledges that the cultural/linguistic model can, to some extent, "accommodate and combine the distinctive and often competing emphases of" the experiential/expressive and cognitivist models (p. 34). The cognitivist model sees religion as primarily concerned with truth claims about objective reality. Of course the models are not always discrete. Consider Paul Tillich's claim that "religion is the substance of culture, and culture the form of religion." Lindbeck see this as an "experiential/expressivist formula" (p. 34). But Geertz and Berger, both adherents of the cultural/linguistic model, would embrace it. Cf. Tillich, *Systematic Theology*, vol. 3, pp. 248ff.

31 In my view analyses such as those of Berger and Geertz are largely compatible with and not unrelated to experiential accounts such as Otto's. Indeed, they seem to subsume them. (This is not to suggest that Berger or Geertz accept the existence of a numinous object.) Lindbeck sees the two models as "alternatives" between which one must choose. They are incommensurable and incompatible. Cf. *The Nature of Doctrine*, ch. 2.

32 Geertz ("Religion as a Cultural System"), Berger (*The Sacred Canopy*), Freud (*The Future of an Illusion*), and others who give naturalistic accounts of religious belief, claim that the question of the truth of such belief is independent of the question of its origin. They are aware of the so-called genetic fallacy. Nevertheless, the accounts they give of the origins of belief, while logically independent of their truth or falsity, do serve to undermine their justification. William Alston claims that the truth of a Freudian explanation for the origin of religious belief need not undermine its rationality if one has independent rational grounds for the belief. William Alston, "Religion, Psychological Explanations of," in Paul Edwards (ed.) *Encyclopedia of Philosophy* (New York: Macmillan and Free Press, 1967). This is a truism and it is puzzling why Alston asserts it in the context he does. After all, in showing what he took to be the real ground of religious belief, Freud thought he was also showing there is no reason to suppose that religious belief was either justified or true (i.e. that Alston's independent rational grounds are not available). In other words, it would be remarkable if religious beliefs were true given the validity of Freud's analysis, and only slightly less so on Berger's or Geertz's account.

Berger claims that his analysis of religion in *The Sacred Canopy* is neutral with regard to the question of the truth of falsity of religious belief. Geertz makes a similar claim in "Religion as a Cultural System." But I doubt this is so in either case. If Berger's sociological theory of religion is correct, then it has implications for questions concerning the truth of religious beliefs – or rather for the justification of such beliefs. The "genetic fallacy" notwithstanding – the analyses by Geertz, Berger and Freud do serve to undermine, *prima facie*, any rational justification for believing in the literal truth of religious beliefs. However, what these analyses also show is that the question of the literal truth of religious belief is not the only important question, and perhaps not the most important, in understanding the significance of religion.

33 I choose Geertz's account for several reasons. First, it is a general account that has been influential and widely adopted. Second, I think it is basically correct and illuminating. Finally, it is useful for my purposes. For discussion of a different view see my "Deep Structure and the Comparative Philosophy of Religion," *Religious Studies*, 28 (1992), pp. 387–99.

Geertz explains "culture" as that which "denotes an historically transmitted pattern of meanings embodied in symbols, a system of inherited conceptions expressed in symbolic forms by means of which men communicate, perpetuate, and develop their knowledge about and attitudes toward life" (p. 89). A symbol is a "vehicle for a conception – the conception is the symbol's 'meaning' " (p. 91).

34 Geertz says,

> Where the more intellective aspects of what Weber called the Problem of Meaning [the existence of bafflement, pain, and moral paradox, p. 109] are a matter of affirming the ultimate explicability of experience, the more affective aspects are a matter of affirming its ultimate sufferableness. A religion on the one side anchors the power of our symbolic resources for formulating analytic ideas in an authoritative conception of the overall shape of reality, so on the other side it anchors the power of our, also symbolic, resources for expressing emotions ... religious symbols provide a cosmic guarantee not only for their ability to comprehend the world, but also, comprehending it, to give a ... definition to their emotions which enable them, morosely or joyfully ... to endure it.
>
> (p. 104)

35 Cf. Susanne Langer, *Philosophy in a New Key* (New York: Pelican Books, 1948), p. 287. The similarities between Geertz's view of religion and Berger's (*The Sacred Canopy*) are extensive. This is not surprising given the overlap of primary sources (e.g. Weber etc.). I could have (almost) as easily used Berger's theory instead of Geertz's.

> Religion legitimates social institutions by bestowing upon them an ultimately valid ontological status, that is, by *locating* them within a sacred and cosmis frame of reference ... Probably the most ancient form of this legitimation is the conception of the institutional order as directly reflecting or manifesting the divine structure of the cosmos, that is, the conception of the relationship between society and cosmos as one between microcosm and macrocosm.
>
> (Berger, *The Sacred Canopy*, pp. 33–4)

36 See, for example, the work of Jacob Neusner, Jonathan Z. Smith and other historians of religion. It has also been influential in certain ecumenical settings. Lindbeck says, "A theory of religion and doctrine cannot be ecumenically useful unless it is nonecumenically plausible" (*The Nature of Doctrine*, p. 8). This is not true since ecumenically useful theories of religion and doctrine are not nonecumenically plausible. Perhaps what Lindbeck means is that for a theory of religion and doctrine to be ecumenically useful *and* rationally justifiable, it must also be nonecumenically plausible. Thus, to the extent that socio-scientific theories are taken to be nonecumenically plausible, they may be ecumenically useful – in the sense of useful and rationally justifiable – and nonecumenically useful. Lindbeck claims that experiential-expressivist models are the ones most frequently employed in religious studies departments (p. 25). I doubt this is the case, but if he is right it is cause for concern. If there is a feature that distinguishes religious studies from theology it is a reliance on the cultural/linguistic model as opposed to the experiential one.

37 Aside from some native American Indian religions, philosophical Taoism – that of the *Tao Tê Ching* – is the most pantheistic. Religious Taoism mixes Chinese folk religion, Buddhism, Confucianism, and very little philosophical Taoism. Few marginal sects attempted to practise philosophical Taoism.

38 Anna Kisselgoff, "Dance: Graham's 'Canticle' Revived," review of Martha Graham's "Canticle for Innocent Comedians," *New York Times*, October 9, 1987, p. C3. " 'Canticle for Innocent Comedians' in Miss Graham's great hymn to nature – a mystery play of no particular religious denomination and more openly pantheist in inspiration." It is unclear how the reviewer recognised the dance as pantheistic. Perhaps Graham described it as such. However, it is possible to imagine art and music that can be construed as pantheistic. The second movement of Beethoven's seventh symphony has been described as pantheistic, and I recognise it as such – though I'm not sure if the recognition came before or after hearing the description. See John Crabbe, *Beethoven's Empire of the Mind* (Newbury: Lovell Baines, 1982). "My miserable hearing does not trouble me here. In the country it seems as if every tree said to me: 'Holy! Holy!' – Who can give complete expression to the ecstasy of the woods! O, the sweet stillness of the woods!" (Beethoven, in Crabbe, p. 105). Crabbe says, "In such utterances Beethoven expresses the sentiments underlying Schelling's Nature Philosophy: an all-pervasive unity of nature and spirit with pantheistic overtones" (p. 105).

39 In Berger's account "humanly constructed nomoi are given a cosmic status" which promotes the legitimation of social institutions and "world-maintenance" (*The Sacred Canopy*, p. 36).

40 Geertz, "Ethos, World View, and the Analysis of Sacred Symbols," p. 141. Geertz seems to suggest that because people draw moral conclusions from factual premises, theories which deny this is justified are mistaken. But he has not established this. Contrary to Hume, granted that not every move from a factual "is" to a normative

"ought" is unjustified, the fact that people reason this way does not show they are justified in doing so. Hume knew that people draw conclusions about value from factual premises and vice versa. But he argued that there is no rational justification for doing so, and his arguments are often regarded as successful.

2.3 Monism

1 Owen, *Concepts of Deity*, p. 65.
2 Arthur Lovejoy, *The Great Chain if Being* (New York: Harper & Row, 1960), pp. 12–13. Lovejoy continues: "psychologically the force of the monistic pathos is in some degree intelligible ... It affords ... a welcome sense of freedom, arising from a triumph over, or an absolute from, the troublesome cleavages and disjunctions of things."
3 J. A. Smith, "The Issue Between Monism and Pluralism," pp. 7–8. Smith quotes William James, *Pragmatism*: "I suspect ... that in but few of you has this problem occasioned sleepless nights ... I myself have come, by long brooding over it, to consider it the most central of all philosophical problems ... I mean by this that if you know whether a man is a decided monist or a decided pluralist, you perhaps know more about the rest of his opinions than if you give him any other name ending in *ist*." Smith intends his view to be taken literally. Either Smith was as mistaken then as he would be now, or times have changed.
4 This is one category of monism which includes many varieties. See Peter Forrest, "Some Varieties of Monism," in R. W. Perrett (ed.) *Indian Philosophy of Religion* (Dordrecht: Kluwer, 1989), pp. 75–91.
5 Most pantheists are not explicit about their notions of Unity or substance, and their idea of Unity is more difficult to discern than that of substance. The pantheists' idea of substance, *if any*, is just what is philosophically current. Spinoza notwithstanding, pantheists are not usually monists. Lao Tzu, Hegel, probably Plotinus, and certainly Whitman, Jeffers etc. were not monists.
6 The notion of substance has been extensively criticised in post-Cartesian philosophy, and theories as to what it is and what the "problem of substance" is have changed. But it remains a viable notion among some contemporary metaphysicians. See Hamlyn, *Metaphysics*, pp. 64–9, "there must be substances in any world with reference to which it is possible to speak of change and identity through time" (p. 69). Cf. David Wiggins, *Sameness and Substance* (Oxford: Basil Blackwell, 1980).
7 Cf. William Charlton, "Spinoza's Monism," *Philosophical Review*, 90 (1981), pp. 503–29.
8 For brief accounts of Aristotle on substance see Hamlyn, *Metaphysics*, and D. J. O'Connor, "Substance and Attribute," in Paul Edwards (ed.) *Encyclopedia of Philosophy* (New York: Macmillan and Free Press, 1967), vol. 8. Page numbers in this section of the text refer to these works. O'Connor says that Aristotle "contrast[s] the independent way

MEANING

of existing proper to substances with the parasitic mode of being of qualities and relations. Substances can exist on their own ... The notion of essences as substances ... seems to be his preferred sense of the term" (p. 37).

9 Secondary substances, in *Categories*, are species of genera of primary substances, "Of secondary substances, the species is more truly substance than the genus, being more nearly related to primary substance" (*Categories* 2$_B$7). See Hamlyn, *Metaphysics*, pp. 60–1. Secondary substances are predicable of a subject. "For instance, 'man' is predicted of the individual man" (*Categories* 2$_A$21–22) (O'Connor, p. 37).

10 Owen, pp. 71–2. Owen does not base his rejection on experience alone, but on other considerations as well; for example, the implications of denying that experience counts against A/R. See p. 72.

11 I discuss and reject the idea that Unity can be based on the idea of substance as "that which is capable of independent existence" in "Pantheism, Substance and Unity," *International Journal for Philosophy of Religion*, 32 (1992), pp. 1–23.

12 Peter Forrest, "Some Varieties of Monism," p. 75. Parts of the reason Forrest gives for undertaking a "taxonomy of varieties of monism" is that it might be useful in helping to determine "whether belief in a transcendent God is compatible with Monism, or whether Monism and Theism together lead inevitably to Pantheism" (p. 75). On my view monism and theism do not lead to pantheism, and in fact usually entail its denial since pantheism (generally) entails the denial of theism. Whether belief in a transcendent God is compatible with monism depends on what is meant by "monism," "transcendent," – and even "God."

Forrest reverses the proper order in which these issues should be addressed. The taxonomy Forrest wishes to undertake, in so far as it is relevant to the above issues in philosophical theology, is only possible after the above and related substantive issues are addressed. A taxonomy of monism relevant to questions concerning, for example, the compatibility of theism and monism, might be impossible to delineate until theism addresses the issue of compatibility. Once done, many varieties of monism will be irrelevant.

13 F. H. Bradley, *Appearance and Reality* (Oxford: Clarendon Press, 1930).

14 Plato Mamo argues that monism does not require an absolute identity of all things, and that Plotinus can be a monist although he denies such an identity. He claims it is a mistake to conclude that Plotinus is a theist on the grounds that he denies such an identity, and argues that J. Rist, following Arnou and Zaehner, is mistaken in his view "that Plotinian mysticism is of the theistic type and not monistic or pantheistic" (p. 199). Plato Mamo, "Is Plotinian Mysticism Monistic?," in R. Baine Harris (ed.) *The Significance of Neoplatonism* (Norfolk: International Society for Neoplatonic Studies, 1976), pp. 199–215.

Rist supposes that monism means the absolute identity of the soul with its source, i.e. the One. He supposes that for the monist the separate self is nothing but illusion and that the typical monistic mystic's utterance is "I am God." Following Zaehner, Rist takes the Vedānta as the paradigm of monistic mysticism and then claims that Plotinus . . . is no Vedāntic mystic and, therefore, he must be a theistic one.

(p. 200)

Mamo explains a "theistic mystic" as one who maintains a gap between created and creator.

The union then becomes one of contemplation, similarity, love, anything short of absorption. The mystic who, in his interpretation of the experience, follows this Christian metaphysical principle [i.e. maintains the gap between creator and creature] is a theistic mystic. The mystic who talks, seriously, of absorption and loss of the self is a monist. But Plotinus, we are told, is no monist because he does not stress the *absolute* identity of God and soul; *ergo* he is a theist.

(p. 200)

[For Plotinus] The transcendent One is the source and origin of all things; it is not identical with them. Nor is there any suggestion that the multiplicity of forms . . . is nothing but illusion.

(p. 201)

This postulate, the ego . . . enables Plotinus to maintain the ultimate identity of the self with its ground; while his more formal system of hypostases enables him to assert the permanence and reality of individual men.

(p. 202)

Cf. J. Rist, *Plotinus: The Road to Reality* (Cambridge: Cambridge University Press, 1967). Mamo says,

If the pantheist wishes to claim that the divine is identical with the material world, that [quoting Rist] "the One and matter are identical and that there is a reconciliation of good and evil" [Rist, p. 216], then clearly Plotinus is no pantheist and Rist is right in dismissing that interpretation. Whether it is necessary to understand pantheism in this narrow sense is, of course, another matter.

(p. 200)

Rist's interpretation of pantheism is inadequate. Mamo's account of Plotinus as a monist can, in various ways, support the distinction I draw between pantheism and monism. Although he does not explicitly discuss pantheism, his analysis of monism is suggestive of ways in which monists (e.g. Plotinus) can be interpreted pantheistically.

15 I use Brahman and God interchangeably here, though the two should not be equated. In this context I mean by "God" what Rāmānuja means by Brahman – whatever that is – and not "God" in any Western theistic context. This use is problematic since Rāmānuja himself uses

the term "God" in its theistic sense at times. Such a use is central to his qualified non-dualism and his doctrine of the world God's body.

16 This is Peter Forrest's description of "Evaluative monism." "Some Varieties of Monism," p. 89. Descriptive monism is a "descriptive thesis expressing a purely theoretical, non-evaluative, belief" (p. 89). He says "Evaluative Monism, while it could be based on Descriptive Monism, does not entail the latter" (p. 90). Forrest recognises that

> descriptive monism, combined with other premisses, might . . . have various implications regarding values. Typical of these extra prem-isses is the premiss that nothing which fails to exist can have (non-aesthetic) intrinsic value, or the stronger premiss that nothing which is unreal can have (non-aesthetic) intrinsic value.
>
> (p. 89)

He notes "Kant took aesthetic value to be independent of existence." The "other premisses" Forrest is referring to are apparently other descriptive premisses. But there are also ways that descriptive Monism can have evaluative implications when combined with other prem-isses, where those other premisses have nothing to do with the fact that value cannot be attributed to that which "fails to exist," or with any other descriptive premiss. Descriptive monism may be combined with evaluative premisses such as views about the value of such a world and the things in it, and so yield implications about value.

17 See section 2.1, note 18.

18 George Burch denies that advaita Vedānta is pantheistic.

> According to pluralistic Vedanta, Brahman is the most real being, but other beings, although created by Brahman and destined to return to Brahman, are also real. According to pantheistic Vedanta, Brahman is the reality within the phenomena, which manifest it. But, according to monistic Vedanta, Brahman is the only reality. Phenomena are neither themselves real nor the appearance of anything real. Brahman is not the first or greatest among many realities, but is "one without a second," as they say, and this is the meaning of the term "non-dualism" (*advaita*), which I am translat-ing as "monism".
>
> (pp. 231–2)

George Bosworth Burch, "Principles and Problems of Monistic Ved-anta," *Philosophy East and West*, 11–12 (1961–3), pp. 231–7. Also see Elliot Deutsch, *Advaita Vedānta: A Philosophical Reconstruction* (Honolulu: East-West Center Press, 1969).

19 See "Some Varieties of Monism," p. 88, for Forrest's account of ways in which an aggregate can have a natural unity without being primi-tive. For example, an aggregate might have a natural unity because "the aggregate is made up of parts which are related in some way, but which are not related in this way to that which is not part of the aggregate."

20 Cf. Paul Henri Michel, *The Cosmology of Giordano Bruno*. It is question-able whether hybrid versions of theism/pantheism are less problem-

atical than either theism or pantheism alone in relation to theism's standard problems.

21 Spinoza was a monist who believed that only one substance exists, that it has an infinite number of attributes, and an infinite number of modes. Attributes and modes are absolutely dependent upon substance for their existence, and persons and things are modes of substance. However, it is unclear if Spinoza's regarding attributes or modes of substance as necessarily dependent upon substance for existence meant he did not, or could not, regard persons and things as individually existent things. Does necessary dependence upon substance for existence undermine their ontological status as individuals?

Leaving aside Spinoza's view, being a mode, attribute or aspect of something (e.g. of an all-inclusive substance) need not imply that such modes etc. cannot properly be regarded as individuals, even if they are necessarily dependent for existence upon something else. Modes of things are not regarded as individuals in some ontologies, but in others they can be. Ontology *per se* cannot decide the issue. Only the plausibility of a particular ontological scheme can resolve it. Descartes, and all theists who maintain the doctrine of divine conservation, believe that the world is necessarily dependent for existence upon God's conserving activity, and that nevertheless the world and God are not co-substantial but ontologically distinct. Did Spinoza think that "everything is either unreal or real to the extent that it is the self-expression of the Absolute"? This is Owen's necessary and sufficient condition for a monist to be a pantheist. I suppose so, since according to Spinoza there is nothing besides substance with its attributes and modes. But this is simply a reiteration of his monism and is not what makes him a pantheist. What makes Spinoza a pantheist, if anything, is what it means to say that for him everything is the self-expression of the Absolute, where this is not explained exclusively in terms of substance lineage.

2.4 Transcendence

1 Owen, *Concepts of Deity*, p. 65.
2 Ninian Smart, "God's Body," *Union Seminary Quarterly Review*, 37 (1981-2), pp. 51-9. See p. 51.
3 See Chin-Tai Kim, "Transcendence and Immanence," *Journal of the American Academy of Religion*, 55 (1987), pp. 537-49. "The ideas of transcendence and immanence are not mutually exclusive but mutually determinative" (p. 537).

Relative to the omni-predicates (e.g. omnipotence etc.) transcendence has been the subject of little attention in contemporary analytic philosophy of religion. This is despite the fact that transcendence as an aspect of God's nature is arguably more central than those other properties. It has implications religiously speaking, in ways that other properties do not obviously have. Not all inquiry concerning aspects of God's nature need be judged in terms of how they translate into practical terms. But issues like transcendence are neglected if the practical is taken as a criterion. Scripturally it is ambiguous whether God is attributed with the omni-predicates as they have been taken up by Perfect Being theory. (Actually it is not ambiguous but clear that he is not.) Transcendence on the other hand is about the relationship of God to the world, and that is central to an account of what is religiously significant.

4 For a discussion of the classical problem of transcendence see Grace Jantzen, *God's World, God's Body*, ch. 6, pp. 101–30.

> But if the transcendence of God is interpreted ... as essential distinction from the world, if God and matter agree in *nothing*, then nothing material could, *qua* material, be in any sense revelatory of God ... if this is so, then we have no positive knowledge of God whatsoever ... Christian theology ... has firmly rejected this view, finding the significant cleavage not between material substance and spiritual substance as Plotinus did, but between the created and uncreated ... If transcendence is defined as utter difference ... such a view would make it difficult to account for any interaction between God and the world.
>
> (pp. 102–3)

Cf. Thomas Aquinas, *Summa Contra Gentiles* I.17.7. Compare Jantzen's account of the problem of transcendence and its relation to immanence with Ninian Smart's discussed below.

5 See Grace Jantzen, *God's World, God's Body*; Ninian Smart, "Myth and Transcendence," *Monist*, 50 (1966), pp. 475–87; William Wainwright, "God's Body," *Journal of the American Academy of Religion*, 42 (1974), pp. 470–81; J. J. Lipner, "The World As God's 'Body': In Pursuit of Dialogue With Rāmānuja," *Religious Studies*, 20 (1984), pp. 145–61.

6 They can only know some things as they asymptotically approach the knowledge of the essence of things which is also a knowledge and understanding of God. Such knowledge approaches the same knowledge that God has of "himself." See *Ethics*, V, Propositions XXIV–XXVII and Demonstrations.

7 W. D. Hudson, "The Concept of Divine Transcendence," *Religious Studies*, 15 (1979), p. 197. Page numbers in the text citing Hudson refer to this article. See the discussion of Otto in section 2.2 above. For an alternative analysis of transcendence see Grace Jantzen, *God's World, God's Body*, pp. 122–30. She argues that "transcendence is compatible with divine embodiment ... God is not reducible to the universe, though the universe is God's body" (p. 127). Jantzen's analysis is relevant to pantheism in various ways. However, it is far closer to a panentheistic view. For a very different account of transcendence see Clyde Nabe, "Transcendence and an Other World," *Sophia*, 26 (1987), pp. 2–12.

To say that the "wholly other" cannot be defined or described means it cannot be *adequately* described and eludes *ordinary* conceptualisation. Taken literally, the claim that some experiences are "ineffable" encounters logical difficulties. I take it those claiming certain experiences are "ineffable" do not mean it literally. It is an honorific title, and no less interesting when taken non-literally.

8 One way of looking at the "beyond description" analysis of transcendence is in terms of "cognitive closure." It may be in principle beyond our capacity to understand certain properties belonging to God or how, for example, God can create the universe or cause other things to occur in virtue of these properties. This may be a fact about human understanding given the way human beings' intellectual capacities are constituted. Since I think the distinction between the "beyond knowledge" and "beyond description" analysis of transcendence breaks down at a point, both analyses could be looked at in terms of cognitive closure. The closure would be more radical in the latter analysis as described by Hudson than in the former – though in practical terms (i.e. what we can know as a matter of fact given our experience and capacities) might be the same.

See Colin McGinn's discussion of what he terms, following Chomsky and Fodor, "cognitive closure" as applied to the mind–body problem. "Can We Solve the Mind–Body Problem?," in *The Problem of Consciousness* (Oxford: Blackwell, 1991), pp. 1–22. He argues that there is a sense in which the problem may not be solvable: "we are cut off by our very cognitive constitution from achieving a conception of that natural property of the brain (or of consciousness) that accounts for the psychophysical link" (pp. 2–3). He traces a similar view to Locke. "Locke held ... only divine revelation could enable us to understand how 'perceptions' are produced in our minds by material objects" (p. 4n). There may be "some property P instantiated by the brain, in virtue of which the brain is the basis of consciousness" (p. 6). But the question of just how that property can give rise to consciousness, how consciousness results from that property, may not be answerable by us either in principle (i.e. it may be logically impossible for us to answer it – though not impossible for other cognitive creatures); or more cautiously, as a matter of fact it may not be possible for us to comprehend how P is the basis of consciousness because of our own inherent cognitive capacities and restrictions on those capacities. "properties (or theories) may be accessible to some minds but not to others" (p. 3).

9 See John Stuart Mill, "Mr. Mansel on the Limits of Religious Thought": "when we mean different things we have no right to call them by the same name, and to apply to them the same predicates, moral and intellectual. Language has no meaning for the words Just, Merciful, Benevolent, save in that which we predicate them of our fellow-creatures ..." (p. 42).

10 See Hudson's discussion of the doctrine of analogy and "affirmation and attitude interpretations" (pp. 204–5). Such interpretations claim that when, for example, one is reciting the Creed one is "affirming intentions or expressing attitudes" rather than "stating descriptions."

11 In Hudson's account, the transcendence of God (understood as "beyond knowledge") can be overcome in part by a "deepening experience of God" while others may be overcome "through clearer

thinking" (p. 208). "Given such a conception ... philosophers who believe in God should take it as their aim to remove any limitations on our knowledge of him which may be due to confused conceptualisation" (p. 210).

12 Ninian Smart, "Myth and Transcendence." Smart denies that God's transcendence and immanence should be interpreted as in tension with one another, and certainly not as contradictory. For a supporting view see Grave Jantzen, *God's World, God's Body*, p. 31. She says, "Thus, where later theologians have sometimes seen immanence and transcendence as in tension and difficult to reconcile with one another, the Fathers, basing all on a doctrine of divine incorporeality, thought of them as complementary concepts. God can truly be immanent and pervade all precisely *because* he is transcendent and incorporeal" (p. 31). She cites Gregory of Nazianzus, *Second Theological Oration* 28.8 and Jeremiah 23: 24.

13 See Smart, "Myth and Transcendence," p. 479, note 5, for the supporting quotation from Tillich.

14 Interpreting Tillich's view of God as pantheistic is not without basis. See Nels F. S. Ferré, *The Living God of Nowhere and Nothing* (Philadelphia: Westminster, 1966), p. 9. "Whitehead and Tillich have both told me at times that they would prefer, in contradistinction from theism, to be called pantheists. In our latest talk in 1965, however, Tillich disclaimed the term, calling pantheism a 'swear word'." Aside from the fact that he saw pantheism as a term of abuse, the difficulty in attributing pantheism to Tillich is that he never operated with a clear notion of what pantheism means. Tillich's view of God is a non-personal one. In the context of his analysis of "God" this suggests more in common with pantheism than with theism. Although Tillich may have tried, one cannot be a theist and maintain that God is not personal.

15 Mill's remarks on the application of predicates to God are applicable here. See John Stuart Mill, "Mr. Mansel on the Limits of Religious Thought."

16 Shu-hsien Liu, "The Confucian Approach to the Problem of Transcendence and Immanence," *Philosophy East and West*, 22 (1972), pp. 45–52. Liu agrees with Mou Tsung-san in claiming that the *Chung Yung* "belongs to the central tradition of Confucianism" (p. 45 n. 1). The translation of *Chung Yung* that Liu follows is in Wing-tsit Chan, *A Source Book in Chinese Philosophy* (Princeton: Princeton University Press, 1963), pp. 95–114. In his introduction Chan says,

> the *Doctrine of the Mean* is a philosophical work, perhaps the most philosophical in the whole body of ancient Confucian literature ... In the *Analects* [Confucius] *chung-yung*, often translated the "Mean," denotes moderation but here *chung* means what is central and *yung* means what is universal and harmonious. The former refers to human nature, the latter to its relation with the universe. Taken together, it means there is harmony in human nature and that this harmony underlies our moral being and prevails through-

out the universe. In short, man and Nature form a unity. Here is an early expression of the theory that was to dominate Chinese thought throughout its history.

(p. 96)

17 It should not unduly concern one that some scholars of Confucianism would deny that it is pantheistic. What exactly is being denied?

18 Macquarrie, *In Search of Deity*, pp. 52–3.

19 D. A. Rees, "Greek Views of Nature and Mind," *Philosophy*, 29 (1954), pp. 99–111.

20 *The Concise Oxford Dictionary*. Animism, as used here, should be distinguished from the other dictionary definitions. One refers to the doctrine of the *anima mundi* (i.e. "that phenomena of animal life are produced by an immaterial soul"), the other to "spiritualism as opposes to materialism." Marcus Ford defines animism as "the position that nature is infused with consciousness – that natural objects and phenomena, such as rocks . . . are alive and have souls." Marcus P. Ford, "William James: Panpsychist and Metaphysical Realist," *Transactions of the Charles Peirce Society*, 17 (1981), pp. 158–70. The term "animism" was coined by the anthropologist Edward B. Taylor. For a critical discussion of Tylor's account of animism and religion generally see E. E. Evans-Pritchard, *Theories of Primitive Religion* (Oxford: Oxford University Press, 1965).

21 Thomas Nagel, "Panpsychism," in his *Mortal Questions* (Cambridge: Cambridge University Press, 1979), pp. 181–95. "By Panpsychism I mean the view that the basic physical constituents of the universe have mental properties, whether or not they are parts of living organisms" (p. 181). For a "scientific" appraisal and argument in favour of panpsychism see Bernhard Rensch, "Panpsychistic Identism and its Meaning for a Universal Evolutionary Picture," *Scientia*, 112 (1977), pp. 337–47. "all matter . . . is protopsychic . . . the physical characteristics are at the same time the protopsychical ones" (p. 347). For a defence of a genetic argument for panpsychism with presupposes emergent evolutionism, see Clark Butler, "Panpsychism: A Restatement of the Genetic Argument," *Idealistic Studies*, 8 (1978), pp. 33–9.

Also see Paul Edwards, "Panpsychism," in Paul Edwards (ed.) *Encyclopedia of Philosophy* (New York: Macmillan and Free Press, 1967), vol. 6, pp. 22–31. "Panpsychism is the theory according to which all objects in the universe, not only human beings and animals but also plants and even objects we usually classify as 'inanimate,' have an 'inner' or 'psychological' being" (p. 22). For a list of some panpsychists see page 23 and his extensive bibliography on pages 30–1. Among them are Thales, Anaximenes, Empedocles, Plotinus and Bruno – all of whom (arguably) are pantheists. Edwards claims that William James was not a panpsychist (p. 24). For a contrary view see Marcus P. Ford, "William James: Panpsychist and Metaphysical Realist." Ford also suggests (p. 166) that in "Final Impressions of a Psychical Researcher" James held pantheistic views.

22 Spinoza's psycho-physical parallelism is a form of panpsychism. Mind

and matter run parallel. "all things are animate in various degrees" (*Ethics* II, XIII, Scholium). "According to Spinoza, matter and soul are the outside and inside aspects, or attributes, of one and the same *thing in itself* (or *things in themselves*); that is to say, of 'Nature, which is the same as God.'" Karl Popper, "Some Remarks on Panpsychism and Epiphenomenalism," *Dialectica*, 31 (1977), pp. 177–86.

23 Paul Edwards says ("Panpsychism," p. 23), "Lotze was particularly concerned to vindicate 'the fullness of animated life' in such lowly things as 'the dust trodden by our feet [and] the prosaic texture of the cloth that forms our clothing' ... uncomely as these 'may appear to us in their accumulations, they at least everywhere and without shortcomings perform the actions permitted to them by the universal order.'" Note however that neither pantheists nor panpsychists are necessarily 'hylozoists." Hylozoism is the view that matter is "intrinsically active" or that "all objects in the universe are in some literal sense alive" (p. 23). Panpsychism implies hylozoism only if, as is usually the case, one supposes that "mind implies life." Edwards also distinguishes panpsychism from the doctrine of a world-soul (p. 24). Hylozoism and pantheism should also be distinguished from this doctrine. However, individuals often hold more than one of these positions concurrently and they are not always clearly individuated.

24 Plato combines both doctrines. See *Timaeus* for his account of the world-soul. But not all doctrines of a world-soul are combined with the macrocosm/microcosm distinction. Parmenides appeared to have held the former but not the latter. D. A. Rees says,

> The most convincing presentation of his [Parmenides] philosophy is that which sees in his One a living and ensouled substance, or alternatively an embodied world-soul, ever-living and divine, exempt from birth and decay, discernible by the intellect because it was itself intellect ... if we apply our distinction of theories which make soul immanent in the universe and those which make it transcendent, Parmenides' does not belong unequivocally to the former type. For he allowed to the objects of perception only a partial reality, and so the living and divine One which I have described as an embodied world-soul was yet somehow beyond the world of the senses.

(p. 102)

D. A. Rees, "Greek Views of Nature and Mind." Rees refers to F. M. Cornford in *Cambridge Ancient History*, vol. iv, pp. 558–62.

25 Donald Levy, "Macrocosm and Microcosm," in Paul Edwards (ed.) *Encyclopedia of Philosophy*, (New York: Macmillan and Free Press, 1967), vol. 5, pp. 121–5, 121–2. "Man the microcosm is a commonplace of Greek thought from Anaximenes, the Pythagoreans, Heraclitus, and Empedocles to the Stoics and Neoplatonists. It is a staple theme for variation in the Orphic, Gnostic, and Hermetic texts and in the literature of mysticism, pantheism, and the occult" (p. 122). Cf. Owen, *Concepts of Deity*, p. 65. Owen describes Stoicism as a form of pantheism. He says, "one Being, the cosmic Logos ('Reason') or

anima mundi ('Soul of the world') . . . [is] identified with Nature's basic elements . . . Each person, they held, participates in this Logos through his own powers of reason. Sometimes they personified this Logos in order to satisfy religious and moral needs. They called it Zeus, addressed prayers to it, and regarded submission to its providence as the sign of true wisdom" (p. 65).

26 "Well into the period of the scientific revolution, the microcosm was an image of the order and harmony, pervading the world. Saying that the universe is controlled by a single principle . . . expressed the unified and self-regulating character of the world as understandable in its own terms, fit for scientific investigation" (Levy, p. 122).

Part II

PHILOSOPHY OF PANTHEISM

The Higher Pantheism in a Nutshell

One, who is not, we see: but one, whom we see not, is:
Surely this is not that: but that is assuredly this.

What, and wherefore, and whence? for under is over and under:
If thunder could be without lightning, lightning could be without
thunder.

Doubt is faith in the main: but faith, on the whole, is doubt:
We cannot believe by proof: but could we believe without?

Why, and whither, and how? for barley and rye are not clover:
Neither are straight lines curves: yet over is under and over.

Two and two may be four: but four and four are not eight:
Fate and God may be twain: but God is the same thing as fate.

Ask a man what he thinks, and get from a man what he feels:
God, once caught in the fact, shows you a fair pair of heels.

Body and spirit are twins: God only knows which is which:
The soul squats down in the flesh, like a tinker drunk in a ditch.

More is the whole than a part: but half is more than the whole:
Clearly, the soul is the body: but is not the body the soul?

One and two are not one: but one and nothing is two:
Truth can hardly be false, if falsehood cannot be true.

Once the mastodon was: pterodactyls were common as cocks:
Then the mammoth was God: now is He a prize ox.

Parallels all things are: yet many of these are askew:
You are certainly I: but certainly I am not you.

Springs the rock from the plain, shoots the stream from the rock:
Cocks exist for the hen: but hens exist for the cock.

God, whom we see not, is: and God, who is not, we see:
Fiddle, we know, is diddle: and diddle, we take it, is dee.

Algernon Charles Swinburne

3

PANTHEISM AND THEISM

pantheism is not a Christian position, lacking as it does, God the creator, a doctrine of personal providence, and capacity for Incarnation.[1]

Nels Ferré

In explaining the relationship between pantheism and theism it is important to reiterate that pantheism, no less than theism, asserts the existence of God. Pantheism is a non-theistic or non-personal type of monotheism. It is simply not true that "to say that the world is God amounts to saying that there is no God" (Hobbes).[2] Nor is true that the exclusion of personality or consciousness from the pantheistic Unity, in anything but an attenuated or equivocal sense (i.e. it contains conscious things), entails atheism. Thus, Coleridge's claim that "Spinozism consists in the exclusion of intelligence and consciousness from Deity – therefore it is atheism"[3] is similarly false. It would be true if the pantheistic unity or God necessarily had to be a (conscious) person – but it does not.

Pantheism's rejection of the idea of God as a person, whatever its basis (e.g. its implausibility), may bring certain satisfactions with it in lieu of the kinds of comforts the idea of a theistic God as father sometimes provides. Religious questions – questions of meaning, value etc. – remain, but no longer is it a person one answers to or looks to for answers. Personhood and consciousness are not taken, as they are in theism, to be unequivocally or supremely valuable. Theism regards them as such because God has these properties. But both their intrinsic and extrinsic value may be questioned – as they are by pantheists. J. A. Smith says,

There was a time when Coleridge declared that the article

147

of faith "nearest to his heart" was "the absolute imperson-
ality of the Deity," and surely many have felt that the
phenomena presented in History by human personality is
so inextricably blended of good and evil that the disappear-
ance of it would not itself be an unmixed evil or its per-
petuity an absolute good.[4]

Granted that personality and consciousness are sometimes valuable, perhaps even intrinsically valuable, they are just something
that the Unity does not have, though it contains things that do.
(They are not always worth having and it is difficult to conceive
of what a conscious all-encompassing divine Unity might be. What
would such a "person" think? The classical theistic answer is clear.
God thinks about himself. Nothing else is, after all, perfect etc.)
The Unity is not, or need not, be conceived of on the theistic
model as being a person or conscious – let alone "perfect." Any
perfections that in fact exist will exist within the Unity. But
some "perfections" or valuable properties may not be central to
the Unity.

Certain material and formal requirements need to be met by
any philosophically adequate version of pantheism. But personality and intelligence cannot be among the necessary conditions
of any materially adequate version of pantheism because there
have been many versions of pantheism in which these are
excluded. The Unity would (does), of course, include various
personalities and consciousnesses, but it does not follow that it
would have to be personal. (Perhaps, contrary to classical theism,
"personality" and "consciousness," no matter how good, can be
taken as intrinsically imperfect or as entailing imperfections.)
Furthermore, it is difficult to see why personality should be taken
as a necessary requirement of formal adequacy. Given that personality and other anthropomorphic features are attributed to "God"
with only greater or lesser degrees of equivocation, and given
that many of the most intractable problems associated with theism
(e.g. evil) have generally followed from the predication of human
properties to God, there appears to be no *prima facie* case for
attributing personality to the pantheistic deity, and plenty of
reason to reject it. Rejecting the idea that God is a person has
usually has been essential to pantheism (e.g. Spinoza and Lao
Tzu). Personality is required of God only in theistic and panthe-
istic/theistic hybrids like panentheism.

Note that if the sense of divinity essential to pantheism's ascription of divinity to Unity is that associated with the numinous, then personality and other rationalistic predicates are not essential. (I have argued, however, that the sense of divinity appropriate to pantheism is independent of the numinous.) These are accretions, and are not part of the original idea of the numinous according to Otto. Pantheism may be seen as a kind of de-anthropomorphised theism. It could be taken as a type of theism (i.e. belief in "god") that dispenses with the personal properties often seen as anthropomorphic projections attributed to God. Given the notion of divinity or holiness I take to be operative in pantheism (i.e. in general terms, the same one as in theism) personality and consciousness are not required.

3.1 DOES THEISM ENTAIL PANTHEISM?

What is the relationship between theism and pantheism? Are they compatible or are they mutually exclusive? I shall argue that there is little reason to believe that they are compatible, and that in the absence of such reasons one should adopt the conventional view which is that they are mutually exclusive. Each view entails the denial of the other. In Part III this will be shown to have implications for questions concerning the practice of pantheism. In that final part of the book I will show that certain common religious practices are intrinsically connected with theism, and are therefore inappropriate when employed to express the different views held by pantheists.

Robert Oakes has claimed that, despite the common assumption that traditional theism entails the denial of pantheism, there is sufficient reason for *believing* that traditional theism entails pantheism.[1] He does not argue that traditional theism entails pantheism, but only that there is sufficient reason to believe that it does. Oakes's thesis is as follows: objects, including persons, that depend necessarily for their perdurance (i.e. lasting existence) upon some rational or "minded" entity are, ontologically speaking, necessarily aspects or modifications of the entity that is their conserving agent. If it is a necessary truth that something depends for its perdurance upon the conserving activity of an agent, then necessarily the dependent thing will be ontologically an "aspect" of the conserving agent. The former entails the latter, or rather the latter fact is a function of the former.

The modal character of the thesis is crucial but ambiguous. Oakes thinks that Aquinas and Maimonides, as examples of traditional theists who believe that the world and everything in it depends for its perdurance upon God's conserving activity, are claiming that it is logically impossible for entities conserved by God to exist apart from God's conserving activity.[2] (Perhaps "subsist" is a better word here.) He denies that they may have been claiming only that physically or empirically it is impossible for such entities to exist apart from the appropriate activity by God. (It is physically, e.g. nomologically, but not logically impossible that such things perdure.) If they cannot logically exist apart from God's conserving activity, then neither can they exist as entities that are not "modifications" of God. His claim is based on an analogy drawn between (a) those things we acknowledge cannot exist apart from the conserving activity of an agent, and therefore exist as "aspects" of the agent, and (b) the "mentalistic" conserving activity of God that allegedly enables persons and things to perdure. Just as thoughts are "merely aspects or modifications" of thinkers, since the former cannot exist apart from the latter, so persons and things are not distinct from God since they cannot exist apart from God's conserving activity. Therefore, just as thoughts, beliefs etc. are aspects or modifications of persons, by analogy objects and persons must be aspects or modifications of God.[3] If Aquinas and Maimonides etc. were only claiming that as a matter of fact (e.g. physically) entities could not exist apart from divine conserving activity, be it mentalistic or some other sort, then this would not entail any identification between God and those entities. Consider a person pushing a button to drink from a water fountain. The fountain of water is dependent upon the conserving activity of the drinker, but they remain distinct. The fountain is not a modification of the drinker.

It is not clear that anything more than factual impossibility is crucial to the conservation doctrine or that anything more is being claimed. Aquinas and Maimonides might be claiming that it is logically impossible that the world perdure apart from God's activity, but they need only claim physical impossibility. Rāmānuja, however does claim that the world cannot, logically speaking, exist apart from God's conserving activity. The dependence here is absolute. Bodies of humans, plants etc. are not "absolutely" ontologically dependent upon their souls (their finite *atman*), though they too are ultimately dependent upon

God (*Brahman*). Nevertheless, Rāmānuja still maintains finite reality is "substantival" and the world is not an illusion.[4]

Oakes recognises that the assertion "the world could not perdure apart from God's activity" does not lead to the conclusion that they are ontologically non-distinct in any pantheistic sense, unless one assumes the impossibility to be logical rather than merely factual (e.g. Rāmānuja). The rejection of Oakes's thesis concerning theism and its entailment of pantheism does not however necessarily depend upon denying this entailment. Even if pantheism is simply interpreted as the ontological identification of God and the world, there are no good grounds for believing theism entails pantheism.

Suppose that Oakes is correct in the examples he gives as cases in which the existence of entities such as thoughts and beliefs – intentional, emotional and perceptual states of human persons – are logically dependent for their perdurance on persons and are therefore not ontologically distinct from persons, but rather aspects of those persons. What he then has to show (though even this is not sufficient for his thesis) is that these cases are analogous to the case in which it is assumed that persons and objects cannot perdure apart from God's conserving activity. Oakes attempts to establish the following:

> It is a necessary truth that the existence of x depends – at every moment of its existence – upon some mentalistic conserving activity/power of C

> entails

> It is a necessary truth that x exists as an aspect or modification of C.[5]

By using (relatively) uncontroversial examples, he has shown that this is so only for certain kinds of mentalistic activity.

For example, he has not shown that if necessarily – where "necessity" is here taken as either "physical" or logical necessity – only I could keep a fountain running merely by thinking, then that fountain and I would be ontologically indistinguishable, or that the fountain would be an aspect of myself. Intuition flounders here. Why assume that God's conserving activity is necessarily on a logical par with mentalistic activity of the sort that does entail ontological unity (i.e. undifferentiated unity) between the conserver and conserved? Even if the activity is mentalistic the analogy does not necessarily indicate that what is ontologically the case between thinkers and their thoughts is also the case between God and the world.[6] It must be shown that the analogy between God's conserving activity and our own is analogous in the relevant respects. To show why this cannot be done we need to ask the following question. Is there a case in which conserving activity is logically necessary to something's perdurance, where this does not entail that what is conserved is an aspect of what is doing the conserving?

Suppose that "life" is a fountain and that God's activity is logically necessary to keep it going. Suppose it is logically impossible that anyone who is not God could enable the fountain to perdure. Is it not possible that the activity be such that only God can perform it without supposing that, ontologically or pantheistically, the entities that are made to perdure are necessarily aspects of God? The issue is ontologically obscure – and pantheistically even more obscure. On some ontologies such an identification may be unavoidable. However, even if such an identification could be made, the case for pantheism is more difficult to establish. I have already argued that any simple ontological identification between God and the world does not suffice for pantheism.

There are more direct reasons for rejecting the idea that theism entails pantheism. For example, the claim that God is the creator and conserver of the universe presupposes that God is ontologically distinct from the universe – that the universe is not an aspect of God but is an "independent existence." If God caused the universe to come into existence or causes its continued existence, or bears any causal relation to the universe whatsoever, then we are committed to the view that God is independent of creation. "A caused B" presupposes that A and B are distinct existences.[7] No matter how we finally choose to analyse the notion of distinct existences, we would not say that A caused B unless we regarded A and B as distinct existences.[8]

The issue of the ontological relationship between God (as creator and sustainer of the world) and the world cannot be resolved by rejecting a model of event-causation in favour of some other. Rather the resolution rests on defending some obscure intuitions concerning ontology. Furthermore, the ontological issue is not the more basic one. By this I mean that *if* one regards God as the creator and sustainer of the world, then even *if* one also believes that the world is in *some sense* an aspect of God, one (i.e. the theist) will not also believe that God and the world are "one" in any ontological (let alone pantheistic) sense. Indeed, theism entails the denial of such a unity of God and the world. One's ontological position will follow from one's view concerning the independence, or lack thereof, of the world from God, and not vice versa.

Oakes is right in the claim that if (1) persons can be the cause of their decisions, actions etc. *and* (2) "A causes B" presupposes that A and B are distinct, then one must hold that persons and their thoughts etc. are not distinct existences. Accordingly, one should not conclude that if the world is caused and conserved by God, and is therefore an aspect of God, then the universe is within God (i.e. that traditional theism entails pantheism). The more likely conclusion, for the theist at any rate, should be that being an aspect or modification of God does not entail that such aspects and modifications of God, and God himself, are ontologically undifferentiated. Being an aspect or modification of God is to stand in a certain causal relation to God, but not in an ontological relation that entails that aspects of God are part of God himself. It must be possible to be an "ontological parasite" of something while not included within the being of that thing.

If one is committed to supposing the independent existence of A from B, where A is the cause of B, then perhaps this supposition only has to do with the concept of "cause" in ordinary usage. The argument that divine conservation entails or suffices for pantheism might be employed to suggest that, metaphysically speaking, it is a mistake to describe God as the "cause" or "conserver" of the universe, since the universe is not independent of God in the requisite sense. Such a description may be metaphorical or analogous to – yet distinct from – ordinary assumptions concerning the independent existence of items in the causal relation. However, there must be sufficient reason to abandon ordinary assumptions concerning the independence of items causally related in the case of God and the universe, and these reasons could only be given in the context of a more fundamental ontological scheme. Ontology is a messy business.

Oakes will claim that his argument has shown that despite appearances the universe is not distinct from God, and yet the two are nevertheless causally related. But then what does this claim amount to? It is a kind of qualified non-dualism. It is a metaphysical claim about the constitution of ontological identity, and the ultimate identity of all things. Ontologically speaking everything is an aspect of God, though they are not themselves God. Specifically, the claim seems to be that everything is ultimately one. The world is ultimately part of, or ontologically indistinguishable from, that which is ontologically prior to it. The world and God are not separate existences. So perhaps Oakes's argument may best be understood not merely as an argument for what he takes to be pantheism, but as an argument for monism as well. After all, Oakes not only claims that everything that exists ultimately constitutes an all-inclusive divine unity as "classical" pantheists do; he also ontologically identifies God with everything in a manner reminiscent of Spinoza. Perhaps Oakes is best understood to be arguing only for monism, since he maintains that the universe and God are distinct existences in some ways (i.e. they are not identical), while also claiming that ultimately they are ontologically the same (i.e. "aspects" in this context are aspects of the same thing). This is the way in which his claim that the world and its contents are "included within the being of God" can be taken. In other words, everything that exists does not constitute a divine unity except in an ultimate ontological sense. The latter view is not pantheistic given what has been said about notions of unity relevant to pantheism.

In accordance with some unspecified principles of individuation, just as one thing will properly be regarded as distinct from another – usually the result of pragmatic considerations – even though it is, under some schemes of individuation, a part of another, so one thing can be regarded as distinct from another, though it is an aspect of another. To deny this is to be unduly restrictive in one's ontology, or at least, it evidences prior ontological commitments. In the absence of a suitable defence of such commitments it should not be assumed that an "aspect or modification" of something cannot also be an ontologically significant thing in its own right. It is possible to have an ontology, a scheme of ontological individuation, where for x to exist as an aspect of something is, nevertheless, to exist as a particular. Thus, for x to exist in an "ontologically significant sense" should be understood to mean *not* necessarily that x is capable of independent existence, but rather that under an acceptable scheme of ontological individuation x is a particular even if it is ontologically/existentially parasitic.[9] It has not been shown that the theist cannot maintain both that the world depends upon God for perdurance and that God and the world are distinct.

Given the doctrine of divine conservation, the question of whether God and the world are distinct existences can be clarified by asking how to interpret the relation "being included within the being of."[10] How does Oakes understand this relation which he argues the world has to God? He denies that any intelligible version of pantheism "entails or involves a defence of the proposition that contingent objects are identical to God." They are included within the being of God, but are not identical to God. He claims that while there is good reason to believe that every constituent of the universe is an aspect of God, it is a "patent absurdity [to maintain] that everything within the domain of God's 'creation' has the property of being *identical* to God."[11] He *appears* to favour a view that regards the relation to God of the contingent universe and its constituents as a relation of parts to a whole. On this view one could not identify the whole (i.e. God) by referring to its parts (i.e. its aspects), and nothing within God's creation (i.e. no aspects) are identical to God. Individually, at least, they cannot be equated with God. As Hegel says, God is not this or that individual contingent thing (e.g. the toaster) and vice versa.

Consider this, however. Although usually I can be identified by my body, I am not identical to any part of my body or the whole of my body unless I am my body. And there are ontologies in which I am regarded as identical with my body. Central State Materialism, in so far as it is committed to an ontology, holds this view – or it is the most obvious one for it to hold. So, whereas Oakes may be correct in suggesting that it would wrong to identify or equate any particular contingent object or aspect of God with God, it is not clear that it is wrong to speak of the totality of contingent objects, even if they are aspects of God, and even if they are necessary rather than contingent, as being ontologically undifferentiated from God. Versions of pantheism that maintain that there is something that makes the totality an ontological item in a non-trivial sense do claim that "contingent objects [along with whatever else exists] are identical to God." Versions of pantheism that are ontologically based in some way would hold that the totality is an ontological item in a non-trivial sense. It is more than a mere totality in the sense of "everything that exists." Oakes denies that any intelligible version of pantheism "entails the proposition that contingent objects are identical to God." But given a suitable interpretation, some versions of pantheism would claim this.

Although Oakes appears to favour the view that the constituents of the universe (i.e. "aspects" of God) are related to God as parts to the whole, he is ambiguous. In his discussion of the problem that the doctrine of divine simplicity poses for his thesis, he says that "neither finite spirits nor assemblages of 'God's ideas' could legitimately be construed (strictly speaking) as parts of God, or things into which God was divisible."[12] If so, then either Oakes must accept that the doctrine of divine simplicity does pose a problem for his thesis, or he is identifying aspects of God with God. He is ambiguous between two notions of ontological independence. One allows him to say that contingent objects, either individually or together, are "parts" or "aspects" of God and not identical to God. The other allows him to uphold the doctrine of divine simplicity by maintaining that contingent objects – what he elsewhere calls "parts," "aspects" or "modifications" of God – are not really (i.e. in the ontologically relevant sense) "parts" or "aspects" of God. But, if they are not really parts of God, and not something other than God, then are they not identical to God? If A is not ontologically distinct from B and is not part of B, then is not A identical to B? Oakes has two concepts of identity at work in his thesis which correspond to the ambiguous usage of "ontological independence." One is identity in the "ontologically relevant sense" (Oakes's term); the other is an informal type of identity based on how we refer to things. The latter kind is not linked to ontological identity. "Strictly speaking," then, the thesis that contingent objects are "aspects" of God conflicts with theism's doctrine of divine simplicity.

Oakes's way of dealing with the problem of divine simplicity introduces the problem of evil into his thesis, because now, ontologically speaking, it is God and not an independent "aspect" of God that is responsible for evil in the world – though this is problematic enough. We now have the peculiar view that God is actually doing evil to God – or God's body (i.e. God's aspects).[13] Ontologically speaking, God is harming no one but God. Yet in theistic circles it is supposed that any plausible solution to the problem of evil, or any account of what the classical theistic problem is, requires that the world, and especially people, are ontologically differentiated from God.

Grace Jantzen disagrees, and the issue is more complex than I am making it out. Jantzen says,

> Although the "in" in "evil is in God" can then [i.e. if the world is God's body] be taken literally (that is spatially), this does not collapse the distinction between the statement, which all Christians must accept, that evil is finally ontologically dependent upon God, and the statement that God himself is evil, which means that he deliberately produces or allows evil without justification. Only if this distinction were collapsed would this be an objection to saying that the world is God's body.[14]

Jantzen does not claim that the problem of evil is resolved in her model of the world as God's body, but that "the new model leaves the problem of evil just where it was before."[15] If this is the case in her model – and this is highly contentious – it is only because such a model by no means abandons, nor of course is it intended to abandon, a theistic conception of God. Her model is meant to be a more adequate representation of the traditional theistic concept of God. In the kind of non-theistic concept of God most relevant to pantheism, however, the "problem of evil" must be completely reinterpreted – as we shall see.

Not only does Oakes want to show the centrality of the conservation doctrine to traditional theism – much of his argument rests on it – but also to provide us with "some reasonable grasp of what it means to claim that God conserves the existence of all 'finite things' at every moment of their existence."[16] The doctrine appears to be intelligible. However, certain statements of it seem so blatantly false when considered apart from some theistic metaphysical context that it becomes difficult to understand what is being claimed. Consider Descartes's statement: "It is . . . perfectly clear and evident . . . that in order to be conserved in each moment in which it endures, a substance has need of the same power and action as should be necessary to produce and create it anew."[17] For this to make sense, let alone be plausible, it must be tied to some metaphysical understanding of substance in relation to creation *ex nihilo*. It is impervious to any contemporary scientific account of what is required to "create" or "sustain" something. Even if true, the theory of divine conservation has no empirically determinable consequences. There is no way to empirically determine the truth or falsity of the doctrine. Of course, if it is true, it has profound consequences for the actual world which (whether ideal or material) would vanish apart from divine conservation.

If we substitute "material object" or "event" for "substance" in Descartes's statement, and assume that what is being produced is not being produced *ex nihilo*, then the conservation doctrine is clearly false. It does not take as much effort to hold a boulder in place on top of a mountain as it takes to roll it up there – unless Sisyphus' tormentor was confused in his method of damnation. It does not take as much effort or force to maintain a house in existence as it takes to build it – though it may sometimes seem that way. Perhaps the most sense to be made of the doctrine is to interpret "conservation" as Berkeley and many classical theists suggest. "Conservation" is really constant creation *ex nihilo*. Since contemporary scientific theory has (properly) little or nothing to say about creation *ex nihilo* (i.e. it is a metaphysical rather than a scientific hypothesis), this version of the conservation doctrine does not conflict with such a theory.

There are additional points about Oakes's thesis that have broader relevance in terms of the relation between theism and pantheism. As Oakes notes, not only is divine conservation insisted upon in traditional theism, the ontological independence of God and the world is also integral. There appears to be a standoff between two equally necessary doctrines. However, he thinks that the thesis of divine conservation is *clearly* necessary to traditional theism, whereas that of ontological independence is not. It is arguable whether many traditional theists or philosophical theologians would agree. Certainly Aquinas would not.[18] Part of Oakes's argument for the necessity of the conservation doctrine to theism rests on his claim that minus the conservation doctrine theistic belief reduces to deistic belief.[19] But this does not follow. For example, one may believe in the efficacy of prayer and not believe the conservation doctrine. Contrary to deism one can hold that God exerts all sorts of powers over the world while maintaining that the doctrine of divine conservation is false. Such a doctrine, like that of divine simplicity, might be viewed as a confused attempt to exalt God. Therefore, if Oakes is correct in his claim that theism entails pantheism, then his conclusion should be that traditional theism is incoherent since it contains two contradictory theses.

Oakes also argues that "Hell," as traditionally conceived, involves separation from God. If he is correct in arguing that theism entails pantheism, then he has shown us a way out of "Metaphysical Hell." If we are aspects of God we cannot be separate from God.[20] What then is the role for "Hell" in traditional theism according to Oakes? If there can be no Hell in his account, and Hell is essential to classical theism, as it seems to be, then does not this too introduce a conflict between traditional theism and his account of theism/pantheism? The conclusion should again be that there is at least a *prima facie* inconsistency in theism. But his account of Hell bears little resemblance to traditional concepts even though separation is central to both. Traditional accounts do not stress ontological distinctness. This is assumed, except by some mystics, and these mystics are not concerned with elucidating an ontological account of Hell. Ontological separation is based on the creator/created distinction in theism. At the most, and at the very least, ontological separation is a necessary but insufficient condition for being in Hell. Rather than ontological separation, what is crucial is a lack of "closeness" to God, deprivation of the beatific vision, "sinfulness" that has not been absolved, and one's moral failings. "Closeness" need not be interpreted ontologically. And, if the arguments presented earlier about how pantheistic Unity is to be understood are more or less correct, then to rest the issue of whether or not some set of beliefs constitutes pantheism on the question of ontological separation is a serious oversimplification.

Central to theism is the belief that there exists a God who, though supra-human, is in crucial respects a "person." God is understood to be a conscious being, sentient in some accounts though not others, capable of at least some intentional states such as believing, knowing and willing, though perhaps incapable of others such as wishing, and also incapable of some emotions and feelings as well (e.g. embarrassment). Any restrictions on what God is able to do or feel are not taken to be limitations of the perfection, power or goodness of God, but are understood to be exemplifications of such omni-properties (i.e. omniscience, omnipotence etc.). They are not regarded as genuine restrictions.

The principal reason – which entails a host of others – why theism does not entail pantheism is because in pantheism God (i.e. the divine Unity) is not understood to be a perfect being. Pantheistic Unity is utterly remote from a conception of a theistic deity. (Again, this is not meant to deny the obvious – that in practice theistic and pantheistic strains are often intertwined.) This is why theism and pantheism are understood to be alternative and mutually exclusive religious views. This is so, even if at times, both practically and doctrinally, there are undeniably elements of each to be found in the other. Generally, the pantheistic Unity is not taken to be a "being" at all, though it is sometimes taken as "Being" itself or some such equivalent technical concept. The conclusion, therefore, is that it is just not possible that theism entails pantheism. Even if they are not always interpreted as antithetical they are, at the most fundamental level, conceptually, though not always religiously, exclusive.

To reiterate: If Oakes is correct in claiming that there is sufficient reason to believe that theism entails pantheism, then there would be reason to conclude that theism was incoherent. Note that although Oakes is not concerned to argue the converse of his thesis – that pantheism entails theism – given his account of pantheism some versions of it would. If it could be shown that some type of pantheism entailed theism, then the conclusion should also be that pantheism of that kind is incoherent. To prove that a type of pantheism entailed theism would be a far more difficult task, however. In part this is because pantheism is a more nebulous concept. But it is also because, while the relationship between the theistic God and the world may be a matter of dispute, the relationship between any pantheistic Unity and the theistic God seems more certain. From pantheism's point of view there is no theistic God, and so to prove that pantheism entailed theism could prove more than merely difficult. Historically this is borne out when one considers the Stoics, Lao Tzu, Spinoza, Fichte, Schelling etc., and more modern pantheists such as D. H. Lawrence and Robinson Jeffers.[21]

There are many other reasons why pantheism and theism are generally, and correctly, understood to be mutually exclusive from a conceptual viewpoint. Although I have argued that some aspects of the concept of transcendence are applicable both to pantheism and theism, it is certain that others are not. God cannot be both transcendent and identical to the world; in Aquinas's sense, "God and prime matter are distinguished: one is pure act, the other is pure potency, and they agree in nothing" (*Summa Contra Gentiles*

I.17.7). Even if God or God's power may at some time be immanent in the world, theism maintains a strong doctrine of ontological or substantial transcendence that is incompatible with
pantheism. At the very least it is not obvious how to reconcile
such an evident incompatibility.[22]

In cases like those of Rāmānuja whose theology appears to
contain both theistic and pantheistic elements (i.e. the world as
God's body), these elements are seen as requiring a reconciliation
of some sort. Rāmānuja himself recognises and addresses the
prima facie incompatibility between aspects of his theology that
are theistic and those that can be seen as pantheistic. Whether
one decides that Rāmānuja is, in the final analysis, a theist or a
pantheist is not relevant either to the question of compatibility
or to the extent to which he was successful in combining the
two.

3.2 THE WORLD AS GOD'S BODY

Several recent arguments have attempted to establish that a doctrine of the world as God's body is either (a) compatible with
classical theism or (b) an improvement on, rather than an abandonment of, the model of God's relation to the world as presented in classical theism. Analogies are drawn between the soul-
body relation of ordinary persons and that of God-world. Thus,
William Wainwright claims that "The 'Platonic' model [i.e.
account of the soul-body relation] enables us to speak of the
God-world relation as a relation between soul and body without
sacrificing classical theology."[1] And as we have already seen, Grace
Jantzen claims:

> If human personhood and particularly the relationship
> between the mental and the physical in human persons is
> still to provide an analogy for the relationship between God
> and the world . . . the analogy will no longer point towards
> a God existing independently of the world . . . God's
> relationship to the world is analogous to the relationship
> between a person and his or her body when this relation-
> ship is understood holistically . . . traditionally this approach
> has been vehemently rejected . . . [However] the new model
> of an embodied God retains what is religiously and philo-
> sophically important in them.[2]

Panentheists such as Charles Hartshorne are closer to Jantzen than to Wainwright since they deny that panentheism is compatible with classical theism. They see it as taking much of what is essential or significant in classical theism and correcting or supplementing the rest.

I shall briefly argue that both Wainwright's claim about the Platonic analogy, and Smart's contention that Rāmānuja's theology may offer a way out of Western theology's "horror of pantheism," are unacceptable from the classical theistic perspective. (Smart would probably agree.) They are unacceptable because they tend to blur the radical ontological distinction, as well as other central distinctions, insisted upon in classical theism. As Smart says "The horror [of pantheism in classical theism] stems from the thought that there must be a gulf between God and creatures..."[3] In terms of classical theism "the world as God's body doctrines" are seen as pantheistic. If such doctrines of the world as God's body are unacceptable to classical theism there is little reason to think that, conceptually or doctrinally, pantheism can find a niche within theism – let alone that classical theism entails pantheism. Jantzen's thesis is (aside from some of the panentheists like Hartshorne, Whitehead and Macquarrie) the most systematically developed. (Maquarrie calls his view "dialectical theism.") It is more intriguing than the simpler and less significant question of compatibility between classical theism and the doctrine of the world as God's body. The answer to the latter question is indeterminate, resting as it does on various presuppositions concerning what is essential to theism. But whether or not Jantzen is successful in establishing that her model is an improvement over the traditional theistic model, rather than an abandonment of it, cannot be taken up here.

Both Jantzen and Smart claim that the doctrine of the world as God's body is pantheistic, and that it is nevertheless acceptable despite the classical theistic tradition in which pantheism is an anathema. Jantzen is explicit in seeing her model as pantheistic and finds it acceptable nonetheless. This requires some discussion.

Whether or not one views the doctrine of the world as God's body as compatible with, or an improvement on, classical theism, such a doctrine should not be taken as pantheistic – or not primarily as pantheistic – but as theistic. This is not so much a matter of definition but instead follows from what has been said about the mutually exclusive elements of theism and pantheism. The doctrine of the world as God's body as deployed by Rāmānu-jua, Jantzen etc., relying as they do on the notion of God as a person etc., just *is* theism – albeit significantly different than classical theism. The same may be said of process theology. From the perspective of classical pantheism which maintains a non-personal (i.e. non-theistic) notion of deity, these particular doctrines of the world as God's body are first and foremost theistic doctrines. And they are theistic doctrines that, so to speak, could not bear to break with theism – though they feel the strain.

Because of the theistic aspects in these doctrines, and their significance for those doctrines, they all have more in common with classical theism and each other than they do with any classically pantheistic doctrine maintaining that "God" (i.e. the Unity) is not a person. The incongruity or incompatibility between such revised theisms, no matter how much revised, and any classically pantheistic doctrine shows itself in pantheism's refusal to accept a personal God. Pantheism is the classical religious alternative to theism. Any doctrine therefore that has as an essential element the belief in a personal God (i.e. the *sina qua non* of theism) is unacceptable to pantheism. The point can easily be made in "religious" terms. Pantheists reject the idea of a personal God and so no doctrine will be religiously acceptable to them that emphatically insists upon it. I am not claiming that the two are incompatible in actual religious practice or traditions where the two simply exist not only side by side but mixed.

From the pantheists' position (i.e. classical, non-theistic or normative pantheism) it is *peculiar* to first revise theism in the way that Rāmānuja, Jantzen or process theologians do and then claim it not only as a kind of acceptable pantheism, but also as compatible with theism – allegedly taking what is best (?) from both theism and pantheism. Their kind of enterprise is possibly less strange from a theistic perspective since it at least seeks to preserve and improve upon what it sees as essential to theism – the notion of a personal loving God etc. These are essentially theistic rather than pantheistic exercises. Pantheism rejects the idea of a theistic God – an omnipotent, perfectly good etc. being. It is (conceptually) unimpressed with Jantzen's or Smart's contention that, to use an example we have been using, the problem of evil is no more of a problem for a doctrine of the world as God's body then it is for classical theism. The problem with theism according to pantheism is that it mistakenly posits a personal God. Other difficulties are subsidiary. Asking a pantheist what it is that they object to in a doctrine of the world as God's body aside from its insistence on a personal theistic deity reminds one of the black joke: "Well other than that Mrs. Lincoln . . . did you enjoy the evening at the theatre?"[4]

Consider William Wainwright's claim that "The 'Platonic' model [i.e. the Platonic account of the soul–body relation] enables us to speak of the God–world relation as a relation between soul and body without sacrificing classical theology." He argues that in various other accounts of the mind–body relationship, any analogy between God and the world as God's body would be rejected by classical theology. He claims that the relation posited between mind and body in these other accounts is incompatible with tenets central to theism. But:

> In the Phaedo, Cebes suggests that the soul may create its own body (or bodies) . . . In later Platonism, the soul creates or produces or emanates its own body. This body (or the lower self cum body) is an image or expression of the soul (or higher self) on a lower level. Furthermore, Plotinus argues that the (higher parts of the) soul are necessary, immutable, and impeccable. While the later Neo-Platonists refused to follow Plotinus on this point, they did agree that the body cannot act upon the soul. Rāmānuja also believes that the defects and imperfections of the body do not affect the soul, and . . . he goes on to argue that just "as the defects or deficiencies of the body do not affect the soul, so . . . the defects of the latter [the world] cannot . . . affect the nature of Brahman. Thus, though Brahman has a body, He is partless . . . and absolutely devoid of any *karma* . . . He is . . . wholly unaffected by all faults and remains pure and perfect in Himself . . ."[5]

Why does Wainwright claim that this Platonic view – similar in some ways to that of Rāmānuja – of the relation between soul and body avoids the "most serious objections" that classical theology has to using the relation as an analogy for the one between God and the world? Wainwright says,

> If body is related to soul in this way and if (as Platonists maintain) a man is essentially his soul, the inference from

"my body is O" to "I am O" (or "some part of me is O")
loses its force. (It has no more force than the inference
from "my hammer (coat) is O" to "I am O" or "some part
of me is O".) . . . If Platonists are correct the inference is
illegitimate. Hence from the fact that the world is God's
body and exhibits various defects and limitations, it does
not follow that God or some part of Him does so.
Furthermore . . . on a Platonic view, the body depends upon
but does not affect the soul, so the world depends upon God
but does not affect God. God's sovereignty and independence are preserved.[6]

Having to rely on a Platonic model of the soul–body relationship
in order to make the analogy of the world as God's body acceptable will of course only be as acceptable as the Platonic model is
in the first place. As Wainwright notes there are problems with
such a model. It appears antiquated.

Leaving this aside, it is not clear what Wainwright's model of
classical theology is, but if it is anything like Aquinas's, then
his emphasis upon the "illegitimate inference" is unlikely to be
accepted as a way out of the classical objections to thinking of
the world as God's body. Aquinas, it will be recalled, claims that
"God and prime matter are distinguished: one is pure act, the
other is pure potency, and they agree in nothing" (*Summa Contra
Gentiles* I.17.7). Given Aquinas's distinction, the fact that one
cannot infer that God has some property merely because the
world does – even if the world is God's body – is not significant.
The model remains unacceptable. However, the legitimacy of the
inference from "the world is O to God is O" is not the heart of
the matter. The classical objections are not as precise as Wainwright thinks they are. Rather, what classical theologians object
to is that God would in any way be related to, or possibly affected
by, creation in anything approaching ways in which persons are
related to their bodies. In fact there is good reason to believe
that this particular analogy remains singularly unacceptable to
classical theology given the kind of attitude towards the notion
of "body" that Jantzen, for example, correctly portrays classical
theology as having. God is allegedly transcendent, and part of
what this means is that God cannot be affected by or connected
with the world. The "illegitimate inference" that can be avoided

on the Platonic model affects only the most radical form of this worry.

Jantzen argues that even in the classical theistic model God is at times seen as being connected to the world and affected by it in ways that are inconsistent with that model's disdain of the body and of pantheism. Some of these connections follow from the fact that God is the creator and sustainer of creation. Thus, on one level, God is ultimately responsible for all of creation – including evil.

> everything that exists is created by God and absolutely dependent upon him in just the same sense if the universe is God's body as it is if the doctrine of creation *ex nihilo* is true, except that God formed it quite literally "out of himself"... The doctrine of creation *ex nihilo* was... adopted partly to preserve the doctrine of God's sovereignty; it was considered incorrect to think that things could exist without God having made them... But if all that exists is in a quite literal sense the self-manifestation of God, then it is clearly not in any way independent of him, as it would be on a Platonic-type theory of pre-existent matter. It would be, literally, God's creative self-manifestation.[7]

If, as Jantzen contends, classical theism, itself, must attribute to God some of the characteristics or properties (or responsibility) associated with creation, the same seems to be true – perhaps more so – of the doctrine of the world as God's body. Smart, for example, argues that given Rāmānuja's adherence to that doctrine, his contention that God's (*Brahman's*) soul or essence remains unaffected by karma or suffering is unconvincing.

> Rāmānuja's attempt to escape the consequence of God's being affected by suffering or karma is not quite successful, since it depends on a rather rigid distinction between the essence of God in Himself and His modal transformations in His body. At the very least, one must suppose that God is displeased with souls who commit evil, for it is on the basis of His pleasure and displeasure that karma itself operates.[8]

Jantzen would nevertheless agree that the Platonic model Wainwright claims is acceptable to classical theism is unacceptable to it. There are simply too many various components of classical theism that remain at odds with seeing the world as God's body.

This is why Jantzen argues that the classical model must be radically altered – even though there are many elements within that model that can and should be carried over.

The analogy between soul–body and God–world remains unacceptable from the classical theistic perspective, whether on the Platonic model of the relation or any of the others discussed by Wainwright. Therefore, it seems unlikely to suppose that any *rapprochement* between classical theism and pantheism which relies on such analogies can be effected. In so far as Jantzen is able to claim that from a theistic perspective the doctrine of the world as God's body may represent a kind of acceptable pantheism, she has moved well beyond classical theism and is operating with her new theistic model. While she would acknowledge this, she does not appear to consider that the model, though it claims to contain what is right in pantheism, or be consistent with pantheism, is unacceptable to pantheism. She is also operating with a notion of pantheism that is anything but classical since she sees it as compatible with theism.

For the most part the above remarks can be applied to Smart's contention that Rāmānuja's theology may offer a way out of Western theology's "horror of pantheism." The way out is unacceptable from the classical theistic perspective. Smart would agree and claim, much like Jantzen and J.J. Lipner, that the classical theistic model would in fact "benefit" from certain revisions in line with Rāmānuja's theology – especially its central doctrine of the world as God's body and much that it can be seen as entailing. But of course this is different from suggesting that the doctrine of the world as God's body is acceptable to classical theism. Many of the alleged advantages that Smart goes on to illustrate are similar or identical to those discussed by Jantzen and Lipner. "God as a person is more accessible." Better sense is made of God's omniscience and omnipotence. Even the doctrine of the trinity can be beneficially interpreted against the backdrop of such a doctrine etc. As Smart says "There are various theological advantages to the doctrine that the cosmos is the body of God."[9] Whether this is so is heavily dependent upon one's commitment to classical Christian doctrine.

The claim that classical theism will find the Platonic model or Rāmānuja's theology to be unacceptable in terms of a model for the God–world relation rests on the classical theistic understanding of the distinction between God and creation. This is so even if, as Jantzen claims, classical theism is, in crucial ways, itself unable to ultimately maintain a stronger distinction between God and the world than can the doctrine of the world as God's body. In this context it is worth noting what Lipner says about Hindu monotheism. "In Hindu thought at least, a monotheist need not be a convinced ontological dualist. Śankara, for example, espoused a theism which was to be sublated ultimately in an uncompromising non-dualism."[10]

The doctrine of the world as God's body, or Rāmānuja's ingenious blend of that doctrine with theism in his effort to combine the strong monism of classical Vedānta with the rise of devotional religion (*bhakti*) and its personal God(s), is not acceptable to classical theism. Yet, it is this doctrine that is interpreted by Jantzen and Smart as being pantheistic – and as beneficial to, rather than ultimately at odds with, much of classical theism. I have contended that such a doctrine is not acceptable to theism, and also that, in so far as the doctrine is interpreted as compatible with theism, it is unacceptable to pantheism. This is not meant to deny that the doctrine is pantheistic in some ways. After all, it is arguing for a kind of Unity of all things. Indeed, the point of the doctrine seems to be to adopt a kind of pantheistic outlook – with its accrued benefits – while maintaining as much as possible of the classical theistic metaphysic. It is the most common theistic version of "pantheism" and it explicitly or implicitly acknowledges various "defects" (call them what you will) of theism.

The ideas both of creation and of evil which have appeared in this section are important in considering the relation of God to the world in the context of classical theistic metaphysics. The next chapters discuss these concepts more systematically as they relate to pantheism.

NOTES

1 Nels Ferré, *Living God of Nowhere and Nothing* (Philadelphia: Westminster, 1966), p. 9.
2 Leszek Kolakowski, *Religion* (New York: Oxford University Press, 1982), p. 110.
3 Thomas McFarland, *Coleridge and the Pantheist Tradition* (Oxford: Oxford University Press, 1969), p. 190.
4 J. A. Smith, "The Issue Between Monism and Pluralism," *Proceedings of the Aristotelian Society*, 26 (1925–6), p. 17.

3.1 Does theism entail pantheism?

1 Robert Oakes, "Does Traditional Theism Entail Pantheism?," *American Philosophical Quarterly*, 20 (1983), pp. 105–12. Reprinted in Thomas V. Morris (ed.) *The Concept of God* (Oxford: Oxford University Press, 1987), pp. 57–71. Oakes's thesis is epistemological. He claims there is sufficient reason for *believing* that theism entails pantheism. What follows is a summary of my reasons for rejecting Oakes's thesis. For a more complete account see Michael P. Levine, "Why Traditional Theism Does Not Entail Pantheism," *Sophia*, 23 (1984), pp. 13–20; "More On 'Does Traditional Theism Entail Pantheism?,'" *International Journal for Philosophy of Religion*, 20 (1986), pp. 31–5; Robert Oakes, "Theism and Pantheism Again," *Sophia*, 24 (1985), pp. 32–7; "Classical Theism and Pantheism: A Victory for Process Theism?," *Religious Studies*, 13 (1977), pp. 167–73; Philip Quinn, "Divine Conservation and Spinozistic Pantheism," *Religious Studies*, 15 (1979), pp. 289–302.

Jantzen also thinks there are pantheistic elements in traditional theism. Cf. *God's World, God's Body* (Philadelphia: Westminster, 1984) pp. 147–50. Paul Tillich says: "Pantheism is the doctrine that God is the substance or essence of all things, not the meaningless assertion that God is the totality of all things. The pantheistic element in the classical doctrine that God is *ipsum esse*, is . . . necessary for a Christian doctrine of God." Paul Tillich, *Systematic Theology*, (Chicago: University of Chicago Press and SCM, 1963), vol. I, p. 324.

2 Oakes, "Does Traditional Theism Entail Pantheism?," pp. 107–8. P. A. Byrne gives an argument similar to Oakes's. Cf. P. A. Byrne, "Berkeley, Scientific Realism and Creation," *Religious Studies*, 20 (1984), pp. 453–64. I discuss this article in "Cartesian Materialism and Conservation: Berkelean Immaterialism?," *Southern Journal of Philosophy*, 24 (1986), pp. 247–59.

3 Oakes, "Does Traditional Theism Entail Pantheism?," pp. 108–10.

4 Cf. J. J. Lipner, "The World as God's 'Body': In Pursuit of Dialogue with Rāmānuja," *Religious Studies*, 20 (1984), pp. 145–61. Lipner says, "if finite being has a totally dependent, that is, derived being, does not the spectre of the world's being . . . an illusion arise? Rāmānuja emphatically rejects this . . . the world does have a substantive reality . . . a reality which cannot be sublated in terms of a 'higher' experience" (pp. 150–1). Oakes's insistence that the modal character of the conservation doctrine is logical rather than empirical is not obviously supported by his quotations in "Does Traditional Theism Entail Pantheism?," pp. 107–8.

5 Oakes, "Does Traditional Theism Entail Pantheism?," pp. 108–10.

6 In the case of Berkeley's "theocentric mentalism," where God's perceiving the world is taken as logically necessary for its perdurance, perhaps pantheism or the view that the world is an aspect of God is entailed as Oakes suggests. But the case seems too far removed from that of the relation between our thoughts and ourselves to claim that the world is an aspect of God. Therefore, it is unclear that Berkeley's

view or the conservation doctrine *per se* entails pantheism. However, Berkeley may have been a pantheist – albeit a theistic one. This interpretation of Berkeley is resisted by commentators for two reasons. First, it seems at odds with interpreting him in the empirical tradition of Locke and Hume. Second, even if is acknowledged that his theism was extraordinary, pantheism is obscure and often regarded as atheism or a term of "abuse."

Cf. Thomas McFarland's superb study, *Coleridge and the Pantheist Tradition*, pp. 300–3, "Berkeley's Idealism and Pantheism." McFarland says,

> His philosophy ... though perhaps not strictly speaking pantheist, is not a defence against pantheism, and in its implications actually favours pantheism ... "the works of Nature, i.e. the far greater part of the Ideas or Sensations perceived by us ... belong to the aforesaid Spirit, *who works all in all*, and *by whom* all things *consist*" (*Principles*, 146). And as pantheism itself looms ... Berkeley refuses to deflect his course: "But you'll say has Nature no share in the Production of Natural Things, and must they be all ascrib'd to the immediate and sole Operation of God? I answer ... if by *Nature* is meant some Being distinct from GOD ... I must confess, that Word is to me an empty Sound, without any intelligible Meaning annexed to it. Nature, in this Acceptation, is a vain *Chimera*" (*Principles*, 150).
>
> Not only does Berkeley's later work not repudiate this identification of God and nature, but his treatise on tar water of 1744 is a veritable anthology of Neoplatonic and Stoic pantheistic lore, lovingly and approvingly set forth by the Bishop. There is the *anima mundi*: "Nature seems to be no otherwise distinguished from the *anima mundi*, than as life is from soul, and upon the principle of the oldest philosophers, may not improperly or incongruously be styled the Life of the world" (*Siris: A Chain of Philosophical Reflexions and Inquiries Concerning Virtues of Tar Water, and Divers other Subjects connected together and arising one from another* (Dublin, 1744) par. 278). Berkeley, significantly, finds no atheism in the conception: "If nature be the life of the world, animated by one soul, compacted into one frame, and directed or governed in all parts by one mind; This system cannot be accused of Atheism" (*Siris*, par. 279).

Cf. Michael P. Levine, "Berkeley's Theocentric Mentalism: Pantheism?," *Sophia*, 26 (1987), pp. 30–41; "Cartesian Materialism and Conservation: Berkelean Immaterialism?"

7 See J. L. Mackie, *The Cement of the Universe* (Oxford: Oxford University Press, 1974), pp. 31–2. Mackie says,

> are there cases where we would not say that X caused Y but would say that X and Y both occurred and that in the circumstances Y would not have occurred if X had not? Would we not have to say the latter, trivially, if X and Y were identical? ... But events ... are

not commonly said to cause themselves. Equally, the penny could not have fallen heads-up if it had not fallen tails-down; but we would not say that its falling tails-down caused its falling heads-up . . . To exclude all such counter-examples, we must say that . . . "X caused Y" presupposes that X and Y are distinct events, and . . . this must be taken in a stronger sense than merely that "X" and "Y" are logically or conceptually independent descriptions. Indeed, it is not even necessary, anymore than it is sufficient for this purpose, that these should be logically independent descriptions. It is legitimate, though trivial, to say that X caused every effect of X . . . what is required is that the cause and effect should be, as Hume says, distinct existences. It may be objected that this requirement is vague or obscure, but it is not, I think, necessary for me to aim at any great precision here. I am discussing only what causal statements mean, and for this purpose it is sufficient to say that someone will not be willing to say that X caused Y unless he regards X and Y as distinct existences.

8 Oakes claims it is improper to use the model of event-causation in arguing that if God is the cause of the universe then the two must be distinct. But given that "creating the universe" is the description of an event, a model of event-causation seems appropriate. The relevance of the point concerning the "independence" of cause and effect need not, however, be restricted to this model. It is just as applicable to object-causation (i.e. causation as a relation between objects) or causation analysed in terms of states of affairs. Oakes, "Theism and Pantheism Again," pp. 34–5.

9 It does seem that ideas, including the Berkelean material world which is a world of ideas, must be "aspects" of the entities on which they depend. Everything in Berkeley's world except finite spirits is an aspect of God, and even finite spirits are conserved by God. As Oakes points out, if this is the case does not Berkeley's idealism suggest pantheism even if it does not entail it? Is the sense in which Berkeley's world is an "aspect" of God one of the acceptable senses of panthe-istic Unity? Berkeley says ideas exist in the mind, but he also says they are "entirely distinct" from the mind (*Principles*, 2). For a dis-cussion of the compatibility of these two claims see Colin Turbayne, "The Berkeley, Plato, Aristotle Connection," in Colin Turbayne (ed.) *Berkeley: Critical and Interpretative Essays* (Minnesota: University of Min-nesota Press, 1982), pp. 295–310.

10 Anselm says "For nothing contains thee, but thou containest all." Cf. *Proslogion*, chs XIX-XX. Paul says "we live and move and have our being" in God (Acts, 17: 28). Cf. Jeremiah (23: 24): "Do I not fill heaven and earth? saith the Lord." Aquinas says "spiritual things contain the things in which they are; as the soul contains the body. So, too, God is in things as containing them. Nevertheless . . . it is said that all things are in God inasmuch as they are contained by Him" (*Summa Theologiae*, vol. I, q. 8, a. 1, reply objection 2). It seems

undeniable, though it usually is denied, that pantheism is intimated in these quotations.

11 Oakes, "Theism and Pantheism Again," p. 32.

12 Oakes, "Does Traditional Theism Entail Pantheism?," p. 111.

13 This is discussed further in section 4.2 on evil. A principal criticism of pantheism has been that it cannot account for evil.

14 Jantzen, *God's World, God's Body*, p. 93. Cf. pp. 90–3.

15 Jantzen, *God's World, God's Body*, p. 93.

16 Oakes, "Does Traditional Theism Entail Pantheism?," p. 107. Cf. Robert Oakes, "Material Things: A Cartesian Conundrum," *Pacific Philosophical Quarterly*, 64 (1983), pp. 144–50. Cf. Philip Quinn, "Divine Conservation, Secondary Causes, and Occasionalism," in Thomas V. Morris (ed.) *Divine and Human Action* (Cornell: Cornell University Press, 1988), pp. 50–73; "Divine Conservation and Spinozistic Pantheism"; "Divine Conservation, Continuous Creation, and Human Action," in Alfred J. Freddoso (ed.) *The Existence and Nature of God* (Notre Dame: University of Notre Dame Press, 1983), pp. 55–79. Also see Jonathan Kvanvig and Hugh McCann, "Divine Conservation and the Persistence of the World," in Thomas V. Morris (ed.) *Divine and Human Action* (Cornell: Cornell University Press, 1988), pp. 13–49.

17 Oakes, "Does Traditional Theism Entail Pantheism?," p. 107. As Descartes uses it "clear and evident" is a technical term.

18 Cf. Thomas Aquinas, *Summa Contra Gentiles* I.17.7.

19 Oakes, "Does Traditional Theism Entail Pantheism?," p. 107.

20 Oakes, "Does Traditional Theism Entail Pantheism?," pp. 105–6. Cf. Jantzen, *God's World, God's Body*, p. 92: "the universe and everything in it, evil not excepted, has no independent existence apart from God ... Hell itself cannot ultimately be outside of an omnipresent God."

21 Cf. F. C. Copleston, "Pantheism in Spinoza and the German Idealists," *Philosophy*, 21 (1946), pp. 42–56. Fichte thought ascribing personality to God was anthromorphic and denied God is personal. Copleston thinks pantheism is atheistic. He says Hegel is not atheistic, but is neither unequivocally pantheistic nor theistic. Similarly, Copleston says "neither the system of Plotinus nor that of Fichte can be termed unequivocal theism or unambiguous pantheism" (p. 49). He describes Schelling's view as "the conception of the Absolute as Spirit and Nature in identity ... standing behind all finite manifestations, all differentiations ... Schelling's conception of Nature ... [is] a totality, a living and dynamic process, a self-organising cosmos ..." (p. 50). Hegel referred to Schelling's system, his romantic apprehension of the Totality, as "the night in which all cows are black." (Coming from Hegel this gives one reason to pause – which must be why it is so often quoted.)

Copleston says pantheism is "logically speaking, deterministic" (p. 48). Spinoza's system is deterministic, but pantheism is not intrinsically deterministic.

22 Grace Jantzen attempts to reconcile aspects of Aquinas's view of

172

God's transcendence, though not others, with classical theism and the idea that God need not be incorporeal to be "perfect." She argues that the model of the world as God's body is more consonant with the principal tenets of orthodox theism than is the model of God as incorporeal, transcendent to matter etc. Of course, this is quite different from trying to reconcile Aquinas's view, and other aspects of the orthodox notion of transcendence, with pantheism. Jantzen, *God's World, God's Body,* pp. 108–14.

3.2 The world as God's body

1 William Wainwright, "God's Body," *Journal of the American Academy of Religion,* 42 (1974), pp. 470–81. Reprinted in Thomas V. Morris (ed.) *The Concept of God* (Oxford: Oxford University Press, 1987), pp. 72–87. Cf. Ninian Smart, "God's Body," *Union Seminary Quarterly Review,* 37 (1981–2), pp. 51–9. Smart claims that Rāmānuja's doctrine of the world as God's body is pantheistic in some ways, but it avoids the "horror" of pantheism seen in Western theology which stems from "the thought that there must be a gulf between God and creatures . . . an identity between nature and God . . . has the flavour of blasphemy" (p. 51). Cf. Lipner, "The World as God's 'Body' "; *Rāmānuja: The Face of Truth* (London: Macmillan, 1985).

2 Jantzen, *God's World, God's Body,* pp. 2, 22.

3 Smart, "God's Body," p. 51.

4 Consider the modifications to theism undertaken by theists who maintain that seeing "the world as God's body" is an acceptable improvement to theism (e.g. Rāmānuja, Jantzen, Wainwright, Smart). Could such modifications be seen as consonant or compatible with the views of Lao Tzu, Spinoza, the Stoics or contemporary pantheists?

5 Wainwright, "God's Body," pp. 479–80.

Rāmānuja defines "body" as follows: "Any substance of a conscious being which can entirely be controlled and supported by that being for the latter's own purposes, and whose proper form is solely to be the accessory of that being, is the "body" of that being." Lipner, "The World as God's 'Body,' " p. 147. Given that finite bodies are not "entirely supported and controlled" by their finite *atmans,* whereas the world as God's body is controlled by Brahman or infinite *atman,* it follows that God or Brahman is more embodied than we are. Brahman is maximally embodied. Compare Jantzen's claim throughout *God's World, God's Body* that under suitable interpretations various properties of God such as omnipotence point to God being more completely embodied than we are rather than less so or incorporeal. Commenting on Rāmānuja's definition of body Lipner says,

> created bring is literally – not metaphorically – Brahman's body, yet not in any obvious sense . . . "body" in the sense described can be predicated of a substance related only to a conscious entity, that is, in fact to the atman or spiritual principle, which in the case of a spirit–matter composite is the immortal centre or "self"

of the composite... [In Vedāntic philosophy even sub-human forms of life have a conscious nature since they too have an atman.]... the concept of "body" so defined prescinds from whether its referent is spiritual or material. *Any* substance, spiritual or material, which is related to a self in the way described is that self's body. This makes it possible not only for material substances but also for spiritual substances, i.e. finite atmans, to be the "body" of the infinite, supreme Self or Atman.

(pp. 147–8)

Lipner is in agreement with Jantzen and Smart when he says, "it would be theologically fertile, both conceptually and devotionally, for Christians to regard the world, and its individual components, as God's body" (p. 159). Cf. pp. 159–61.

6 Wainwright, "God's Body," p. 480.
7 Jantzen, *God's World, God's Body*, p. 135.
8 Smart, "God's Body," p. 55. Cf. J. J. Lipner's discussion of Rāmānuja's attempt to keep God independent of the world which is his body. This is central to Rāmānuja's theory of "identity-in-difference" (*visistadvaita* or "the non-duality of differenced being"). Neither Smart, Jantzen or Lipner think that the doctrine of the world as God's body is completely successful in maintaining the distinction between God and his body in places where it might seem advantageous to do so (e.g. regarding evil). They all think this can be turned to a theological advantage – arguing for example that a God who suffers is "preferable" to one who does not; and that this is in line with important aspects of classical theism.
9 Smart, "God's Body," p. 51.
10 Lipner, "The World as God's 'Body,'" p. 145n.

4

PROBLEMS OF PANTHEISM

4.1 CREATION

Whatever the doctrine of creation is, it is not a scientific explanation for the origin of universes . . . creation *ex nihilo* is . . . a theistic label to the mystery of why there should be something rather than nothing . . .

"He that formed the eye, shall he not see . . ." (Psalm 94: 9–10 AV) . . . the one who originated our ability to perceive can hardly be without that ability himself; the creator of persons is personal.[1]

Grace Jantzen

for the same reason that the maker of the table . . . must be different from the table . . . the maker of the . . . universe . . . must be a being separate from . . . the universe; which is a sufficient answer to the reasoning of Spinoza, who, making the universe itself to be God, did, in fact, deny that there was any God.[2]

Joseph Priestley

emanationism does not necessarily lead to pantheism, but it does imply that in some sense God is in the world and the world is in God. Creation out of nothing, as understood by classical theism, places the world outside of God.[3]

John Maquarrie

The concept of the Tao precludes the theory of divine creation.[4]

R. Young and R. Ames

How pantheism addresses and avoids some fundamentally problematic issues in theism is the topic of this and the next three sections. Do the same or similar problems arise for pantheism? If pantheism is to be regarded as an alternative to theism such juxtapositions and comparisons are, as they always have been, unavoidable. They are also useful, since pantheism's own philosophical positions are clarified in distinguishing them from theism's.

"Why is there something rather than nothing?" Pantheism rejects the theistic response that God exists necessarily and freely creates the universe from nothing. But does pantheism require an alternative doctrine of creation? What might such a doctrine be? Roughly, the conclusion will be that, for pantheism, creation remains somewhat problematic and even mysterious. However, difficulties associated with the theistic doctrine of creation *ex nihilo* (i.e. God creating the world out of nothing) vanish. Abandoning an unacceptable theistic doctrine is a step towards a pantheistic position. If pantheism requires a creation doctrine, some type of emanationism seems most plausible. This is the type usually associated with, and probably most congenial to, pantheism (e.g. Taoism, the Stoics, Plotinus) – although pantheists can also eschew such doctrines.

Mystery is associated with the theistic account of creation from the start, and that account is not alleged to penetrate the mystery of existence. Consider Aquinas and Augustine. Aquinas did not think it could be proved that the world did not always exist. It is only on the basis of revelation that Christians can justifiably believe the world and time began when God created it *ex nihilo* (*Summa Theologiae* 1a.46.2). "*Ex nihilo*" means from nothing at all. It does not mean out of himself (e.g. his substance), from pre-existing formless matter as with Plato's demiurge, or from anything whatever. But the idea of creation *ex nihilo* is fraught with difficulties. Given that every conceivable instance of creation seems to be a case of creation from something rather than from nothing (i.e. "*ex nihilo nihil fit*"), why suppose it possible to create something *ex nihilo*? Augustine – a formulator of the doctrine – entertains various questions about creation, including: "What made God create heaven and earth then, and not sooner? (*City of God* 11.4). But there is a point in this questioning beyond which Augustine will not, or thinks one cannot, go.[5]

Theism maintains that God freely created the world *ex nihilo*, but there are numerous views of what this means. Leaving aside difficulties with "creation *ex nihilo*," "free" also presents problems. According to Augustine, "God freely creating" the world does not mean "that God might or might not have created the world; or that he might have created it very differently; or that he may respond to what happens in it in a personal way. God, being wholly immutable, had to create precisely this world" (Ward).[6] For Augustine, then, God's "freely" choosing to create the world does not mean what one ordinarily would take it to mean – which is that God chooses to create this world and not some other etc. This *seems* to be Aquinas's view. But Keith Ward argues that it is not Aquinas's position either if that position is interpreted apart from his questionable senses of "necessity." And if Aquinas's suspect notions of "necessity" are employed, the doctrine no longer means what it appears to – that God is "free" to create or not create.[7]

Before considering pantheistic views about creation it is useful to list some difficulties associated with the theistic doctrine. God is allegedly "timeless" and "eternal," but is the concept of eternity coherent, and can one conceive of a "timeless" being? Did time begin when the universe did? Where was God "before" creation? How can something be created out of nothing? Why did creation take place when it did and not before – and what was God doing in the "meantime"?[8] Why did God create this world and not some other – better – world? *Should* God have created anything at all? Is divine omniscience compatible with human freedom and responsibility? (If God knew how creation was going to turn out, are people responsible for their actions?) Are the doctrines of divine immutability, impassibility and simplicity compatible with the doctrine of creation? (How can an immutable being create?) Are they compatible with human and divine freedom and responsibility? If God created he universe and there is evil in the universe, then is God *in some sense* responsible for evil? (Ward argues that given Augustine's doctrine of creation God is responsible.) Is immutability etc. compatible with the efficacy of prayer and God's responsiveness to human action? Surely "response" appears to require change? Is omniscience compatible with immutability, simplicity etc.? Is God's timelessness compatible with biblical theology and the doctrine of redemption?[9]

Although many classical theists still regard the doctrines of divine simplicity, immutability and timelessness as both intelligible and essential to theism, most contemporary philosophical theists probably reject these doctrines and modify their conception of the God accordingly.[10] Of course pantheism (like atheism) can dispense with these problematic ingredients of theistic metaphysics outright.

If questions of origin are important for religious positions *per se* then pantheism must take account of them. Creation doctrines may be indispensable in theistic traditions because of the centrality of the notion of God as creator and the ways it is connected to essential theistic tenets. (For example, God is worthy of worship partly because he is the creator.) Creation doctrines are usually part of the entire story a religion tells. They are a foundation for a world-view – for an account of how things are and why they are that way; and usually for why it is "good" they are that way despite seeming evidence to the contrary. It is because they constitute an important ground for a world-view and ethos that they are doctrinally significant. But creation doctrines are more central to some religions than to others. They are less relevant to non-theistic traditions with their very different notions of reality. Taoism is a perfect example. (This not only gives the basis for Taoism's rejection of a theory of divine creation, but foreshadows what I shall say about the pantheistic conception of evil, and the objectives and practice of pantheism.)

> The concept of the Tao precludes the theory of divine creation. In his [Lao Tzu's] allusions to the process of creation there is no hint of any anthropomorphic concept of deity, and in his notion of following the natural course there is no mention whatsoever of religious observances. On the contrary, he rejects the concept of a purposeful, active Heaven, and subordinates the earlier idea of a supremely powerful and absolutely good Heaven to the heterogeneously formed Tao. Thus, in the Tao Te Ching we have a clear statement of a naturalistic Heaven which is wholly indifferent to the struggles of human life. In Lao Tzu's philosophical system, it is man's lot to cope with the problems of the human sphere, and this can best be accomplished by emulating the pattern of the universe – the Tao – and developing according to our intrinsic natures. By developing according to what is natural, we not only realise our full human potential, but further, we do not interfere with the cosmic harmony.[11]

If accounts of origin are relevant to pantheism and other non-theistic traditions, then they will be embedded in a comprehensive non-theistic storyline of their own, and will function similarly in some ways to the way they do in theistic doctrines.

Creation is crucial to theism because it is an essential ingredient of its entire storyline beginning on the very "first day" and ending with judgement and salvation or damnation. It cosmically locates individuals and institutions by providing the world-view and ethos – the intellectual and affective wherewithal – necessary for avoiding and coping with meaninglessness and "anomie" (i.e. chaos and disorder). This is a universally necessary task according to Geertz and Berger. It is what constitutes the "problem of meaning" in human life or, though they do not use this description, "the human condition."[12]

Pantheism rejects the theistic storyline in its entirety because it rejects so much of what it is based on – like the theistic God. Spinoza employs some theistic terminology (e.g. blessedness, eternal), but, like Lao Tzu, he believes none of the theistic account including its creation doctrine. Pantheists see the theistic story as neither intellectually convincing nor emotionally satisfying; and so they are unable to employ the theistic strategy, with both its intellectual and affective aspects, for comprehending the world. Thus, even if pantheism must formulate its own story about creation, by rejecting theism it naturally avoids the problems mentioned generated by the theistic conception of God in relation to creation, as well as additional ones engendered in the Genesis myth.[13]

Assuming pantheism does require a doctrine or view about creation, what can be said positively about it?[14] Pantheism has a range of options unavailable to theism since the theistic doctrine is extrapolated from scripture. A pantheist might be a kind of existentialist with regard to questions like "Why is there anything at all?" Pantheists could believe existence is a brute fact, with no explanation possible. This might be seen as a refusal to deal with the issue of creation – as rejecting the idea that pantheism requires a theory of creation suited to the notion of a divine Unity. But this is not necessarily so. For all its seeming negativity, this is a positive position and not one that simply denies other views. It is a theory of origin or creation that could be acceptable to some pantheists.

Believing existence to be a brute fact in no way entails that a pantheist is committed to other existentialist theses. Like Sartre and Camus, pantheists may think that important questions of how to live, our attitude towards life and what we do, must take this brute fact into account. However, unlike such existentialists, this bare inexplicable fact of existence will not be the determinative factor in how one lives. The ultimate meaninglessness in life that some atheistic existentialists see as entailed by the bare fact of existence may be thoroughly mitigated for pantheists by the existence of a divine Unity. For the pantheist who believes existence is a brute fact, it is not only this belief that is determinative of the character of their life, but more importantly, it is the belief in the existence of a divine Unity. Pantheists need not interpret the existence of such a Unity as itself necessary or ultimately explicable. To do so may be to move towards theism.

One reason any account of origin, including the view of existence as a brute fact, might be rejected as being especially relevant to pantheism is that the account is not thought to be intrinsically connected to the notion of Unity. Indeed, pantheists might reject the idea that they require an account of creation intrinsic to their idea of Unity. Instead, *any* account that does not conflict with the way in which Unity is conceived of might be accepted. This is the view that pantheism, *qua* pantheism, requires no doctrine of creation.

It is unclear that pantheism requires a theory of creation; but if it does, must it be a specifically pantheistic account? Should the account be connected to the claim that "everything constitutes a Unity" in such a way that creation and Unity are essentially related? If not, then various theories of creation – though not that that required a personal creator – could be adapted to various models of pantheism. Any account of creation that did not conflict with the account of Unity could be acceptable. However, there would be nothing necessarily pantheistic about it, and any connection between creation and Unity would be extrinsic. Still, depending on how Unity was conceived, some accounts of origin could be more acceptable than others.

If there are any intrinsic connections between accounts of origin and Unity, the place to look is among the models of Unity outlined in section 2.1. The "genealogical model of the explanation of unity" is clearly *a propos*. In that model the idea of common origin – a kind of creation doctrine – is essential to Unity. Pantheism (i.e. Unity) is predicated on the basis of a common origin. Christopher Rowe says, "Thales, Anaximander, and Anaximenes, the Milesian monists appear to have claimed that what unifies the world is that it sprang from a single undifferentiated substance."[15] In the first instance at any rate, Unity is here predicated in terms of a common origin from a common substance. It is unclear if what is crucial to Unity is the common substance, the common origin from that common substance at a certain time (i.e. a common beginning in time), or both.

Apart from also positing the presence of a unifying principle that has an evaluative aspect, the idea of a common origin in terms of either substance or time seems too thin to support the claim of Unity. It is too close to unity in the bare logical sense rejected earlier as inadequate to pantheism. As was argued in section 2.1, even if facts about the world suffice to ensure Unity, an explanation of why this is so must in part be evaluative. A common origin in terms of substance or time does not carry evaluative implications in any obvious way. And in the case of the Milesians it might be a mistake to emphasise the significance they saw in a common origin. If they did believe in the Unity of all things, the belief may have had less to do with origin than Rowe supposes.[16]

We have seen that there must be an intrinsic connection between creation and pantheism for there to be a properly "pantheistic account of creation." But if creation is explained apart from any evaluative aspect, for example merely in terms of substance or time, then the connection between creation and pantheism must remain extrinsic. However, if creation is itself interpreted evaluatively, if there is an evaluative reason or basis for creation, this could be the basis of a belief in the existence of an all-inclusive Unity that is intrinsically linked to a theory of creation.

Theism explains why God created the world in partly evaluative terms. Creation is regarded as a good thing, and God creates the world "because" of his perfect goodness. This is so even though theism maintains that, although God freely chose to create the world, it would not have detracted from his perfect goodness had he not created the world, or had created some other world instead. But a pantheistic account of creation must first explain creation in terms of value and then show that it is necessarily connected to Unity (i.e. the basis of Unity), without referring to

181

the theistic God. So the evaluative basis for creation available in theism (e.g. God's perfect nature) is not available to the pantheist who wants a specifically pantheistic doctrine of creation. That is – it is not available to the pantheist who wants to interpret creation evaluatively so as to posit an intrinsic connection between creation and Unity.

John Leslie postulates a theory that explains creation solely in terms of value. If correct it could provide a basis for a truly pantheistic account of creation. It would provide such a basis if the "ethical requirement" that explained creation was also necessary for an account of Unity.[17] (I am not suggesting that Leslie thinks his account is pantheistic, or that it is necessarily pantheistic. He does not discuss pantheism.) He says,

> In an absence of all thinking beings and other existents, what could there be to serve as a creative factor? The only realities would be ones to do with possibilities: the eternal fact, for example, that a good universe (unlike a round square) really might exist, and the eternal need for it to do so. Might such a need have acted creatively, so perhaps deserving the name "God" which Platonist theologians would use here? Or can armchair reasoning, or experience of life's evils, prove its powerlessness to create anything?[18]

Thus, Leslie favourably considers the possibility that it is "the eternal need" for the existence of a good (i.e. valuable) universe that is the creative force which explains its existence. The "need" can create. He argues not for the possibility, but for the plausibility of the supposition that the universe exists because of an "ethical requirement" that it do so.[19] On Leslie's account, given the "ethical requirement" that it exist and the requirement's "creative effectiveness," the universe cannot fail to exist.

If Leslie is right, then his account of creation could play the kind of direct role in a pantheistic account of Unity that is required of a theory of creation if it is to be logically related to pantheism. Unity would be posited on the basis of a common origin in terms of value. The "ethical requirement" that the universe exist would explain why there is something rather than nothing in so far as any explanation is possible, and this would also be the grounds for positing a Unity. Furthermore, the goodness of the universe is presupposed in Leslie's account since the ethical requirement or "need" is for the existence of a good universe. Thus, a related ground for positing Unity may be the "goodness" attributed to the universe overall – a view shared by pantheists as diverse as Spinoza and Robinson Jeffers. There may be other ways of positing an intrinsic connection between a doctrine of creation and pantheism, but this appears to be the most direct.

If Leslie's hypothesis proves unsatisfactory, as I shall argue it does, then one could go back to supposing that pantheists need not have their own doctrine of creation. There may be no intrinsic connection between *any* theory of creation and any evaluative reason for believing a divine Unity exists. Unity will then be evaluatively based in a way unrelated to an account of creation. "Goodness," for example, may be attributed to the universe overall apart from an account of creation like Leslie's.

The principal and sufficient reason for rejecting Leslie's hypothesis is the obvious one that it is not clear how "an ethical requirement" in the absence of everything could create anything. Leslie says, "Contemplating the idea of ethical requiredness seems to me no guide to whether such requiredness is ever creatively effective, nor does it give the preference to any figure for the '*a priori* likelihood' of its effectiveness" (p. viii). But this frank admission misses the major objection. The difficulty does not have to do with what the chances might be for the creative effectiveness of an ethical requirement, or whether such requiredness is ever creatively effective. It has to do with making sense of the idea that such a requirement can by itself create. Leslie mentions various philosophers (e.g. Plato, Aristotle etc.) for whom the idea of "value" or the "good" plays a role in explaining creation. But where is it suggested that it is "value" itself, or an "ethical equirement" itself, that creates or explains existence? It is easy enough to see how such a requirement might be one factor among others that are together sufficient for creating something, but it is unclear how such a "requirement" by itself could be creative.[20] Considerations of "value" might inform intentions to create; or God's perfection may require God to create – though classical theism, as we have seen, denies this. But how could the world (or God) exist because it is ethically necessary that it do so?

Leslie's hypothesis is no advance over the doctrine of creation *ex nihilo*. It is no less mysterious, though it may be conceptually advantageous in that it does not require the timeless existence of a theistic God, thereby avoiding difficulties the concept of such a God poses in connection with creation.[21] Leslie does not explain *how* an ethical requirement can be creative. What does it mean? But an explanation is necessary for there to be reason to believe that such a concept is coherent (i.e. that such a requirement can account for creation).

Leslie says,

> Axiarchism is my label for theories picturing the world as ruled largely or entirely by value ... Until this century most philosophers had axiarchistic beliefs ... the one I find most intriguing views the universe as the product of a directly active ethical requirement, a requirement which *as a matter of fact* proves sufficient to create things ... It avoids proposing such brute facts as the inexplicable creative ability of an inexplicably existing benevolent deity.
>
> (p. 6)

It is clear that Leslie's theory does not avoid positing the brute facts he claims it does, and no reason is given for why he thinks it does. At best he substitutes one brute fact for another. In place of "the inexplicable creative ability of an inexplicably existing benevolent deity" he substitutes the brute fact of "a directly active ethical requirement." Neither the "requirement's" creative ability is explicable, nor its existence – and Leslie makes no effort to explain it. As far as "brute factuality" is concerned, the "creative ethical requirement" is at least on a par with the inexplicable creativity of an inexplicably existing deity. It may even be "more of a brute fact" since God's existence is ultimately explicable according to theism in terms of his nature (i.e. his "necessary" existence) – although this is simply a cipher for a brute fact as well. The "ethical requirement," however, merely proves sufficient to create things "*as a matter of fact* ... it sufficiency is far from guaranteed *as a matter of logic, deducible from definitions*" (p. 6).

Leslie's idea that an "ethical requirement" can create is not given enough content for its coherency to be judged. Instead of providing such content Leslie addresses the general question of whether the universe and order in it, including life, requires an explanation as opposed to being regarded as a brute fact. He focuses on teleological arguments for the existence of God. But suppose Leslie could show what Hume claims it is impossible to show: that the existence of the world requires an explanation.

184

He will still not have shown that his explanation in terms of an ethical requirement is a possible, let alone likely, explanation unless he can give content to the idea that such a "need" can literally create. His explanation is not even as acceptable as a theistic one, since despite difficulties inherent in the idea of creation *ex nihilo,* one at least understands how a being who already exists can create something – even if not from nothing.

Leslie's thesis is problematic for other reasons. It presupposes *strong* moral realism. Not only must at least some morally normative claims be true, but "value, for extreme axiarchism's purposes, must be a mappable reality, it cannot be one of any kind picked upon by [for example] naturalism" (p. 16). By "mappable reality" Leslie presumably means that value has a real ontological status. He says, "no mysteries need intrude here. In picturing a thing's constitution as making that thing's existence required or justified, we indicate only that the thing, *through being of a certain sort, is self-justifying...* That is, *can itself supply SOME ethical grounds for itself"* (p. 17). According to Leslie, even if no humans existed, "value" would exist, and it would exist not just as an abstraction like numbers can, but as a reality. Value has the kind of "reality" that is required for it to be (very) creative.

Whatever one's position towards moral realism in general might be Leslie's version is particularly problematic. It is similar in some respects, certainly in strength (i.e. ontological commitment), to the kind of moral realism that is presupposed in a divine command theory of ethics. Certainly his claim concerning the lack of any "intruding mystery" is questionable. On the "mystery scale," how the constitution of a thing might make the thing's existence ethically required arguably rates alongside creation *ex nihilo.* Leslie summarily dismisses emotivism, and prescriptivism as well as ethical naturalism.[22] Yet, his theory requires a more complete moral philosophy than he gives. Axiarchism rests on assumptions concerning the meaning, logical status, use, and more generally "metaphysics" of moral statements.

Leslie talks of the "need for a good universe" and not of the "need for a perfectly good universe," but if this is intended to allay the kinds of questions about evil so apparent in theism's creation doctrine it is hard to see that it can do so. If the need for good (i.e. the "ethical requirement") created the world then why is there evil? Was the ethical requirement's creative power something less than it might have been? Was the requirement "perfect" but the fulfilling of it less than perfect? What could be the reason for this failure given that nothing else existed? Or perhaps some other requirement existed as well; some other possibility that conflicted with the ethical requirement that there be a good universe? Should there not be a sufficient reason for evil explainable in terms of the "requirement" itself?

As Leslie seems to suggest, standard theodicies (i.e. justifications of God's goodness given the existence of evil) can probably be employed in his account even if "God" as the name of the creative requirement is dropped. For example, it could be argued that a world with free human beings capable of performing atrocities is better than one without such beings, and therefore the existence of evil does not necessarily conflict with the ethical requirement that a good, even perfectly good, universe exist. Such theodicies, though continually marketed, are wildly implausible. But there is no reason to suppose that both the "problem of evil" and associated responses to it are not present in Leslie's account of creation. There would be no reason, for instance, to prefer Leslie's account on the grounds that it bypasses some of the intractable problems, like the existence of evil, that beset theism in relation to its doctrine of creation.

The question "Can the 'good' create?" is relevant to the pantheist who wants to posit Unity on the basis of such a creative factor. But since it makes little sense to suppose the answer to the question is "yes," creation remains mysterious and Leslie's account fails. Since the account is unacceptable it is also inapplicable to pantheism. Unless some other intrinsic connection between Unity and creation can be found, one should assume either that pantheism does not require its own doctrine of creation or that such a doctrine will be extrinsic to the reasons the pantheist may give for positing a divine Unity. If so, pantheism's "improvement" over theism as regards the question of creation would best be seen as significant but limited. It is significant in that it does away with the array of difficulties generated by the theistic doctrine. However, it is limited in that creation remains a mystery, and pantheists, *qua* pantheists, have little to say by way of explaining it. Thus, a distinctive pantheistic view about creation probably has little to do with what pantheists believe or do.

It is useful to show why I think Leslie is unsuccessful in refuting Hume's principal objection(s) to the teleological argument, even though if he were successful it would not help establish his positive thesis concerning creation. Leslie's argument is worth discussing because, if Hume is mistaken, the pantheist may be forced into supposing (contrary to what pantheists like Lao Tzu and probably Spinoza do suppose) that there must be an explanation for creation, for perceived order and for the existence of Unity. However, pantheists can *either* accept or ignore Hume's objection, so long as pantheism is not concerned with showing that there is a reason for the existence of either the universe or the Unity – i.e. a reason that requires an explanation. Pantheism claims only that Unity exists and explains what constitutes it. It need not explain its existence or claim an explanation is possible. After discussing Hume's main objection to the teleological argument and Leslie's failure to meet it, I discuss the argument in relation to pantheism.

The teleological argument is an argument from analogy that attempts to show there is good reason to believe the universe has a designer (i.e. that God, or a designer, exists). Hume objects to the view that the world and its apparent order (e.g. its provision of the "unlikely" conditions that made life possible etc.) requires an explanation; can be explained; or that the "order" reasonably suggests that a "designer" created the world.[23] Hume's main objection is that, owing to the uniqueness of the universe, it is not logically possible to determine – or even make an educated guess – what the probability is of the existence of the order we discern in the universe. For the same reason we cannot determine what the probability is of the universe existing rather than not existing. We cannot say that the order we discern is less likely to have occurred in the absence of God (or some other reason for it) than if we suppose God exists and so constitutes an explanation for it. Hume's logical point can be summed up in the assertion that "there are no *a priori* probabilities." If we have no experience of other universes, which by hypothesis we cannot have given that this universe, in the sense of all that ever exists, is unique, then it is not possible to say what the probability is of there being such order as there is in the universe in the absence of a designer. There is no logical basis *whatsoever* for supposing a designer is responsible for the order. The order cannot, to any extent, indicate that it is more probable than not that a designer is responsible for it. The probability of there being such order apart from God is wholly indeterminate.

Contrary to the supposition that it is unique, suppose this universe were one of ten (or one of two). Hume would then say that if no other universe, or only a few others, had any of the regularities this one has, then if we reason in accordance with past experience we should conclude that there is something responsible for the order in this universe.[24] We should suppose that there is some reason for the order, even if we do not know what it might be, since on the basis of our experience of other (orderless) universes we can conclude that such order is to some extent otherwise improbable. If, *per impossibile,* our universe could be shown on the basis of experience to be relevantly different from the others in terms of being ordered, then we would be "justified" in positing something that caused the order. It would still be possible that it was just chance that our universe was ordered and the others were not. However, on the basis of (hypothetical) past experience with unordered universes we "should" suppose there was a reason for the difference – some relevant difference between our universe and the others. We could justifiably seek some explanation as to why our universe was ordered when the others were not. But of course there are no other universes with which to compare this one.

We have been supposing there is a discernible real "order" in the universe, but Hume questions even this. Hume questions if the "order" we discern really is "order" in the relevant sense of resulting from something other than chance. By his account we cannot say that it is. For all we know or are justified in believing, anything at all may follow anything else. The fact that all Bs we have seen follow all As we have seen does not show that this is "order" in the relevant sense of there being a reason for it, rather than it resulting from chance. We have no way of knowing the universe is actually structured in any way – that the order we discern is the result of structure or informing "laws" of any kind.[25] (Similarly if we had no experience with a pair of dice, or a relevantly similar pair, we would have no way of knowing that the dice turning up "twelve" every time they were ever thrown was not due to chance rather than, for example, "six" being written on all faces of both die.) According to Hume, for all we know, the laws of nature (which are merely universal descriptive generalisations on Hume's account) may change tomorrow.[26] For Hume there is ultimately no justification for claiming that the "order" we discern (e.g. Bs following As) really is "order" in the sense of there being any reason for it at all.

Richard Swinburne claims that Hume's principal objections to the teleological argument are decisive against supposing there is a reason for one kind of regularity (i.e. "regularities of co-presence" such as spatial regularities), but not against supposing an explanation (e.g. God) for another type of regularity (i.e. "regularities of succession" – or the laws of nature).[27] He argues that the uniqueness of the universe is not an obstacle to rationally supposing that it is likely that there be an explanation for the latter kind of order. He further claims that even as applied to unique situations – and all situations are unique in some respect – we can rationally make predictions about the situations' outcome. In short, he argues that it is not true that "there are no *a priori* probabilities." Swinburne gives no account of what Hume's response would be, but Hume would clearly reject his argument. Hume would say that either the kind of cases that Swinburne cites as examples of unique cases in which probabilities may be determined are not really unique, in that they are partially analogous to other cases of which we have experience, or else no determination of the probability in question can be made.[28]

Neither Swinburne nor Leslie recognise the logical character of Hume's objection, or if they do recognise it they do not direct their arguments against it. They think that some *kind* of order (this type rather than that), or some *amount* of order, or some combination of both, can suggest that it is probable that there is a reason for such order. But Hume's point is that, given the uniqueness of the universe (i.e. a uniqueness that *nothing else has* for the purposes of determining probability), no matter what kind or how much "order" there is, it is not possible to say whether it is indicative of a reason for the order (e.g. God), rather than the result of chance. The order might just be a brute fact and it is *impossible* to justifiably say otherwise. It does not matter that everything is unique in some respect. For Hume, the assertion that there are no *a priori* probabilities applies in an absolutely unique way to the universe. There is no analogy to be drawn between the sense in which the universe is unique and the sense in which anything else is unique. The universe is a kind of thing of which we have no experience of any other and can have none. Other things will be unique in some ways but not in others. Where probabilities are concerned, the uniqueness of the universe as a whole is *logically speaking* a special case. No determinations can be made concerning the probability of it either having or lacking some feature it actually has or lacks. And no determination can be made as to the likelihood of there existing some explanation and reason (e.g. God) for its having or lacking some feature (e.g. order) that it in fact has or lacks. Leslie asks: "when life as we know it balances on a razor edge, does this not suggest that it was placed in balance there?" (p. 122). Hume's answer is that it does not suggest this and logically it cannot. It is not possible to decide if the chances of life appearing in the universe instead of no life are 1 in a billion or a billion to 1. It cannot be determined which of these probabilities is at all more likely.

Consider the relevance that a teleological argument and the preceding has for pantheism and creation. Suppose that, as claimed previously, Unity is usually evaluatively based on a naturalistic ordering principle or force of some kind. (What follows is also applicable for Unity posited on other grounds, though in a less obvious way.) The pantheist is not concerned with proving the existence of something responsible for the ordering principle itself. Instead, the pantheist is concerned only with showing that she is justified in believing order exists, and that there is an ordering principle which accounts for the order. The existence of the ordering principle itself may be a brute fact. As far as Hume is concerned, if the pantheist tries to show there is a reason for such a principle, and so for the order that follows from it, then she will be in the same indefensible position as anyone who employs the teleological argument.

The pantheist, while accepting Hume's logical point concerning "no *a priori* probabilities," is in a better position to respond to Hume than is the theist who attempts to defend the teleological argument. Instead of defending the teleological argument, the pantheist argues for the more easily defensible position that there is a discernible order attributable to a discernible ordering principle(s). The pantheist can defend this view while accepting Hume's principal, and correct, objection to the teleological argument. The ordering principle, as far as the pantheist is concerned, is not indicative of a designer. Given the uniqueness of the universe we have no way of knowing what the probability would be of such a principle existing in the absence of a reason that explains it. Therefore we cannot say that the existence of such a principle is indicative of a "designer." In the absence of a specific pantheistic doctrine of creation, all of creation, including the existence of whatever ordering principle (or alternative basis) Unity is predicated upon, may be regarded as ultimately inexplicable by the pantheist. There may ultimately be no reason for the Unity.

Hume claims that the discernible "order" does not make it in any way probable that there is something that accounts for the order and so makes it explicable. And if no explanation is needed for the order – indeed for all we know *there is no "order" to explain* – then certainly none is needed for any ordering principle one might posit (without justification according to Hume) as responsible for the order.[29] The pantheist however claims both that there really is order, and that there is something responsible for the order such as a Unifying principle. But to reiterate: the pantheist need not claim there is anything responsible for the ordering principle itself. To do so would leave one open to Hume's logical objection to the teleological argument.

It is important to see that Hume's principal objection to the teleological argument ("there are no *a priori* probabilities") does not rest on his view that one cannot justifiably say that there is "order" in the world, or "forces" responsible for order, or laws of nature that are more than descriptive universal generalisations. His objection to the teleological argument is independent of these other views which Hume seeks to defend only in the context of his wider metaphysics.[30] This is why the pantheist, along with anyone else, can accept Hume's objection to the teleological argument while rejecting his other far more contentious claims. Only one who accepts a Humean analysis of causation, which rests on an acceptance of his metaphysical empiricism, will accept these other outrageous claims (e.g. that we are not justified in believing that a book will drop when we let go of it).

The pantheist accepts Hume's point that there are no *a priori* probabilities. Therefore, there is no reason to suppose that there is an explanation for the existence of some unifying principle – which in turn is the basis for alleging the existence of the divine Unity. There is no reason to suppose the existence of Unity requires or is capable of an explanation beyond explaining the grounds for positing the Unity. "Why" it exists in terms of some doctrine of creation is a moot point for the pantheist. The pantheist *may* just accept the existence of the divine Unity as a brute fact. But if a further explanation were sought, it would probably be extrinsic to the pantheistic position.

Some additional features of pantheism's treatment of creation can be discussed by considering the quotations cited at the beginning of this section. Jantzen says, "Whatever the doctrine of creation is, it is not a scientific explanation for the origin of universes."[31] The pantheist agrees. It is confusion to mistake theories of physical cosmology about the origin of the universe with theories intending to explain the causes and reasons (i.e. the "why?") of the origin conceptually prior to the point at which physical cosmology even begins. In principle, any doctrine of creation that really is a doctrine of creation and not admittedly (e.g. "creation science") or implicitly a scientific theory is compatible with *any* physical cosmologist's account of the beginning of the universe. This assumes of course that the cosmologist's account really is a scientific one and not admittedly or cryptically also a creation doctrine. There are no differences in the kinds of positions that the theist and pantheist can maintain with regard to *bona fide* theories of physical cosmology.

As a pantheist, one has no more to say about the acceptability of theories of physical cosmology than *qua* theist, the theist does. If Unity is based, for example, on a naturalistic model (e.g. a unifying principle), or even on a genealogical model (i.e. a common origin), this should not be interpreted in a way so as to conflict with scientific theories of the origin of the universe, or scientific theory of any kind. If "principle" or "origin" are interpreted evaluatively, as it was argued they must be if they are to be the basis of Unity, then whatever principles, laws of nature or accounts of origin that science can in principle account for, cannot strictly speaking be those that pantheists are fundamentally concerned with. Thus, pantheists probably do not require any special pantheistic account of creation. However, whatever creation theory they do have (if any) should not conflict with anything that physical cosmologists say about origin. Moreover, pantheism in general should not conflict with a *properly* scientific account of the world (i.e. an account that is not also philosophical).

The sense in which Spinoza and Berkeley claim that their theories are compatible with (correct) science is only partially the same as the sense in which it is being claimed that creation doctrine, or pantheism generally, must be compatible with science (e.g. cosmology) to be acceptable.[32] What Spinoza and Berkeley meant is that their theories were not inconsistent with what "science" could show to be true, and did not entail anything that science could show to be false. In this respect, creation doctrine, and pantheism in general, should be compatible with science (i.e. physical cosmology). (Berkeley and Spinoza thought their theories could account for the findings of science.) But what is being claimed here that is different and conflicts with what Spinoza and Berkeley say about science in relation to their philosophical theories is that creation doctrine is logically independent of scientific accounts of creation. They are different kinds of theories. That is why creation doctrines are impervious to empirical testing or finding, and also why they should be compatible with any physical cosmological account. The scientist who claims that it is "scientific" to deny that creation (in the relevant ultimate sense) is due to something "totally other" is confusing scientific cosmology with creation doctrine.

Concerning the second part of the quotation from Jantzen, she claims that what is important to the composer of Psalm 94: 9–10 is "that the one who originated our ability to perceive can hardly be without that ability himself; the creator of persons is personal." No explanation is given as to why the creator of persons must be a person except that theism requires it.[33] The claim may rest on the kind of metaphysical principle which some medievals and Descartes accepted: that a cause must have as great (or more) a degree of "reality" or "being" as its effect. But it does not even clearly follow from this that what is responsible for the existence of persons is personal.

Pantheists deny that the creator of persons – or what is responsible for the conditions that made the existence of persons possible – is personal. If evolution can adequately account for persons it seems both false and superfluous to claim that persons were created by something personal. Given an evolutionary account of the origin of persons, the claim that something personal (e.g. God) created persons is best interpreted not as a scientific claim that could conflict with evolution but as part of a theory or doctrine about creation. It is best taken as the claim that (i) something created the material universe in which persons evolved and (ii) only a person is capable of doing this. So indirectly something personal created persons. God, for example, made the Big Bang possible. This is neither a scientific account of the origin of persons nor an account of why the creator had to be a person. The view that the creator of persons must be a person is a natural theistic assumption made in a context in which the belief that God is a person is presupposed and absolutely central. As such, the pantheist rejects it.

Pantheists view this assumption about creation, along with the theistic concept of deity generally, as anthropocentric and anthropomorphic. This is what is most unacceptable to the pantheist. Whether the anthropomorphism relates to a creation doctrine or to doctrines of sin, grace and salvation, its rejection is central to a non-anthropocentric pantheistic world-view.

Joseph Priestley claims that "the maker of the . . . universe . . . must be a being separate from . . . the universe; which is a sufficient answer to the reasoning of Spinoza, who, making the universe itself to be God, did, in fact, deny that there was any God." Pantheism rejects the idea that "the maker" must be a being separate from the universe since, as we have seen, it rejects the idea that the maker must be a being, or even that there must be a maker. Pantheism also rejects any blanket separation or identification of the divine Unity and the universe – as have numerous Christian theologians with respect to the theistic God and the universe.[34] Pantheism maintains that in some ways, though not in others, the divine Unity and the universe are separate. As was argued in the section 2.1 on Unity, there is no complete or straightforward identification of the divine Unity and the universe for the pantheist. At any rate, even where pantheism does have an account of creation, as for example where the Tao is seen as engendering the "myriad things," there is no question of a personal creator.

The arguments in Chapter 3 show that "being separate from" can be understood in various ways, and that even in theistic terms not all of them are such that "being separate from the universe" is a necessary condition of being its creator. It is not even clear, to use Priestley's analogy, that "the maker of the table . . . must be different from the table." Why? What Priestley probably means, in part, in claiming that the maker of the universe must be "a being separate from the universe" is what theists generally mean: that the maker is capable of existing apart from the universe and possibly precedes it, whereas the universe cannot exist apart from the creator. Pantheists deny this because it denies theism. But it also denies that the divine Unity is "separate" from the universe, or that creation demands it, where such separation is seen to conflict with the all-inclusive nature of Unity. Priestley contends that Spinoza, or anyone who in some way identifies God and the universe (i.e. pantheists generally), is an atheist. This has been argued against in both Chapter 1 and section 2.1. The basis of such a claim is theistic chauvinism.

In distinguishing between creation *ex nihilo* and emanationism as he does, Macquarrie makes it easy to see why emanationism is often closely associated with pantheism. Emanationism is the view that "creation" is not a "making," but in some sense a "flowing forth" from God or its origin, as Macquarrie puts it. And, what "flows forth" "maintains a closer relation to [its] origin. It participates in the origin, and the origin participates in it."[35] He says, "emanationism does not necessarily lead to pantheism, but it does imply that in some sense God is in the world and the world is in God."

Even though doctrines of creation *ex nihilo* do not necessarily conflict with that central pantheistic claim, they are usually seen as doing so – partly because they are associated with other incompatible theistic elements (e.g. the creator is a person). On the other hand, emanationism appears to provide a doctrine which – if not an explicit ground on which to base pantheism – is at least one that is seen as congenial. As a doctrine of creation, it may even provide a partial basis for pantheism – as it has (arguably) for Plotinus,[36] Eriugena, and even for Spinoza where "God" is the immanent cause of all things. The view that God is the "immanent cause" of things is a kind of creation doctrine for Spinoza and a basis for Unity. So far as Lao Tzu has a doctrine of creation it too is emanationist. "The Tao engenders one, One engenders two, Two engenders three, And three engenders the myriad things" (*Tao Te Ching*, XLII). The Tao is "the primordial natural force, possessing an infinite supply of power and creativity."[37] Not only does the Tao create things – it is responsible for, or makes possible, their growth. "It nourishes them and develops them . . . provides for them and shelters them" (*Tao Te Ching*, LI).

Emanationism tends to affirm rather than deny a common ontological, substantial and evaluative base among everything that exists (e.g. whatever it is which creatively emanates, it is "Good"). It is therefore seen as in keeping with the central tenets of pantheism, and where pantheists adhere to a doctrine of creation it tends to be emanationist. Since Unity must partly be explained evaluatively, the fact that emanationism is often linked to the "Good" provides further reason for supposing it consonant with pantheism. Thus, although Macquarrie is right in claiming that the emanationist view of creation "does not necessarily lead to pantheism," the implication is that it often does. I have given some reason why this is not unexpected. Macquarrie denies, often mistakenly in my view, that positions to which emanationism is as central as the idea of a personal creator is to theism, are pantheistic. He does not, however, deny they contain important pantheistic elements.

4.2 EVIL

Pantheists are bound to find the fact of evil (and especially moral evil) an enormous embarrassment. It is difficult enough to square this fact with belief in an omnipotent and infinitely loving Creator. It is much more difficult to square it with the view that an evil world is an actual expression of God's perfect nature.[1]

H. P. Owen

This attempt to reconcile God's wisdom with human misery is especially characteristic of all currents within Christianity which – from Erigena to Teilhard de Chardin – succumbed to the temptation of pantheistic belief in the total absorption, at the end of time, of whatever this history of the world has produced. From this standpoint evil is ultimately not evil at all; we only think of it as such because the complete history of salvation is beyond our reach, because we absolutize certain fragments of it without realising that in the divine plan they serve the cause of good. Thus the question of evil is not so much solved as cancelled, since all the things we imagine to be evil are merely bricks for building a future perfection.[2]

Leszek Kolakowski

[Lao Tzu] felt that if there was a purposeful, knowledgeable providence, these terrible calamities would not occur.[3]

R. Young and R. Ames

I shall argue that the problem of evil is basically a theistic one that is not directly pertinent to pantheism. It is not, as Owen claims, "an embarrassment," intellectually speaking, to pantheists, nor can it be. The "problem of evil," as it appears in classical theism, cannot be relevant to pantheism, and this is not surprising since pantheism rejects all of the aspects of theism that are essential to generating the problem. The "problem of evil" is peculiar to theism. This conflicts with the common view among Spinoza's earliest critics that pantheism, unlike theism, can neither account for evil nor offer any resolution to the problem of evil.[4] It is my contention that the reason for claiming that pantheism cannot account for evil usually rests on an unwarranted conflation of pantheism with monism, and on the even more untoward supposition that the pantheist's "God" is "theistic" in important respects.

I am not claiming that pantheism need not address the existence of evil and associated moral issues. It offers both its own formulation(s) of a "problem of evil" and its own responses. However, the very idea of evil may be something the pantheist wishes to eschew. "Evil" is essentially a metaphysical rather than a moral concept; or it is moral concept with a particular theistic metaphysical commitment. The pantheist may prefer, as most contemporary ethical theorists do, to talk of what is morally or ethically right and wrong. The term "evil" could be retained and applied to particular (usually extreme) instances of moral wrongness, but it would be understood in a sense that divorces it from its original theological and metaphysical context.

Before returning to some of the reasons given for why pantheism is allegedly unable to cope with evil, it is necessary to examine the problem of evil as it is conceived of in its theistic context. For reasons that will be made clear, this is the only context in which the problem can be formulated. I shall also briefly examine some proposed solutions (i.e. theodicies) to the problem as it is theistically conceived. A theodicy is a vindication of God's goodness despite the evil that exists in the world. Theodicies attempt to show there is nothing irrational or otherwise improper in believing in the existence of a perfect God despite the existence of evil.[5] The purpose of doing so is, of course, not to prove that theistic responses to the problem are necessarily inadequate. Instead, I merely want to indicate why there is a *prima facie* case for supposing that theism cannot adequately resolve its problem of evil, while also showing that evil is not the problem for pantheists that theists remarkably have claimed it is.

After examining the theistic problem of evil and proposed theodicies, the applicability of prominent theistic theodicies to pantheism will be questioned and rejected. But this will not show that pantheism is at a logical disadvantage compared with theism in the attempt to make sense of evil. Rather, the theistic theodicies fail to apply to pantheism because pantheism dispenses both with the problem of evil itself and the need for any proposed solutions.[6]

4.2.1 Evil is mysterious

Although there are classical theistic doctrines of both creation and evil that attempt to "explain" and account for them in some way, these are among the most prominent issues that theism designates as "mystery." We *cannot* know, in this life at any rate, all there is to know, or even what we would like to know, about creation and evil. The theistic view is that some of the problems associated with these doctrines are cognitively impenetrable. Even revelation does not satisfactorily explain creation or evil, although the hope or belief often associated with theism is that in a life "after death" when one no longer sees "as through a glass darkly" some of the mystery may disappear.

Assigning the status of "mystery" to evil is one of the points, the principal point, of the story of Job. If God's "response" to Job, whirlwind and all, is regarded as a solution to the problem of evil, or an explanation as to why evil befell Job, the point of the story is lost. Interestingly, God refers to creation in his response to Job and intimates that the mystery associated with it carries over, or is in some sense similar, to the apparent lack of understanding Job shows with regard to his own situation. Job is at a loss, and it is classical theism's view that he is necessarily at a loss. From the human point of view there is no complete and adequate explanation. It is a mystery.

The same point is made by Dostoyevsky in *The Brothers Karamazou*. What Ivan is telling Alyosha is that there can be no intelligible reason why some of the evils that occur do occur given God's existence. There can be no rational justification for it. Ivan is rejecting any humanly intelligible vindication of God's goodness in view of such evil. He is rejecting theodicy *per se*. Ivan appears to acknowledge the mere possibility that there may be an explanation for the evil, and so a vindication of divine goodness, but in the end he rejects this. Since he does not see any conceivable way in which there could be a justification, he rejects the notion there is one, and defiantly rejects God as a result. Ivan wants not just a logically possible explanation for evil but some plausible explanation. And he sees the lack of any plausible explanation as grounds for rejecting any meaningful possibility of there being one.

That theism itself regards evil, and probably creation, as being penultimately mysterious is often overlooked by those who think that evil is, for example, simply to be explained in terms of the free will which human beings have and which an omnibenevolent God graciously gave us. (It is only penultimately mysterious because there may be some answers forthcoming in "life everlasting".) That evil is and remains a problem in this life is central to classical theism. Those who simply attribute it to the devil, in the case of physical evil, or free will in the case of persons, disregard the nature and character of the problem as it is seen within an important, even pre-eminent, strand of classical (and biblical) theism.

Despite Alvin Plantinga's denial, the Free Will Defence (discussed below) to the problem of evil is a theodicy, the defence is generally not meant simply as an argument for the *compatibility* of God's goodness with moral evil in the world. It is meant to be a theodicy. Even for Plantinga the Free Will Defence does not appear to be an argument for mere possibility. Free will is given as a plausible explanation for evil. Plantinga says,

> St. Augustine believes that natural evil ... is *in fact* to be ascribed to the activity of beings that are free and rational but non-human [i.e. devils]. [This is a *theodicy* and opposed to a *defence*.] The Free Will Defender, on the other hand,

need not assert that this is *true*; he says only that it is *possible*... He points to the possibility that natural evil is due to the actions of significantly free but non-human persons. We have noted the possibility that God could not have actualised a world with a better balance of moral good over moral evil than this one displays. Something similar holds here ... [7]

The natural reading of the Free Will Defence is to see it as an explanation for the evil, as an explanation of why God allows it, and how despite the evil he can remain perfectly good. The Free Will Defence *is* a theodicy. And since it is offering a kind of explanation *cum* justification for evil it is a classical misrepresentation of the nature of the problem – at least as the problem is illustrated in Job. Thus, Plantinga is engaged in theodicy and the kind he is engaged in is a type that at least some theists find fundamentally flawed – that of finding a rational justification for evil. Plantinga is a prime example of those contemporary theists that disregard the nature and character of the problem of evil as it has been traditionally conceived.[8]

It will be shown that for the pantheist evil need not be regarded as a mystery. People freely commit "evil" (i.e. do the morally wrong thing) and are responsible for it. But there is nothing cognitively impenetrable about this. The pantheist does not need to account for the fact of evil in view of an essential supposition concerning God's (or the Unity's) perfect goodness. And it is only this needing to "account for" or explain evil that generates the sense of mystery associated with evil for the theist. For some theists it may generate hopelessness more than mystery (e.g. Ivan).

4.2.2 Theism's problem with evil

The classical problem of evil concerns the alleged incompatibility between the existence of an omniscient, omnipotent and perfect good God with the existence of evil in the world. Is it *possible* for a morally perfect God who is omnipotent and omniscient to allow evil? Alternatively, the problem may be posed in terms of what is probable. Is it *probable* that God would allow such evils if he existed? If one looks at the problem of evil, and at the way in which pantheism has thus far been explicated, it is puzzling to see how one can think of the problem as arising for pantheism.

As indicated above, there are two forms of the argument from evil against the existence of God – the "logical argument" and "the empirical or probabilistic argument."[9] The logical argument from evil against the existence of God claims that the theist is committed to accepting all three of the following propositions: (1) God is omnipotent, omniscient and perfectly good; (2) God would prevent all preventable evil; (3) the world contains preventable evil. The argument alleges that these three propositions are inconsistent.[10] If God is perfectly good then he would prevent any evil that is preventable. Given that God is perfectly good, omnipotent and omniscient, he should prevent (preventable) evil. But there is evil in the world and it does not appear to be logically unpreventable – indeed some of it we prevent ourselves. Therefore the existence of an omnipotent etc. being is incompatible with the existence of evil. God "cannot" exist if evil does. The empirical argument from evil claims that the existence of evil makes it *highly unlikely* to suppose that a theistic God exists.[11]

Much of the argument is based on what is meant by preventable evil and what a perfectly good God would allow. Would a perfectly good God permit evil that is required for a greater good, rather than preventing all evil? Can God prevent all evil (e.g. by not creating anything at all)? Must a perfectly good God create the best of all possible worlds even if such a world contained evil? Or would a perfectly good God simply not allow any evil – even if it meant creating nothing at all? It might be argued that in not allowing evils which are logically required for a greater good, God would be allowing a greater evil than is necessary. So perhaps God's perfect goodness requires that any and all evil will be permitted if it is required for a greater good. What constitutes a "greater good" anyway? These are just some of the complexities involved in the problem at the outset.

The most immediate "way out" of the problem in either its logical or empirical form is to deny the truth of one of the propositions.[12] Thus, it has at times been denied that there really is evil in the world or that it is logically preventable.[13] Sometimes, as suggested above, it is argued that evil is necessary for a greater good, and so God (i.e. a perfectly good, omnipotent etc. being) would not prevent all preventable evil, but only evil that did not result in a greater good. It could be that by preventing certain evils God would thereby be allowing the occurrence of greater evils, and this is something, it is claimed, God would not do. The Free Will Defence is a version of this kind of argument.

"Vale of soul-making" theodicies are also versions of this kind of argument though less obviously so.[14] God could have created us so that our souls were, so to speak, "already made." However, this theodicy claims it is "better" that as free human beings we work towards the establishment of a relationship with God. It claims it is better that we "make our souls" and freely choose to relate to God, even if this involves the occurrence of evil. A relationship entered into as the result of God coercing us would be less valuable than one we sought to establish even though evil results from our having this freedom. A greater good allegedly results from God allowing individuals the freedom to develop in such a way that their doing evil, or even being unjust victims of it, is not precluded. People can only achieve full spiritual development by living life complete with its evils, vicissitudes, pains and joys. Not only is committing various evils oneself part of the learning process, but so is being the unjust victim of evil. Although Hick defends this theodicy he also calls attention to some of its obvious difficulties. He says, "so far as we can see, the soul-making process does in fact fail in our own world at least as often as it succeeds."[15] Hick's estimate is clearly optimistic and this theodicy is a half-lovely but wholly unconvincing idea. Is it *probable* that the evils in this world, both moral and physical, can each be traced back to some necessary role they play in the preparation of some soul? If there are any (let alone *many*) evils that cannot be accounted for in this way the theodicy fails.

The Free Will Defence is the argument most often employed to counter the logical argument from evil. I shall discuss it briefly before turning back to pantheism and evil.

The Free Will Defence claims that a world which contains free human beings capable of choosing between good and evil, and who sometimes choose to do evil but freely perform more good than evil, is on the whole more valuable than a world in which there is no freedom of choice and also no evil. According to the Defence, the reason for moral evil is basically freedom. The world is "better" if it has free human beings capable of doing evil, but who do more good than evil, than if there were no freedom – and so no evil. It is at least possible that moral evil is necessary if we are to have the amount of moral good in the world that this world has. If it were possible to create human beings so that we always freely chose to do the good then it would be possible to have a world with as much moral good in it as this one has without also having moral evil. But, according to Plantinga, we cannot be *created* so that we always freely choose to do the good.[16] Being free creatures we are not compelled to do evil, but nevertheless we will freely do evil. It is possible that we always freely choose to do the good (i.e. we are not compelled to do evil), but in fact we do not always choose good over evil. Alvin Plantinga states the Free Will Defence (minus some complications) as follows:

> A world containing creatures who are sometimes significantly free (and freely perform more good than evil actions) is more valuable, all else being equal, than a world containing no free creatures at all. Now God can create free creatures, but he cannot *cause* or *determine* them to do what is only right. For if he does so, then they are not significantly free after all; they do not do what is right *freely*. To create creatures capable of *moral good*, therefore, he must create creatures capable of moral evil; and he cannot leave these creatures *free* to perform evil and at the same time prevent them from doing so ... The heart of the Free Will Defence is the claim that it is *possible* that God could not have created a universe containing moral good (or as much moral good as this one contains) without creating one containing moral evil.[17]

Would not a better or more valuable world contain creatures like ourselves (or ourselves) who because of their natures did not choose any (or as much) evil as they do? Is not this the world that God, if he existed, would have created? Is such a restriction in terms of our natures a serious impediment to freedom? And even if it is, why is it not worth it overall? Contrary to J.L. Mackie and Anthony Flew, Plantinga argues that it is not possible for God to create free human beings who always freely choose to do the good. He argues against "compatibilism" – the position which maintains the compatibility between causal determinism and free will.[18] According to compatibilism God could causally determine us to always freely choose the good. God could create us with natures such that, given those natures, we were free to do evil, but we always chose not to.

203

If on one occasion we can choose to do the good freely why cannot we always choose to do the good freely? Why did not God create us with natures so that we did always choose to do the good? Plantinga sees the idea of God creating us with natures such that, because of those natures, we never choose to do evil as a serious restriction on human freedom. For the time being, let us grant it is a restriction on human freedom. It seems implausible to suppose that God would not have chosen (been morally required) to create us with that kind of limitation on our freedom. After all, no matter what kind of nature we have there are limitations that go with it. Suppose that God created us with "better" natures, morally speaking, than we do have. If this would have been a restriction on human freedom, then it is unclear that we should not have been created with such restrictions. Suppose we had much worse natures, morally speaking, than we in fact have. Suppose people went out of their way to "do evil" and did a great deal more of it than they do now. God could have instead created us (i.e. less moral versions of us) with those (worse) natures, but he did not.[19] Should the fact that we are morally better than what could have been the case be taken as a restriction on our freedom? Suppose given the limitation on what makes a "nature" a "human" nature God could not have created us so that, with such natures, we always "freely" choose to do the good. Is it implausible to suppose God could have made us with slightly better (i.e. morally better) natures than we do have? Would it be a restriction on human free will if people just did not even think of committing the kind of atrocities they do – or at least refused to act on them – usually or even always? And to reiterate, if it is a restriction on free will, is it plausible to maintain that God should not have so restricted us?

Plantinga fails to show that "it is *possible* that God *could not* [my emphasis] have created a universe containing moral good ... without creating one containing moral evil"; and he fails for reasons similar to those for why one cannot show conclusively that it is *possible* that God *could* create a universe containing moral good without creating one also containing moral evil. (Whether or not the "possibility" Plantinga addresses is a "plausible" supposition is a different matter.) In this case it is just not clear what is and what is not possible. Plantinga may seem right about the "possibility" he speaks of because one can always imagine that whatever evil there is such evil might be necessary for a greater good. No matter how it taxes one's imagination to think of how all such instances of evil might be required, how can one prove that it is not *possible* that the evil is required for the greater good? (If free will is regarded as of maximum value, or close to it, and freewill is taken as incompatible, or factually incongruous, with humans always freely choosing to do the good, then whatever evil is performed can always be taken as necessary to, or promoting, a greater good – namely free will.) In this case imagination is a poor test of coherence. The "possibility" Plantinga argues on behalf of must be tested against the "possibility" of a state of affairs with which it is inconsistent; a state of affairs such that if it were possible it would show that Plantinga must be mistaken in what he argues is possible. Plantinga claims to have refuted the possibility of just such a state of affairs in an argument against a view held by Mackie and Flew. He argues that compatibilism is essential to their view, and that compatibilism is incoherent. But is he right?

Mackie and Flew argue that if it is logically possible for humans to freely choose the good on one occasion, then (a) it is logically possible that they can freely choose to do the good on every occasion, and (b) God could have created them so that they always freely choose to do the good. Leaving Mackie and Flew to one side for the moment, it is not clear that this view requires compatibilism. No mention is being made of God "causally determining" how people choose. It might be possible that, given how humans were created (i.e. their natures), they freely choose to do the right thing and could choose otherwise on every occasion. Whenever one acts one always acts in accordance with one's nature and so it might be claimed that every action is unfree if "acting in accordance with one's nature" means that one's actions are always causally determined. In general, to talk of acting in accordance with one's nature does not commit one to the view that one's action is causally determined. Indeed, it is more natural to suppose that one is causally determined when one is acting out of character – i.e. not in accordance with one's nature. However, even if the Mackie–Flew view does rest on compatibilism it is not clear that compatibilism is false. If I have a certain nature (e.g. a totally good one) and act in accordance with it, then even if I am causally determined to act that way given my nature, why is that necessarily a restriction on my free will? I am acting in accordance with my nature and I am choosing to do so. That is part of who I am given my nature. I might even be seen as being more free (i.e. not constrained by evil impulses).

In short, it seems possible that humans could have been created so that they always freely choose to do the good, and this does not obviously entail that one is causally determined to do the good. But even if it does entail causal determination, it is not clear that such determinism rules out free will. And of course it neither entails, nor in any way suggests, that a perfectly good God would not have put at least certain constraints on what human beings are "free" to do.

Theodicy requires more than merely showing that God's goodness is logically compatible with the evil that exists in the world.[20] It involves a justification of such goodness in the light of evil – where "justification" involves more than showing the logical consistency of there existing evil and God. Job could not care less about the logical consistency of the position – as could Ivan in *The Brothers Karamazov*. The question of consistency can be no more than a prolegomena to a theodicy. Both Adams and Plantinga seem to be concerned not with just showing the consistency of believing in God's goodness despite the existence of evil, but also in justifying God's goodness despite the evil. In so far as they do this they misunderstand Job and trivialise the problem.[21]

Job's problem was that he could see no justification for the evil that befell him – not that he took it to be inconsistent with God's moral perfection. We can assume Job rejects the Free Will Defence as grounds for his misfortune. The rejection is implicit in the story. Similarly we can assume that Job would reject Adams's thesis and happily trade places with his "significant other" (i.e. the person who he is almost identical with) in the better world in which the misfortunes did not occur. What troubles Job is that he does not see how God could have allowed the misfortune to befall him and still be the perfect being he always took him to be. What bothers Job is not the question of whether the existence of evil is compatible with God's existence. Indeed Job *knows* that God exists and does not doubt it for a minute. What bothers Job is that he does not see how to reconcile God's goodness with the evil.

I have claimed that efforts to prove that it is logically possible that evil may be necessary for a greater good are inconclusive. If free will is regarded as incompatible with God having created us to always choose to do the good, and is valued so highly that the possession of it outweighs whatever value there might be in constraining it, then it is logically possible that no matter what the evil is or how much of it there is, so long as it is freely done it is a morally better world with it than without it. Although the arguments are inconclusive, if one does assume that it is logically possible that evil is necessary for the greater moral good, then God's perfect goodness entails that he would allow them rather than prevent them.

Given, for example, that the Free Will Defence against the logical argument from evil cannot conclusively be shown to be mistaken, the empirical version of the argument from evil seems to be the more viable or useful one. Anyone who is employing an argument from evil against the existence of God should not be troubled by the move from the logical to the empirical version of the argument since the alleged logical possibility of the evil in the world actually being required for a greater good remains, for them, *merely a possibility* (e.g. as improbable as it can get and still remain possible). It suffices that the existence of some evils seems so unnecessary and horrific, or not horrific but just evil, that it is not just psychologically impossible to believe they are required for a greater good but epistemically unjustified (in the extreme) as well.[22]

4.2.3 Pantheism and the theistic problem of evil

Given the classical argument from evil in either its logical or empirical version it is surprising that anyone should think evil presents any problem whatsoever for the pantheist; e.g that evil counts against the existence of the pantheistic Unity in a way similar to the way in which it counts against the existence of the theistic God. Evil *might* be taken to be indicative of a lack of pantheistic Unity, as evidence of some kind of chaos instead. But it cannot count against the existence of a pantheistic Unity in the way it can count against the existence of a theistic God. The argument from evil states that given the following propositions it is either impossible that God exists or it improbable that God exists. (1) God is omnipotent, omniscient and perfectly good. (2) God would prevent all preventable evil. (3) The world contains preventable evil. The pantheist rejects the proposition needed to generate the problem to begin with. The pantheist accepts (3) "The world contains preventable evil." The pantheist also accepts that *if* there was a theistic God, which for the pantheist *ex hypothesi* there is not, then (2) "God would prevent preventable evil." But the pantheist rejects (1) "God is omnipotent, omniscient and perfectly good." Undeniably there is evil in the world that could be prevented, and supposing there was a theistic God one would assume that he would prevent it. But since there is no such God why suppose that proposition (3) requires some kind of special explanation or is cause for any "unease" on the part of the pantheist? The existence of preventable evil, for all that has been said thus far, does not even constitute a *prima facie* reason for rejecting either the coherence of a pantheistic notion of Unity or the probability of the existence of Unity. (3) is not incompatible with anything the pantheist believes to be true. Certainly it is not incompatible with (1) since the pantheist denies the truth of (1), and it is not incompatible with (2) which is only hypothetically true for the pantheist. The pantheist has no need *either* to explain evil or to *explain evil away* – at least not in any way resembling theism's need to do so.

Evil may be a problem for the pantheist, but it is not the kind of problem that it is for the theist. It does not even conflict, *prima facie*, with the existence of a divine Unity. Pantheism does not claim that its divine Unity is a "perfect being" or being at all (generally), or that it is omniscient etc. Surely it is mistaken to interpret Spinoza's "God" as "perfect" and "omniscient" etc. in anything like the way these predicates are interpreted theistically as applying to God. It might be supposed that the existence of evil is inconsistent or incongruous with the "divinity" of the Unity. But this would have to argued. In theism it is assumed that what is divine cannot also be (in part) evil. But why assume this is the case with pantheism? Even in Otto's account of the "holy" the holy has a demonic aspect. There seems little reason to suppose that what is divine cannot also, in part, be evil. At any rate, there is little reason for the pantheist to argue that what is divine can also be evil, since they can deny that evil falls within the purview of the divine Unity. To say that everything that exists constitutes a divine Unity (i.e. pantheism's essential claim) need not be interpreted in such a way that it entails that all parts and every aspect of the Unity is divine or good. There can be a Unity and it can be divine without everything about it always, or even sometimes, being divine.[23]

It would be a mistake however to think that evil is fundamentally, or only, a problem in moral philosophy for the pantheist (i.e. that it has nothing to do with one's pantheism). It is a mistake unless "moral philosophy" is interpreted rather broadly so as to include various metaphysical assumptions. (All moral philosophy, whether or not it explicitly acknowledges them, requires metaphysical assumptions.) Evil – or "morality" in general – will have a religious dimension for the pantheist because answers and approaches to some of the fundamental questions of moral philosophy must be connected in various ways to one's understanding of the nature of the divine Unity. An "evil" action for a pantheist will be one that works against the Unity. It will be one that is seen as disruptive of the Unity in some way. If pantheism is a genuinely religious position there will have to be intrinsic connections between its understanding of the divine Unity and what the pantheist regards as the right or valuable thing to do etc. This is an affirmation of Geertz's claim that a religion's world-view and ethos are dynamically interactive; and that what it is that a particular cultural system (i.e. religion) sees as morally right and wrong reflects the way in which it understands the nature of ultimate reality (i.e. how it thinks things really are).[24]

Because pantheism, like any other religion, is fundamentally concerned with the "problem of meaning," and because "evil" is always a central ingredient of that problem, pantheism must concern itself with "evil" – though not the theistic formulation of the problem. In fact, evil is the primary concern of various pantheists. Arguably, it is the principal concern of Spinoza and the central topic of his *Ethics*. It does not present the kind of challenge in terms of consistency or plausibility that the theistic problem of evil presents for theism. Nevertheless, for Spinoza, evil is a problem and it takes the entire *Ethics* to show that it can only be overcome through a special kind of knowledge and understanding of "God or Nature."

4.2.4 Pantheism and evil: no worries

I now return to the widely held view that evil is as much of a problem, or more of one, for pantheism as it is for theism. Owen claims "It is difficult enough to square this fact [i.e. evil, and especially moral evil] with belief in an omnipotent and infinitely loving Creator. It is much more difficult to square it with the view that an evil world is an actual expression of God's perfect nature." A claim similar to Owen's is made by Spinoza's early critic Pierre Bayle in his *Historical and Critical Dictionary*.[25] Fredrick M. Barnard says,

> Bayle described Spinoza's philosophy as "the most absurd and monstrous hypothesis that can be envisaged, contrary to the most evident notions of our mind." Bayle's antagonism to Spinoza's philosophy arose primarily from his dissatisfaction with monism as a solution to the problem of evil. That such an extreme evil as war could exist among men who are but modes of one and the same infinite, eternal, and self-sufficient substance seemed particularly outrageous to him.[26]

In one of the passages Barnard is referring to Bayle says:

> Here is a philosopher [Spinoza] who finds it good that God be both the agent and the victim of all the crimes and miseries of man ... that there should be wars and battles when men are only the modifications of the same being, when consequently, only God acts ... is what surpasses all the monstrosities and chimerical disorders of the craziest people who were ever put away in lunatic asylums ... modes do nothing; and it is the substances alone that act and are acted upon.[27]

As Barnard notes, Bayle's objection is directed particularly to Spinoza's monism. Since Owen claims that "pantheists are monists," his view that evil ("especially moral evil") is an especially severe problem for pantheism should also be seen as directed primarily at monism's rather than pantheism's alleged inability to deal with the problem of evil. Since I have distinguished monism from pantheism, the kind of objection Bayle raises against Spinoza in particular, and Owen raises against pantheism generally, will miss its mark against any pantheistic view that is not fundamentally based on substantival monism. Given what has already been said about the basis of pantheism and Unity, and how inconsequential monism is to it, the Bayle–Owen objection will apply to only very few versions of (monistic) pantheism. It may not even be applicable to Spinoza's pantheism unless it is understood in a way that sees it resting exclusively on his substance monism. Spinoza would not deny that it is modes of the single substance that are warring. But why see this as objectionable? Bayle seems to think of it as a single person split in two and committing atrocities against itself – a kind of ontological schizophrenia. But no single "person" is posited by pantheists – only a Unity. Furthermore, the relevance of the kind of ontological consideration Bayle thinks so crucial is dubious. Bayle never says why it is important.

Nevertheless, in view of the classical theistic doctrine of creation and the problem of evil, there is something more fundamentally problematic in the Bayle–Owen criticism. Bayle finds it "monstrous" that wars can exist among modes of the same substance. And Owen finds it difficult to imagine how pantheism can account for evil if the world and the evil in it "is an actual expression of God's perfect nature." Bayle and Owen claim, implicitly and explicitly, that pantheism, because of its monism, is "substantially" (pun intended) worse off than theism when it comes to explaining or justifying evil. Yet surely theism fares no better in terms of this kind of "ontologically" related responsibility for evil. Given the doctrine of creation *ex nihilo* God must be (as both Grace Jantzen and Keith Ward acknowledge), in some sense, responsible for evil in the world.[28] Theism's claim that God and the world are ontologically distinct hardly resolves the aspect of the problem with evil that is objectionable to both Bayle and Owen. Suppose one grants the theistic hypothesis that the world and God are not co-substantial but are ontologically distinct. Why would Bayle find "warring" less "monstrous" among people who are not modes of the same substance but are nevertheless created by an infinite, eternal, self- subsistent and perfectly good substance? Pantheism is at least no worse off than theism here. What is so particularly objectionable about modes that fight? Perhaps it disrupts the kind of Unity posited by pantheists. But this would have to be established and Bayle does not do so. What is more objectionable about modes fighting than people (who are not modes) fighting? And why would Owen think that the idea of "an evil world [which] is an actual expression of God's perfect nature" is considerably more difficult to make sense of, or "justify," then a world that is freely created *ex nihilo* by God and contains evil? Leaving these questions aside, the pantheist is not committed to the view that Owen thinks she is; that the evil in the world, or "an evil world," "is an actual expression of God's perfect nature."

According to classical theism, people from Adam on down are responsible for the evil present in the world since they freely choose to commit it. (This refers to moral evil but not to physical evil such as earthquakes. The "devil" is sometimes taken to be responsible for physical evil – as he (possibly) is, for example, by Alvin Plantinga. Thus, physical evil is also a type of "moral evil" attributable to free (devilish) agents.)[29] It is peculiarly alleged that the human race is partly responsible for Adam's sin of disobedience and so is being punished for it. Nevertheless, an aspect of responsibility must adhere to the creator as well. If not, why not? And "if not," then why suppose the pantheistic Unity must bear more of, or a different kind of, responsibility for its modes than God does for his creation? A lot of weight is being put on the significance of substance by Bayle and Owen here – more than pantheists themselves put on it, or should put on it. If pantheists are not monists, then what Bayle and Owen are really arguing for is that monism cannot account for evil – or rather that the problem of evil cannot be resolved in a monistic metaphysical context. But even this claim is unconvincing. Given that God created the world which contains evil, why should not monism be able to offer explanations for evil not too different from those hypothesised in the context of theistic pluralism? The idea that monism cannot give an account of evil is itself based on a theistic assumption that the monistic "One" must be good, whatever else it is, and if it is good then no evil can come from it. This is an odd supposition to make in the context of theism since, given the theistic doctrine of creation, God created a world that has evil in it and so in effect evil, like everything else, comes partly from God.

There are no cases I know of in which pantheism's alleged inability to account for evil is based on some contemporary theory of ethics or purely ethical considerations. Instead, as with Bayle and Owen, cases of pantheism's alleged inability to deal with evil are often based on the acceptance of some aspect of theistic metaphysics (e.g. concerning the nature of evil) and on the conflation of pantheism with monism. It is then claimed that monism cannot account for evil. For example, "evil" is sometimes conceived of in theistic metaphysics not as being anything "positive" but only as "privation." An argument by Paul Siwek illustrates this. He says,

Evil is a privation. How could this exist in a Being who, by hypothesis, exists all alone? Since he alone possesses exist-ence, he exists only by his own strength: it is quite clear that in this case he owes absolutely nothing to others. Now, how could such a being lack any reality or perfection, which is due to him? Limitation, Spinoza affirms, can only come from outside . . . But, also according to Spinoza, outside of God nothing exists. Moreover, the Being who exists by virtue of his own essence, must possess being in all its fullness, and is therefore necessarily infinite. How then could such a being ever find itself affected by a privation of any kind? . . . the only reality that so exists, God, is confused by the Pantheists with universal being . . . universal being does not admit in itself any limitation, any restriction, conse-quently it admits no imperfection. How then could Evil be introduced into the world? . . . there is no room for Evil in pantheistic monism. That which we call "Evil" would be an illusion . . . [30]

The pantheist rejects the medieval theistic notion that evil is a privation in the sense that it is nothing real but is only constituted by a lack of "being" of reality or perfection. The sense in which evil might be associated with the notion of "privation" for the pantheist would be a very different one. Evil may at times reflect disunity or the absence of whatever it is the pantheistic Unity is predicated upon. Siwek thinks that pantheism claims there is a "Being who, by hypothesis, exists all alone." But pantheism (i.e. non-personal pantheism) rejects the idea that the Unity is a "Being" and it also rejects the idea that the Unity must "exist all alone." (Siwek focuses on Spinoza, but he too rejected the idea that God is a Being.) Unity must "exist alone" only if it is inter-preted trivially as "all that exists." The idea that evil comes from "limitation" or other kind of "privation" is based in the theistic idea that God who is perfect, infinite etc. cannot be limited or deprived in any way. Therefore, it is supposed that whatever is evil cannot be attributed to or associated with God who has the highest degree of reality possible. Only that which is finite can be (indeed must be) limited or deprived. But the pantheist rejects (or should reject) all of this, since she does not accept the existence of a perfect infinite God to begin with. Pantheism is the view that there exists an all-inclusive divine Unity. It is not (necessarily) the view that there exists a perfect and infinite God. There are other reasons to reject this view as well – including its intelligibility. The notion of "degrees of reality" plays no role in contemporary metaphysics.

Another reason evil is taken to be an irresolvable problem for pantheism is because pantheism is equated with Spinoza and his strict determinism and determinism undermines moral responsibility. According to Spinoza, "freedom" properly understood has nothing to do with free will. Free will is an illusion. But if everything is strictly determined and free will is an illusion then there can be no human moral responsibility since such responsibility presupposes freedom. Henry Oldenburg, the secretary of the Royal Society, made this point in a letter to Spinoza. "If we men are, in all our actions, moral as well as natural, under the power of God, like clay in the hands of the potter, with what face can any of us be accused of doing this or that, seeing that it was impossible for him to do otherwise? Should we not be able to cast all responsibility on God?"[31] This was, and perhaps still is, one of the principal objections to Spinoza's view of "freedom" and his entire metaphysical system – that it undermines morality. Determinism of the Spinozistic variety was also seen as undermining any purpose and meaning in life. Spinoza, of course, denied this as well. For Spinoza real purpose and meaning (i.e. what constitutes meaning and purpose in life) could only be understood in the context of his system, but this is not to say that purpose and meaning are not generally a part of people's lives according to Spinoza.

Although strict determinism may be intrinsic to Spinoza's system it is in no way intrinsic to pantheism *per se*. Pantheists will claim that whatever the conditions of freedom are that are necessary for, or presupposed by, the notion of genuine moral responsibility, these conditions obtain in the Unity. Why suppose that the inclusion of these conditions is not consistent with a pantheistic criterion of Unity? Pantheists do not deny free will and they do not deny moral responsibility. Determinism is the exception, not the rule, in pantheism. Neither meaning nor purpose in life, moral responsibility, nor freedom are denied by pantheists.

In so far as evil is interpreted in terms of theistic metaphysical doctrines pantheism rejects the interpretation. Where evil, or immorality, is considered apart from theism and put in the context of some ethical theory of goodness and account of what makes an action a moral one, various options for discussing what is right and wrong, good and bad, are open to pantheism. But there is no problem of evil in any theistic sense. To speak of a "problem of evil" is already to speak of a fundamentally theistic problem in the context of a fundamentally theistic framework – all of which the pantheist rejects. For the pantheist, evil is not something that has to be accounted for or interpreted in such a way so as to be consistent with God's perfect goodness. The problem of evil as such arises only for the theist and only because the theist maintains, as essential, the belief that God is perfectly good, omnipotent etc., and must then explain why and how evil occurs given this view of God's nature.[32] That is what theodicy is about. The pantheist's ethical views will be related in significant ways to her account of Unity, but this has nothing to do with the theistic problem of evil. This just reflects that ethical analyses and concepts of all kinds – theistic, atheistic or whatever – are connected to various metaphysical views.

Bayle and Owen are not alone in conflating monism with pantheism and then denying that pantheism, because it is a form of monism, can adequately account for evil. If Marcus Ford is right, William James's argument against believing in a monistic universe (and the monistic "subspecies of pantheism" which he called "the philosophy of the absolute") and for believing in a "pluralistic universe" (and the pluralistic subspecies of pantheism which he called "radical empiricism") was motivated by his concern that monism could not account for evil. According to Ford, James's pluralism is fundamentally related to his "*ad hoc*" solution to the problem of evil and certain related philosophical assumptions. Ford says,

> Unable to deny the existence of real evil in the world, and unable to deny God's absolute goodness, James chose to assert that God is not all-inclusive – that there are other things (evil things, for example) which exist apart from God ... Ironically, pluralism ... is not a central tenet of pluralistic pantheism; it is simply an *ad hoc* solution to the classical problem of evil once James assumed that to be included in another's consciousness constitutes being controlled or determined by the other being ... it is only his *ad hoc* solution ... that distinguishes his "pluralistic" pantheism

from the monistic alternative . . . James's philosophy is itself essentially monistic; its pluralism is only accidental.[33]

James not only conflates monism with pantheism; he also conflates the pantheistic Unity with a kind of theistic God. Both the monistic and pluralistic varieties of pantheism he distinguishes are associated with theism in this way. The significant alternative for James is not theism or pantheism – they are too closely related – but rather monism or pluralism. Inherent in theism is a kind of pantheistic unity for James. In this regard James is not different from numerous other theistic mystics who take pantheism to be a natural extension of theism that is borne out in their experience.

In the cases discussed it is clearly monism rather than pantheism that presents what pantheism's critics see as its inherent inability to cope with the problem of evil. Once it is denied that there is a logical connection between pantheism and monism, then whatever problems evil is seen as causing for monism – however the existence of evil is seen as undermining or defeating monism – the same reasons will not necessarily hold against pantheism.

At any rate, just supposing that the world and God are ontologically or substantially distinct (i.e. just denying monism) does not appear to offer a basis for some fundamental resolution to the problem of evil.[34] The theistic responses to at least the empirical argument against the existence of God, devil and all, strain one's credulity. (Even where the existence of God is not questioned, proposed solutions to the problem are rebuffed by theists like Job.) The only advantage the theistic supposition that the world and God are distinct seems to offer is that there is no longer a sense in which God himself (e.g. via his attributes and modes) is performing the evil "against" himself. But this is hardly an advantage when one realises that pantheists, including Spinoza, are not operating with a notion of God as a person. The criticisms of Bayle and Owen assume that pantheists are operating in important ways with a theistic notion of deity. If pantheists are not employing a theistic concept of God, then why is it objectionable to suppose that modes of one and the same substance might war? Why is it objectionable to suppose that an evil world, or evil in the world, is an actual expression of God's (perfect) nature? It is theism, not pantheism, that claims God is perfect. Pantheistic Unity need not be "perfect" and so pantheism avoids various problems generated by "perfect-being theology" – including "evil," the "biggest" of them all.

What is it about evil, exactly, that Bayle and Owen thinks requires an explanation? Looking at the classical theistic problem of evil, it is difficult to discover any pantheistic analogue for it. It is a uniquely theistic problem and one that the pantheist can shrug off since its formulation entails an essentially theistic doctrine of deity. The criticisms of pantheism having to do with evil, taken to be so devastating for so long, have no force. Furthermore, the sense in which evil does present a real problem for pantheism, as it does for any religion, has been ignored. It is ignored because critical discourse in philosophical theology has been dominated, as it still is, by classical theism. It sets the agenda by setting the questions and treating the theistic context as a given. Bayle's and Owen's criticisms in particular fail because they rely on a quasi-theistic notion of deity that pantheists – including Spinoza who is their main target – do not accept. Given the classical theistic doctrine of creation, divine conservation etc. the view that pantheism is less able to cope with and account for evil than is theism is without foundation.

As soon as one disassociates pantheism from both monism and theism, the specific problems that evil may present for monism (from a theistic perspective) or theism are no longer applicable. Whether evil is an irresolvable problem for monism is beside the point here, but of course Spinoza denied that it was. In fact he claimed that *only* for monism was evil not a problem. From what has been said, evil is seen as a problem for monism primarily in the context of a theistic metaphysic. But the philosophical monist – *and there are no other kinds* – might well reject assumptions such as "evil is a privation." There is nothing intrinsic to monism that makes evil any problem at all for it – let alone an irresolvable one. The theistic attempt to show that evil is a problem for monism and pantheism rests on the illegitimate exportation of a problem that only makes sense in the context of theism.

Just as idealism "went quietly" from Anglo-American philosophy in the first part of this century, monism tended to go with it. Of course there are still idealists and idealism has had some recent defenders, including some in the analytic tradition (e.g. John Foster and Howard Robinson). But idealism and monism are no longer generally taken to be philosophically defensible positions. The pantheist, then, would be wise not to rely on assumptions that can only be made in the context of such positions. In this way it may be possible to distance pantheism from whatever untoward metaphysical commitments such positions entail. The pantheist, having abandoned a theistic world-view as untenable, will not want to opt for some other view that appears equally, or more, untenable.

4.3 ETHICS AND ECOLOGY

In a Word, every Thing in the Earth is organic... this justifies my Answer to a German Inn-Keeper, who impertinently importuned me to tell him, what Countryman I was? The Sun is my Father, the Earth my Mother, the World's my country, and all Men are my relations.[1]

John Toland

... the view that man in any sense rules over nature inevitably presumes that nature is not itself divine.[2]

John Passmore

The universe is altogether composed of eternal and indestructible matter. All matter is one infinite whole... Nature. It is however, incessantly combining and recombining into forms, or "modes". When portions of it combine into the mode of man, it becomes active... in all other forms it is passive. It follows from this community of matter that the interests of the whole material universe are intimately the interests of every individual man. This is the basic truth of morality.[3]

Bertrand Bronson (Remarks on the philosophy of John Stewart: "Walking Stewart")

If pantheism and monism were as closely related as H.P. Owen and others have taken them to be, then pantheistic ethics would have to be discussed in the larger context of monism and ethics. This was done to some extent in section 4.2. I shall assume, however, that whatever the relation between pantheism and monism is, and despite Spinoza, it is possible to give a general account of pantheistic ethics without referring in any essential way to the monism that pantheism may or may not be associated with. It is not "monistic ethics," but "pantheistic ethics" I shall be discussing.

I begin with an account of what the pantheist's ethical position is formally likely to be (e.g. objectivist etc.). I then discuss the relationship between pantheism and ecology in the context of the search for the metaphysical and ethical foundations for an ecological ethic. It is claimed that it is no accident that pantheism is often looked to for such foundations. Next, I draw a parallel between pantheistic ethics and a theistic divine command theory of ethics. Despite its implausibility, the divine command theory captures something about the relation between God and morality that is similar to what the pantheist wants to say about the relation between the Unity and what is morally correct. I conclude this selective examination of pantheistic ethics with the claim that, despite differences, pantheistic ethics are broadly speaking Aristotelian.

Pantheists, like theists, tend to be "moral realists." They believe it is an objective fact that some kinds of actions are ethically right and others wrong, and what is right and wrong is independent of what any person thinks is right and wrong. With the exception of religious ethics, moral realism has not been a widely accepted philosophical position in recent times.

According to Geoffrey Sayre-McCord the reason moral realism has not been accepted is because of "the common (mistaken) assumption that the only realist positions available in ethics are those that embrace supernatural properties and special powers of moral intuition" (i.e. non-naturalistic positions as explained below).[4] Theists, of course, do not regard this assumption as mistaken; or at least they see no reason to reject moral realism because it does "embrace supernatural properties and special powers of moral intuition." According to the theist, even if Sayre-McCord is correct in claiming that moral realism need not rely on such properties and powers (and it is unlikely that the theist would grant him this), it is not objectionable if it does. The pantheist, like the theist, will not be troubled by the fact that her moral realism is based on certain metaphysical assumptions that some will regard as otiose or unacceptable. Even if the pantheist eschews any notion of "supernatural" properties, her moral realism will be based on some non-natural property that will be equally objectionable to the new breed of moral realists who, as others before them have tried to do, base their realism on ethical "naturalism."[5]

"Natural properties" are properties such as being a certain

219

colour, shape, temperature or height, causing pain, "producing the greatest good for the greatest number" etc. They are properties that one can, in principle, verify that an object or action has or does not have. Some ethical "naturalists" (e.g. some Utilitarians) claim that moral properties are identical with natural properties. For example, a morally right action is sometimes equated with the action which "produces the greatest good (or happiness) for the greatest number." Others claim that moral properties are entailed by natural properties. Pantheists, however, generally believe that moral properties are distinct from natural properties and are not entailed by them. Thus, they are usually "non-naturalists."[6] Furthermore, pantheists, like theists, generally think that moral judgments, and value judgments generally, are not empirically verifiable – at least not in the way one verifies matters of fact generally. Paul Taylor describes non-naturalism in ethics as follows:

> In the view of the nonnaturalist . . . a value judgment is not a factual assertion about people's attitudes, nor indeed is it an assertion about *any* empirical fact or set of facts . . . value-predicates, such as "good" and "right," are names of special value-properties of things, and value-properties cannot be reduced to empirical [natural] properties . . . These properties (one might call them "objective values") are ultimate and irreducible . . . How do we *know* whether a given value judgment is true or false, according to nonnaturalism? . . . *by intuition* and by *self-evidence*.[7]

Contrary to non-naturalism, naturalism entails that moral claims are (to some extent) empirically verifiable in ways identical to those by which other matters of fact are usually verified. If one knows that having a particular moral property is entailed by the possession of certain natural properties, then showing that some action has such properties will thereby show it also has the moral property.

Despite their non-naturalism, pantheists, like theists, reject G.E. Moore's contention that these properties (i.e. goodness and badness) are ultimate and irreducible. For the theist the fact that "X is wrong" will be explained, and partially analysed, in terms of (even if not reducible to) nonnatural facts about God's will and nature. And for the pantheist the fact that "X is wrong" will be explained, and partially analysed, in terms of (even if not reducible to) non-natural facts about the divine Unity.[8]

Certainly, the pantheist, like most theists, would want to deny that their non-naturalism, unlike anti-naturalism according to Swinburne, can be undermined by what has been termed the "problem of supervenience." The anti-naturalist allows the logical possibility of two objects "being exactly alike in their natural properties, but differing in their moral properties – e.g. two actions of killing a man in exactly the same circumstances differing only in that the one action is right and the other wrong" (Swinburne).[9] If, as Swinburne claims, anti-naturalism does allow for the logical possibility described above, and if such a possibility is incoherent as Swinburne suggests, then not only is anti-naturalism incoherent, but any ethical theory that accepts the possibility described will similarly be incoherent.

Non-naturalism is the position most congenial to pantheism, but a pantheist could make a case for being an ethical naturalist – just as Swinburne makes a case for a naturalistic theistic ethics.[10] Pantheism leaves the option between ethical naturalism and ethical non-naturalism open. For the pantheist, though perhaps not for the theist, value properties and predicates may be empirical or natural, or supervene upon natural properties, even if they are not entailed by such properties. So pantheists may be ethical naturalists. This may be the case even if assertions containing value predicates are not taken to be empirically verifiable in any straightforward way as they often are for naturalism. Such value predicates are not "empirical" in a narrow sense in which facts in the physical or even psychological sciences are empirical; but neither are they facts about some *transcendent* reality. Pantheism may, in a sense, deny the existence of any properties that are not "natural." It depends on how much one is willing to broaden one's notion of "natural." But if, as Adams claims, "a nonnatural fact is one which does not consist simply in any fact or complex of facts which can be stated entirely in the languages of physics, chemistry, biology and human psychology,"[11] then the pantheist, like the theist, will maintain that ethical facts are non-natural facts. Given Adams's account of "non-natural," the fact that "X is wrong" is a non-natural objective fact according to the pantheist. Of course, classifications such as "objectivist" and "non-naturalist," constitute only a partial explanation of what pantheists' ethical views are.

It is not accidental that pantheism is often taken to be a view inherently sympathetic to ecological concerns. This makes a decision to deal with ecology alongside pantheistic ethics less artificial than it might be if I were discussing, for example, theism and ethics – or a particular normative theory of ethics. There is a tendency to picture pantheists (i.e. pantheists other than Spinoza) outdoors and in pastoral settings. This has roots in the Stoics' veneration of nature, and in the much later nature mysticism, and perhaps pantheism, of some of the nineteenth-century poets such as Wordsworth and Whitman. It has been fostered in the twentieth century by pantheists such as John Muir, Robinson Jeffers, D.H. Lawrence and Gary Snyder who explicitly "identify" with and extol nature, and claim people's close association and identification with "nature" and the "natural" is necessary to well-being. The belief in a divine Unity, and some kind of identification with that Unity, is seen as the basis for an ethical framework (and "way of life") that extends beyond the human to non-human and non-living things. The divine Unity is, after all, "all-inclusive." Consider some examples of alleged connections between pantheism, ethics and ecology.

In his article on "The Apprehension of Divinity in the Self and Cosmos in Plotinus," Hilary Armstrong says,

> Plotinus may give us a lead to a better understanding of the world and may help us to adjust our attitudes and evaluations in a way which may help us to deal with some of the most pressing problems of our time, and especially to do something towards closing the gap between man and non-human nature which has been widening through the Christian and rationalist centuries with, as we are now beginning to see, disastrous results.[12]

Armstrong sees in Plotinus a metaphysical basis for an environmental ethic. He suggests ways in which aspects of Plotinus' thought can serve to engender an adjustment in our "attitudes and evaluations" concerning non-human nature.

Grace Jantzen makes a claim similar to that of Armstrong's in regard to her own model of the world as God's body. She regards this model as pantheistic in important respects.

> The model of the universe as God's body helps to do justice to the beauty and value of nature, the importance of conser-

vation and ecological responsibility, the significance and dignity of the human body and human sexuality ... Those who have once seen themselves and the world about them, as the embodiment and self-manifestation of God are unlikely to continue to treat it in a cavalier way or feel it utterly alien or devoid of intrinsic significance and worth.[13]

Armstrong's view concerning Plotinus, and Jantzen's view concerning the implications of her model for ethics and ecology, are, as I have said, sometimes taken to be true of pantheism in general. For religiously inclined non-theists, pantheism is supposed to have the resources capable of (in Armstrong's words about Plotinus) "closing the gap between man and non-human nature which has been widening."

Whatever critics allege the shortfalls of pantheism to be, there is a prominent, if not prevalent, view that its implications (if it were true) would be a good thing for ecology, and for aspects of ethics having to do with the non-human (and the human). Thus, Genevieve Lloyd points to "Some contemporary philosophers concerned with ethical issues related to the environment [who] are looking to Spinoza in the hope of finding a firm metaphysical basis for environmental ethics." And she goes on to say,

Such a hope is by no means entirely misplaced. Spinoza ... is concerned with the integration of metaphysics and ethics, and with the metaphysical bases of ethical positions. A very dominant theme in his thought, moreover, is the cultivation of what can only be described as an attitude of reverence for nature ... Despite all this, it would, I think, be quite misplaced to claim Spinoza as patron philosopher of the environmental movement ... Anyone who looks to the *Ethics* for a viable, coherent metaphysical system to ground belief in the rights of the non-human will look in vain.[14]

Yet despite this, she attempts to extract from Spinoza some metaphysical ground for environmental ethics, and argues that this can be done even without assigning *rights to the non-human* on the basis of his system.

She suggests that Spinoza's metaphysical system can be the basis of a useful corrective not only to the environmentally unconcerned, but also to the approach of deep ecologists who think it important to assign rights to the non-human.[15] She says, for example,

> Spinoza cannot say: "Things (such as butterflies, whales, rainforests) are good, or have value, or have rights, independently of man." But he can say; "It is *good for man* to perceive things as independent of himself. It is good for man, that is, to perceive things as they really are.
>
> (p. 307)

And, it is clear that "seeing things as independent of himself" is, on Lloyd's view, "good" environmentally speaking – so much so that it is an attitude that we should engender in children.

> Children educated to regard themselves as "part of nature," would, for the most part, surely, orient themselves differently towards other species from those who are explicitly taught that man holds a privileged position in the universe. At least some of our exploitative responses to the non-human rest on the implicit belief that the rest of nature exists for us; and can be expected to wither away if this implicit belief is brought into the open and rejected.
>
> (p. 308)

Why does Lloyd think that seeing non-human things as "independent" can help ground an environmental ethic? According to Spinoza all things exist for their own sake and not for anything else's and they are all capable of their own form of self-realisation. But how can this be the basis for the kind of change in attitude that Lloyd rightly claims would be a good thing for the environment? A whale may be independent of me and I may recognise that I am part of nature and that the rest of nature does not exist for me etc. But why should I not use that whale "to my advantage" – just as Spinoza says I should – and anything else I can if I so desire? Granted that Spinoza does stress the importance of "seeing things as independent of oneself" there is no logical, or even psychological, connection between such a perspective by itself and a rejection of an exploitative approach to nature as Lloyd claims.

George Sessions points out a different metaphysical basis for an environmental ethic in Spinoza and, like Lloyd's, it is one that has nothing to do with attributing rights to non-humans. It is in our self-interest to preserve the environment and Spinoza endorses that which is done for self-preservation. Sessions does not call it this but the basis he finds in Spinoza seems to be that of an ethical egoist. What is ethical is what is in my self-interest.[16] Sessions says,

> It is clearly to our "advantage", as individuals and as a species, that the delicate equilibriums of ecosystem functioning, upon which our lives literally depend, remain viable. Thus, the very concept of what is involved in "seeking one's advantage" or "persevering in one's being in a rational way" [Spinoza's concept] is now seen to be open-ended and necessarily subject to revision in the light of new knowledge.[17]

Sessions does not mention ethical egoism and he certainly wants to base an environmental ethic in Spinoza's metaphysics in some other non-egotistical and non-anthropocentric way. Nevertheless, whatever Sessions' wider views, he has pointed out a basis in Spinoza for an approach to environmental ethics that does not rely on attributing rights to the non-human.

Ethical egoism is not an adequate basis for an environmental ethic however. Only given an unrealistically broad interpretation of what is in our "self-interest," and what is "good for persons," can these be supposed to be the basis for an adequate environmental ethic. Certainly Sessions, and probably Lloyd, does not regard self-interest as, by itself, a sound or adequate basis for environmental ethics. Only if one takes the definition of "self-interest" to be that it is in our self-interest not to (generally) "harm" living and non-living things can self-interest be seen as providing such a basis. A more plausible understanding of self-interest can provide a basis for many, but clearly not all, principles that are arguably necessary for an ethical approach to the environment. It is in our interest that we do not poison the air, but not (necessarily) that some species of fish survives – as opposed say to building the dam. Ethical egoism (like utilitarianism) may provide the "right" answers to environmental moral questions much of the time, but it will not do so all of the time, and it will do so for the wrong reasons. It fails as a general normative principle and basis for environmental ethics for the same reasons it fails as a basis for ethics generally. Pantheists do not, however, rely on ethical egoism or consequentialist theories such as utilitarianism as the normative basis for either their ethics generally or their environmental ethics. They rely instead on a metaphysical basis that tries to connect what is morally right and wrong with their own natures, the nature of other things and the nature of the divine Unity. Pantheists agree with Stuart Hampshire's claim that for Spinoza "Ethics without metaphysics must be nonsense; we must first know what our potentialities are and what our situation is as parts of Nature."[18]

Thus, although Spinoza is the best known pantheist, looking towards his metaphysics for a foundation for environmental ethics is, as Lloyd points out, not without its difficulties. After all, Spinoza rejected animal rights, and despite his view that man is part of nature (i.e. there is nothing else) this view is in "apparent tension" with "his treatment of morality as circumscribed by what is good for human beings ... [and his view] that other species can be ruthlessly exploited for human ends" (Lloyd).[19]

Whether or not Spinoza provides a suitable metaphysical basis for an environmental ethic depends, in part, on whether his metaphysics and ethics are acceptable. For that reason alone one might be suspicious of grounding an environmental ethic in Spinoza's philosophy. It is, by all accounts, obscure in many places and most certainly wrong in some of its fundamental contentions – e.g. its monism. But leaving Spinoza's particular system aside, it is often supposed that pantheism, *if it were "true,"* could offer a more suitable basis for an environmental ethic, and perhaps for ethics generally, than the Judeo-Christian tradition, or some non-religious alternatives such as utilitarianism, contractarianism, Kantian views etc. Some utilitarians etc. might disagree, but they might not. They could simply deny that pantheism is true. It is unlikely, however, that the committed theist, utilitarian etc. would, or can, agree that pantheism offers a better basis for an environmental ethic than their own ethical theory. This is because of meta-ethical considerations. The meaning of key ethical terms and the conditions governing their use in normative ethical theories are described in terms of normative principles characteristic of a particular system. The utilitarian cannot allow that a pantheist's ethical reasoning provides a sound basis for moral deliberation unless "utility," defined in terms of "happiness" or some other "greatest good," is the pantheist's supreme normative principle – which it is not.

Harold W. Wood Jr, a founder of the Universal Pantheist Society, claims that pantheism provides the foundation for an environmental ethic that the Judaeo-Christian tradition fails to. He says:

> Instead of a "conquer the Earth" mentality, pantheism teaches that respect and reverence for the Earth demands continuing attempts to understand ecosystems. Therefore, among religious viewpoints, pantheism is uniquely qualified to support a foundation for environmental ethics ... by learning to celebrate and revere such natural events ... people would be less likely to permit unfettered pollution to take place ... acid rain would not be seen as merely an inconvenience, but as a travesty against a holy manifestation ... the pantheist view provides a rationale ... which makes environmental conservation tantamount to loving God ... an ethical pantheist does not practice conservation out of simple self-interest, but rather as a religious motivation ... Pantheism does not advocate an ethics derived *from* natural phenomena ... The source of pantheist environmental ethics is not the natural behaviour of other animals as role models. Pantheism confirms the uniqueness of humanity, and its ethics derives from ... human abilities for empathy, compassion, and a mystical oneness with the rest of the natural world. Pantheist ethics has as its goal a closeness with nature ... a relationship with nature equivalent to traditional religion's relationship with God. It is a closeness based not upon imitation, but upon reverential communion.[20]

Wood takes pantheism to be the identification of deity with the forces and workings of nature – or simply with nature.[21]

Whether or not the "Judaeo-Christian tradition is one which motivates arrogant dominance or humble stewardship on our part towards nature" is of course debatable. The issue has been discussed by John Passmore, Robin Attfield and others.[22] But regardless of what one's views are concerning the attitude engendered by the Judeo-Christian tradition (e.g. Genesis 1: 26–30) towards nature; it seems to be presupposed by pantheists, and not only by pantheists, that the "attitude" pantheism engenders is metaphysically advantageous to the formulation of a much improved, and much needed, morally sound ecological ethic. Whether pantheism is advantageous in these ways, and just what the ecologically advantageous "attitude" that pantheism allegedly engenders is, needs to be critically examined. This is especially so given that it is, as we have seen, highly problematic to regard Spinoza's pantheism as providing either a metaphysical basis for an environmental ethic or as engendering an "attitude" that might prove environmentally beneficial. Presumably, even if a pantheistic environmental ethic has an essential affective component, being objectivist it must be based on something more than an "attitude."

Wood says, "The modern pantheist views the opportunity to interact with God-as-nature as an ethical religious pursuit compatible with a sound understanding and respect for the *natural* world as opposed to *supernatural* fiction" (p. 161). He claims, therefore, that pantheists should not take the following view of Reinhold Niebuhr as a criticism. Niebuhr says, "Pantheism inevitably strengthens those forces in religion which tend to sanctify the real rather than to inspire the ideal" (p. 161). But Wood is mistaken if he thinks pantheists would not take issue with Niebuhr. If Niebuhr is taken to mean that theism inspires the ideal at the expense of (i.e. by demeaning) the "real," then it *is more likely* that some theists (though only some) would take Niebuhr's view as a criticism. However, pantheists will also object to Niebuhr and claim that their emphasis on the "real" engenders more rather than less ideal inspiration. Both the theist and pantheist reject Niebuhr's dichotomy as a false one. The character of what a religion (or anyone) takes to be "ideal" is always determined by what is taken to be "real." Even in Vedānta where only Brahman is regarded as "real," "ideal" behaviour and goals are explained in terms of Brahman.

Wood is also mistaken in characterising pantheism as avoiding the speculative metaphysics he associates with what he terms theistic "*supernatural* fiction." He himself describes a pantheistic "relationship with nature [as] equivalent to traditional religion's relationship with God ... based ... upon reverential communion." The pantheist may deny that there is a "supernatural," if this means something outside of, or other than, the divine Unity. But positing a divine Unity and speculating about its nature is no different in type from theistic speculation. Even if the pantheist identifies Unity with nature (and this is not the usual case), she is not thereby avoiding metaphysics or necessarily refusing to postulate something transcendent. Surely what Wood understands by "nature," its value etc., is vastly different from "nature" as seen by the natural sciences.

Of course, for some, any alleged grounding of an environmental ethic in a pantheistic metaphysic is as pointless as a reliance on a theistic one. It is mysticism and religion – once again. I take it this is Andrew Brennan's view in *Thinking About Nature*. He argues that a variety of "frameworks" and perspectives are necessary for resolving ecological problems, but there is no room in that interdisciplinary approach for the religious. New attitudes and practices towards nature must depend on what "scientific ecology" tells us about humans, rather than on "ecological holism," or the speculations of other kinds of "metaphysical (non-biological) ecology."[23]

Brennan draws on an important distinction between "having moral rights" and having "moral considerability or standing." Thus, following Joel Feinberg, Michael Tooley and others, Brennan says that *perhaps*, "only items with interests can be possessors of rights, and thus be represented as suffering benefits and harms as a result of my behaviour." But he denies "that anything like the point about rights holds for moral considerability." Brennan says, "What is the nature of moral standing? It is the *value* that something has by virtue of the fact that concern for it enters, in a certain constraining way, into the deliberations of a moral agent" (pp. 139–40).[24] Thus, natural things (i.e. non-human and non-living things) may have moral claims in virtue of their moral standing even if they do not have rights.

Brennan argues that the foundation for a proper environmental ethic (i.e. "ecological humanism") is what he calls "ethical or moral holism."[25]

> [Ethical or moral holism] . . . involves a perspective on human nature. It takes seriously the idea that humans are social beings, finding their fulfilment in social living. Human beings are autonomous . . . they are . . . lacking in intrinsic functions. Who they are is then to some extent a matter of the commitments they take, the groups to which they attach themselves . . . Unlike the crow, humans have a choice over which identifications they will make . . . In terms of ecological humanism, our alienation from nature is also

a kind of alienation from ourselves, a failure to recognise ourselves in our real location in the world ... any ethic by which we are to live has to recognise our location in natural and social systems, and take account of our place in history ... Objects, systems, even the land forms around me deserve my respect, deserve ethical consideration simply by being what they are, where they are and interacting with other items in the way they do.

(pp. 194–5, 197, cf. pp. 192–3)

Brennan alleges that his "ecological humanism" takes account of what he sees as the principal deficiency in utilitarian, contract-arian and deontological ethical theories. "In each case, the trouble is that the theories try to give an account of persons who live in a society in a way that ignores the force of the claim that what I am is a function of where I am" (p. 179). But defenders of the theories Brennan criticises as inadequate – both on the general grounds cited above, and specifically as unable to provide a foundation for an environmental ethic – would deny Brennan's charge.[26] They need not deny that "what I am is [in part] a function of where I am," but they would deny this has the moral force Brennan claims it has. It may have more to do with an analysis of personal identity than with ethics.

The ethical theorists Brennan criticises would of course reject his solution to our ecological situation. That solution is a broad one and it is stated in terms of a reappraisal of the commitments we choose, and a reassessment of "our real location in the world." They would also reject his more basic positions of "ecological humanism" and "ethical polymorphism." "Ethical polymor-phism" is the view that "an ethic by which to live is not to be found by adopting one fundamental, substantive principle relative to which all our deliberations are to be resolved. Instead, we are prey to numerous different kinds of considerations originating from different directions, many of them with a good claim to be ethical ones."[27] They would regard both Brennan's solution, and more basic position, as fundamentally *ad hoc*. It is not just that Brennan's position lacks any supreme normative principle of the kind one finds, for example, in utilitarianism and Kantianism. (In the place of any such ultimate principle there is the dictum "what I am is [in part] a function of where I am." Perhaps in some ways this is taken to be a functional equivalent of a supreme normative principle?) Rather, what appears to be missing from Brennan's ethical holism are firm criteria for determining which, among the many ethical principles Brennan advocates, is overriding or applicable in particular cases. Brennan does not see this open-endedness as a drawback, but instead as integral to the "ethical polymorphism" he advocates. Yet, in the absence of a supreme normative principle, and criteria that enable us to choose between various principles that at times conflict, some might see his "ethical polymorphism" as epistemologically speaking implying ethical intuitionism. This is so despite his objectivism, moral realism and naturalism.

Pantheists and theists will respond to Brennan in the same way as do the ethical theorists he criticises. I am *not* here claiming that they would be correct in their response; only that (i) this is the approach they are likely to take, and (ii) more is needed to show that they would not be correct. The ecologically astute pantheist, and environmentally concerned theist, will agree with Brennan's ecological humanism which holds that "our alienation from nature is also a kind of alienation from ourselves, a failure to recognise ourselves in our real location in the world ... [and that] any ethic by which we are to live has to recognise our location in natural and social systems, and take account of our place in history." However, the pantheist, like the theist, utilitarian, existentialist or whatever, disagrees with Brennan as to what our location and place in history is. As Brennan recognises, so far as these theories employ an account of human nature – and some, such as contractarians and existentialists, attempt (unsuccessfully in Brennan's view) to eschew any such account – the accounts they rely on are quite different from his own. Yet, what one takes to be one's "real location" is not independent of one's view of human nature or ultimate reality.

Since "ecological humanism" itself rests on metaphysical assumptions, Brennan's dismissal of what he takes to be needlessly metaphysical and religious approaches to environmental ethics is premature. One cannot eschew such approaches *in general* and then employ particular metaphysical positions in defence of one's own meta-ethical and normative position. Brennan's position concerning the irrelevance of certain metaphysical and religious positions cannot be shared by those who have a different view from his of "man's place in nature." This point can be generalised. In asking "Why reject a religious (specifically pantheistic) framework as a basis for environmental ethics?" Brennan's position is being used primarily as a foil.

Brennan criticises "deep ecology," while maintaining that many of their insights are consistent with his ecological humanism. His critique is relevant to pantheism because it shows ecological humanism to be anthropocentric. For pantheists, however, this anthropocentric view is an anathema and a basic ingredient of environmental disaster. He characterises deep ecology as the view "which develops the central theme that things other than humans, or humans and a select group of other animals, have value or worth of a non-instrumental kind" (p. 141).[28] In Brennan's view, a view he claims is supported by scientific ecology, "natural communities have no ends to serve, no purpose in their development, and no goods of their own . . . the attempt to fund moral respect for nature on some notion of systemic good or value thus has to be abandoned" (p. 156). Brennan's rejection of deep ecology rests not only on his view of natural communities, but also on his anthropocentrism. It is not just that he finds no basis for funding moral respect in terms of systemic good or intrinsic value attributable to natural communities. He claims it is unlikely that the non-anthropocentric view held by deep ecologists could be the basis for a practical environmental ethic.

> it may prove impossible for us, as human beings, to take seriously the judgement of the non-anthropocentric perspective. But that may be not so much a matter of morals but a reflection of what we are. Even if morality succeeds as a device for counteracting limited sympathies within the human community, it is unlikely to succeed as a device that will enable us to yield priority over human concerns and interests to the good of things "natural, wild and free."
>
> (p. 30)

I doubt Brennan is mistaken in his assessment. If so, this would not show that a non-anthropocentrically based environmental ethic is mistaken, but only that it cannot succeed. Combine this with the view that *only* a non-anthropocentric view such as pantheism can provide the foundations of an acceptable ethic and the prognosis is worse than gloomy.

A pantheistic ecological ethic will not be anthropocentric. This rules out the notion of man as a "steward of nature," whether his own or God's, who is responsible for nature. It also rules out utilitarian, contractarian and Kantian approaches as providing an ultimate basis since they are anthropocentric. It does not, however, rule out contractarian etc. principles as useful guides to making and justifying environmental decisions. Applying anthropocentrically conceived principles to environmental issues would suffice in many cases, but not all, to sound reasoning about the environment. (The practical problem environmentally speaking has been that almost no principles have been applied until recently. Selfish economic "forces," i.e. people, have ruled without restraint.) The situation here is no different from that with respect to theism. For the theist, ultimate justification of ethics resides in a view about the nature of God. But the theist is not prevented, *qua* theist, from invoking less ultimate ethical principles.

The pantheist's ethic, her environmental ethic and her ethics more generally, will be metaphysically based in terms of the divine Unity. It will be based on the Unifying principle which accounts for an important commonality, and it will be the grounds for extending one's notion of the moral community to other living and non-living things. Everything that is part of the divine Unity (as everything is) is also part of the moral community. Aldo Leopold says, "The land ethic simply enlarges the boundaries of the community to include soils, waters, plants, and animals, or collectively, the land . . . A thing is right when it tends to preserve the integrity, stability, and beauty of the biotic community. It is wrong when it tends otherwise."[29] Looking towards pantheism as a metaphysical justification of, for example, Leopold's "land ethic" is not unreasonable – or rather no more unreasonable than pantheism itself is.

An anthropocentric view of morality can at best make the non-human and non-living world an object of moral consideration. But it cannot, according to some, provide a basis for regarding those things as having a "good" of their own or as being non-human members of a moral community. This may satisfy those who think, as Brennan does, that an environmentally sound ethic need not or cannot rely on "enlarging" our notion of the moral community in the sense in which Leopold or the deep ecologists advocate; and that regarding the non-human and non-living world as having "moral considerability" from an anthropocentric perspective suffices. Indeed, it had better suffice in Brennan's view since it is the only basis that can be rationally justified and

233

provide morally adequate reasons for action. His reasons, as we have seen, partly have to do with his notion of personal identity; but they are enforced by his claim that an anthropocentric view should not be abandoned because, practically speaking, it cannot be. What he means by an anthropocentric view is an egoistic one. The only practical basis for a feasible environmental ethic is one that enforces a belief in the congruence between what is good for the environment and what humans regard as serving their ends. What is morally speaking environmentally right must be seen as good for humans.

Others, however – including pantheists and theists – will generally reject any environmental ethic as unsound if it fails to regard the non-human world as a full-fledged member of the moral community. In their view, to do otherwise is ultimately to rest the prospects of environmental well-being on the good will of the only members of the moral community there are – humans. This is seen as resting the welfare of colonies on the good will of the colonisers. In order to enlarge our understanding of the moral community in the appropriate ways a metaphysical basis for an environmental ethic is needed which limits the significance of the anthropocentric view.

Furthermore, it is clear that those, like deep ecologists, who argue that our notion of the moral community must be enlarged to include the "good" of the non-human and non-living, and that it is metaphysically correct to do so, also claim that practical consequences *are* involved. The issue is not merely one of providing a rational basis for an environmental ethic. The results that both deep ecologists and Brennan think are desirable coincide to some extent, though they differ significantly as well. Brennan thinks these desirable goals can only be obtained through "ethical polymorphism" and ecological humanism. These views do not rely on a radically different concept of "moral community" and reject "systemic value." But the metaphysically minded deep ecologist, or pantheist, claims that the desired results can only be obtained by changing our concept of what constitutes the moral community.

It may seem that pantheists can claim that ethics and an approach to ecology should be kept separate from, or that they are separate from, the more general pantheistic view that asserts the existence of a divine Unity. A kind of "separation between church and environment" might be proposed. But I doubt that such a separation is possible. The pantheist, like the theist or atheist, takes the nature of reality as determinative of ethical requirements. Since Unity is predicated upon some evaluative consideration (e.g. the divine Unity being constituted on the basis of "goodness"), value is a focal point for the pantheist and a principal concern. This situation in regard to pantheism is not too different from the one for theism. For the theist, ethical requirements and evaluative concerns of all sorts are connected with God's alleged goodness and overall nature.

Despite a seeming incongruity, a useful parallel can be drawn between a theistic divine command theory of ethics and a theory of pantheistic ethics. The incongruity is that in the divine command theory there is a theistic God to issue commands that are in some way taken to be constitutive of moral requirements, whereas in pantheism there is no personal God to issue or "reveal" divine commands.[30] After giving a brief account of the divine command theory, I claim that this incongruity is not a serious problem for the parallel I draw, and argue that a pantheistic version of a "divine command theory" is not susceptible to the same kinds of criticisms the theistic theory is. (Divine command theories are often taken to be compatible, in varying degrees, with other ethical theories as well – at the normative if not the meta-ethical level. The same should be true of pantheistic ethics.)

The issue that is at the centre of the divine command theory was raised in Plato's *Euthyphro*, 9e. Are actions morally obligatory or forbidden because God commands or forbids them; or does God command or forbid them because they are morally obligatory or forbidden? Does God's commanding them make them obligatory or forbidden; or are some actions obligatory or forbidden apart from, God's commanding them? The divine command theory states that "ethical wrongness *consists in* being contrary to God's commands, or that the word 'wrong' in ethical contexts *means* 'contrary to God's commands.' "[31]

There are various objections to this form of the theory. As Robert Adams notes, it is clear that not everyone does mean "contrary to God's commands" by the word "wrong" in ethical contexts. For one thing, many people do not believe in God and still use the word "wrong" in ethical contexts. For this reason he thinks the scope of any divine command theory, including his "modified" one (to be discussed), should be restricted to "the meaning of 'wrong' in Judeo-Christian religious ethical discourse."[32] Even with this restriction, however, the theory is not plausible.

It is implausible to suppose that even in Judeo-Christian religious ethical discourse "wrong" and "contrary to God's commands" can mean the same thing. A way of showing they do not mean the same thing, even within Adams's suggested restriction of scope, is that even if one does believe X to be commanded by God, it makes sense to ask "But is it wrong to do X?" If X simply meant "commanded by God" it would not make sense to ask whether or not a commandment of God's was ethically right or wrong.[33] The idea that it does not make sense to ask this, because at least part of what one means by "X is wrong" is that it is "contrary to God's command" is stipulative. It is not, as Adams thinks, indicative of a logic internal to religious discourse. And it is something that most theists – anyone who does not hold a divine command theory – would reject. The believer may have little reason to question the morality of what she takes as a commandment from God, but that does not entail that it would *not make sense* to do so. The way in which one would question the morality of a command could make essential reference to other things one believes about God. But this does not show that it makes no sense for the theist to question the morality of some particular command. Attention to the "grammar" (i.e. rules governing usage and the application of concepts) of Judeo-Christian religious discourse does not reveal a syntax that supports any divine command theory of ethics. No doubt there are complex relations between the believers' ethical discourse and their belief about God and God's commandments; but these relations do not support the claim that the "meaning" of "morally wrong" and morally right" are "It is contrary to (or in accord with) God's commandments."[34]

The difficulty with the divine command theory, including Adams's modified version, is basically the same. The divine command theory unduly burdens the theist with an exaggerated and indefensible account of the way in which their ethical discourse is linked to God's commands.[35] The motivation for a divine command theory seems to be that (i) only if the link between discourse and command is taken to be one of strict implication (i.e.

"wrong" implies "contrary to God's commands"), or (ii) only if it is supposed that religious ethical discourse would be undermined (i.e. would be impossible) if the morality of any of God's commands were questioned, could the believer's ethical discourse and life be seen as having a sufficiently "serious" reliance on God's commands. The view seems to be that for the reliance to be meaningful it must be "intrinsic" in some strong logical sense. But no divine command theory is needed to make God's commands central to the life of the believer. They *are* central – and for reasons having nothing to do with the kinds of issues (e.g. the "implication" relation) raised in the divine command theory. Given God's alleged moral perfection, and the theistic worldview, it follows that the believer will regard what she takes to be God's commands as the morally right thing to do. This does not mean that a believer might not question whether or not some command is moral. In most cases, if what is commanded blatantly conflicts with the believer's understanding of the nature of God, or conflicts with her understanding of what is morally right and wrong, then it is possible for the believer to reject the command as being genuine, and it is probable that this is what occurs. It is difficult to imagine a case in which this would not be possible.

The believer may also change her mind as to the nature of God, or what is right and wrong. But this appears less likely, since changing one's views about the nature or character of God in some substantial way would tend to undermine belief in God altogether; as, for example, when one stops believing in God due to a failure to see why God allows some types of evil. And it is also difficult to see that one would change one's sense of right and wrong even if one did believe God commanded cruelty, or something equally paradigmatically immoral. This is because moral notions are embedded in one's life in various ways, as Adams notes, and not only with religious ethical discourse. For example, if God commands cruelty it is difficult to imagine changing one's views so that one now thinks cruelty is morally good.

The divine command theorist is correct in claiming that there are complex relations between the theists' ethical discourse and their belief about God and God's commandments, but mistaken in claiming they have to do with *meaning*. The pantheist's ethical discourse has similarly complex relations with what she takes to be the nature of the divine Unity. The pantheist tries to discern and live in accordance with the Unity and the kind of value intrinsically associated with it. This is clearly seen in Taoism. To act correctly one acts in accordance with the Tao (the way) which is the unifying principle. In the context of the *Tao Tê Ching* (Taoism's primary "scripture") what the Tao is and how to act in accordance with it are explained in terms of one another. The *Tao Tê Ching*, like most other primary scriptural sources, is at one and the same time an ethical treatise on how to live and a metaphysical treatise analysing reality. One does not understand the Tao unless one understands what it means to live in accordance with it. Ethics are intrinsically related to the Tao, and "value" is associated with it at the most basic levels.[36]

The Indian doctrine of karma can also be interpreted pantheistically in a way that takes ethical discourse to be reliant on action in accordance with, or in defiance of, an all-pervasive principle that by its very nature is associated with value. It promotes the good. The doctrine of karma is not a theistic doctrine.

Pantheists do not, any more than theists, claim that what they *mean* by ethically right and wrong is something like "living in accord with the 'commandments' of the Unity." Instead, they claim that living in accord with the Unity is ethically good and violating it in some way, going against it etc., is ethically wrong. What is right and wrong is to be explained by reference, essential reference in some cases, to the divine Unity, just as what is right and wrong for the theist is, in some cases, to be explained by reference to the nature of God. Neither the theist nor the pantheist need be saddled with anything more elaborate than this (e.g. a divine command theory) to explain the connection that exists between ethical discourse and God.

I have argued (contrary to Adams) that even if the divine command theorist takes what is right and wrong not to be independent of God's will, she can still maintain that it is logically impossible that God command certain things we commonly and paradigmatically take to be wrong. The same is true for the pantheist whose ethics are intrinsically related to (their understanding of) the nature of the divine Unity. There may be a lot of room for interpretation as to what does and does not accord with the divine Unity, but certain things will clearly be wrong and cannot be otherwise given one's understanding of the Unity.

Living an ethical life and a "good" (i.e. valuable) life for the pantheist means, in part, living a life in accordance with the way in which ultimate reality is constituted. In attempting to conform to the way in which reality is constituted, the pantheist is no different than the theist, Taoist, Confucian, Buddhist or atheist existentialist. Pantheists strive to live in accord with the divine Unity of which they are a part. The nature of the Unity is the metaphysical basis for a regulative ideal of how one should live. One only lives "happily" to the extent one pursues and, to some extent, achieves the ideal. Living in accordance with the Unity is to live in accordance with one's nature, and with the nature of other things and conditions in the world generally.

In discussing pursuit of an ideal and the realisation of "the good" in life (and many different kinds of lives come under that rubric), the notion of an ethical and valuable life is linked to the idea that there is a kind of *telos* or goal in life. Thus, in ways that will be elaborated upon in the next chapter, pantheistic ethics are partly Aristotelian. Pantheistic ethics, however, are connected not only with the Aristotelian notion of "well-being" and the Good Life, but also with what in theistic terms is the notion of "salvation." Pantheism, like Aristotelianism and theism, has both its own notion of what the *telos* in life is (i.e. what in theism constitutes salvation) and its own concept of the Good Life.

The pantheistic "alternative" to the divine command theory – an alternative that in some ways parallels that theory – is that what is morally correct will be in accord with the Unity. There is a sense in which what makes something "right" is the fact that it conforms to the Unity. The pantheistic view, however, does not have the difficulties that divine command theories in general have – or that Adams's theory in particular has.

4.4 SALVATION AND IMMORTALITY

How close pantheism, anti-hierarchical leanings, and pagan leanings really were even in the countryside we learn from a few rare outbursts. A case in point is the vulgar pantheism of a half-literate village miller in the sixteenth century, recently discovered in Venetian inquisitorial acts. The man went around preaching, with a missionary zeal, that the Church, its hierarchy, and doctrines are a self-serving fraud. We are all God in the same measure; the universe is one huge wheel of cheese, spirits and angels the worms in it. Salvation can only come through this knowledge.[1]

Amos Funkenstein

Walking Stewart . . . scoffed at the idea of the perpetuation of the individual consciousness after death . . . the Child of Nature . . . will not look for reward to the consolations of a Christian or Pagan heaven, but will find his adequate satisfaction in the joy that follows from the sublime contemplation of his unity with the whole sentient universe, as he feels his happiness in all things and all men through eternity.[2]

Bertrand Bronson

I believe that the universe is one being, all its parts are different expressions of the same energy, and they are all in communication with each other, influencing each other, therefore parts of one organic whole. (This is physics, I believe, as well as religion.) The parts change and pass, or die, people and races and rocks and stars; none of them seems to me important in itself, but only the whole. This whole is in all its parts so beautiful, and is felt by me to be so intensely in earnest, that I am compelled to love it, and to think of it as divine. It seems to me that this whole alone is worthy of the deeper sort of love; and that there is peace, freedom, I might say a kind of salvation, in turning one's affections outward toward this one God, rather than inwards on one's self, or on humanity . . . [3]

Robinson Jeffers

Like the term "evil," "salvation" may be rejected by pantheists as being too integral to the theistic world-view they reject. It is a term borrowed from theism and one not consonant with pantheism. I use the term "salvation" with this in mind.

I have claimed that pantheistic ethics are, in some ways, Aristotelian, and that for pantheism the notion of "the good life" as a regulative ideal – a *telos* or end to be strived for – is an aspect of salvation. This can be explained by examining some similarities between pantheistic ethics and Aristotelianism. The pantheist has what Paul Taylor calls "an essentialist conception of happiness." Like the Aristotelian, Platonist and theist, the pantheist's conception of happiness "presupposes that there is such a thing as an essential human nature."[4] They all disagree, however, as to what that essential nature is. The pantheist's conception of human nature (i.e. her philosophical anthropology) is perhaps generally broader and less specific than the others.[5] When goals are stipu-

240

lated that man *qua* man should achieve this is indicative of an essentialist conception of human nature.

Furthermore, in an essentialist conception of happiness (i.e. one which presupposes that there is such a thing as an essential human nature), "happiness" is largely a function of how well one fulfils one's essential nature. Pantheism's wide conception of human nature allows for a correspondingly broad range of ways for people to achieve happiness. There are, in other words, fewer ways for the Aristotelian or theist to achieve happiness than there are for the pantheist.

Taylor says,

> According to the essentialist conception of happiness, a truly happy life is identified with the Good Life for Man ... Happiness (*eudaimonia*, well-being) is the kind of life that is suitable or fitting for a *human* being to live, and a *human* being is one who exemplifies the essential nature (or essence of) man. Thus happiness is not to be identified with any kind of life a person might actually want to live. Instead it characterises the kind of life we all *would* want to live if we understood our true nature as human beings. Happiness, then, may be defined as that state of the "soul" or condition of life which all human beings, *insofar as they are human*, ultimately aim at ... This essence of man is not only a set of properties common to all human beings and unique to them ... it is also a set of properties which define the good for man as such, a Human Good that is fundamentally different from an animal's good or a plant's.
>
> (pp. 132–3)

To the extent that a human being is able to achieve "happiness" by actualising the properties that "define the good of man as such" (i.e. by exemplifying the essential nature of man), they will be leading an intrinsically good or valuable life. "Happiness" is then the standard by which to judge the non-derivative (i.e. intrinsic) value of a person's life.

> When this conception of happiness is used as the standard of intrinsic value, the standard becomes identical with the essentialist's standard of human perfection or virtue. What determines the intrinsic goodness of a person's life is the realisation of an ideal; in living a truly human life, the

person is realising the good for man as man. Not everyone fulfils this standard to the same degree, but to the extent that a person does, his life takes on a worth, a perfection, that gives it value in itself, independently of any consequences it might have in the lives of others.

(p. 133)

For the theist the goal, or *telos*, of life is salvation in the form of personal immortality, and a special kind of happiness. In heaven one will have a more intimate relationship with God than was possible in life on earth. "Blessedness" or "happiness" (*beatitudo*) is the Christian theist's goal, and human nature is defined in terms of this. To be human is to be a finite creature whose happiness and well-being is ultimately dependent upon a relationship with God. The pursuit of this goal involves what Christians regard as a distinctive way of life. Those who achieve salvation are allegedly no longer subject to the difficulties of this life, and their personal immortality is assured.[6]

The Platonic view, though very different from theism's, is similar in claiming that there is personal immortality, and that supreme happiness is only possible after death.[7] The pantheist is like the Aristotelian in denying personal immortality and any doctrine of salvation in which an afterlife plays a role. The pantheist, like the Aristotelian, explains the *telos* of human life in terms of this life, albeit in the context of what comes before and after one's life.

Pantheism has a non-anthropocentric conception of human well-being. The human good is characterised partly in terms of relational properties. One must have a certain kind of relation to the Unity in order to live "properly." The set of properties common and unique to humans, which also define the good for humans as such, include relational properties. When a person exemplifies their essential human nature in this way – and it can only be exemplified in this relational way – they are living the "good" life and can thereby achieve well-being and happiness. This non-anthropocentric conception of human well- being constitutes pantheism's standard of human perfection and virtue. It is a standard of intrinsic value.

As in the case of Aristotle's essentialist conception of the nature of things, the human good (defined as it is in terms of human nature) will be different from an animal's good or a plant's good.

For the pantheist, however, the good of these other things must also be understood partly in terms of their relation to the Unity. Furthermore, the good associated with various things (humans, plants etc.) is incommensurable. (This is true of Aristotle's conception of these goods as well, although there is also a sense in which he does compare them in a hierarchy of goods.) What this means is that there is no standard external to each kind of thing by which all things can be measured in terms of perfection, or virtue, or intrinsic value. There is no such thing as intrinsic value *per se* given an essentialist account of the nature of things which includes essentialist standards of perfection. It is not just wrong to say that a human being is intrinsically more valuable than a tree. It is also nonsense. Of course this does not mean that trees should not be used by people.

Taylor claims that according to the essentialist conception of human nature the value achieved in human life by fulfilling the standard of intrinsic value is independent "of the consequences it might have in the lives of others." If Taylor is correct, then the pantheist will reject any unqualified account of the essentialist's standard of human perfection and virtue. (Indeed, I think an Aristotelian need not hold such an absolute non-consequentialist account either.) Intrinsic value is, of course, value that is non-derivative. But, what determines the intrinsic goodness in a person's life will, for the pantheist, rely on that person's relationship to the Unity. A person's "good" is partially constituted by the divine Unity of which everything is a part. In pantheistic terms it makes little sense to speak of the intrinsic value of a human life as measured against a standard independent of how that life affects others, since for the pantheist all such value (even so-called "intrinsic value") is partly derivative. The standard of intrinsic value and perfection (e.g. well-being) cannot be determined without reference to the divine Unity. In other words, a person's essential nature and well-being (or anything else's) cannot be analysed apart from its context in relation to the Unity and everything it includes. The good for humans cannot be explained by reference to humans alone.

This situation is similar to theism where it makes little sense to describe what is good for persons without reference to God. For the theist, a person's essential nature is partly determined by what persons are in relation to God. Although both theism and pantheism have essentialist conceptions of human nature, well-being on either of those accounts cannot be achieved apart from one's relation to others, or the consequences of one's actions for others. And the pantheist and theist are not the only kind of essentialists for whom consequences and relations matter. For the Aristotelian, in order to achieve well-being it is necessary to develop a certain kind of character. This requires, in part, certain virtues (e.g. courage, temperance etc.). Since the development and display of character and virtue is connected in significant ways with the consequences of an individual's actions in relation to other people, the concept of one life having "intrinsic value" apart from how it affects any other life is vacuous. Aristotle's account of the virtues makes a practical impossibility of living a "good life" that is fundamentally bad for others. Plato too claims that the virtuous life has its rewards for all. Thus, essentialist conceptions of human nature and the good need not preclude, and may even entail, an account of persons in relation to other things. For the pantheist, "realising the good for man as man" must be interpreted in terms of the Unity. Spinoza, for example, explains "happiness" in terms of "God or Nature."

In Confucian thought the kind of life a person should lead is determined by a person's own nature, the nature of "man" as such, and by the nature of an ultimate and all-encompassing principle or power – "Heaven" (*t'ien*). Shu-hsien Liu gives an account of an aspect of Confucian thought that illustrates this. It is particularly relevant to pantheism in that *t'ien* is an impersonal unifying principle. Confucianism (or at least Confucius) attempts to distance itself from metaphysical speculation in ways that philosophical Taoism does not. Nevertheless, like Taoism, the Confucian account of the nature of things is pantheistic.

> Heaven seems to be the ultimate creative power which works incessantly in the universe without exhibiting any personal characteristics, and man is to take heaven as the model to follow ... Mencius [says] "He who exerts his mind to the utmost knows his nature. He who knows his nature knows Heaven. To preserve one's mind and to nourish one's nature is the way to serve Heaven" ... not only is there no need to depart from the way of man to realise the way of Heaven but to follow the way of man is the only way to realise the way of Heaven. Mencius has established the basic model for later Confucian scholars to conceive the relation

between Heaven and man. There is no simple dichotomy between the natural and the supernatural, the secular and the sacred.[8]

Taoism and Confucianism, although very different from each other, both have accounts of the human good congruent with a pantheistic metaphysic. Although different from one another, their respective ideals of perfection also comport well in pantheistic terms.

For pantheism, an essentialist account of human nature does not suggest that there is necessarily only one kind of ideal person or way to achieve happiness. How to live, and what the good life is, varies as both Plato and Aristotle recognise to a degree. However, Plato and Aristotle thought that people's rational capacities were what made them distinctive. In terms of a hierarchy of the "good life," those that were most capable of understanding how things really were, and so most capable of determining what constituted the "good" (i.e. those that were most rational), were those capable of leading the most valuable and happy lives. Both Plato and Aristotle conclude that those most capable of supreme happiness are the philosophers. (This is ample cause for dismay – surpassed only by Plato's not insignificant claim that the person best fit to rule is a philosopher.)

An essentialist conception of human nature may recognise a range of human natures compatible with "human nature" as such. Just as various plants are constituted in such a way that their different requirements must be met if they are to thrive and flourish (i.e. what constitutes their well-being varies), so too will conditions for a person's "well-being" vary from person to person. The pantheist maintains that there is no such thing as *an* (i.e. one) essential human nature – although some properties are shared. Yet given *various* human natures, well-being can only be achieved to the extent that the individuals satisfy their own nature (i.e. achieve their own potential) in their particular circumstances in relation to the Unity.

Pantheists eschew hierarchies that have as a criterion for the "good life" any particular intrinsic feature that certain human beings may have which others lack. A good mind used in a good way may help one lead a better life, but so will good looks and a good job. Having a good mind, like anything else, may be overrated. There is no simple correlation between intelligence and well-being. Indeed, there is a far more direct correlation between money and well-being – despite the fact that "money cannot buy happiness." In his introduction to *Leaves of Grass* Whitman says,

> To carry on the heave of impulse and pierce intellectual depths and give all subjects their articulations are powers neither common nor very uncommon. But to speak in literature with the perfect rectitude and insouciance of the movements of animals and the unimpeachableness of the sentiment of trees in the woods and grass by the roadside is the flawless triumph of art.[9]

Whitman is here talking specifically about literature, and more especially about poetry. But it is clear in *Leaves of Grass* that he sees his sentiment and thought regarding poetry as applicable to life in general. It is an important aspect of his pantheism. The point here is that intellectual prowess is not necessarily a key to well-being and may even interfere with it.

Despite their essentialism, neither Plato nor Aristotle interpreted the good life exclusively in terms of intellect or the ability to discern things as they really are. All of the virtues necessary to being a perfectly virtuous person will not be found in a single person – and of course (to paraphrase Confucius) it is a mistake to expect them to be. Nevertheless, the pride of place they assign to cognitive powers and to certain kinds of lives and professions as opposed to others is undeniable. The pantheist maintains an essentialist account of human nature but rejects some of the criteria – probably the central criterion (i.e. "rationality") – that Plato and Aristotle employ in their respective evaluations. For the pantheist, happiness (or salvation) depends on living in accord with one's own nature in relation to the Unity. The pantheist thus concurs with the form, but not the substance, of the theistic, Platonic and Aristotelian salvific prescription.

It has been argued by Kai Nielsen, Kurt Baier and others that the idea of human beings having a "nature" in the sense of "purpose" is degrading to persons.[10] Unlike knives and can-openers, people do not have any intrinsic purpose; a purpose, for example, for which they were created, or a nature to fulfil. People have purposes that are extrinsic – they choose them for themselves. Accordingly, no kind of life is intrinsically better to live than some other on the grounds that it is a way to fulfil an intrinsic purpose.

It is simplistic, however, to regard the idea of persons as having a purpose fundamentally related to their nature as degrading. An Aristotelian notion of perfection does not liken the value of persons to the instrumental value of some object. The well-being of a thing must be understood in terms of a thing's nature according to Aristotle. A thing's "purpose" is to fulfil its nature. But this purpose is not something extrinsic to the individual and imposed. In claiming that having a purpose simply in virtue of being a human is degrading, Nielsen's and Baier's primary target is theism. God allegedly creates people for the purpose of worshipping God etc. – and so theism, if true, is degrading. But the theist does not regard this purpose as simply imposed by God, but as intrinsic to human nature. According to theism, in seeking a relationship with God, persons are perfecting their own intrinsic natures and are seeking to become the kind of persons, that *qua* human being, they should become. It is misleading to say that people are *created for the purpose* of worshipping God etc. Rather, human nature is such that the pursuit of personal well-being is linked to the worship of God. By worshipping God people seek their own happiness and well-being.

Of course, God created humans with the natures they have, but it remains an oversimplification to say God created us such that our purpose, like the purpose of useful objects we create, is to worship. According to theism, people have the ability to freely choose whether or not to "seek" God, and given our natures we should do so if we desire well-being. For the theist, the essentialist conception of human nature undermines the notion that we are created by God to fulfil an externally imposed purpose. What would it mean not to have a particular kind of nature? In the essentialist conception of nature, whether Aristotelian, theistic or pantheistic, whatever kind of nature a thing has (including persons) there is necessarily a corresponding purpose. It is not an imposed purpose but a matter of becoming what one essentially is – of realising a natural potential.

Essentialists do not regard it as degrading that a person's well-being is determined by the extent to which the ideal standard of happiness and perfection (i.e. the human *telos*) is realised when measured by the degree to which an individual exemplifies their essential nature. For the pantheist, to describe salvation in terms of "well-being" and how well the individual lives in accordance with their nature in relation to the Unity is not to regard a person as "made for some purpose." It is not to suggest that all human beings should, *qua* human, do the same things with their lives or pursue the same kind of lifestyle. It means that given what persons are well-being will be achieved in varying degrees by different people living within parameters dictated by their own natures and the all-inclusive Unity.

Pantheists deny personal immortality. There is no life after death in the sense that it is "they" who survive. Historically, the denial of personal immortality is one of pantheism's most distinctive features. This is partly because it is in clear opposition to the theistic view. But, it is primarily significant because it is constitutive of the pantheist's world-view and ethos, and so has implications for pantheistic practice. Believing that one is not going to live again after one dies, just as believing one will live again, has implications for one's choices in this life. There is, of course, nothing like a direct correlation in terms of what one believes concerning immortality and how one chooses to live. But for some people, seeing death as the permanent end of one's existence, or alternatively as a prolegomenon to another life, will be a constitutive factor of the ultimate context in which to live. The goals they choose to pursue, the relationships they have, their vocations, may to varying degrees be affected by their belief that death is or is not the permanent end of the individual. The pantheist need not believe that it would be tedious to live forever – as, for example, Bernard Williams claims it would be.[11] They just claim that no one does. This fact is not so much something to be lived with, as to be lived in terms of. The denial of personal immortality is as determinative of how the pantheist lives as the belief in an afterlife is for the theist.

The fact that pantheists (e.g. Spinoza) deny personal immortality is at times given as a reason why pantheism is atheistic. The doctrine of immortality is so central to classical Christian theism that rejecting the former is taken as entailing the denial of the latter. Yet, denying personal immortality can hardly be regarded as grounds for atheism unless theism, with its insistence on personal immortality, is taken to be the only position asserting the existence of a "God" that is not atheistic. The doctrine of personal immortality is not even essential to all forms of theism. Since many theists, e.g. many Jewish theists, deny immortality, it would seem that this denial is neither a necessary nor a sufficient condition of atheism.

But, even if it is not regarded as sufficient grounds for atheism, the denying immortality may be taken, as it was by Leibniz, as beyond "the bounds of reason," and so as grounds for rejecting pantheism. Leibniz said Spinoza's doctrine "destroys... the immortality of souls and degrades humankind, or rather all living creatures, from their proper place."[12] Yet given the *prima facie* evidence against a person's survival after death (i.e. the dissolution of the body necessary to sustaining life in this world), the denial of immortality, even if a mistaken view, seems not to be "beyond the bounds of reason."

According to some (e.g. Anthony Flew), it either is or should be only personal immortality that is of interest to individuals concerned with immortality. People who seek personal immortality, or at least survival after death, are primarily interested in their own (and others') personal continued existence. One who seeks life after death may have little, if any, interest in the prospect of their "soul" surviving death, if their soul's survival did not ensure their personal survival.[13] A person's own continued survival includes a continuation of themselves as a locus of experience. Their conscious memories, personality etc. must remain the same after death if it is "they" who are to survive death.

People who are interested in personal immortality, like people who are not interested (perhaps because they do not believe people survive death), may nevertheless be concerned with continued existence in an impersonal sense. Impersonal forms of "immortality," or surviving death, can include "surviving" in people's memories, being remembered for one's work, a bone in a reliquary, or becoming another part of the matter/energy cycle once again. One may want to remembered for what one has accomplished, or for the person one was. Impersonal "immortality" may seem to pale next to the theists' insistence on personal immortality and the meeting again of people known in this life. Nevertheless, people's notions of impersonal immortality may be important in various ways. Whether or not they believe in personal immortality, it matters to some people how they will be thought of. No doubt, people who believe in personal immortality are also generally concerned with the impersonal forms. Some may even value being remembered for something they produced as more important than personal survival after death. But typically, the person who believes in personal immortality regards it with a concern that they do not have for various impersonal types of survival.

Some pantheists believe in various types of non-personal immortality (e.g. Spinoza and Robinson Jeffers), and they regard this as significant for reasons other than, or in addition to, the reasons non-pantheists give. They reject the view that personal immortality is more valuable than impersonal immortality. This is not to say that if pantheists believed there was personal immortality they could not regard it as desirable. Perhaps they could even though the idea is anthropocentric and generally uncongenial to pantheism. But pantheists do not believe in personal immortality, and they regard some types of impersonal immortality as important on distinctively pantheistic grounds.

In the quotation at the beginning of this section Robinson Jeffers suggests that what may be important to the pantheist, and regarded as "a kind of salvation," is neither the realisation of the theist's hope for personal immortality, nor the atheist's (or theist's) desire to be remembered in certain ways – although the pantheist can desire this as well. Instead, what is distinctively significant is the recognition of the individual as a part of the Unity – what Jeffers calls the "one organic whole ... this one God." The "parts change and pass, or die, people and races and rocks and stars," but the whole remains. He says, "all its parts are different expressions of the same energy, and they are all in communication with each other, influencing each other, [and are] therefore parts of one organic whole." Part of what Jeffers is suggesting is that "salvation" (or immortality) is not so much a matter of the fact of one's survival in some form; rather, "salvation" consists in the recognition of the "oneness" or Unity of everything. "[T]his whole alone is worthy of the deeper sort of love; and that there is peace, freedom, I might say a kind of salvation, in turning one's affections outward toward this one God, rather than inwards on one's self, or on humanity." This is impersonal rather than personal immortality or salvation, but it is different from the kinds of impersonal survival discussed above. It may even be regarded as a kind of personal salvation, since Jeffers suggests that salvation can be experienced for oneself while alive – and only when alive. Such "salvation" resembles neither the impersonal forms of immortality mentioned above nor the theist's personal life after death.

Jeffers's explanation of his poem "The Tower Beyond Tragedy" illustrates his account of immortality and salvation.

> Orestes, in the poem, identifies himself with the whole divine nature of things; earth, man, and stars ... they are all one existence, one organism. He perceives this, and that himself is included in it, identical with it. This perception is his tower beyond the reach of tragedy; because, whatever may happen, the great organism will remain forever immortal and immortally beautiful. Orestes has "fallen in love outward" not with a human creature, not with a limited cause, but with the universal God. That is the meaning of my poem.[14]

Jeffers here, as elsewhere, disregards the relevance of personal immortality. There is a kind of satisfaction in knowing that the world goes on – even if one personally does not. And, although it is not clear from his explanation, there is also a satisfaction in knowing that one will not go on forever (i.e. that there is no personal immortality) because only then is one beyond the reach of tragedy. But Jeffers also thinks that there is a sense in which each of us does continue. If the whole is immortal then so too are we who are parts of it, or better yet, "identical" with it – though this is a metaphor.

Although it is not the only one, this is a distinctively pantheistic approach to the concept of salvation. It does not fit neatly into the category of either personal (i.e. usually theistic) or impersonal (i.e. usually humanistic) concepts of immortality. In general but still meaningful terms, it is consonant with Spinoza's account in *Ethics*, Book V, of "blessedness," "peace of mind," "human freedom," happiness, love and knowledge. In short, it is Jeffers's account of a Spinozistic conception of "salvation."

In his *Dialogues Concerning Natural Religion* Hume raises the question of whether the material Universe, rather than the theistic God, might not be the "necessarily existent Being" that theists claim must exist. Speaking through Cleanthes, one of the characters in the *Dialogues*, he says:

Cleanthes: It is pretended, that the Deity is a necessarily existent Being, and this Necessity of his existence is attempted to be explained by asserting, that, if we knew his whole Essence or Nature, we should perceive it to be impossible for him not to exist as for twice two to be four ... Why may not the material Universe be the necessarily existent Being, according to this pretended Explication of Necessity?[15]

The sense of "necessary" Hume employs in the above indicates he thinks the theist believes God is a logically necessary being (i.e. that the denial of God's existence involves a logical contradiction). A logically necessary being's non-existence is logically impossible.

However, the relevant modal notion in classical theism is not that of logical necessity but metaphysical necessity. The theist takes God to be a "metaphysically necessary" being. According to Aquinas, whose account is based on Aristotle's metaphysics, a being is *metaphysically necessary* if and only if it has neither the active or passive potentiality for non-existence. Such a being has no tendency to cease to be, nor are there forces that can bring about its non-existence. A being is *metaphysically contingent* if and only if it has either the active or passive potentiality for non-existence. Such a being contains within itself the tendency to cease to be, or there are forces which can bring about its non-existence.

There are two kinds of metaphysically necessary beings according to Aquinas. One kind has its necessity *caused by another* necessary being. Such a being's lack of active or passive potentiality for non-being is caused by another necessary being. The second kind of necessary being has its necessity *of itself.* Such a being's lack of active or passive potentiality for non-being is not caused by any other thing. Aquinas thought that angels, human souls and heavenly bodies were necessary beings whose necessity was caused by another necessary being (i.e. God). God, however, according to Aquinas, is a necessary being who has necessity of itself.[16]

Given the theistic view of creation *ex nihilo* the theist must deny that the universe can be a metaphysically necessarily existent being whose necessity is caused *of itself.* If the universe, or parts of it, do exist necessarily, then it has its necessity from another necessary being, God, who has its necessity of itself. The pantheist will not regard the universe as logically necessary. There is no logical contradiction in supposing it could not exist. But will pantheists regard it as metaphysically necessary? How is this connected to a pantheistic view of immortality?

The pantheist need not care about the world being a necessarily existent being, if it is one, in the way that a theist cares given the theistic account of creation. Yet, a pantheistic view about immortality such as Jeffers's may be connected to the idea that the divine Unity, and the material universe partly constitutive of the Unity, exists necessarily of itself. (There is no reason for the pantheist to posit some other necessary being, one who has its necessity of itself, as the cause of the Unity's necessary existence.) If the Unity (and world) always exists, as it must if it necessarily exists, and if one identifies with the world (i.e. the Unity), then in a non-personal sense one also always exists and cannot fail to exist. The significance of the idea that the world always exists seems to be this.

Jeffers's pantheistic notion of immortality might be captured more simply by the idea that the world always exists rather than that it exists necessarily. This would also imply that, since the world exists for ever, individuals in a sense also exist forever. But the world's existence, and one's own immortality, would not be (metaphysically) guaranteed as would be the case if the world's existence was metaphysically necessary. The idea that the universe is a metaphysically contingent thing that happens by chance to exist forever might suffice for the pantheistic type of immortality Jeffers espouses. But it might also be seen as undermining or making the notion precarious. On such a view everything could, after all, simply go out of existence. Furthermore, on some views – including Aquinas's – if a thing has the potential for non-existence, then at some time it will not have existed or will not exist. I am therefore inclined to think that pantheists with views about immortality like Jeffers tend to regard the world and Unity as metaphysically necessary.

The idea of immortality was taken by the Presocratics as one of the defining features of the "divine." Something is divine if it is immortal. But immortality may also have to do with Unity. Unity may be predicated partly on the basis that all things are part of one thing that always exists (i.e. the Unity is metaphysically necessary of itself). In section 2.1 I quoted Michael Stokes as saying: "Aristotle . . . maintains that the early monists had believed in the unity of all things in the sense that their one substance remained the same through change, without coming-to-be or passing-away."[17] Thus, Jeffers's view of immortality, and perhaps of Unity, may not be too different from the view held by some of the Presocratics.

In contemporary terms, the view that things remain the same throughout change and last forever is reminiscent of the view that matter and energy are conserved (i.e. the law of conservation of mass/energy) and that the physical universe is naturally indestructible. To say that the universe is "indestructible" is to claim that it exists necessarily in some sense. If time began with the creation of the universe, then the universe can be thought to have always existed. Perhaps it can be regarded as a metaphysically necessary being whose necessity is of itself – having neither the active nor passive potential for non-existence – and at no time ever having not existed. Alternatively, the pantheist might claim that even if the universe did not always exist, and that it makes sense to speak of a time "before" the Big Bang, the divine Unity has nevertheless always necessarily existed.

At any rate, for the pantheist, and for the Presocratics as well, the significance of the Unity being "indestructible" has to do with one's relation to the universe and one's being part of something that is indestructible and everlasting (i.e. it has to do with "immortality"). Neither the pantheist nor the Presocratics appear to be concerned about the modal status attributed to the Unity *per se*. And it is probably a mistake to equate early notions of "indestructible" and "neither coming-to-be, nor passing-away" as applied to "substance" with their latter day modal cousin – the idea of a "necessarily existent" universe, as opposed simply to a universe that has no beginning or end in time.

The fact that there is no personal immortality is not something the pantheist regrets. Indeed, the pantheist might regard such immortality, if it existed, as a misfortune. As I have said, it is a fact that determines a disposition towards life. Atheist existentialists like Sartre and Camus thought that atheism, and the subsequent denial of immortality, was necessary for human freedom. How the individual was to live had to be decided against the background of this belief. Bertrand Russell, too, thought that recognition of ultimate extinction, not just of individuals but of the solar system (i.e. art, music, philosophy etc.), was significant in terms of how one chooses to live.[18] Whether the denial of personal immortality influences the pantheist more or less than the belief in it influences the theist is basically a psychological issue. It will depend on the individual and how the individual regards the question of immortality. In any case, as can be seen in Spinoza and Jeffers, the pantheist is not devoid of beliefs concerning immortality and salvation. There is no apparent reason to suppose that their beliefs are less consequential than the theist's. Pantheists reject the view that the only kind of immortality that is worth having – that should be of personal interest – is personal immortality. Such a view, according to pantheists, is narrowly theistic and anthropocentric.

For the pantheist, salvation must occur, if at all, in this life and without the help of a messiah. In theism, salvation is often represented, for example by Augustine, as an either/or "all or nothing" proposition. It is decided after death, or in some Protestant views, oddly enough, before one is born. In pantheism, salvation is not something one achieves or fails to achieve *in toto*. It is a progressive task; one that is lifelong, and as Kierkegaard said of his own notion of salvation (i.e. "inwardness" and "subjectivity") it is the only task worth ultimately pursuing in terms of one's own existence. After all, it involves achieving one's potential and becoming one's self.

How well one lives this life is relative. It involves the avoidance of living certain (probably most) kinds of lives and the pursuit of others more integral to one's natural self and the Unity. As for Aristotle, the "good life" for the pantheist is associated with happiness. This state of well-being is achieved by various people in varying degrees, and (happily) by the same person to different extents at different times. For the pantheist, "well-being" is the only *personal* form of salvation there is. It includes the realisation of and identification with the Unity.

The pantheistic notion of salvation may sound humanistic, but it is very different from the notion of "salvation," if there is one, that atheist humanists such as Bertrand Russell put forward.[19] (Humanists, like pantheists, tend to reject the term "salvation.") A humanist notion of "salvation" (e.g. an account of one's purpose and goal in life) might take the form of an account of the "meaning of life" – e.g. that there is no meaning except the meaning we create. Like the theistic account, the humanist one is anthropocentric (i.e. it is *humanist*), whereas a pantheist one – because of the role the divine Unity plays in it – is not. Any notion of a divine Unity, or anything extra-human, that involves parameters in terms of which people should live is rejected by (atheist) humanists. Like (atheistic) existentialism, ethical humanism is explicit in its denial of the existence of not only God, but anything like "god" (e.g. the divine Unity) as well. For ethical humanists and atheistic existentialists, any acceptable doctrine of what constitutes meaning, purpose or "salvation" must be formulated without reference to anything other than humans themselves.

Given the pantheist's denial of personal immortality what is her attitude towards death? For the pantheist, the fact that there is no personal immortality is not something to be regretted. This does not, however, mean that death is not to be regretted, and may not in some ways, and at some times, be regarded as a bad thing. There are various reasons needed to explain why death may be bad and regrettable, but one of the mains ones is that it may deprive us of the possibility of experiencing and doing further good.[20] Death precludes the possibility of further pleasure and, for some, significant achievement. For the pantheist, as for others who do not believe in personal immortality, death is regrettable because it deprives us of future goods that we would have if we lived longer.

Nevertheless, the kind of immortality or "salvation" that one may achieve in this life (e.g. according to Spinoza and Jeffers) should take much of the sting out of death. For one who has achieved the kind of identification with the Unity that Jeffers describes, or the "blessedness" Spinoza describes in *Ethics* V, death, whether one's own or someone else's, is not ultimately regrettable or bad. And death is not ultimately bad even if one does not reach such states. Other people's deaths deprive us, as well as themselves, of future goods and so their death may be a cause for regret. For the pantheist, however, the death of others is ultimately no more regrettable than one's own.

The theistic position is often presented, by both theists (e.g. Tolstoy) and atheists, as claiming that if there were no personal immortality, then one's death, along with one's life, would be essentially meaningless.[21] Death in the absence of personal immortality is regarded as "meaningless," or as a bad thing in some other way by the theist. However, since the theist believes that personal immortality is assured, death should not ultimately be a cause for great regret and cannot ultimately be regarded as a bad thing – unless one expects to go to Hell.[22] This is not to say that theists have no grounds for regret even with belief in immortality. They do for reasons mentioned above.

The theistic attitude towards death and immortality is not altogether different in the case of pantheism. Pantheists do not believe there is personal immortality and they deny the significance theists claim for it. Nevertheless, given pantheism's belief in a kind of immortality, and its significance, death – at the "right" time and in the right way – is not an evil. If pantheists did not believe in any immortality, in any kind of salvation, then their attitude towards death would be different. It would be regarded as a greater cause for regret and a much worse thing than it is given their beliefs about the divine Unity and immortality.

NOTES

4.1 Creation

1 Grace Jantzen, *God's World, God's Body* (Philadelphia: Westminster, 1984), pp. 131, 77. See her discussion of creation and rejection of the doctrines of Augustine and Aquinas, pp. 131–54. The creation doctrine she favours, and her model of the world as God's body, incorporates what she thinks is right in pantheism into Christian theology. "If Pantheism is thus understood as an affirmation that all reality is God's reality, that there can be nothing without God or utterly apart from him, then pantheism is not an alternative to Christian theology but an ingredient in it. The idea of the universe as God's body draws out this aspect of pantheistic thought, stressing as it does God's immanence and totality while still rejecting reductionist accounts which plunge us into mechanistic determinism" (pp. 149–50).

2 Joseph Priestley, *Theological and Miscellaneous Works*, John Towill Rutt (London, 1817–32; reprinted New York, Garland, 1972), vol. III, p. 324. Spinoza denies that God (i.e. substance) creates the world. Cf. Spinoza, *Ethics*, I, Proposition 18: "God is the immanent and not the transcendent cause of all things." Demonstration: "All things which are, are in God, and must be conceived through Him (Prop. 15) and therefore (Corol. I, Prop. 16) He is the cause of the things

which are in Himself..." Spinoza's *Ethics*, ed. James Gutmann (New York: Hafner, 1949). Similarly, for Spinoza, motion is not an effect of God, as it is for Aristotle's unmoved mover or Aquinas's first mover; rather motion is part of the nature of God.

3 John Maquarrie, *In Search of Deity* (London: SCM, 1984), p. 35. Cf. J. J. Lipner, "The World As God's 'Body': In Pursuit of Dialogue with Rāmānuja," *Religious Studies*, 20 (1984), pp. 145–61. Lipner says:

> Rāmānuja regarded Brahman as being, at the same time, the "substrative cause..." and the "efficient cause..." of finite being... Rāmānuja (and the other Vedāntins) would find quite unsatisfactory a doctrine of "*creatio*", i.e. the production of the world by God out of nothingness, such as has traditionally been held in Christianity. To hold such a view would do scant justice to those scriptural texts and images... which point to Brahman as the very ground of being... Rāmānuja wanted no ontological, "creational" gap between the infinite source of being and its finite effects... From the point of view of the world's existence, Brahman is the substrative cause of the world. The world is produced out of him, continues to subsist in him, and is finally re-funded into him.
>
> (p. 156)

4 Ch'en Ku-ying, *Lao Tzu, Text, Notes, and Comments*, translated and adapted by Rhett Y. W. Young and Roger T. Ames (Republic of China: Chinese Materials Center, 1981), p. 45 of the introduction by Young and Ames.

5 Cf. Keith Ward, "God as Creator," in Godfrey Vesey (ed.) *The Philosophy in Christianity* (Cambridge: Cambridge University Press, 1989), p. 118. He quotes Augustine: "This I thought to handle without affirming, that my readers may see what questions to forbear as dangerous, and not hold them fit for farther inquiry' (*City of God*, 12.25). Cf. Macquarrie's account of theism on creation in *In Search of Deity*, pp. 34–5ff. In discussing the implications of creation doctrines for the relation of God to the world he says: "deism is a sorry departure and deterioration from classical theism, just as is pantheism in the opposite direction" (p. 35).

6 Ward, "God as Creator," pp. 106–7. Ward rejects the positions of Augustine and Aquinas because he sees no possibility of contingent states of affairs in the world in their accounts. Cf. pp. 114–16. For a defence of theistic creation doctrine see Richard Swinburne, *The Coherence of Theism* (Oxford: Oxford University Press, 1977), ch. 8.

7 In Aquinas's account, although God is necessary, immutable and simple, he "freely" creates the world. The world is neither necessary nor necessarily created, and God could have created some other possible world or none at all. But given his account of God's nature, it is questionable if Aquinas can meaningfully claim that God could have created another world and that there is genuine contingency in this world. Cf. Ward, "God as Creator." Ward claims Aquinas's doctrine of God is incompatible with his claim that creation is contingent. Ward says: "Though God creates a world that seems to us to

be one logical possibility among others, there is nothing that God could do other than what he does ... [I]t may be doubted whether it [Aquinas's doctrine] captures the sense of Divine freedom that is so strong in the Bible, or whether it can adequately cope with the Christian belief that God was free to create or not to create any world he chose" (pp. 115–16). Ward concludes that the classical doctrine(s) of creation, along with the doctrine of God's immutability etc., should be abandoned (i.e. modified) for one which views God as partially immutable but also "endlessly creative" and contingent. God should be seen as capable of change, choice, action and response (p. 118). Cf. Nelson Pike, *God and Timelessness* (London: Routledge, 1970).

8 Augustine answers his question, "What made God create heaven and earth then, and not sooner?" by rejecting the supposition he thinks it rests upon. Augustine, like Boethius, denies God exists in time. God did not exist for a period of time before commencing with creation, nor does God exist "in" time afterwards. God exists time-lessly. Augustine says "in the Eternal nothing passes, but the whole is present" (*Confessions*, Book 11). Augustine's view is that "There is no past ... there is no future ... there is no present ... There is one unchanging reality, subject to no temporal relations whatsoever" (Ward, p. 99). Of course, Augustine's way of dealing with his question raises other questions about the intelligibility of the concept of a timeless being.

9 Cf. Eleonore Stump and Norman Kretzmann, "Eternity," in Thomas V. Morris (ed.) *The Concept of God* (Oxford: Oxford University Press, 1987), pp. 219–52.

10 Cf. Ward, "God as Creator"; and Nelson Pike (*God and Timelessness*) for problems associated with these related doctrines (e.g. omniscience and human freedom, and God's responsibility for evil). For a defence of the Doctrine of Divine Immutability and of the Doctrine of Divine Simplicity (e.g. its compatability with human and divine freedom) see William E. Mann, "Simplicity and Immutability in God," in Thomas V. Morris (ed.) *The Concept of God* (Oxford: Oxford University Press, 1987), pp. 253–67. For a defence of Boe-thius's doctrine (e.g. its compatability with divine and human free-dom etc.) see Stump and Kretzmann, "Eternity." For an obscure defence of Thomistic views concerning God's immutability etc. in relation to creation, see James F. Ross, "Creation," *Journal of Philo-sophy,* 77 (1980), pp. 614–29. The widely accepted position that the doctrines of divine timelessness, changelessness and simplicity are liabilities for theistic metaphysics is, of course, contentious. I find neither Mann's nor Stump and Kretzmann's arguments convincing. Mann's defence of Divine Simplicity rests on a questionable notion of "simplicity" and on the coherence of the idea of God's eternality presented by Stump and Kretzmann. Stump and Kretzmann, in my view, fail to show that the concept of God's timelessness is coherent.

11 Ku-ying, *Lao Tzu, Text, Notes, and Comments,* p. 45 of the introduction by Young and Ames.

12 Cf. Clifford Geertz, "Religion as a Cultural System," in his *The Interpretation of Cultures* (New York: Basic Books, 1973), pp. 87–125, or Peter Berger, *The Sacred Canopy: Elements of a Sociological Theory of Religion* (New York: Doubleday, 1967). Indian creation myths may serve to justify and sanction the caste system and this is a good example of how such myths can function.

13 Consider the Genesis myth. It is a basis for pride of place for humans, and all this entails; a patriarchal society; a divine command theory of morality; a doctrine of original sin and "sin" in general; a shameful attitude towards the body.

14 If one association "doctrine" with revealed religious texts and institutionalized responses, dogma etc, it is misleading to discuss a pantheistic "doctrine" of creation at all.

15 Christopher Rowe, "One and Many in Greek Religion," in Adolf Portman and Rudolf Ritsema (eds) *Oneness and Variety* (Leiden: E. J. Brill, 1980), p. 57. Rowe's claim, at least concerning Anaximander, is disputed. Cf. note 19 in section 2.1.

16 Cf. Michael C. Stokes, *One and Many in Presocratic Philosophy* (Washington, DC: Center for Hellenic Studies, 1971), p. 64. He claims the Milesians did not believe in the unity of all things. Stokes is referring here only to the doctrine of the "world's unity in one stuff."

17 John Leslie, *Value and Existence* (Oxford: Blackwell, 1979), p. 7. "Every chain of explanations must end somewhere. If ethical grounds for existence are ever really creatively effective, then this fact must contain an inexplicable component; the best that can be done is to reduce its size."

18 Leslie, *Value and Existence*, p. vii. Leslie quotes a number of philosophers whom he regards as having a similar view (p. vi). Among them are Plato, Aristotle, Plotinus, Aquinas, Spinoza, Kant and Hegel. The similarity of some is suspect, but others do have similar positions. One of the closest to Leslie's is A. C. Ewing. "God's existence will be necessary because it was supremely good that God should exist. The hypothesis that complete perfection does constitute an adequate ground for existence seems to me the only one which could give an ultimate explanation of anything." See J. L. Mackie's discussion of Leslie's argument in *The Miracle of Theism* (Oxford: Oxford University Press, 1982). Cf. Richard Swinburne, "Argument From the Fine-Tuning of the Universe," in John Leslie (ed.) *Physical Cosmology and Philosophy* (New York and London: Macmillan, 1990), pp. 154–73.

19 Leslie claims that taken as a creative factor this "requirement" has often been equated with God. But this is of subsidiary interest to Leslie. He says, "God" is sometimes used as another name for the "need for a good universe to exist" that acts to create the universe; or the name certain theologians have given the creative factor. According to Leslie however one need not associate "God" with the creative factor.

If we are to speak of God in this doctrine ... then we may be speaking just of the principle that some set of ethical needs is creatively powerful. God-as-a-person is then only a mythical personification of this principle. But... the doctrine might instead be joined with belief in a God who is not any abstract force but a supremely perfect individual; for such an individual's existence might be supremely needful.

(*Value and Existence*, p. 6)

If God is taken to be a supremely perfect individual, then his existence, which in turn explains the existence of the universe, might itself be explained by an "ethical requirement" that he exist. Instead of applying the requirement directly to the universe it is first applied to God. But the ultimate explanation of why anything existed would be that it was "ethically required" that it do so.

20 Leslie sometimes talks of a "creative force [e.g. God] which has an ethical aspect" as the reason for existence, rather than an "ethical requirement" or "ethical necessity" itself being the reason. But what he means here too is that it is the ethical necessity that is creative (i.e. the ultimate explanation for creation) and not God. If God creates, it is because it is ethically necessary that he do so; or else God and/or the world were created because it is ethically required that they exist. The "ethical requirement" has creative force. Cf. *Value and Existence*, ch. 1.

21 In their article "Eternity," Stump and Kretzmann defend the coherence of the concept of eternity (i.e. God's "eternality") and especially the concept of "ET-simultaneity" (i.e. eternal-temporal simultaneity) that is crucial in making sense of the notion of a timeless (i.e. eternal) God. But their defence is primarily a negative one. They argue that the notion of ET-simultaneity is not more problematic than that of ordinary "temporal simultaneity" given relativity theory. They say:

> These difficulties in spelling out even a very crude acceptable definition for temporal simultaneity in the light of relativity theory foreshadow and are analogous to the difficulties in spelling out an acceptable definition of ET-simultaneity. More significantly, they demonstrate that the difficulties defenders of the concept of eternity encounter in formulating such a definition are by no means unique to their undertaking, and cannot be assumed to be difficulties in the concepts of ET-simultaneity or of eternity themselves.

(p. 230)

But they have not shown there is a useful analogy between temporal simultaneity and ET-simultaneity. Relativity theorists would see no useful analogy whatsoever, and Stump and Kretzmann have not shown that the concept of God's eternality is coherent. What they have shown is that, if the concept is coherent, then problems inherent in the doctrine can be resolved.

22 Cf. Paul Taylor, *Principles of Ethics* (Encino, Calif.: Dickenson, 1975). I discuss ethical naturalism in section 4.3.

23 See Hume's refutation of the teleological argument in David Hume, *The Natural History of Religion and Dialogues Concerning Natural Religion*, ed. A. Wayne Colver and John V. Price (Oxford: Clarendon Press, 1976). Hume has a host of reasons for rejecting the argument, and the relevant passages in his *Dialogues Concerning Natural Religion* are among the most well known in natural theology. I am concerned here only with his principal and most important objection.

24 For a discussion of Hume's principles of *a posteriori* reasoning, and an account of the sense in which for Hume one might be *relatively justified* in believing something on the basis of experience, see my *Hume and The Problem of Miracles: A Solution* (Dordrecht: Kluwer, 1989). All *a posteriori* reasoning (i.e. reasoning based on experience) is ultimately *unjustified* according to Hume. But Hume employs a notion of relative justification. One is relatively justified in believing something to the extent that it is reasoned on the basis of experience in accordance with his principles of *a posteriori* reasoning.

25 This is related to Hume's claim that inductive reasoning is ultimately unjustified. Not only are we not justified in believing that things will occur in the future as they have occurred uniformly in the past, but we are not justified in believing that there was any "real connection" between events that occurred uniformly in the past. If, as Hume claims, there is no discernible connection and none can justifiably be posited, then why say the fact that all Bs follow all As is indicative of "order" in any real sense – a sense that suggests there is an explanation for Bs following As?

26 For further discussion of Hume's rejection of *a priori* probabilities see Neil Levi and Michael P. Levine, "Robinson on Berkeley: 'Bad Faith' or Naive Idealism?," *Idealistic Studies*, 22 (1992), pp. 162–77.

27 Cf. Richard Swinburne's discussion of the teleological argument in *The Existence of God* (Oxford: Oxford University Press, 1979).

28 The probability one is trying to determine might be related to an event's occurrence, or the presence of some property, in the past – e.g. the activity of a "designer" – which allegedly makes some current or future situation probable; or it might relate to the likelihood of something happening later if something else occurs now.

29 Contrary to Hume, the pantheist believes the order discerned is real and is not, for all we know, accidental. Contrary to Hume, the pantheist, along with everyone else, claims we are justified in believing the regularity in nature to be indicative of a structure that provides the grounds for explaining why things happen the way they do. Regularity in nature is due to ordering principles and these principles (e.g. laws of nature) are not merely descriptive universal generalisations. Such principles or laws determine the way in which things happen. They are efficacious in bringing about the order which in turn can be explained only by reference to the principles. Hume however would claim that, just as we cannot say that there really is "order," so we cannot know there is "an ordering principle" if we mean by this that such a principle is more than descriptive (e.g. genuinely regulative). If we are not justified in believing that things

happen other than merely by chance, then of course we are not justified in believing that they happen in accordance with genuinely regulative principles.

30 Cf. David Hume, *A Treatise of Human Nature*, ed. L. A. Selby-Bigge (Oxford: Clarendon Press, 1978), Book I; or *Enquiries Concerning Human Understanding and Concerning the Principles of Morals*, ed. L. A. Selby-Bigge (Oxford: Clarendon Press, 1975). For a discussion of the connection between Hume's analysis of causation and what is unacceptable in his naive empiricism, see my *Hume and The Problem of Miracles: A Solution*.

31 "The function of a scientific explanation for any event is to give an account of how that event can be subsumed under a general law, or of how it can be inferred by piecing together other general laws. Clearly, however, we do not have available any general laws about the origin of universes" (Jantzen, *God's World, God's Body*, p. 131). This oversimplifies the function of scientific explanation, but it suffices for the distinction Jantzen draws between a doctrine of creation and a scientific account of the origin of the universe – the difference between a scientific explanation and what she calls a "personal or theistic one." For a discussion of "personal" explanation and creation see Swinburne, *The Coherence of Theism*, pp. 131–41. Paul Davies, in a number of recent books, treats creation doctrine as a scientific account; or alternatively he believes that science can explain creation (i.e. that it can answer the question "why is there something rather than nothing?"). In my view, Davies fundamentally obfuscates, confuses and conflates the philosophical with the scientific issues involved in creation.

32 Berkeley claims that his idealism, including his unusual idealistic account of creation, is consistent with science and is the only philosophical account of the "material" world that is. For Berkeley, "creation" is a matter of God's perceiving the world rather than producing it. For the Stoics the question of conflict between cosmology and creation theory could not arise since the two were as intertwined as their "science" and religion in general.

33 Jantzen, *God's World, God's Body*, pp. 74–100. She argues that although divine perception can be accounted for by a doctrine of God's incorporeality, once one understands what is meant by God's perception and what is significant about it, it is better accommodated in a doctrine of a *more* rather than a less embodied God. Her model of the world as God's body conceives of God as maximally embodied.

34 John Macquarrie (*In Search of Deity*) discusses some theologians that reject Priestley's contention. Macquarrie makes a case for rejecting it to some extent not only in his own "dialectical" theism (i.e. panentheism), but also in Plotinus, Dionysius, Eriugena and others. In each case Macquarrie denies they are pantheists, though he acknowledges there are pantheistic elements, good and bad, in these doctrines. But in the analysis of pantheism undertaken thus far, these people can be seen as pantheists rather than theists. They are not classical theists, and in some cases (Plotinus) they are so distant

263

from classical theism and its notion of God as a personal creator that it is implausible to suppose they are theists at all. Macquarrie understands pantheism is a narrower sense than is argued for in this book. He says, for example, "pantheism [acknowledges] a uniform diffusion of the divine through the cosmos" (p. 78). The claim that Eriugena's views are pantheistic is not based simply on his assertion that "God is all things everywhere" (cf. Macquarrie, p. 88). There are enough statements like that in classical theism. It is based instead on the centrality of the notion of a divine Unity for Eriugena, and also on his denial of some central tenets of theism (e.g. the separation of God and the world).

35 Macquarrie, *In Search of Deity*, pp. 34–5.

36 Cf. H. P. Owen, *Concepts of Deity* (London: Macmillan, 1971), p. 62. Owen quotes Copleston as follows:

> It is quite true that for Plotinus the world proceeds from God *secundum necessitatem naturae* and that he rejects free creation *ex nihilo*; but it should also be remembered that for him the prior Principle remains "in its own place" ... always transcending the subordinate being ... [W]hile rejecting free creation out of nothing on the ground that this would involve change in God, Plotinus equally rejects a fully pantheistic self-canalisation of the Deity in individual creatures ... he tries to steer a middle course between theistic creation on the one hand and a fully pantheistic or monistic theory on the other hand. We may well think that (since an ultimate dualism does not enter into the question) no such compromise is possible.

37 Ku-ying, *Lao Tzu, Text, Notes, and Comments*, p. 6 of the introduction by Young and Ames.

4.2 Evil

1 H. P. Owen, *Concepts of Deity*, p. 72.

2 Leszek Kolakowski, *Religion* (New York: Oxford University Press, 1982), p. 35.

3 Ku-ying, *Lao Tzu, Text, Notes, and Comments*, p. 49.

4 The idea that pantheism cannot account for evil or that it cannot resolve the problem of evil has been a major criticism of pantheism at least since Spinoza. It was one of Bayle's principal objections. Pierre Bayle, *Historical and Critical Dictionary: Selections*, tr. Richard Popkin (Indianapolis: Bobbs-Merrill, 1965). Cf. Kierkegaard: "So-called pantheistic systems have often been characterised and challenged in the assertion that they abrogate the distinction between good and evil, and destroy freedom. Perhaps one would express oneself quite as definitely, if one said that every such system fantastically dissipates the concept of *existence*. " Søren Kierkegaard, *Concluding Unscientific Postscript*, tr. D. F. Swenson and W. Lowrie (Princeton: Princeton University Press, 1944), p. 111.

5 Naturally I shall be selective. For what is still a good overview of the problem of evil and proposed solutions see H. J. McCloskey, "God and Evil," *Philosophical Quarterly*, 10 (1960), pp. 97–114. Also see Nelson Pike, *God and Evil: Readings on the Theological Problem of Evil* (Englewood Cliffs: Prentice Hall, 1964); Marilyn McCord Adams and Robert M. Adams (eds) *The Problem of Evil* (Oxford: Oxford University Press, 1990).

6 Some pantheists will dispense with the problem of evil because the concept of evil may be seen as an essentially theistic one, explainable only in terms of other theistic concepts such as God. This is one reason why the problem of evil – indeed, the very notion of "evil" – may be regarded as inapplicable to pantheism.

7 Alvin Plantinga, "God, Evil and the Metaphysics of Freedom," in Marilyn McCord Adams and Robert M. Adams (eds) *The Problem of Evil* (Oxford: Oxford University Press, 1990), pp. 83–109, at 108.

8 He is by no means the only example. See, for example, Peter Van Inwagen, "The Problem of Evil, the Problem of Air, and the Problem of Silence," in James Tomberlin (ed.) *Philosophical Perspectives* (California: Ridgeview, 1991), vol. 5, pp. 135–65. Van Inwagen claims that the existence of evil does not constitute any evidence *whatsoever* against the existence of God. Also see R. M. Adams, "Must God Create the Best?," in T. V. Morris (ed.) *The Concept of God* (Oxford: Oxford University Press, 1987), pp. 91–106. My present concern is not to argue for the sheer implausibility of their theses, but merely to register the fact that their essays, in a sense, constitute a refusal to address the problem of evil.

9 William Rowe says, "It is one thing to argue that the existence of evil is logically incompatible with the existence of the theistic God and quite another thing to argue that the world contains evils that render the existence of the theistic God unlikely. The former is the logical argument from evil; the latter is the empirical argument from evil." The empirical argument is also called the "evidential," "probabilistic" and "inductive" argument. William Rowe, "The Empirical Argument from Evil," in Robert Audi (ed.) *Rationality, Religious Belief and Commitment* (Ithaca: Cornell University Press, 1986), pp. 227–247, at 227.

10 The logical argument is often stated more simply in terms of it being "inconsistent for anyone to believe both of the following two propositions: I. The world is the creation of a God who is omnipotent, omniscient, and wholly good. II. The world contains evil." Terence Penelhum, "Divine Goodness and the Problem of Evil," in Marilyn McCord Adams and Robert M. Adams (eds) *The Problem of Evil* (Oxford: Oxford University Press, 1990), pp. 69–82, at 69.

11 Cf. Rowe, "The Empirical Argument from Evil"; "Evil and Theodicy," *Philosophical Topics*, 16 (1988), pp. 119–32. Also see the exchange between Rowe and Stephen Wykstra in Adams and Adams, *The Problem of Evil*. Although most versions of the argument from evil against the existence of God have been of the "logical" rather than the "empirical" (or "probabilistic") type, Rowe's empirical argument is

more successful than any logical argument can hope to be. This is because it is unlikely to suppose that one can ever "prove" that there is an incompatibility between some alleged essential property of God and the existence of some evil. It is always *possible* to claim the evil is necessary for a greater good. The empirical argument is more straightforward in this regard. It denies the plausibility, not the possibility, of assuming that at least some evils are necessary for a greater good. Some of these apparently "useless" evils may not result from human free will, and so it cannot be claimed that free will is a value that far exceeds the evil that results from it – especially given that more good than evil is done overall. Of course it is always possible to posit the devil and to suppose that God limiting the devil's choices is a greater evil than allowing the devil to do what he will. Cf. Plantinga, "God, Evil and the Metaphysics of Freedom," pp. 107–9.

12 Alternatively, as a "way out" of the problem of evil, one might deny the truth of one or more of the conjuncts in the first premise, and so the truth of the premise itself. It could be denied that God is omnipotent, omniscient or perfectly good. This is not the way out usually taken, however, since proposition (1) in its entirety is regarded as essential to theism. One does not reject (1) without abandoning theism.

13 Solutions that deny the reality of evil must rest on some kind of appearance/reality distinction (i.e. things are not really always what they seem to be). Consider the claim that "evil is only apparent." Here is an argument. "If looked at not from our partial perspectives, but from an all-encompassing, divine, or eternal perspective we would see that the apparent 'evil' in this world is necessary for a far greater good. There cannot be the good that there would be if not for the apparent 'evil' in this world. Therefore, from the perspective of one who can see the greater good, the apparent evil is not really 'evil' at all but an ingredient necessary in the circumstances for the greater good." But even if some allegedly "merely apparent" evil is necessary for a greater good is it not an evil anyway? Does its "being required for a greater good" mean that it is not a real instance of evil? If an evil is transmuted to a greater good is it always (or ever) the case that what we took to be the evil before it combined with other factors to produce a greater good, was not then a real evil? And does it not remain an evil? If Hitler was killed as a baby would not that have been a real evil – albeit a fortunate one? There are many other kinds of difficulties with views that deny the reality of evil. Suppose a child's early death would lead to a greater good. How is it good *for that child* to have died young no matter what kind of good it leads to? (Ivan makes a similar point in *The Brothers Karamazov*.) But if it is not good *for that very child*, then that child is being treated not as an autonomous individual but as a means to someone else's end.

14 For a defence of the "vale of soul-making" theodicy see John Hick, "Soul-Making and Suffering," in Marilyn McCord Adams and Robert

M. Adams (eds) *The Problem of Evil* (Oxford: Oxford University Press, 1990), pp. 168–88. Reprinted from John Hick, *Evil and the God of Love*, rev. edn (New York: Harper & Row, 1978), pp. 255–61, 318–36.

15 Hick, "Soul-Making and Suffering," p. 188. Hick borrows the phrase "the vale of soul-making" from John Keats. In a letter to his brother and sister in April 1819 Keats says:

> The common cognomen of this world among the misguided and superstitious is "a vale of tears" from which we are to be redeemed by a certain arbitrary interposition of God and taken to Heaven – What a little circumscribed straightened notion! Call the world if you Please "The value of Soul-making" ... Do you not see ... how necessary a World of Pains and troubles is to school an Intelligence and make it a Soul?

Quoted from Hick, "Soul-Making and Suffering," p. 171 n. 4. The letter is in M. B. Forman (ed.) *The Letters of John Keats*, 4th edn (London: Oxford University Press, 1952), pp. 334–5.

16 The fact that God cannot create us so that we always freely choose to do the good is not generally regarded as conflicting with God's omnipotence. It is not a restriction on God's power that he is unable to do what it is logically impossible to do. The usual view is that God's omnipotence consists in being able to do everything (and only those things) that it is logically possible to do.

17 Plantinga, "God, Evil and the Metaphysics of Freedom," pp. 85–6. For reasons that will be discussed, even if Plantinga is right in showing that "it is *possible* that God could not have created a universe containing moral good ... without creating one containing moral evil" he will not have addressed the issue in its most potent form (i.e. the empirical argument). Plantinga discusses the empirical argument in "The Probabilistic Argument from Evil," *Philosophical Studies*, 35 (1979), pp. 1–53.

18 Cf. Anthony Flew, "Are Ninian Smart's Temptations Irresistible?," *Philosophy*, 37 (1962), pp. 57–60; J. L. Mackie, "Theism and Utopia," *Philosophy*, 37 (1962), pp. 153–8. Ninian Smart, "Omnipotence, Evil, and Supermen," *Philosophy*, 36 (1961), pp. 188–95; "Probably," *Philosophy*, 37 (1962), p. 60; Plantinga, "God, Evil and Metaphysics of Freedom," p. 83–109. For a defence of "compatibilism" see Fred Dretske, "The Metaphysics of Freedom," *Canadian Journal of Philosophy*, 22 (1992), pp. 1–14.

19 I forgo a detailed discussion of Robert M. Adams's essay "Must God Create the Best?" Like Plantinga, Adams has based a kind of theodicy on contentious assumptions concerning what God can possibly do. His argument also rests on dubious criteria of personal identity. Adams argues that a "creator would [not] necessarily wrong someone (violate someone's rights, or be less kind to someone than a perfectly moral agent must be), if he knowingly created a less excellent world instead of the best that he could" (p. 92). He says, "A merely possible being cannot be (actually) wronged or treated unkindly. A being who never exists is not wronged by not being created, and there is

no obligation to any possible being to bring it into existence" (p. 93).

20 Suppose Plantinga, Adams and others have shown that the existence of evil is consistent with the existence of God. The more significant question is whether there is reason to believe it is *probable* that God exists given the amount and kind of evil there is. Is it plausible to suppose there is a morally sufficient reason for every evil such that God would allow it? Is it plausible to suppose that free will is so valuable God would not prevent its exercise in some cases in which there appears to be an overwhelming *prima facie* case for doing so? Cf. William Rowe, "The Empirical Argument from Evil"; "Evil and Theodicy."

21 Peter Van Inwagen says:

> a moral for students of the problem of evil: Do not attempt any solution to this problem that entails that every particular evil has a purpose, or that, with respect to every individual misfortune, or every devastating earthquake, or every disease, God has some special reason for allowing it. Concentrate rather on the problem of what sort of reasons a loving and providential God might have for allowing His creatures to live in a world in which many of the evils that happen to them happen to them for no reason at all.

Peter Van Inwagen, "The Place of Chance in a World Sustained by God," in Thomas V. Morris (ed.) *Divine and Human Action* (Ithaca: Cornell University Press, 1988), pp. 211–35, at p. 235.

This quotation could be taken as suggesting that a plausible rejection of the argument from evil against the existence of God must not rely on the kinds of claims that are often used against the logical version of the argument; for example, that it is *possible* that such and such an evil leads to a greater good so God must allow it. But, Van Inwagen's "moral for students of the problem of evil" is far more applicable to those who wish to refute the empirical argument. It is more applicable for those who claim that it is *plausible* to suppose that such and such an evil leads to a greater good so God must allow it. Still, one wonders why Van Inwagen thinks he needs the "moral" he issues. After all, the most common defence against the argument from evil is the Free Will Defence, and in that defence it is not assumed or argued but *denied* "that every particular evil has a purpose, or that, with respect to every individual misfortune, or every devastating earthquake, or every disease, God has some special reason for allowing it." The Free Will Defence maintains that there is an overall reason for God allowing such evils, but no special reason for any particular evil. When Van Inwagen says "Concentrate rather on the problem of what sort of reasons a loving and providential God might have for allowing His creatures to live in a world in which many of the evils that happen to them happen to them for no reason at all" he seems to have come face to face with Job. He acknowledges the force of the logical and empirical arguments from evil while denying the conclusion. This is a great advance (i.e. a qualitatively different approach) over the kinds of defensive approaches that, for example, Plantinga or Adams take. A way of putting this is to say that Van Inwagen accepts and understands Job's problem, whereas Plantinga and Adams deny he has one. Still, Van Inwagen's "moral for students of the problem of evil" is applicable only to the crudest of those who offer defences against the argument from evil. Who, after all, seriously maintains that every particular evil has a purpose?

22 Michael Peterson generalises the point about the priority of the empirical over the logical argument from evil when he says,

> The more interesting and important formulation of the problem of evil is not as an *a priori* problem of the internal consistency of theism. The problem is more powerfully formulated as an *a posteriori* matter regarding the acceptability or probability of theism in light of relevant external considerations. The problem must be moved from the sphere of purely formal logic into the arena of human thought and decision, into the realm where rational and moral persons assess theism in the light of their values, ontological commitments, and existential orientations. Indeed, this rendition of the problem of evil pervades the classical and contemporary literature ... the atheologian ... at best ... can claim that theism is unacceptable or improbable according to the external considerations which are present and central to his evaluation, and not that it is essentially irrational. The theist, on the other hand, may claim that theism is reasonable because it makes quite good sense of experience, is morally acceptable, and so on.

Michael L. Peterson, "Evil and Inconsistency," *Sophia*, 18 (1979), pp. 20–7. See p. 27 n. 11 for Peterson's examples of the literature that concerns itself with "the problem of *prima facie* gratuitous evil."

23 Some account of what it is to be "divine" is needed here. I forgo such an account in the present context noting only that while anything "divine" is also taken to be perfectly good by some theists, the two properties are not, and should not, be taken as mutually entailing one another by pantheists. In Rudolf Otto's account of the "holy" he explicitly separates the concept of goodness and moral perfection from that of holiness. See Rudolf Otto, *The Idea of the Holy*, 2nd edition (Oxford: Oxford University Press, 1950).

24 Cf. Geertz, "Religion as a Cultural System"; "Ethos, World View, and the Analysis of Sacred Symbols," in his *The Interpretation of Cultures* (New York: Basic Books, 1973), ch. 5, pp. 126–41.

25 Pierre Bayle, *Dictionnaire historique and critique*, 2nd edn, Rotterdam, 1702. Bayle argues against Spinoza in several ways. For example he claims that the supposition that "men are modalities of God" leads to a contradiction.

> If it were true then, as Spinoza claims, that men are modalities of God, one would speak falsely when one said, "Peter denies this, he wants that, he affirms such and such a thing"; for actually ... it is God who denies, wants ... from which it follows that God

hates and loves, denies and affirms the same things at the same time ... for it cannot be denied that, taking all these terms with all possible rigor, some men love and affirm what other men hate and deny ...

(pp. 309–10, in the Popkin edition of Bayle's *Dictionary*)

Bayle would deny that he is commiting the fallacy of composition, since he thinks that only substances, not modalities, can act or be acted upon (p. 311). But Spinoza would deny that God (or substance), as he understands the term, denies and affirms the same thing at the same time. This illustrates some of the difficulties concerning the relation of ontology to pantheism discussed in section 2.3.1 and again in connection with Robert Oakes's thesis that "theism entails pantheism." Any attempt to resolve a substantive issue relating to pantheism by resorting to the kind of ontological consideration that Bayle does will be unsatisfactory. Indeed, I am inclined to generalise and say that fundamental ontological considerations (e.g. what exists) are for the most part not relevant to determining what pantheism is or resolving conceptual issues related to it – e.g. if pantheism should account for evil, and if so, why?

26 Frederick M. Barnard, "Spinozism," in Paul Edwards (ed.) *Encyclopedia of Philosophy* (New York: Macmillan and Free Press, 1967), vol. 5, p. 541. Cf. Bayle, *Historical and Critical Dictionary*, p. 296, for the "monstrous hypothesis" quotation. Bayle uses the term "monstrous" many times in the article on Spinoza and not always about Spinoza. He calls the *Tractatus theologico-politicus* "a pernicious and detestable book" (p. 293). Hume also referred to Spinoza's philosophy as that "hideous hypothesis." Unlike Bayle, it is difficult to imagine that Hume was not being sarcastic.

27 Bayle, *Historical and Critical Dictionary*, p. 311.

28 Cf. Jantzen, *God's World, God's Body*, ch. 7; Ward, "God as Creator." For a recent argument that God is not morally culpable for human sin, see William E. Mann, "God's Freedom, Human Freedom, and God's Responsibility for Sin," in Thomas V. Morris (ed.) *Divine and Human Action* (Ithaca: Cornell University Press, 1988), pp. 182–210.

29 The supposition that it is actually the devil who is responsible for earthquakes etc. may seem anachronistic and jarring – or worse. But there is not or need not be anything extraordinary about the claim to one who accepts the bulk of the theistic world-view. This too one may find unsettling.

30 Paul Siwek, "How Pantheism Resolves the Enigma of Evil," *Laval Théologique et Philosophique*, 11–12 (1955–6), pp. 213–21, at 213–14. For Spinoza, evil is a kind of illusion, an "inadequate idea" resulting from inadequate knowledge. Siwek goes on to claim that "evil loses any intelligible meaning in Spinoza's doctrine, that it is metaphysically impossible" (p. 214).

31 Spinoza, *Epistolae* LXXVII. Quoted in Thomas McFarland, *Coleridge and the Pantheist Tradition* (Oxford: Oxford University Press, 1969),

p. 88. Spinoza claims that people are nevertheless morally responsible for their actions. Cf. Paul Siwek, "How Pantheism Resolves the Enigma of Evil," p. 220. Kant objected to Spinoza on various grounds – including his notion of freedom. Given Spinoza's account "Freedom could not be saved ... man would be a marionette, or an automaton, carpentered together and put on strings by the highest master of all crafts, and though self-consciousness would make it a thinking automaton, the consciousness of its spontaneity, if this spontaneity were equated with freedom, would be a mere illusion" (Kant, *Werke*, iii, pp. 567–8). Quoted in McFarland, p. 90. Kant may be right in claiming that Spinoza's determinism undermines freedom in various ways, including the sense of freedom necessary for morality and meaningful moral discourse. But note too that in this quotation Kant is attributing to Spinoza the concept of something like a theistic God, even though Spinoza's God was nothing at all like the theistic God.

32 For a discussion of how the problem of evil is "dissolved" in the context of an "immanentist" non-anthropomorphic metaphysical framework (e.g. Spinoza and Nietzsche) see Chin-Tai Kim, "Transcendence and Immanence," *Journal of the American Academy of Religion*, 55 (1987), pp. 537–49.

33 Marcus P. Ford, "Pluralistic Pantheism?," *Southern Journal of Philosophy*, 17 (1979), pp. 155–61, at 159–60.

34 Note too that this distinction suffices for dualism, but not for theism.

4.3 Ethics and ecology

1 John Toland, *Pantheisticon* (New York: Garland, 1976); reprint of the 1751 edition, pp. 32–3.

2 John Passmore, *Man's Responsibility for Nature: Ecological Problems and Western Traditions* (New York: Scribner's, 1974), p. 10. Cited in George Sessions, "Spinoza and Jeffers on Man in Nature," *Inquiry*, 20 (1977), pp. 481–528, at 516 n. 11.

3 Bertrand Bronson, "Walking Stewart," *University of California Publications in English* (Berkeley and Los Angeles: University of California Press, 1943), vol. xiv, pp. 146–7. Quoted in McFarland, *Coleridge and the Pantheist Tradition*, p. 100.

4 See Geoffrey Sayre-McCord's "Introduction: The Many Faces of Moral Realism," in Geoffrey Sayre-McCord (ed.) *Essays on Moral Realism* (Ithaca: Cornell University Press, 1988), pp. 1–23, at 13. The reason the assumption is mistaken according to Sayre-McCord is because, as Alexander Rosenberg says,

naturalism – has again become fashionable in metaethics. This is the brace of theses that (a) the conditions that make some moral claims true are facts about the world and its denizens, ontologically no different from the facts dealt with in physics or psychology, and (b) the way in which we come to know such claims to be true is identical to the ways in which scientific claims are acquired ... To be plausible, moral realism needs to avoid any tincture of ethical intuitionism or metaphysical mystery mongering. Naturalism is the only option available to realism for avoiding the charge that its metaphysical and epistemological foundations are untenable.

Alexander Rosenberg, "Moral Realism and Social Science," in *Midwest Studies in Philosophy,* 15 (1990), pp. 150–66. The view that in order to be plausible moral realism must rest on moral "naturalism" as described above is of course rejected by those theists and pantheists who are non-naturalists. The idea that non-naturalist moral realism (e.g. some types of theistic or pantheistic moral realism) is "metaphysical mystery mongering" or that naturalism as described above is at least *prima facie* more plausible than non-naturalism – or even that it avoids "metaphysical mystery mongering" – is of course contentious and question begging.

5 There are also theistic and (possibly) pantheistic forms of moral naturalism. Richard Swinburne gives a theistic naturalistic account of ethics in *The Coherence of Theism,* ch. 11. Presumably, naturalistic accounts such as Swinburne's run afoul of Sayre-McCord's criteria for acceptable foundations for moral realism on the grounds that a connection between theism and naturalism renders naturalism untenable.

6 The claim that pantheists and theists are "non-naturalists" is complicated by the fact that, although to say, "moral properties are non-natural" means they are distinct from natural ones, it does not (necessarily) mean that moral properties are not entailed by, or do not *supervene* upon, the possession of natural properties. Some ethical naturalists believe that possession of a moral property is the possession of a natural property. But one need not believe this to be an ethical naturalist. Those who hold that moral properties are *non-natural* because they are logically distinct from natural properties may also be *ethical naturalists* if they believe that moral properties are entailed by, or supervene upon, natural properties.

This kind of naturalism (i.e. one which holds that moral properties are non-natural but supervenient upon natural ones) is not to be confused with what Swinburne calls "anti-naturalism" which also holds that moral properties, being distinct from natural properties, are non-natural properties. He describes anti-naturalism as the view that "possession of natural properties never entails possession of moral properties. Moral properties are logically distinct from natural properties, and so it is logically possible that any moral property be possessed by an object with any combination of natural properties." (Swinburne, *The Coherence of Theism,* p. 185).

7 Taylor, *Principles of Ethics,* pp. 177–8.

8 Cf. G. E. Moore, *Principia Ethica* (Cambridge: Cambridge University Press, 1965). Also see Robert M. Adams, "A Modified Divine Command Theory of Ethical Wrongness," in his *The Virtue of Faith and Other Essays in Philosophical Theology* (Oxford: Oxford University Press, 1987), pp. 105–6. Adams does not explain "non-natural" in terms of

empirical verifiability. Instead, he says, "A non-natural fact is one which does not consist simply in any fact or complex of facts which can be stated entirely in the languages of physics, chemistry, biology and human psychology" (p. 105). Adams says,

> Given that the facts of wrongness asserted in Judeo-Christian ethics are nonnatural . . . in what do they consist? According to the divine command theory . . . insofar as they are nonnatural and objective, they consist in facts about the will or commands of God . . . It is clear, I think, that in stating that X is wrong a believer normally commits himself to the view that X is contrary to the will or commands of God. And the fact (if it is a fact) that X is contrary to the will or commands of God is surely a nonnatural objective fact.
>
> (p. 106)

It is one thing to say "that in stating that X is wrong a believer normally commits himself to the view that X is contrary to the will or commands of God." It is another thing to maintain, as the divine command theorist does, that "facts of moral wrongness . . . insofar as they are nonnatural and objective . . . consist of facts about the will or commands of God."

9 Swinburne, *The Coherence of Theism*, p. 185. Swinburne follows R. M. Hare's account of the problem of supervenience. Cf. R. M. Hare, *The Language of Morals* (Oxford: Oxford University Press, 1952), pp. 80f. Whether the "problem of supervenience" is an insuperable problem for anti-naturalism is questionable. Less extreme anti-naturalists may deny the possibility of objects "being exactly alike in their natural properties, but differing in their moral properties," that Swinburne and Hare claim anti-naturalism entails.

10 Swinburne, *The Coherence of Theism*. According to Swinburne, theism maintains (or should maintain) that "moral properties are distinct from natural properties" but "possession of the former is entailed by possession of certain of the latter" (see pp. 184–7). Thus, Swinburne disagrees with R. M. Adams's claim that "typically, the Judeo-Christian believer is a nonnaturalist." Adams says, "that X is contrary to the will or commands of God is surely a nonnatural objective feat." Nor does this non-natural fact appear to be entailed by, or supervene upon, any natural properties according to Adams – he does not say so at any rate. Adams, "A Modified Divine Command Theory of Ethical Wrongness," pp. 105–6. But on Swinburne's account this does not suffice to make theistic ethics non-naturalistic. Granted that "X is contrary to the will of God" is a non-natural objective fact, this will not be, in many cases, what *makes* an action wrong.

11 Adams, "A Modified Divine Command Theory of Ethical Wrongness," p. 105.

12 Hilary Armstrong, "The Apprehension of Divinity in the Self and Cosmos in Plotinus," in R. Baine Harris (ed.) *The Significance of Neoplatonism* (Norfolk: International Society for Neoplatonic Studies,

1976), pp. 187–98, at 188. Armstrong denies that Plotinus was a pantheist, but there are significant pantheistic elements in Plotinus.

13 Jantzen, *God's World, God's Body*, pp. 156–7.

14 Genevieve Lloyd, "Spinoza's Environmental Ethics," *Inquiry*, 23 (1980), pp. 293–311, at 293–4. Cf. Arne Naess, "Environmental Ethics and Spinoza's Ethics. Comments on Genevieve Lloyd's Article," *Inquiry*, 23 (1980), pp. 313–25; "Spinoza and Ecology," *Philosophia*, 7 (1977), pp. 45–54. Also, see Freya Mathews, *The Ecological Self* (London and New York: Routledge, 1990). Mathews is original in her pursuit of fundamental Spinozistic themes in relation to the metaphysical bases of ecological issues.

15 Lloyd, "Spinoza's Environmental Ethics," pp. 306–10. In the deep ecology movement's search for a metaphysical basis for their environmental ethic they have focused mostly on Spinoza, but other pantheistic systems might serve them better. However, since a well-developed general pantheistic metaphysic is lacking (i.e. there are only specific systems like Spinoza's Plotinus's etc.) deep ecologists would probably find themselves constructing rather than discovering the required metaphysic. This is a task philosophically minded deep ecologists might turn themselves too – as most already have to varying degrees.

16 Cf. Taylor, *Principles of Ethics*, p. 31. "A person's only duty is to promote his own good as much as possible . . . being moral . . . never requires a sacrifice of one's own long-range interests."

17 Sessions, "Spinoza and Jeffers on Man in Nature," p. 508.

18 Stuart Hampshire, *Spinoza* (London: Penguin Books, 1951), p. 115. "[Spinoza's] metaphysics and dependent theory of knowledge are designed to show man's place in nature as a thinking being. Spinoza always argued that, until this is understood, nothing can be said about the nature and possibility of human happiness and freedom" (p. 115). Cited in Sessions, "Spinoza and Jeffers on Man in Nature," p. 519 n. 25.

19 Lloyd, "Spinoza's Environmental Ethics," pp. 293–4. Perhaps the principal reason for not looking towards Spinoza as a basis for environmental ethics is that "the whole is too abstruse and, in some crucial respects, too alien to modern thought" (p. 294).

20 Harold W. Wood, Jr, "Modern Pantheism As An Approach to Environmental Ethics," *Environmental Ethics*, 7 (1985), pp. 151–63, at 157, 160–1. I discuss Wood's views further in Part III.

21 Wood, "Modern Pantheism As An Approach to Environmental Ethics," p. 152. His pantheism is distant from Spinoza's identification of God with nature, and much closer to nature mysticism. In fact it *is* nature mysticism. He talks about interacting with "God-as-nature." With the important exception of Spinoza, pantheists generally do not equate God with nature. But Wood's account of pantheism is not altogether inconsonant with a naturalistic model of pantheistic Unity, one that predicates Unity on the basis of a unifying force(s) or principle(s). The idea of unifying principles is also present in nature mysticism, which is really what Wordsworth's and the other Romantics' pantheism is. It is also in classical literature and music (e.g.

"pantheistic overtones" in Beethoven's music). The idea that Unity is rooted in nature is what types of nature mysticism (e.g. Wordsworth and Robinson Jeffers, Gary Snyder) have in common with more philosophically robust versions of pantheism. It is why nature mysticism and philosophical pantheism are conflated and confused with one another. But they are distinguishable in theory – even though they both talk about unity and are partly the result of the same intimations and feelings. Nature mysticism, however, is as compatible with theism as it is with pantheism.

22 Cf. Andrew Brennan, *Thinking About Nature: An Investigation of Nature, Value and Ecology* (London: Routledge, 1988), p. 134. Robin Attfield has argued that the Judaeo-Christian tradition does not promote an exploitative ethic towards the environment and non-human world, but embodies the attitude that we are "custodians and stewards of a precious natural order." *The Ethics of Environmental Concern* (Oxford: Basil Blackwell, 1983), p. 63. For a different view see John Passmore, *Man's Responsibility for Nature: Ecological Problems and Western Traditions*, 2nd edn (London: Duckworth, 1980). Cf. J. J. Lipner, "The World as God's 'Body.' " Lipner says,

> Rāmānuja's body-of-God theology, in its very choice of the "body" term . . . looks positively on the world of materiality . . . but, Rāmānuja's articulation introduces a much-needed note of radical ambiguity to the "body" idea. Though in its microscopic application the self-body relation is intended to be a benign one . . . the relationship remains an open one in that the body . . . (really, in this context, one's material body, but by extension, the material world) may "rebel" . . . and thwart the true goal(s) of the self . . . [M]atter has to be understood . . . for what it is and what it can do – its "co-operation has to be sought". Allied to this insight is a much-needed corrective for the western world . . . with its Nature-exploitative and anti-ecological ethics derived from Genesis 1: 26–30. We subdue and dominate, rather than co-operate.
>
> (p. 160)

23 See Brennan, pp. 31–5, for the distinction between scientific and metaphysical ecology.

24 See Brennan, p. 139, for references to others to give an account of "the *moral considerability* of non-human beings."

25 "Ethical holism" is not to be confused with "ecological holism." For Brennan's discussion and rejection of ecological holism see pp. 180–2, 202.

26 For Brennan's critique of various ethical theories and a defence of his claim that "modern ethical theory . . . suffers from ignoring ecological facts of life" (p. 174), see *Thinking About Nature*: Chapter 11, "The Environment and Conventional Moral Theory"; Chapter 12, "Beyond the Social Contract."

27 For a discussion of "ethical polymorphism" see Brennan, p. 186; cf. pp. 186–90. "Ethical polymorphism" as it is characterised here is somewhat reminiscent of Joseph Fletcher's "situation ethics." A

common criticism of "situation ethics" is that it is *ad hoc.* That it is *ad hoc* can also be seen as its principal virtue. See Joseph Fletcher, *Situation Ethics* (Philadelphia: Westminster, 1966).

28 Brennan notes that some deep ecologists would "be suspicious" of his account of their position. For the original paper on deep ecology see Arne Naess, "The Shallow and the Deep, Long-range Ecology Movement," *Inquiry,* 16 (1973), pp. 95–100; cf. Arne Naess, "Identification as Source of Deep Ecological Attitudes," in M. Tobias (ed.) *Deep Ecology* (San Diego: Avant Books, 1983); "The Deep Ecological Movement: Some Philosophical Aspects," *Philosophical Inquiry* 8 (1986), pp. 10–29; J. B. Callicott, "Traditional American and Traditional Western European Attitudes Towards Nature," in R. Elliot and A. Gare (eds) *Environmental Philosophy* (Milton Keynes: Open University Press, 1983).

29 Aldo Leopold, "The Land Ethic," in *A Sand County Almanac* (New York: Oxford University Press, 1949), pp. 219, 240.

30 For a discussion of the divine command theory see Adams, "A Modified Divine Command Theory of Ethical Wrongness," p. 97. This essay originally appeared in Gene Outka and John P. Reeder, Jr (eds) *Religion and Morality* (Garden City, N.Y.: Anchor), 1973, pp. 318–47. Adams abandons this "modified" version in "Divine Command Metaethics Modified Again," in his *The Virtue of Faith and Other Essays in Philosophical Theology* (Oxford: Oxford University Press, 1987), pp. 128–43. I critique Adams's original position in "Adams' Modified Divine Command Theory of Ethics," *Sophia,* forthcoming.

31 Adams, "A Modified Divine Command Theory of Ethical Wrongness," p. 97. Adams calls this the "unmodified divine command theory of ethical wrongness." He distinguishes this theory which he takes to be indefensible from his "modified" version which he thought was defensible before later abandoning it in "Divine Command Metaethics Modified Again."

32 Adams, "A Modified Divine Command Theory of Ethical Wrongness," p. 98. Adams abandons this restriction in "Divine Command Metaethics Modified Again," pp. 128–43. See pp. 128, 139.

33 Cf. Kai Nielsen, *Ethics Without God,* rev. edn (Buffalo, N.Y.: Prometheus Books, 1990).

34 Furthermore, there is no reason to suppose, as Adams does, that religious ethical discourse would fail to operate for the believer who believed that God was commanding something they took to be clearly morally objectionable. This claim is central to Adams's modified divine command theory.

35 The divine command theory is just one indefensible and *unnecessary* theory mistakenly attributed to theists by philosophical theologians who are theists. Another recent example is Alvin Plantinga's strange assertion that, for what he terms "the mature theist," belief in God is a "properly basic belief." He claims the believer is justified in believing in the existence of God apart from other beliefs she may hold by way of justification. The "mature theist" does not, according to Plantinga, base belief in God on other beliefs she has. Plantinga

claims this was Calvin's view, and that it is the view of "reformed epistemology" generally. What is most odd about the theories of both Adams and Plantinga is not so much their epistemology (although Plantinga is wrong about belief in God being a properly basic belief), but that they attribute to the theist wildly implausible views that theists generally do not hold, and regard their claims as *descriptive*. The first thing that should be said by way of criticising their respective theories is that *plainly theists do not generally hold these views*. Certainly Calvin and Luther never held the view Plantinga attributes to them. I discuss Plantinga's claim in my review essay of Alvin Plantinga and Nicholas Wolterstorff (eds) *Faith and Rationality: Reason and Belief in God* (Notre Dame: University of Notre Dame, 1983), in *Philosophia*, 16 (3–4) (1986), pp. 447–60; and in *Hume and the Problem of Miracles*.

36 The Chinese folk religion found in religious Taoism (i.e. Taoism as practised) often predates Lao Tzu's thought and the *Tao Tê Ching*. Its basic pursuit is "longevity" rather than the "harmony" and "tranquility" of philosophical Taoism. The pursuit of longevity involves worship and prayer. Alchemy and other folk practices have little to do with the Taoism of the *Tao Tê Ching*.

4.4 Salvation and immortality

1 Amos Funkenstein, *Theology and the Scientific Imagination from the Middle Ages to the Seventeenth Century* (Princeton: Princeton University Press, 1986), p. 46.

2 Bertrand Bronson, "Walking Stewart", pp. 146–7. Quoted in McFarland, *Coleridge and The Pantheist Tradition*, p. 100. McFarland agrees with Thomas De Quincey's description of Stewart's philosophy as "a sort of rude and unscientific Spinozism."

3 Robinson Jeffers in a letter to Sister Power; cited in Sessions, "Spinoza and Jeffers on Man in Nature," p. 512.

4 Paul Taylor, *Principles of Ethics*, p. 132.

5 There are varieties of pantheism that looks towards some special sort of awareness of interconnection and relation to Unity for the final achievement of true happiness (e.g. Spinoza's). In such cases, perhaps the pantheist ethic is not so clearly separate from that of Plato and Aristotle or theism. However, generally, pantheism will not maintain the view that happiness relies on some univocal sort of awareness of interconnection and relation to the Unity. The achievement of happiness – if not in terms of structure, then in terms of form – is pluralistically conceived.

Some versions of pantheism have narrower conceptions of human nature (and a corresponding ideal type of person) than others. In Taoism, the ideal person – who is also the ideal ruler – is the sage. The sage embodies not so much an essential nature (i.e. the emphasis is not on this) as the knowledge enabling her to achieve her potential; help others to achieve theirs; and to attain the state of "vacuity" and "tranquility" that the Taoist seeks. It is a salvific state. (I discuss

277

this further in section 6.2.) It is possible, however, to see the sage as just one type of person manifesting an essential human nature within a broader Taoist conception of human nature.

6 For a very useful discussion of the notion of "salvation" in the broader context of religious ethics in the Judaeo-Christian tradition, and in the context of a theory of religion, see John P. Reeder, Jr, *Source, Sanction and Salvation* (Englewood Cliffs: Prentice Hall, 1988).

7 Cf. *The Four Socratic Dialogues of Plato*, tr. Benjamin Jowett (Oxford, Clarendon Press, 1903). Where "immortality" plays a role in pantheism it is not personal immortality, and it is achievable in this life, not after death. R. Baine Harris gives the following account of Plotinus's goal.

> Salvation, as Plotinus sees it, is essentially a technique involving three processes: (1) catharsis, or the purification of the soul through morality, (2) dialectics, or the practice of the discipline of philosophy; and (3) illumination, or enlightenment... – a state of ecstasy wherein the soul finally comes into direct communion with that part of the One that is already within it. The way of salvation is a journey from soul to mind to the One during which the soul progressively sees itself as an element of the Ultimate. Salvation is not from above, it is from within; and it is not free – it is very expensive and rarely achieved. By most men it is only relatively achieved, depending upon which level they succeed in attaining...
>
> Seen in its boldest profile, then, Nepolatonism is an effort to reconcile Aristotelianism with Plutonism through an appeal to a still higher unifying principle than is found in either of the two, namely an Ultimate First Principle that is *both* transcendent and immanent in all nature, indefinable *and* knowable, self-sufficient *and* creative throughout the universe without an act of will.

R. Baine Harris, "A Brief Description of Neoplatonism," in R. Baine Harris (ed.) *The Significance of Neoplatonism* (Norfolk: International Society for Neoplatonic Studies, 1976), pp. 6, 8. As Harris describes it, the neoplatonic "higher unifying principle" certainly "sounds" like the Tao.

Given the above account, Neoplatonism is pantheistic. But the method outlined for achieving "salvation," and the salvific state, is different from, for example, Spinoza's – and even more distant from that of the *Tao Tê Ching*. Pantheists can stop well short of the Plotinian aim of mystical union with the One. They do not even seek mystical union with the Unity which they are a part of. A pantheist's aims are usually more modest than the Neoplatonist's.

8 Shu-hsien Liu, "Commentary: Theism from a Chinese Perspective," *Philosophy East and West*, 28 (1978), pp. 413–18, at 413. Liu says, "As for the Taoist philosophers, they also taught a philosophy of union between Heaven and man, only they interpreted Heaven in a totally

different way as to contradict the Confucian understanding of Heaven. But in no way can we interpret the Heaven of the Taoist philosophers as an equivalent of the Western God" (p. 413).

9 Walt Whitman, *Leaves of Grass*, First (1885) Edition, ed. Malcom Cowley (New York: Viking Press, 1959), p. 12.

10 Nielsen, *Ethics Without God*; Kurt Baier, "The Meaning of Life," in E. D. Klemke (ed.) *The Meaning of Life* (New York: Oxford University Press, 1981), pp. 81–117.

11 Bernard Williams, "The Makropoulos Case," in his *Problems of the Self* (Cambridge: Cambridge University Press, 1973), ch. 6. Cf. Richard Swinburne's discussion in "A Theodicy of Heaven and Hell," in Alfred J. Freddoso (ed.) *The Existence and Nature of God* (Notre Dame: University of Notre Dame Press, 1983), pp. 37–54. "A man who had molded his desires so as to seek only the good and its continuation would not, given the Christian doctrine of God, be bored in eternity" (p. 43). "those whom he [Williams] pictures as necessarily bored in eternity seem to me persons of limited idealism" (p. 53 n. 11).

12 Quoted in McFarland, *Coleridge and the Pantheist Tradition*, p. 168. Cf. pp. 167–8 for an account of Leibniz's critique of Spinoza and "the doctrine of a universal spirit" in general. McFarland says, "Leibniz, like Coleridge, was attracted by that corollary of the doctrine of a universal spirit by which nature becomes enriched with divinity, and by which all things are unified . . . But after this flirtation with Neoplatonist pantheism, Leibniz settles down to an unequivocal opposition to the further implications of the universal spirit, for they constitute Spinozism" (p. 168).

13 Anthony Flew, "Immortality," *Encyclopedia of Philosophy* (New York: Macmillan and Free Press, 1967), vol. 4, pp. 139–50. Also see his *God and Philosophy* (London: Hutchinson, 1966).

14 Quoted in Sessions, "Spinoza and Jeffers on Man in Nature," p. 513. Sessions cites it from G. J. Nathan, "The Tower Beyond Tragedy," in *Theatre Book of the Year, 1950–51* (New York: 1951); and Arthur B. Coffin, *Robinson Jeffers: Poet of Inhumanism* (Wisconsin: University of Wisconsin Press, 1971), p. 255.

15 David Hume, *The Natural History of Religion and Dialogues Concerning Natural Religion*, ed. A. Wayne Colver and John V. Price (Oxford: Clarendon Press, 1976), Part IX, p. 216. Cf. Paul Davies, *God and The New Physics* (London: Penguin Books, 1990), originally published by J. M. Dent, 1983. In Chapters 2–4 Davies considers, among other things, the hypothesis that the universe may exist necessarily. He claims that the new physics can be brought to bear on the traditional cosmological arguments for the existence of God. Yet what his discussion reveals is that he is either considering the cosmological argument from a philosophical perspective in which few, if any, scientific as opposed to philosophical hypotheses are brought to bear, or else he is considering scientific issues like whether time existed before the Big Bang – an issue whose relevance to the causal version of the cosmological argument he considers is minimal and probably nil.

The fact that science can now explain, for example, the "appearance of matter without antimatter" (p. 31) does not undermine a religious hypothesis concerning God as creator. The fact that there may have been no such thing as "time" before the Big Bang does not seriously undermine the hypothesis that God "caused" the Big Bang because "cause and effect are temporal concepts, and cannot be applied to a state in which time does not exist" (p. 39).

16 These distinctions are crucial to Aquinas's cosmological arguments. See his *Summa Theologica*, Part I, Question 2. This discussion of Aquinas is based partly on lecture notes of Michael Tooley's.

17 Stokes, *One and Many in Presocratic Philosophy*, pp. 13–21, 34.

18 Bertrand Russell, "A Free Man's Worship," in E. D. Klemke (ed.) *The Meaning of Life* (Oxford: Oxford University Press, 1981), pp. 55–62. Despite the superficial similarity between Russell's position and Camus's they are quite different. Russell thinks that one must resign oneself to ultimate extinction and live in spite of it. Camus however thinks the "absurdity" of existence is not simply something to be got over, but is instead something that one should constantly live in terms of. Camus recommends an attitude not of spite but of scorn.

19 Russell's view is basically that one should strive to accomplish certain things for the satisfaction they bring – despite the fact that ultimately, with the extinction of the solar system, all accomplishments will be forgotten and lost. Russell would not, however, want to equate this with a doctrine of salvation. His point is that the meaning of life is the meaning that we create for ourselves with our own pursuits, accomplishments etc. It is independent of God or anything like God, and none of our achievements will ultimately last. Cf. Bertrand Russell, *Why I Am Not a Christian and Other Essays* (London: George Allen & Unwin, 1975); "A Free Man's Worship."

20 Cf. Thomas Nagel, "Death," in his *Mortal Questions* (Cambridge: Cambridge University Press, 1979), pp. 1–10. Nagel claims that "something essential is omitted from the account of the badness of death by an analysis which treats it as a deprivation of possibilities" (p. 8 n. 3). For a recent defence of "the traditional view that death is bad (when it is bad) primarily because it deprives the deceased of goods – the goods he would have enjoyed if he had lived" see Fred Feldman, "Some Puzzles About the Evil of Death," *Philosophical Review*, 100 (1991), pp. 205–27. Cf. Anthony L. Brueckner and John Martin Fischer, "Why is Death Bad?," *Philosophical Studies*, 50 (1986), pp. 213–21. This article attempts to explain why it is not irrational to fear death as Epicurus and Lucretius both claimed it was.

21 In fact, I think this misrepresents the theistic position. See my articles "Camus, Hare, and The Meaning of Life," *Sophia*, 27 (1988), pp. 13–30; "What Does Death Have to Do With The Meaning of Life?," *Religious Studies*, 24 (1988), pp. 457–65.

22 For a discussion of some problems raised by the theistic concept of heaven see my article, "Swinburne's Heaven: One Hell of a Place," *Religious Studies*, 29 (1993). Herman Melville asks, "How is it that we still refuse to be comforted for those who we nevertheless maintain

are dwelling in unspeakable bliss . . . Faith, like a jackal, feeds among the tombs, and even from these dead doubts she gathers her most vital hope." Herman Melville, *Moby-Dick* (London: Penguin, 1972), pp. 130–1. First published as *The Whale* in 1851.

Part III

METHOD

Leaves of Grass
[15]
The city sleeps and the country sleeps,
The living sleep for their time . . . and the dead sleep for their
  time,
The old husband sleeps by his wife and the young husband sleeps
  by his wife;
And these one and all tend inward to me, and I tend outward to
  them,
And such as it is to be of these more or less I am.

[26]
I think I will do nothing for a long time but listen,
And accrue what I hear into myself . . . and let sounds contribute
  toward me.

I hear the bravuras of birds . . . the bustle of growing wheat . . .
  gossip of flames . . . clack of sticks cooking my meals.

I hear the sound of the human voice . . . a sound I love,
I hear all sounds as they are tuned to their uses . . . sounds of
  the city and sounds out of the city . . . sounds of the day and
  night;

[30]
All truths wait in things,
They neither hasten their own delivery nor resist it,

They do not need the obstetric forceps of the surgeon,
The insignificant is as big to me as any,
What is less or more than a touch?

Logic and sermons never convince,
The damp of the night drives deeper into my soul . . .

[31]
I believe a leaf of grass is no less than the journeywork of the
    stars,
And the pismire is equally perfect, and a grain of sand, and the
    egg of the wren,
And the tree-toad is a chef-d'oeuvre for the highest,
And the running blackberry would adorn the parlors of heaven,
And the narrowest hinge in my hand puts to scorn all machinery,
And the cow crunching with head depressed surpasses any statue,
And a mouse is miracle enough to stagger sextillions of infidels,
And I could come every afternoon of my life to look at the
    farmer's girl boiling her iron tea-kettle and baking
    shortcake . . .

[32]
I think I could turn and live awhile with the animals . . . they are
    so placid and self-contained,
I stand and look at them sometimes half the day long.

They do not sweat and whine about their condition,
They do not lie awake in the dark and weep for their sins,
They do not make me sick discussing their duty to God,
Not one is dissatisfied . . . not one is demented with the mania
    of owning things,
Not one kneels to another nor to his kind that lived thousands
    of years ago,
Not one is respectable or industrious over the whole earth . . .

[48]
I hear and behold God in every object, yet I understand God not
    in the least,
Nor do I understand who there can be more wonderful than
    myself.

METHOD

Why should I wish to see God better than this day?
I see something of God each hour of the twenty-four, and each
   moment then,
In the faces of men and women I see God, and in my own face
   in the glass;
I find letters from God dropped in the street, and every one is
   signed by God's name,
And I leave them where they are, for I know that others will
   punctually come forever and ever.

Walt Whitman[1]

5

WHAT PANTHEISTS SHOULD NOT DO – AND WHY

But make nature your God, elevate creatureliness, and you can count on gross results. Maybe you can count on gross results under any circumstances.[2]

Saul Bellow

Alasdair MacIntyre claims that "Spinoza ... rationalist metaphysician, is of all philosophers the one whose life has least apparent connection with his work."[3] How can this be substantiated? From accounts of his life that include his refusal of a professorship – choosing to polish lenses instead; refusing financial assistance; his reaction to his excommunication in 1656 by the Jews of Amsterdam from the Congregation of Israel;[4] and accounts of his general demeanour; it seems that Spinoza's life was intimately related to his philosophy. Spinoza's philosophy *seems* integral to his life in ways that, for example, Hume's sceptical reasoning, by his own admission, had relatively little influence on his life. MacIntyre's contention, however, raises an interesting question. How can a pantheist's beliefs be reflected in action? What kinds of practice would have had to be evident to convince MacIntyre that Spinoza's life was connected to his beliefs? Surely accepting the prestigious appointment he was offered at Heidelberg was not the only (kind of) way to make the connection between his philosophy and his life apparent. For Spinoza, refusing it was another way.

My aim in Part III is to determine what pantheists, religiously speaking, should and should not do. Can pantheists employ traditional modes of theistic and non-theistic practice such as worship, prayer, and meditation? What form, if any, might a distinctively pantheistic type of practice take? To address these

287

issues some account must be given of the relation between belief and practice – specifically, between religious beliefs and actions they engender. This is a vast topic. In effect, it is a fundamental question addressed by theoretical social anthropology, and related aspects of sociology, in their effort to explain how to interpret systems of thought and action different from our own (e.g. "traditional" societies).

The relation between belief and practice has philosophical, theological and psychological dimensions – as well as anthropological and sociological ones. Philosophically, the issue is directly related to the nature of rationality and relativism, and less directly to an account of "meaning." It can also involve metaphysical issues such as truth, realism, anti-realism, idealism etc. Theologically, the question involves the nature and function of doctrine. What kinds of doctrine and practice are consonant with particular traditions, and how are traditions related to doctrine? How are doctrinal differences related to practice and why are some differences central and others not?[5] To what extent can doctrines change? The relationship between belief and practice also has an obvious psychological dimension. There are various psychological accounts of how religious belief is acquired and sustained, and of why people undertake certain religious practices. Freud, Jung, William James and Abraham Maslow give divergent accounts of belief and practice, and of the value of religion in general. Although it involves all these dimensions, the relationship between belief and practice can be investigated without reducing it to basic psychological or theological issues, or to the more fundamental question of the nature of rationality.[6]

Actions are usually explained by an agent's desires and beliefs. But the situation in regard to religious action is more complex. As Freud, Durkheim and many others have argued, where religious practices such as rituals are not clearly accounted for by beliefs, other kinds of explanation may be in order. And, of course, they also claim that even when practices do appear to follow from beliefs, the correct explanation of them may not be the belief that appears to explain them. The accounts examined presuppose that sense can be made out of religious practices even if their connection with belief is not always clear, and even if references to agents' beliefs are not always necessary. Where a practice appears irrational, an underlying rationality is assumed that makes it subject to explanation.

My interest is in determining what practices should be associated with pantheistic beliefs. Only on the assumption that one knows how to explain the relation between belief and practice is it possible to judge that certain practices do or do not fit, or seem to follow from belief – and vice versa.

It should also be possible to explain disparities between what one expects in terms of practice given certain beliefs and what actually takes place. Asking about the nature of the relation between religious belief and practice is another way of asking about the nature of religion. These questions are prerequisite to determining the kind of practices pantheists could suitably undertake given what they believe. For present purposes it should suffice to examine some prominent accounts of belief and practice most relevant to the question of how to practise pantheism.

5.1 BELIEF AND PRACTICE

Those who were acquainted with him [Spinoza], and the peasants of the villages where he had lived in retirement for some time, all agree in saying that he was sociable, affable, honest, obliging, and of a well-ordered morality. This is strange; but, after all, we should not be more surprised by this than to see people who live very bad lives even though they are completely convinced of the Gospel.[1]

Pierre Bayle

People who come to have different beliefs about whether there is a God, what he is like, and what he has done, will, if they are pursuing the good, do different actions.[2]

Richard Swinburne

Pantheists believe in a divine Unity. Yet, in pantheism there is no apparent community of believers organised around their common (though not identical) beliefs by an established body of religious teaching and scripture.[3] Without these traditional constituents of religion pantheists may find themselves wanting to practise their faith – seeking to relate their actions to their beliefs – and yet wondering how to go about it. Pantheists have to ask themselves what they should do given what they believe.

The admonition to "practise what you preach" seems straightforward when heard at mother's knee. Who would quarrel with the idea that acting in accordance with one's (morally correct and true) beliefs is a good thing, and something we should endeavour to do?[4] Interpreted as a warning against hypocrisy it is clear what "practise what you preach" means. Yet, all sorts of beliefs give rise to all sorts of practices. The same or similar religious beliefs result in distinct practices, all allegedly connected to and explained by those beliefs. However, it is also the case that practices and rites may be invariant while beliefs that allegedly inform and explain them vary. In this case, it may be action that should be used to explain belief, instead of belief explaining action.[5] (Should we also be told to "preach what you practise"?) If the connection between belief and action is fluid, and either may at times be used to account for the other, then acting in accordance with one's beliefs (or believing in accordance with one's actions), and avoiding hypocrisy, may not be so easy.

Consider the following commonplace: theists sometimes do not pray in situations where expected; but atheists sometimes unexpectedly do pray. There are theists who never pray, and atheists who frequently pray. This indicates that while certain kinds of practice may be associated with certain kinds of belief, there is no steadfast link between them. There is no direct correlation between belief of a certain kind (e.g. theistic belief) and practice of a certain kind (e.g. prayer). Whereas one might be astonished to overhear Sartre whispering the "Our Father" over coffee in *Les Deux Magots*, it is neither astonishing or troubling that many avowed atheists will, on occasion, find themselves praying. There are explanations, typically psychological ones, as to why this occurs, and it is a mistake to assume that sincere prayer must indicate belief in God. (Only a myopic theist would claim "there are no atheists in foxholes" and not see the peculiarity in doing so.)

Although modes of behaviour are usually explained by the reasons given for them (i.e. beliefs), I have noted that on some accounts beliefs do not explain regular forms of behaviour. It is argued (e.g. V. Pareto) that sometimes the action (e.g. ritual practice) explains the reasons given for them. Beliefs may be a rationalisation for practices undertaken for other reasons. "Where forms of action are constant, but 'rationalisations', 'ideologies', or 'derivations' vary ... we should conclude that explanation goes from action to the beliefs which apparently inform it, and not vice versa" (see note 5, p. 330). An alternative but related view held by some "Wittgensteinians" is that in religion (and elsewhere) belief and practice are inseparable and must be interpreted together. To understand what people believe it is necessary to look both at what they do and what they say. Belief and practice together are constitutive of "forms of life." Thus, even if my belief that my thirst will be quenched if I drink water, and my desire to quench it, explains my drinking, my religious refusal to light a match on Saturday, or to be tattooed, or my burial in a plain pine box, will certainly require a more complex explanation and may require a different kind of explanation.

Furthermore, even if we are not at all clear about what pantheists should do, it may seem we are relatively clear about what they believe. However, if theorists who claim that action sometimes explains belief or that action and belief must be understood together are right, then it follows that we do not yet know what pantheists believe. Indeed, in so far as pantheists lack a distinctive practice, they may be taken not to believe anything (pantheistically) at all. Such theorists claim that systems of belief and practice, if not individual beliefs and practices, are intrinsically related so as to define one another – and they develop together. Therefore, it may not be possible to keep the question of pantheists' belief distinct, or totally distinct, from the question of what they do. Indeed, one need not accept such theories to believe, as a matter of commonsense, that belief and practice are connected in such a way that they cannot be adequately understood apart from one another.

Some prominent accounts of the relation between religious belief and practice are considered below. This should enable us to partially determine what is involved in practising pantheism, by explaining how what a pantheist does relates to what she believes. It will also set pantheism in the context of some influential theories of religion.

5.1.1 The Wittgensteinian "non-realist" interpretation

I shall argue that the connection between belief and practice is not the one posed by Wittgenstein in his "lectures on religious belief," or his other later writings; nor, to the extent they differ, is it the one Wittgensteinians, such as D. Z. Phillips or Peter Winch, and Don Cupitt hypothesise.[6]

What is the "Wittgensteinian" position? John Hick refers to Phillips, and others influenced by Wittgenstein's later philosophy, as giving a "non-realist interpretation of religious discourse."[7] They claim that such discourse is not about what it appears to be about. This analysis of religious discourse is also an analysis of religion. The non-realist

> understands [religious discourse] throughout as referring, not to realities alleged to exist independently of ourselves, but to our own moral and spiritual states. Thus to say that God exists is not to affirm the reality of . . . a person without a body (i.e. a spirit) who is eternal . . . That "God exists" means that there are human beings who use the concept of God and for whom it is the presiding idea in their form of life.[8]

D. Z. Phillips, for example, has a non-realist account of immortality. He says, "Questions about the immortality of the soul are seen not to be questions concerning the extent of a man's life . . . but questions concerning the kind of life a man is living."[9] The non-realist does not claim, as for example Freud does, that believers are mistaken in thinking they know why they believe in God. The non-realist claims, in effect, that believers do not mean what they seem to mean if taken literally. Believers are mistaken if they think their beliefs in immortality are literally about surviving death. Non-realist accounts are based on the Wittgensteinian theory of "meaning as use." The meaning of a concept or an expression is its use. Phillips and others interpret this as implying a non-realist construal of religious discourse, but the theory does not entail this patently false account.

The case is complicated since in the Wittgensteinian view "literal" meaning is not what it is ordinarily understood to be. Literal meaning must be interpreted in terms of the way in which the assertion is used – the role it has in the life of the language-user. The non-realist typically claims that believers do understand their own discourse, but their understanding shows itself in the application of religious concepts in their lives, and not in what they say they mean. What believers mean, and their own understanding of what they mean, "shows" itself in their judgments and in what they do. In this Wittgensteinian view, religious discourse is no different from any other kind of discourse. To understand what a person means, one must look at what they do. Belief and practice are conceptually and linguistically linked.

If "meaning is use" *simpliciter* (i.e. nothing but use) and the expression of some religious belief X results in practices a or b, then the meaning of X is a or b. Thus, in MacIntyre's account of the anthropologist Edmund Leach: "Myth is to be understood in terms of ritual, saying in terms of doing. To interpret any statement made by primitive people which appears to be unintelligible, ask what the people in question do . . . Leach writes 'myth regarded as a statement in words "says" the same thing as ritual regarded as a statement in action.' "[10]

In this non-realist analysis, since similarly stated religious beliefs are not used (acted upon) in a univocal way, a highly relativised account of their meaning follows. Even if each believer "says" the same thing about what they believe (i.e. uses the same words), they will mean different things by it since the role the belief plays in the life of the speaker differs from person to person. Since practice always differs among persons to a degree, their associated beliefs must always differ as well.

Some of the difficulty in non-realist and "fideistic" positions is a result of conflating what a person believes with how that belief affects her life. (The fideist claims that a form of life must be shared to be understood. One must "believe" in order to "understand." And to "believe" as believers do, one must say and do as believers do, since that is what it means to have such beliefs. This allegedly follows from "meaning as use.") In realist and non-fideistic accounts the fact that people act on beliefs in different ways is not taken to imply they believe different things. That insight into what is believed is gained by looking at what is done does not show that beliefs resulting in different practices are not the same beliefs – nor is Leach committed to this view. It is not always possible to understand what is said without taking it in a wider context of belief and action. But this does not support the non-realist and fideistic positions.

In the non-realist view it may appear impossible to suppose that persons can ever *not* practice what they believe since what they believe is "shown" in what they do. But this is not the case. To recognise when a believer is acting hypocritically, for example, one must understand the rules governing the application of concepts such as hypocrisy in the life of the believer. Hypocrisy is recognised by placing what is said or done in the wider context (the "form of life") of the believer's beliefs and actions.

John Hick criticises the non-realist position as follows: "Whereas the central core of religious discourse interpreted in a realist way constitutes, if true, good news to all mankind, on a non-realist interpretation it constitutes bad news for all except a fortunate minority."[11] The "fortunate minority" are those who attain the kind of "salvation" that according to the non-realist must be achieved in this life, if at all (i.e. not after death), and is the only kind possible. "Salvation" is in principle available to everyone, but only a few achieve it according to the non-realist.

Hick's criticism is not the most basic one. It is not an argument against non-realism at all since it merely points out what the consequences of such a position would be if it were true. If non-realism were correct it would be "bad news," but Hick does not say why it is not correct. Indeed, if the non-realist regards the fact that there is no afterlife as lamentable, then she will agree with Hick that her view is bad news. The basic criticism of the non-realist position is that their analysis implausibly rejects both the believer's and the "outsider's" account of the literal meaning of religious discourse. It denies the believer *can* believe in life after death taken as a life not in this world or current life.

Whatever the insights the non-realist is able to give concerning the role religious discourse has in the life of the believer, it fails as an account of the meaning of that discourse. The relation between belief and practice implied by this analysis is also mistaken. The plausible supposition that belief has to be explained and understood partly in terms of practices related to it is not sufficient reason to accept non-realism. Even if one accepts "meaning as use," it does not follow that what the believer means by immortality must be interpreted as about *this-worldly* expectation. An adequate theory of "meaning as use" should see it as impossible for a believer not to mean what they think they mean about straightforward existential propositions, and *most* other beliefs.

What does this have to do with the practice of pantheism? Even if non-realism were correct it could not help answer the substantive question of how to practise pantheism – or what they believe. Whatever the pantheist did would be interpreted as reflecting what she believed. To know what pantheists believed, one would look at the criteria for the application of pantheistic concepts among the community of pantheists – a community that lacks cohesion. And, if a pantheist wanted to know what to do as a pantheist, all she could do to find out is look at what she and other pantheists already do. Unless the communal practice of pantheism were already in place, the non-realist could not give an account of what they believe or should do given their beliefs. Non-realism, it seems, is necessarily mute concerning the kind of normative concern a pantheist may have about what she should do. From the Wittgensteinian perspective it is doubtful that it makes sense to ask "what to do" if one is a pantheist. The only information that can be gleaned is from practices already identifiable as pantheistic and already in place. Thus, the non-realist interpretation of religious discourse is irrelevant for the questions about pantheism being asked. The fact that it is irrelevant is suggestive of other grounds for rejecting it.

Non-realists are mistaken not only in their account of religious discourse, but also – because connected – in their understanding of religion. A realist account of religious language (and religion) takes it at face value to refer, often symbolically, to independent reality.

Clifford Geertz, whose account of religion was discussed above in "Divinity," interprets religious discourse symbolically but "realistically." (He is a realist as opposed to a non-realist.) "A religion is a system of symbols which acts to establish powerful, pervasive, and long-lasting moods and motivations in men by formulating conceptions of the general order of existence and clothing these conceptions with such an aura of factuality that the moods and motivations seem uniquely realistic."[12] Unless religious discourse is construed by the believer to refer to independent realities as in the realist view, religion could not function as it does. (Compare this with Emile Durkheim's view that, if believers accepted his "symbolist" account of religious belief and practice, this would have an important effect on religious life.)[13] A non-realist account of religious belief *on the part of believers themselves* is not possible in a Geertzian account, although this is what Phillips and especially Cupitt call for. John Hick says,

> Phillips does not argue that the classical users of God-talk . . . consciously accepted or were even aware of this kind of non-realist interpretation. They . . . believed in a real and powerful divine person and in a literal conscious existence

after death . . . Phillips' contention is rather that in the light of twentieth-century philosophy . . . we are now in a position to distinguish between its merely literal and its authentically religious meaning.[14]

If Phillips is right about "authentic religious meaning," and if this account is accepted by believers, then it is impossible for religion to function as Geertz sees it as functioning.

A non-realist account denies what is crucial to Geertz's realist account: that the believer seeks to formulate a way of life that accords with an independent reality. Geertz says

> Sacred symbols function to synthesise a people's ethos . . . and their world-view – the picture they have of the way things in sheer actuality are . . . In religious belief and practice a group's ethos is rendered intellectually reasonable by being shown to represent a way of life ideally adopted to the actual state of affairs the world describes, while the world-view is rendered emotionally convincing by being presented as an image of an actual state of affairs peculiarly well-arranged to accommodate such a way of life.[15]

Since Geertz's account is essentially a realist one, it is surprising that, although Don Cupitt's explanation of religion seems similar to Geertz's, Cupitt is a non-realist. Cupitt says, "Religion . . . consists in a set of symbolic forms and actions by which human beings relate themselves to the fundamental conditions of their existence."[16] Since one cannot consistently hold Cupitt's non-realist account and Geertz's realist one, Cupitt's idea of religion must be different from Geertz's despite a superficial likeness. For Cupitt, the "fundamental conditions of existence" are not realities independent of believers. Cupitt claims that if religious beliefs are about supernatural beings etc. they are "manifestly false." He also claims that "religious forms of life and belief can continue, and indeed be enhanced, when the language is deliberately construed in a non-realist way" (Hick).[17] Neither Geertz nor ordinary believers could agree with the latter claim.

Non-realism is atheistic humanism in another guise. But, non-realists like Phillips and Cupitt obfuscate their position by claiming that, properly understood, religious discourse supports what *they* think is important about religious truth claims. The believer, however, claims that what is important about religious truth claims is their literal truth. Atheistic humanism can be construed religiously in Geertz's terms. But in doing so its symbol system must be taken as distinct from the one operative in traditional theism. Phillips and Cupitt, however, think that traditional religious symbols can be transposed and reinterpreted without loss of efficacy.

Given the failure of non-realism, pantheism's belief in a divine Unity should be construed in a realist manner about an independently existing reality. Like all believers, pantheists are implicitly if not explicitly "realist" in their account of both religious discourse and religion. The practice of pantheism, like that of theism, depends on it. In Geertz's analysis, the pantheist's symbol system will be different from that of the theist. But like the theist, what pantheists do will be a function of their particular world-view and ethos. Therefore, to understand pantheistic practice, the pantheist world-view and ethos must be examined. The picture one gets of these from Spinoza is different from what one gets from the Presocratics, Bruno or Robinson Jeffers, the pantheistic world-view and ethos being no more univocal than the theistic one. But there are similarities among pantheists with very different overall views.

5.1.2 Intellectualist and symbolist approaches

As we have seen, since an account of the relation between belief and practice is inseparable from a general theory of religion, the question of how to practice pantheism is answerable only in the context of such a theory. Rejection of the non-realist position leaves the "literalist" and "symbolist" analyses of religion, and they greatly differ from each other (see note 16).

"Literalism" includes "intellectualism." Both distinguish between traditional and modern religion. Intellectualism gives an account of the origin and persistence of "traditional" religion, religion in cultures "insulated from the explosion of scientific knowledge, [and] the resulting leap in men's ability, to control their natural environment" (Skorupski).[18]

> On the intellectualist view traditional religion pre-eminently takes the form of a cosmology whose basic explanatory category is that of *agency*; its pantheon of gods and spirits . . . can be invoked to explain why this rather than that event

occurred; and it affords a means by which men, through influencing the will of the gods, can themselves hope to influence the course of events. Modern religion, on the other hand, has relinquished the explanation and control of nature to science, and restricts itself to other functions . . . which religion has either always had or has gradually acquired. Religious – and also magical – activities in traditional societies . . . are . . . intended ways of bringing about desired events or avoiding feared ones; and the ideas which give them point are to be taken literally as cosmological in character. What is more – and here we come to the distinctive feature of the intellectualist view – the explanation . . . of this cosmological emphasis is taken to be that traditional religious thought originates and persists as an attempt . . . to explain and control the natural environment.

(p. 2)

Intellectualism [develops] a complete pattern of explanation . . . a theory . . . whose domain of reference goes beyond what is given in experience . . . traditional systems of thought originate and persist as . . . "transcendental hypotheses".

(p. 12)

Although pantheism has been concerned with explaining the natural environment partly through "transcendental hypotheses," it has been less concerned with controlling it. And being nontheistic, there has been no pantheon of gods invoked to explain or influence things – no "basic explanatory category of *agency*." The emphasis in Taoism, the Presocratics, Spinoza etc. is first on understanding nature, and then on living in accordance with it. Control and manipulation is not a principal pantheistic concern; or rather one "controls" nature by living in accord with it instead of by influencing gods. Pantheism is therefore more of a "modern" religion given the above distinction, and its purposes and practices must be seen accordingly. Intellectualism recognises that impersonal forces sometimes play the role of "gods" in traditional religion. Forces, along with gods, need to be understood and controlled. But pantheism does not seek to control forces as in traditional religion either. Even if pantheism originated to "explain and control the natural environment," as with the Presocratics, these purposes are not consonant with Taoist, Spinozistic and other versions of pantheism. The sense in which pantheism seeks to explain and control is not identical to the way traditional religion as described above does so. Thus, although not all of the intellectualist approach is inapplicable to pantheism, some important aspects of it are.

The intellectualist approach gives a *literal*, as opposed to symbolic, account of the meaning of religious belief and practice. Religious beliefs literally refer to and are about gods or the world. Religious practice is explained instrumentally by those beliefs. But literalism does not entail intellectualism. One can be a literalist and reject the "distinctive intellectualist thesis"; its account of the origin and persistence of religious beliefs in terms of explanation and control. (This account of the origin of religion is basically compatible with Hume's and Freud's.) For reasons already mentioned, and especially where the notion of "agency" is involved, this thesis is inapplicable to pantheism. The denial of this thesis helps differentiate pantheism from theism or polytheism.

Skorupski explains the intellectualist programme (e.g. E. B. Tylor and J. G. Frazer) as having four stages.

> Why do people in certain cultures perform certain types of *actions?* The answer . . . [imputes] *beliefs* to the actors, which . . . give an understandable rationale for doing them. How do the actors first acquire these beliefs? . . . by being socialised into them. Why do these beliefs go on being held? . . . [because of] attitudinal and structural blocks to their falsification. Finally, Stage IV . . . How did these beliefs originate in the first place? . . . out of a need to understand and control the natural environment – a function which they still fulfil.
>
> (p. 9)

Stage IV contains the "distinctive intellectualist thesis." It is not entailed by I-III. Skorupski calls "the broader consensus" which leaves open the question of origin in Stage IV "*literalism*" (p. 11). Intellectualism entails literalism but not vice versa.[19] But much of the intellectualist programme is accepted by literalists.

Skorupski continues:

> one can perfectly well accept (a) that traditional religious

299

beliefs are to be interpreted at face value as beliefs about the *natural* world ... (b) that they are deployed for the purposes of [explanation and control] ... and yet still believe [c] that these goals are not the only ones to be grasped if traditional religious thought is to be understood – that there are important needs and preoccupations, significantly different from the activist, this-worldly ones of explanation and control, which from the first shape and form the content of religious thought.

(pp. 10–11)

Along with (a) and (b) the intellectualist can accept [c]: that religion is concerned with other "needs and preoccupations" (i.e. other than explaining and controlling the natural environment) that must be "grasped" if religion is to be understood. Intellectualism's distinctive thesis does not involve a denial that traditional religion has additional functions and concerns – ones in common perhaps with modern religion. The programme would be implausible if it did deny this. The psycho-sociological explanations of religion that literalists and intellectualists give do not generally deny but account for religion's others concerns. This broader account of intellectualism is more congenial to pantheism. Although the intellectualist's distinctive thesis is not very helpful for understanding pantheism, except by way of distinguishing it from religions whose basic explanatory category is that of agency, pantheism has concerns in common with other religions. Intellectualism and literalism may try to account for these.

If intellectualism fails it is not because it does have a sufficiently broad notion of how religion functions. Instead, it fails either because its thesis about the origin of religion is wrong, or because *literalism* is an essential part of it. It is the literalist aspect of intellectualism that "symbolist" approaches claim is fundamentally mistaken.

What is important about intellectualism for present purposes is not its account of the origin of religion, but its literalism. There is nothing in intellectualism that prevents a literalist account of some pantheistic beliefs and practices. It is not intellectualism but literalism that is basically opposed to the symbolist approach to explaining religious belief and practice.

"Symbolists" explain religious belief and practice as symbolically representing social relations and other ideas in their cultures.[20] The representations serve various purposes such as contributing to a society's cohesiveness by helping to legitimise the political and social *status quo*. They do so through the affective influence of these representative rituals.

There is almost no agreement between symbolism and intellectualism.

> The symbolist approach ... sees a difference between science and religion or magic as forms of life – a difference in the concerns, even the logic, of the two kinds of activity ... beliefs and rituals ... constitute a symbolic system which describes the pattern of social relations in the society ... it distinguishes between the literal meaning of religious and magical discourse and the perhaps overtly intended meaning of religious or magical actions on the one hand, and their symbolic meaning ... Explaining ... ritual ... is a matter of coming to understand what is conveyed, in the performance of such rituals, of the system of social relationships, actual and ideal, in that society. It consists of "decoding ritual messages" by ... relating them to social structures; it has little to do with searching for the causes which produced the overt, surface form of ritual beliefs.
>
> (Skorupski, p. 18)

For the symbolist, religion is not a system of thought and action comparable to scientific theory – albeit mistaken. Since the symbolist denies that traditional religion can be understood as pseudoscience, she cannot claim that modern religion is to be distinguished from traditional religion in relinquishing the goals of explanation and control to real science. (Although the symbolist denies that religion can be understood as a means of explaining and controlling nature, most symbolists allow that religion sometimes functions to explain and control.)

Skorupski further contrasts the symbolist and literalist as follows:

> Whereas the literalist emphasis is unambiguously on explaining magico-religious *actions* in terms of the beliefs which give them their point, and then going on to a further

and independent explanation of the beliefs, our alternative theorist... suggest[s] that it is the "rite" which needs to be seen as "prior" to "the belief"... [T]he unit of significance is the *action*... behaviour whose meaning needs to be understood by grasping the purposes and ideas expressed in it... Whether or not it [the symbolist] grants that there *is* a level at which rituals... are instrumental it claims that at the level at which understanding of them is to be sought they are not instrumental at all; they must be grasped as symbolic... if the beliefs which form the background of ritual... are... more than mere rationalisations – if, that is, their link with ritual actions is to be preserved as the deeper level of significance – then they too must be understood as symbolically or metaphorically expressed.

(pp. 11–13)[21]

Although it may seem plausible to suppose the symbolist analysis of a particular belief/ritual complex correct in some cases, and a literalist account right in others, Skorupski appears to deny that the symbolist approach (e.g. Durkheim's)[22] is ever the right one.[23]

Consider one of Skorupki's reasons for rejecting the symbolist approach.

If the symbolist account is the right one... then to talk of gods and spirits is to make symbolic reference to social groups... When a man says "The crown is mighty in the land, I fear it", he is making not a literal reference to the crown, but a symbolically expressed reference... the object of his fear is not the crown, but the powers of the institution of monarchy... The Durkheimian thesis invites us to assimilate religious discourse to such examples as this, so that religious emotions and attitudes are emotions and attitudes towards gods and spirits *only* in the sense in which the fear is fear of the crown. If it is right in this, then pointing that fact out should make no fundamental difference to the beliefs and feelings of the religious. But Durkheim is clearly correct in thinking that acceptance of his account by religious believers could not, to put it minimally, fail to affect religious life.

(pp. 34–5)

Skorupski claims that if Durkheim's analysis is correct "then pointing that fact out should make no fundamental difference to the beliefs and feelings of the religious." He gives no argument to support his claim, and contrary to Skorupski's view it seems clear why it *should* make a fundamental difference. For Durkheim, the symbolically expressed reference in the case of the crown is crucially different from that in religious discourse. The fact that they are both cases of "symbolically expressed reference" is not a reason to equate them. In the case of the "crown" the speaker is aware of the symbol. Her beliefs and feelings will not be affected by a literal account of what she actually fears – and she may be able to explain it herself. But in the case of the believer the symbolically expressed reference is something the believer is not aware of in the same way. Durkheim does not think that ritual participants can give an account of the symbolic referents of their rituals. If believers did therefore accept Durkheim's account, there is reason to suppose their beliefs and feelings would change. Beliefs and feelings about the social groups to which religious discourse makes symbolic reference is not at all the same as beliefs and feelings about those groups when (and if) they are referred to literally. Durkheim would certainly not deny this. Thus, it is wrong to claim "that religious emotions and attitudes are emotions and attitudes towards gods and spirits *only* in the sense in which the fear is fear of the crown," and Skorupski's simple argument fails. Symbolist analyses cannot be dismissed in all cases for the reason he gives. In the end, it seems that Skorupski is objecting to a rarefied version of the symbolist approach – one that few symbolists hold. Furthermore, the extent to which symbolists accept aspects of literalism would not be taken by them to undermine what they see as a fundamentally symbolist approach.

In defending literalism against the "symbolist approach" Skorupski is not suggesting there is no need to interpret symbols. Analysis of symbols is part of an acceptable literalist approach. Aspects of ritual, ceremony and some kinds of interaction between people are neither possible nor understandable without symbolisation.

When anthropologists, studying various cultures from widely differing theoretical perspectives, have given a descriptive analysis of how magico-religious beliefs are actually understood by people within those traditions, the account that invariably emerges is "literalist" ... Within this framework there is usually a great deal of explicit symbolism and allegory ... but the symbolism is religious ... it is given its meaning by the framework of literally accepted transcendental belief – and not sociological.

(p. 35)

Although thought and action ... are linked, the idea that a degree of sensitivity to symbolism is especially necessary in the understanding of ritual behaviour *can* legitimately be separated from an ultimately philosophical concern with what basic categories – literalist or symbolist, realist or anti-realist – are appropriate for the understanding of traditional modes of thought ... rituals might turn out to have a dimension of symbolic meaning consistent with a realist and literalist approach to the framework of ideas which informs them.

(p. 70)

Of course, as Skorupski realises, symbolists like Durkheim do not deny people give literalist accounts of their beliefs. They simply claim this does not show that the literalist explanations that believers give are the correct ones.

Despite his stress on the significance of symbol for understanding religion, Skorupski rejects the symbolist approach – an approach that has been a staple of anthropological analysis since Durkheim. The literalist approach he defends leaves room for symbols but not for symbolists.

Contrast Skorupski's view with that of Geertz who takes symbolists to be *incontrovertibly* correct at least sometimes. Geertz says,

Yet one more meticulous case in point for such well-established propositions as that ancestor worship supports the jural authority of elders, that initiation rites are means for the establishment of sexual identity and adult status, that ritual groupings reflect political oppositions, or that myths provide charters for social institutions and rationalisations of social privilege, may well convince a great many

304

people ... that anthropologists are, like theologians, firmly dedicated to proving the indubitable.[24]

Although this does not prove Skorupski wrong in rejecting the symbolist approach, social theorists, social anthropologists, philosophers and those in comparative religion (i.e. Skorupski's audience) should be wary of a thesis that excludes interpretations that many anthropologists etc. with different theoretical perspectives regard as conclusively established. Skorupski's exclusive reliance on literalism and complete rejection of the symbolist approach is an extremely marginal position in the context of theoretical anthropology, and one not likely to be accepted by many.

A Geertzian would accept the first three stages of the intellectualist programme as providing explanations only in certain cases; and these explanations would never be regarded as adequate without a wider account of religion's nature and function. Geertz could only partly accept the intellectualist account of the origin of religion. Along with non-reductionistic intellectualists and literalists, the Geertzian will insist "that there are important needs and preoccupations ... different from ... this-worldly ones of explanation and control, which from the first shape ... religious thought." Geertz dismisses the "pseudo-science view of religious belief," while allowing that beliefs often do explain religious actions.[25] A Geertzian accepts some literalist explanations.

Geertz's account of religion is very different from, and much broader than, either the intellectualist's or the symbolist's. Religion is concerned with various threats to "our powers of conception." Explaining and controlling nature is only one significant aspect of man's attempt to contain "chaos."

> The thing we seem least able to tolerate is a threat to our powers of conception ... without the assistance of cultural patterns he [Man] would be functionally incomplete ... a kind of formless monster with neither sense of direction nor power of self-control, a chaos of spasmodic impulses and vague emotions. Man depends upon symbols and symbol systems with a dependence so great as to be decisive for his creatural viability and, as a result ... even the remotest indication that they may prove unable to cope with one or another aspect of experience raises within him the gravest sort of anxiety.
>
> (p. 99)

The intellectualist's distinction between traditional and modern religion must be seen by Geertz as an oversimplification. The role that traditional religion once had of explaining and controlling nature may be relinquished to science by modern religion. But for Geertz, this role is just part of the *function*, more broadly construed, that religion and culture *necessarily* retain even in the modern world. The distinction between traditional and modern religion should not obscure the fact that according to Geertz religion retains the same basic functions it always had: that of enabling people to cope with anomie by establishing a sense of order without which people (literally) could not be people.

Though religion is no longer instrumental in controlling nature, it must function to address the "three points where chaos ... threatens to break in upon man: at the limits of his analytic capacities, at the limits of his powers of endurance, and at the limits of his moral insight" (Geertz, "Religion as a Cultural System," p. 100). Geertz's account implies religion is universal. *Everyone* – atheist, theist, whatever – must "formulate conceptions of the general order of existence" and address the problem of "meaning" (i.e. avoid chaos). They must do so by means of a cultural system to which symbolisation is essential. In Geertz's terms this makes everyone "religious." And in the context of his theory, this is not a trivialisation of the term "religious," but its most important sense.

Geertz's theory denies that religion can be understood as the literalist (e.g. Skorupski) claims it should be. This is so even though religion as Geertz sees it is a way of explaining and controlling both nature and other aspects of life; and even though he grants that literalist explanations of belief and action are often right. The idea of "explaining and controlling" is part of religion according to Geertz. But even as applied to nature this function is not interpreted in the strict "instrumentalist" manner literalism describes. Literalism is superficial on a Geertzian account. It tends to be reductionistic because it acknowledges only a small part of the cultural dimension of religion. It basically ignores the significance of symbols; and it fails to distinguish the distinctive "religious perspective" or world-view from the scientific and other types. As a way of construing the world the religious perspective differs from the scientific, the commonsensical and the aesthetic. It "differs from ... the scientific perspective in that it questions the realities of everyday life not out of institutionalised scepticism... but in terms of what it takes to be wider nonhypothetical truths. Rather than detachment, its watchword is commitment; rather than analysis, encounter" (Geertz, "Religion as a Cultural System," pp. 111–12). Although in a Geertzian account it is not possible to see religion as in much the same business as scientific theory, it is possible to sometimes see science as a religion. Science is a strategy for interpreting and controlling the world, and it can enable one to believe and feel they are living in accord with reality. In Geertz's account, this is how everyone wants to live – and how everyone must live.

Skorupski's view of the Geertzian position is best evident in his brief remarks on functionalism.[26]

> Anthropologists writing from a functionalist perspective have given painstaking accounts of how religious beliefs can support and legitimate social positions... But no one has ever explained how any of these acutely observed effects of magico-religious beliefs are relevant to explaining the origins or persistence of magic and religion in society. At best one might fall back on the familiar observation that beliefs which justify attitudes, opinions, or a way of life which one wants to retain are harder to reject and easier to accept than others. In this sense, functionalism does not propose a theory of magic or religion; since this fact is now generally recognized, and since my interest is specifically in such theories, I have sharpened the distinction between accounts of the social functions of ritual and the symbolist approach as such.
>
> (p. 24)

Skorupski claims that because functionalism gives no account of the "origin and persistence" of religion it "does not propose a theory of religion." This claim is baffling.

The functionalist *explains* how the effects of religious beliefs are relevant to accounting for their origin and persistence in terms of their function. They originate and persist *because* of their functional role. (Similarly, in explaining how religious beliefs function Freud is giving an explanation of their origin and persistence.) Why does Skorupski think that "the familiar observation that beliefs which justify... a way of life which one wants to retain..." does not explain (in part) the origin of those beliefs? In a Geertzian view, this observation takes account of an

307

important group of factors that a plausible intellectualism must regard as relevant.

Skorupski's distinction between the "social functions of ritual and the symbolist approach as such" is valid. Neither intellectualism or literalism deny social functions of ritual, and one can be a functionalist without being a symbolist. However, in cases in which a symbolist analysis is the correct one (if any), could a ritual's social function be recognised without accepting the symbolist analysis? Neither the ritual nor its function could be understood apart from the symbolist analysis. Skorupski says, "As I have presented it, this thesis [i.e. the Durkheimian thesis] concerns the meaning of religious discourse as distinct from the social function of religious practice" (p. 23). But could the function of a practice be understood apart from the meaning of its related discourse?

5.1.3 The practice of pantheism and the theory of religion

Literalism, the narrower intellectualism, the symbolist approach, and Geertz's theory of "religion as a cultural system" all give different – though not always mutually exclusive – accounts of religious discourse, the relation between belief and practice, and of religion in general. But literalist and Geertzian theories are useful in formulating an account of pantheistic practice in ways the symbolist approach cannot be. This is not because symbolist analyses are always mistaken, but because it makes little sense to suppose pantheists can self-consciously construct religious practices that in Durkheimian fashion symbolically represent social relations in their cultures. The symbolist approach assumes believers are not consciously aware of why their practices take the form they do, what the referents of their rituals are or what they mean. It presupposes a lack of conscious awareness or understanding of the relation between belief and practice. If believers were aware of these things, their religious life could not continue as before. But pantheists endeavouring to find actions that reflect their beliefs must be aware of the referents and meaning of their practices in ways precluded by the symbolist approach.

The symbolist approach might be applicable to explaining pantheistic practices in traditional religions. In attempting to construct an account of what the contemporary pantheist should do, it would be useful to examine practices that pantheists have traditionally undertaken. But it makes no sense to suppose that contemporary pantheists could replicate the representation of social relations that pantheistic rituals might be analysed as having by a symbolist account. If a pantheistic ritual symbolically represents social relations, it represents those of its own society. At any rate, the point is largely moot since the practice of pantheism has *never* been associated with ritual practice but with a way of life. Thus, Lao Tzu explicitly eschewed ritual, and Spinoza thought that while ordinary religious practice, ritual etc. was a good idea for the common people since it inculcated valuable ideals, it was beside the point for him. The fact that pantheistic practice has never been associated with ritual may partly explain why pantheism has not been practiced communally – e.g. in a church.

In literalist or Geertzian terms it makes sense to ask what to do, given certain beliefs, in a way it does not for a symbolist. The kinds of practice suitable to pantheism are explicable in terms of beliefs literally and symbolically understood; and especially (in Geertz's account) in terms of a world-view (e.g. belief in a divine Unity) and corresponding ethos. Thus, Lao Tzu describes the Tao as a metaphysical reality; as natural law or system of self-regulated principles; and also as a principle, pattern and standard for human conduct.[27] One emulates the Tao after discerning its manifest characteristics in the phenomenal world, and to emulate the Tao is to practise Taoism. In "Song of Myself" Whitman articulates a world-view and evokes the connected ethos he envisages. For Spinoza, examining the nature and implications of Unity (substance) in the *Ethics*, and trying to live in accord with that account, was itself a form of pantheistic practice. Similarly, in writing and living as depicted in "Song of Myself," Whitman practised the pantheism he preached. The relationship between the thought and practice of Hegel, Plotinus, Bruno etc. is less apparent, but should be of interest to pantheists. If pantheists find any of the various world-views and ethos described as consonant with their own, they may pattern their practices after those associated with such views. However, in just having a particular pantheistic view of the nature of things, certain practices and a way of life must, to an extent, follow.

The idea of looking to religions with pantheistic practices for examples of what to do may seem promising in a literalist or Geertzian approach. Similar kinds of practice should follow similar beliefs. The difficulty is that there seem to be no pantheistic traditions to examine – not even Taoism, since, as practised, it is not pantheistic. In traditional religions, practices that might be identifiable as pantheistic are always seen in the context of wider religious (e.g. theistic) practice. In traditions that are partly pantheistic like some native American Indian religions, it is difficult to discern how practices relating to pantheistic beliefs can be distinguished from various kinds of god and spirit worship. Since pantheism has largely been non-communal, individual pantheists, not traditions, must be examined.

Religious practice is usually prescribed by teachings and doctrine, and informed by other beliefs widely held among the community of believers. Since there is no widely recognised body of scriptural or other religious teaching in pantheism and never has been (there is little doctrine and no church), there should be little in the way of prescribed practice. As already noted, the philosophical Taoism of the *Tao Tē Ching* is pantheistic, but it has never been widely practised and there is no body of ritual associated with it.

Nevertheless, as outlined above, literalist and Geertzian theories do offer a general approach to determining pantheistic practice. The kind of activity undertaken by a believer ideally reflects (i.e. is explainable in terms of) the way in which the religious object, and one's relation to it, is conceived. Differences in practice are the products of varying views on the nature of God and the world – set in the context of a more comprehensive worldview. Since pantheistic and theistic accounts of God and the world are best regarded as mutually exclusive, it is likely that the practices of each would be dissimilar. Theistic practice, the intent and so forth, is inappropriate for the pantheist, and vice versa. Pantheists will not want to practise a religion other than pantheism, since such practice reflects beliefs they do not hold.

If specific pantheistic practices could be identified, these might be adapted to modern pantheism. Yet, to talk of adapting practices in this way is artificial. As a whole, practice neither precedes nor follows the body of beliefs formulated and codified by a religious community. It develops along with them. Even where religious beliefs are taken (e.g. Durkheim) to be rationalisations of practices that precede them, practice occurs in a context of shared conceptions, beliefs and concerns, and – whether literally or symbolically – is expressions of these. Ritual, and religious practice generally, is a product of conscious and unconscious, literal and symbolic, communal religious reflection. Given (and one wonders why) that there has been little structured pantheistic *communal* reflection, despite the fact that there are many pantheists, there is no identifiable pantheistic practice. There are only identifiable pantheistic world-views and beliefs. This does not explain why individual pantheists have not developed recognisable rituals, unless a community of believers (i.e. a church) is necessary for such practices. The practice of pantheism seems confined to individuals acting in ways they see as according with the nature of things.

Despite Harold Wood Jr's suggestion that pantheists might construct rituals around certain kinds of natural occurrences like solstices, little in the way of pantheist ritual has been taken up. If contemporary pantheistic ritual exists, it is scarce. (Is the solstice gathering at Stonehenge pantheistic?) The extent to which one can self-consciously set out to construct a ritual is, for reasons already given, suspect. But, given that one can consciously construct symbols that address a community's concerns, there seems no reason why pantheistic rituals cannot be formulated. Indeed, various theistic rituals are self-consciously created. Furthermore, ritual is only one aspect of religious practice, and pantheists may develop other ways to express their beliefs in action. Since belief and practice are interdependent and evolve together, if some future pantheistic communal reflection results in doctrines, then it is likely to result in practices of various sorts as well. Other than the fact that they have lacked what seems to be requisite in terms of a community of pantheists, there may be additional or alternative explanations of why pantheists have not developed rituals. Maybe the lack of community can just as easily be explained by the lack of a developed mode of practice as vice versa.

There may be aspects to the kinds of belief typically held by pantheists that structurally block their expression ritualistically, or even their communal non-ritualistic expression. For some reason pantheism tends towards private expression in the way that other religions tend toward quietism. Alternatively, there may be something in the nature of ritual not conducive to the expression of typical pantheistic beliefs. Both of these factors are probably true. Worship and prayer are part of most ritual, and if pantheists reject these as relevant forms of pantheistic practice, they will also reject ritual in which these practices are prominent. Since, as intellectualism maintains, ritual is theistically oriented, rituals that involve gods are inappropriate to pantheism.

I claimed that for the most part pantheists lack scripture and an established body of doctrine and discourse that could help establish the nature of pantheistic practice. However, it is important to reiterate that this is not entirely true. The pantheist, to some extent, can rely on traditional religious scripture that is recognisably pantheistic; e.g. some Taoist texts and some Western and non-Western theistic scripture. Pantheists also have recourse to numerous philosophical sources – Spinoza etc. But, the pantheist is not without alternatives to the scripture and discourse that theists have at their disposal. To some extent, the pantheist too will know what to do to practise pantheism. Art, music, literature and poetry fulfil the same kinds of roles in pantheism as they do in theism. As representations of cultural patterns they reflect and sustain a world-view and ethos. In Geertz's terms they symbolically function as both a model *of* reality and a model *for* reality. "Culture patterns are 'models' . . . they are sets of symbols whose relations to one another 'model' relations among entities, processes or what-have-you . . . they give meaning, that is objective conceptual form, to social and psychological reality both by shaping themselves to it and by shaping it to themselves" (Geertz, "Religion as a Cultural System," p. 93). Pantheists recognise cultural patterns and symbolic representations that "model" their beliefs. Given such beliefs, and the efficacy of symbolic representations of those beliefs, certain other beliefs, actions and attitudes will be regarded, cognitively and affectively, as appropriate and correct.

In theistic traditions, prayer – which is a type of worship – and sometimes meditation are the principal forms of religious practice. They are often set in the context of ritual. Theism gives a variety of reasons why prayer and worship are appropriate and necessary forms of theistic practice. But, what about for the pantheist? In principle, pantheists will not do things that literally conflict with the beliefs they express. They will not worship if worship implies the recognition of an independent and superior god, since this theistic belief is antithetical to a central tenet of pantheism. Are prayer and worship appropriate kinds of practice for the pantheist? Given that the pantheist should not pray to or worship a theistic God, can she worship the pantheistic Unity?

Can prayer and worship be recast in a version suitable to pantheism? What is a pantheist to do?

5.2 WORSHIP AND PRAYER

Their religion, or rather their superstition, consists besides in praying; but, O mon Dieux! what prayers they make! In the morning, when the little children come out from their cabins, they shout, "Come, Porcupines; come Beavers; come Elk" and this is all of their prayers.[1]

R. G. Thwaites

[T]he religious attitude in face of this supra-personal aspect of the numen must be different from the ordinary attitude in personal intercourse by petition, prayer, colloquy.[2]

Rudolf Otto

Friendship with persons involves acknowledgment of their worth. So friendship with God, the supremely good source of being, involves adoration and worship.[3]

Richard Swinburne

In pantheist religion, worship becomes a devotion to the universe, a celebration of life ... Pantheist worship may involve artistic expression, nature observation, or various forms of outdoor activities ... Pantheist communion with nature does not require an overly intellectual approach[4]

Harold W. Wood, Jr.

My purpose in this section is to argue that worship and prayer, the principal forms of theistic practice, are not suitable to pantheism. I also indicate difficulties in the theistic idea of worship that pantheism avoids.

It has often been claimed by theists and atheists that pantheistic worship (e.g. worshipping the Unity) is idolatrous. It is worshipping a false god. Unlike the theist or atheist, however, the pantheist believes a divine Unity exists – a kind of god. So pantheists, if they do worship the Unity, reject the idea that they are worshipping a false god. What is wrong with pantheistic worship is not that it is idolatrous, but something more basic having to do with both the nature of worship and Unity. Even if the Unity exists, worshipping it would not be proper pantheistic practice.

Pantheistic worship might naively be thought to be a kind of self-worship, worshipping something which one is a part of or identified with. This too is a mistake. As we have seen, pantheism is not the view that "everything that exists," including oneself, is god; and it is not the view that every particular thing or person is equally god. If worship is not acceptable religious practice for pantheists, it is for reasons other than that such practice involves adoring and venerating (i.e. worshipping) oneself.

As forms of religious practice, worship and prayer are not consonant with pantheism. Like "evil" and "salvation," they are intrinsically connected to the theistic world-view that pantheists reject – and theistic practice makes little sense outside of a theistic context. Therefore, except in a highly derivative sense (i.e. derivative from theism) worship and prayer are types of practice that – Harold Wood Jr's remarks (quoted above) not withstanding – are not acceptable to pantheists. Devotion to the universe, artistic expression, nature observation etc. are not types of worship as theistically understood – though they may be ways of respecting, honouring and revering. If they are understood as ways of respecting . . . etc., then these notions should not be taken to mean what they do in theism. Supposing Wood is right claiming that "communion with nature" is an "authentic religious experience," one not requiring an "overly intellectual approach"; it does not follow that in pantheism "worship becomes devotion to the ıuniverse."

How does the fact that worship and prayer are connected to a theistic conception of reality make worship unsuitable for pantheism? And what are some other reasons why worship is something the pantheist will want to avoid?

Ninian Smart says, "In worship one addresses the focus of worship . . . worship is a relational activity; one cannot worship oneself."[5] From a theistic perspective, not only can one not worship oneself, but one cannot worship that to which one is already ontologically related – for example, as a part to a whole. It seems pantheism rules out worship simply because the kind of separation between the object of worship and the worshipping subject required by theism as a condition for worship is, *ex hypothesis*, not present in the Unity. But to suggest this as the principal reason why worship and prayer, theistically conceived, are unavailable to the pantheist is misleading. It is a theistic way of stating the issue based on the supposition that God, the primary object of worship, and creation are ontologically distinct.

I have claimed that pantheistic Unity is not predicated fundamentally on ontological grounds in the first place. There is no reason to think, for example, that Unity should be understood ontologically in a way that would rule out worship on the grounds that the theistic condition of ontological separation is not met. What makes worship and prayer inappropriate for the pantheist is not the lack of ontological separation from the Unity that theism claims God has from the world. If there is a sense in which pantheists *are* ontologically, or in other ways, distinct from the divine Unity, worship and prayer are still inappropriate. If a necessary condition of worship is that it has to be in some significant sense "other regarding," then worship would not on that account be inappropriate to pantheism. What makes it unsuitable is that worship, and especially prayer, are basically directed at "persons" – or at a being with personal characteristics separate and superior to oneself.[6] Whether one's reasons for worship are petitionary or devotional is irrelevant; and so is one's motivation – whether a Freudian way of coping with guilt, or a rationally based sense of duty. Objects of worship are not oneself, and perhaps not even ontologically distinct from oneself as theism claims, but they are generally taken to be conscious, personal and superior.

The idea that worship is fundamentally relational and addressed to a personal deity is not often disputed. It is affirmed, for example, by Otto in the quotation at the beginning of the chapter. He says that one's attitude towards a personal deity will be different from that towards the "supra-personal" aspect of the numen (i.e. "holy" object). The attitude towards a deity conceived and experienced in personal terms involves petition, prayer and colloquy. These are appropriate to "personal intercourse," but not for relating to the supra-personal.

Thus, Otto's claims that what is appropriate as a response to a deity experienced as personal is inappropriate for a deity experienced as "supra-personal." This is somewhat obscured by his assertion that reference to the supra-personal or impersonal aspect of the numen is essential to prayer. It seems he is suggesting that an impersonal deity, or the "numinous and non-rational" aspect of God, can itself be prayed to and worshipped. He says that when the deity is referred to in "impersonal neuter terms ('It')," this is meant to "indicate the mysterious overplus of the non-rational and numinous, that cannot enter our 'concepts' because it is too great and too alien to them; and in this sense they are quite indispensable even in hymns and prayers." But, Otto is not claiming that prayer is appropriately addressed to a non-personal deity or aspect of deity. He is saying that when addressing a theistically (and Christianly) conceived God by means of the impersonal neuter pronoun "It," one is acknowledging its essentially non-rational, numinous and supra-personal aspect. One is not thereby denying its personal aspect. Thus, the quotation from Otto tends to support the view that a God conceived of impersonally would not be worshipped or prayed to.

Consider the concept of moral praiseworthiness essential to theistic worship. Part of the superiority of God one is acknowledging in worship is moral superiority. For a person to be the subject of praise or blame they must (generally) have freely intended to do the praiseworthy action. We attribute praise and blame only if the agent is responsible. *Roughly*, the agent will be morally responsible for an action only if it is intentionally undertaken. And they will be morally responsible for the result of their action only if the action was undertaken for a purpose they intended to realise by the action.[7] Given this intrinsic connection between praise, blame and intentionality, if intention is missing, praise and blame are inappropriate. Thus, a necessary condition for moral agency is the possession of a mind and the ability to perform free actions. Unless pantheists are prepared to attribute intentionality to the Unity, it cannot be morally praiseworthy. (Intentionality is usually taken to entail consciousness, though many accounts of artificial intelligence deny this.) Attitudes and judgements that presuppose their object to be conscious and capable of intentional action are not conceptually appropriate for the pantheist to have or make about the Unity. Ideally, such attitudes would not even arise. There are, of course, kinds of attitudes and evaluations other than moral ones that are directed to people and things for which they are not responsible. We judge people and things for attributes they possess but are not responsible for. We praise something as beautiful even if it just happens to be that way. The Unity could be the object of some of these attitudes. It could be judged "good" – but such judgment would be divorced from its being praiseworthy in any moral sense. It would be an evaluative judgment but not a moral one.

The emphasis on the conscious and personal nature of most objects of worship is not meant to deny that inanimate and non-personal objects are worshipped and even petitioned. But in many such cases the "personal" is related to the object. Despite appearances it is not an inanimate object being worshipped, but a spirit residing temporarily in the object. In other cases it may be questionable whether it is worship that is taking place rather than veneration or something related to worship. But, even if non-personal objects are, without confusion, sometimes worshipped, the principal point remains. Because worship and prayer are usually (even if not necessarily) addressed to persons, they are to that extent unavailable as modes of pantheistic practice. As Spinoza, Lao Tzu and others have realised, they are incompatible with (non-personal) pantheism.

As already noted, worship is an expression of another's superiority. Ninian Smart says, "The words 'Thou art my Lord and King' signalise my difference from God – my inferiority, his superiority. I am at the same time recognising that God is the sole source of holiness, of that substance by which I am saved."[8] There is nothing in pantheism that corresponds to the inferiority/superiority dichotomy taken here as essential to worship.[9] Given that "an object of worship is holy and the adherent conversely unclean and sinful," pantheism rejects the idea that there can be any object of worship whatsoever because it rejects the notion that adherents are "unclean" and "sinful." The theist claims that "It is necessarily true that God (if He exists) is worthy of worship."[10] The pantheist may accept this as true of the theistic God, but will reject its applicability to the pantheistic Unity. It is not necessarily true that the Unity, if it exists, is worthy of worship. Indeed, for the pantheist, it is most likely necessarily false.

Smart says "the Focus of worship is transcendent... it is not to be identified with the particularities... through which he is manifested."[11] In pantheism there is no object that is regarded as transcendent in the sense in which classical theism claims God is transcendent. (This is so despite my contention in section 2.4 that the concept of transcendence has many of the important applications in pantheism as it has in theism.) Every particular, in so far as it is part of the Unity, may be regarded as manifesting that Unity and part of it. This does not mean that for the pantheist any object is as worthy of worship as any other, or that any object at all is suitable for worship. Indeed, none are. For the pantheist, *if there was* a focus of worship, it would not have to be identified with particulars even if they were part of the Unity.

The Unity is not identified with or by any particular and it is not a sum of all particulars. However, for the pantheist there is neither a focus of worship transcendent to particulars nor any focus of worship at all. Neither particular things, nor the divine Unity itself is taken as superior or personal. In short, the properties that according to theists make God worthy of worship are not constitutive of the Unity, and there are no other proper objects of worship for the pantheist.

Dispensing with worship is important both in considering the practice of pantheism and in distinguishing it from theistic practice. But even if pantheists do not worship, they may nevertheless have *some* of the feelings and attitudes associated with worship in relation to the Unity that others have in relation to God. Some feelings and attitudes, both positive (e.g. awe) and negative (e.g. sinfulness), remain inappropriate. The Unity may be the focus of some relational activities and attitudes associated with worship – even though it is not itself an object of worship.

Is the pantheist "missing out" on something in not worshipping? There may be ways of practising pantheism that fulfil some of the functions of worship, while some of its other functions may be otiose. It is worth examining a recent explanation of the theist's duty to worship. If the justification for this duty is found wanting, then perhaps whatever benefits (e.g. psychological) accrue through worship, they would willingly be forgone by the conscientious pantheist. After all, the psychological benefit is partly a function of believing one has a duty to worship.

Swinburne claims it is not merely appropriate, but morally obligatory, to worship God. Although he considers "what properties a being needs in order to be worthy of worship," he bases his claim that one ought to worship God primarily on an analogy he draws between God and human benefactors.[12]

> The theist argues that the duty to worship is a consequence of certain moral principles. The main one is that one ought to show explicit respect to those persons with whom one has to do, having regard to the qualities and status which they possess.
>
> (pp. 283–4)

Friendship with persons involves acknowledgment of their

worth. So friendship with God, the supremely good source of being, involves adoration and worship.[13]

If we should be grateful to human benefactors than we should be all the more grateful to God to whom we owe our existence. God deserves respect and recognition in a manner similar to, but far greater than, what we give to fellow human beings. Swinburne draws an analogy between duties and responsibilities owed or appropriate to humans from humans on the one hand, and those owed God by humans on the other. If we should recognise excellence in humans then we should recognise it in God.

Is the analogy a good one? It should be rejected on the grounds that there is not enough similarity between its subjects to make it acceptable. How does Swinburne get from the fact that "friendship with persons involves acknowledgment of their worth" to the conclusion that "friendship with God . . . involves adoration and worship?" What is the basis of the alleged analogy between gratitude owed to human benefactors and what we owe towards God? It makes sense to be grateful to human benefactors in a way that it does not to God. God, for example, is morally perfect, omnipotent and omniscient. Human benefactors are not. Human benefactors might or should be appreciative of gratitude, as well as *sometimes* owed it, in a way that God cannot be. In being a benefactor it may be supposed that a person makes some kind of sacrifice, and/or that the benefactor is recognising some unique personal qualities in the one she is helping. The notion of helping someone in a way that requires some kind of sacrifice might be the basis for the obligation people regard as owed to a benefactor – even when no real sacrifice is made. But what sort of sacrifice is God making in creating or sustaining us? If it in no way inconveniences God to help or create us, then why should one be grateful (e.g. to the point of worship) if God bestows some favour upon us which – though we do not "deserve it" and it is not owed us – nevertheless does not "cost" God anything? Swinburne acknowledges this to some extent. He says, "The greater the benefit which we receive, and *the more costly it was for the benefactor to give it* [my emphasis], the greater the respect which he deserves" (p. 285).

Gratitude towards benefactors does not always rest on the supposition that any real cost is involved to the benefactor. Nevertheless, if it is right to suppose that gratitude for something bestowed may have been based on the idea that we are getting something from someone that they could themselves use, this would further weaken Swinburne's analogy. Whatever one's obligation to worship God might be, its source would be totally different from the one Swinburne and other theists frequently point to. Indeed, a distinction is drawn in ethics between what we are obliged to do and those actions that we are not obliged to do but which are nevertheless good actions. This distinction may rest in part on the kind of effort or sacrifice that a person would have to make in order to do what is not morally required but would be morally good nevertheless (i.e. supererogatory). If, as in the case of God, no effort of any kind is required, to "help" people, keep them in existence, create them etc., then the notion of what is morally obligatory and supererogatory in the case of God may have to be drawn differently than it is in the case of human beings. God created human beings. Why should he not be morally required to care for them if (*ex hypothesi*) it takes no effort to do so?[14] Given God's powers it seems that his bestowing existence etc. is *at best* absolutely minimally supererogatory instead of obligatory.

At any rate, suppose one does owe a debt of gratitude to a benefactor. Then if God is our benefactor we owe God a debt of gratitude. But how does one get from gratitude and acknowledgment of worth to "worship" and "adoration?" The move Swinburne implicitly suggests is natural – from gratitude in the case of human benefactors to worship and adoration in the case of God – has no apparent warrant. On the basis of Swinburne's analogy one *might* conclude that since God is a very great benefactor we owe God a great deal of gratitude and we should acknowledge God's great worth. But the claim that worship and adoration are appropriate responses is neither explained nor examined. The relationship between "gratitude" and "worship" central to Swinburne's account is opaque. He says

> It follows from these considerations about the duty of respect, that a person who had most of the properties which I have been discussing would deserve to be shown considerable respect. If he is our creator ... he is indeed our benefactor. If he is omnipotent, omniscient, or perfectly free, and so perfectly good, he deserves respect for his unequalled greatness and goodness. But to worship ... is more than just to show respect. It is to show respect towards

a person acknowledged as *de facto* and *de iure* lord of all. Such a person deserves a peculiar kind of respect for two reasons. Firstly, whatever our dependence on other beings, they depend on him. He is our ultimate benefactor, and has the right to be such. Secondly, he has incomparable greatness; if greatness deserves respect, he deserves a peculiar respect.

(pp. 287–8)

There is no justification above for the move from "worthy of respect," even a "peculiar respect," to "worthy of worship" where worship means *more* than peculiar respect. (Is Swinburne suggesting that worship just is "peculiar respect?") Nor is there a justification for the move from acknowledging God as "lord of all" to the claim that he ought to be worshipped.[15]

Swinburne claims his account of the duty to worship is similar to Aquinas's.[16] But the idea that we should worship God because he is our benefactor is not altogether congenial to the classical theistic view. Central to this view is that God should be worshipped because of his moral perfection, incomparable greatness and "otherness." This is also part of Swinburne's claim, but it is overshadowed by his emphasis on gratitude owed God for his beneficence. Swinburne's account of worship has a medieval ring to it – like serfs worshipping their lord.

Swinburne ignores psychological reasons for worship and prayer – whether positive or negative. Can it be that fear and wish-fulfilment have *nothing* to do with worship; not only as reasons and motivations to worship, but also as having to do with the nature and function of worship? Something more than, and different from, gratitude is central to worship. Swinburne is not only concerned with a justification of worship but with an explanation of it; and by omitting to mention its psychological and other functional aspects he omits its central features.

Given that the nature of worship is problematic, and there seems to be no justification for the view that one morally ought to worship God or anything else (e.g. Unity), pantheists will avoid such practice. Spinoza and Lao Tzu had it right. Worship is not part of pantheistic practice. *Not* worshipping may even be essential to pantheism.

Although Swinburne is a "literalist" in some ways, the literalist account of worship conflicts considerably with his. Literalists see

321

religion as primarily concerned with explanation and control. They take petitionary prayer as the paradigmatic form of worship since it is the type most overtly concerned with control.[17] Other types of ritual worship, including prayers of adoration, are interpreted as more oblique ways of attempting to control the gods. Although reasons believers give for worship may include some of those Swinburne cites, in the literalist account what is behind the adoration and gratitude is not so much an acknowledgment of God's worth as the attempt to get God on one's side.

Geertz's account of worship is more consistent with literalism. A Geertzian explains worship and prayer as an effort to conceive of the nature of ultimate reality, and an intention to live in accordance with it. Through prayer and worship one is oriented to the cosmic *status quo* and reaffirms its nature. Religious practice is understood as an attempt, direct and indirect, to deal with the "problem of meaning." Thus, worship and prayer are concerned with explanation and control. But what is involved in this is far more complex than literalists such as Skorupski acknowledge.

It may appear that on a Geertzian account worship is not ruled out as a justified form of pantheistic practice. But this is not the case. Given that the pantheist does not believe in a personal deity, any kind of worship and prayer addressed to a person, as most instances of worship are, is conceptually speaking unavailable. The way in which one attempts to live in accordance with reality must (ideally) be consistent with the way in which one conceives it. Since pantheists do not believe that a personal deity exists they will not address it through worship. If adoration and gratitude are deemed appropriate primarily or exclusively to a person, then such attitudes will be inappropriate to the pantheist. The pantheist will not adore the Unity or regard it as a benefactor. The way pantheists employ a symbol system as a "model of and model for reality" must involve practice. But it cannot properly involve symbols modelling a reality that the pantheist rejects.

A brief account of some additional analyses of worship will support my principal contentions concerning worship and pantheism.

Bernard Dauenhauer cites characteristics he claims that "every object of ritual worship" must have.

> First, the object [of ritual worship] must have some aspect whose efficacious presence does not occur automatically.

Thus, there can be no ritual worship of physical objects or events *qua* such. Whatever is or comes to be present and efficacious in its entirety by any kind of natural necessity is not a fit object of ritual worship. So, for example, the sun *qua* celestial body . . . cannot be an object of ritual worship. Nor can an Aristotelian Unmoved Mover. A naturally occurring and efficacious force or entity can be an object of ritual worship, but only if it has an aspect whose efficacious presence occurs only in relation to ritual worship, and thus not automatically.[18]

This analysis requires that the object of worship be conscious and personal. It must be if it is to be "efficaciously present" (partly) as a result of worship rather than "in its entirety by any kind of natural necessity." How could the object be efficaciously present by occurring (responding?) "only in relation to ritual worship," instead of automatically by "natural necessity," if it were not capable of intentional action? If so, then given that pantheistic Unity is not predicated on the basis of consciousness (i.e. it is neither conscious nor a person), it could not be a proper object of worship.

If "God" is moved solely by natural necessity, then in Dauenhauer's analysis, Spinoza's God, or the Unity, could not be an object of worship. And, it is clear that although Spinoza was not troubled by the fact that ordinary believers pray and worship – indeed, he thought it could be beneficial – he did not think that "God" was a proper object of worship, or that prayer was useful for anyone who, like himself, understood something of God's true nature. For Spinoza, knowledge of a certain kind, rather than worship, is necessary for a proper relation to "God." In fact, knowledge *constitutes* the relation. Knowledge rather than worship is salvific in that it is ultimately necessary for, and constitutive of, what he means by "blessedness" or "happiness."

What makes Unity inappropriate to worship in Dauenhauer's analysis is not that it is subject to natural necessity and likened in this respect to Spinoza's God. Pantheism in general is not committed to the absolute determinism apparently essential to Spinoza's system. The Unity is not anything material at all, and so cannot be subject to the kind of natural necessity (i.e. laws of nature etc.) a celestial body is. Unity is predicated on the basis of value of some type. What makes worship inappropriate is that the Unity is non-personal. It cannot be "persuaded" or made efficacious by prayer; and the Unity cannot be regarded as "superior" in a way that suggests worshipping it makes sense. Even if pantheists believed they could influence an impersonal principle or value on which Unity is predicated, worship remains incongruent with the Unity's impersonal nature. The forms of practice that influence would take would be different from the interpersonal forms they take in the case of theistic practice.

It is unclear if the other two characteristics Dauenhauer cites (below) as necessary to objects of worship rule out pantheistic worship, because it is unclear if these characteristics are applicable to Unity. All three characteristics appear to presuppose that an object of worship is "personal" if not theistic in a more complete way. He says,

> Second, the proper object of ritual worship . . . does not fall under the control of those engaged in ritual worship . . . Whatever man can acquire control over cannot be the object of his worshipping activity . . . [third], the object must be such that men can address it somehow. It must be such that human activity is not completely irrelevant to its manifestations of itself.[19]

It is questionable whether one can or cannot "acquire control over" the Unity – or what it would mean to do so. Therefore, the fact that the pantheist cannot control the Unity does not necessarily mean that Unity has Dauenhauer's second characteristic. The issue is unclear. Incidently, given this second characteristic, depending on what is meant by "control" and how it is distinguished from "influence," the theistic god may not be a proper object of worship in Dauenhauer's account.

Concerning the third characteristic: there is no reason to suppose that human activity is irrelevant to the Unity or its manifestations; that it is inaccessible to human activity; or that the Unity is such that people cannot address it. Perhaps the pantheistic Unity does, in some way, have the third characteristic that, according to Dauenhauer, a proper object of worship must have. But this is questionable since the sense in which the object must be such that it can be addressed, and accessible, seems to require that, much like a theistic God, it is personal.

All three characteristics required of an object of worship in Dauenhauer's account imply that the object must be personal, but oddly he never says it. Smart claims there is an "internal relationship between the concepts of god [i.e. a personal god] and worship."

> worship is relational; it typically involves ritual; this ritual expresses the superiority of the Focus . . . the experience which worship tries to express is the numinous, and the object of worship is thus perceived as awe-inspiring; worship involves praise, but addressed direct to the Focus; this Focus transcends, however, the manifestations. All this implies the personalised character of the Focus . . . it becomes evident that the foci of worship, God or the gods, needs to be understood in the context provided by worship. That is, there is an internal relationship between the concepts of god and of worship. Thus, we might seem to accept that naive and simplistic analytic truth: that a god is to be worshipped (analytic since a god is defined as a being who is to be worshipped) . . .[20]

According to Smart, the focus of worship is a god with a "personalised character." Thus, even if the pantheistic Unity is in some sense a god (e.g. divine), in this account it lacks the character he claims is necessary for something to be a "focus of worship" or a god. Pantheism rejects Smart's contention that a god is, by definition, to be worshipped. This may be true of the theistic god, but it is not true of the pantheistic divine Unity. Pantheists can agree, however, that objects of worship are "personal."

George D. Chryssides has attempted to "refute the [standard] view that the concept of worship demands that the object which is worshipped must be a *being*, and someone (or even something) distinct from the worshipper."[21] He says, "To believe in God one does not have to believe in a person or an entity which exists apart from the universe, and on whose existence the universe depends. It is possible to view God as a principle which runs through the universe – a natural flow of things" (p. 369). I agree with this, and indeed Chryssides' notion of God is a pantheistic one. But Chryssides conflates the issue of the nature of God with that of the nature of worship. He says, "To worship would be to submit one's own life to the principle of order which is inherent in the world . . . the ascertaining of the will of god is the ensuring that one's emotions and actions are in harmony with the flow which is the source, guide and goal of the world" (p. 371).

Granted that God can be conceived in non-personal terms, and also the "value of using personalistic metaphors in the context of a radical model of God" (p. 370), it does not follow that a non-personal God could appropriately be worshipped.[22] Taoism, which Chryssides cites in support of his view, does not support the idea that a non-personal "god" such as the Tao should or could be worshipped.[23] Philosophical Taoism does not support this view, and Lao Tzu emphatically eschews ritual worship. Chryssides also cites Buddhism. "The Buddha or bodhisattva who is the focus of devotion is typically addressed and prayed to ... yet even a cursory acquaintance with Buddhist philosophy will make it plain that these beings cannot really be 'out there', distinct from the devotee" (p. 371).[24] But the fact that worship occurs in Buddhism, Taoism or among some atheists does not suffice to show that worship is conceptually *appropriate* in these non-theistic traditions. In asking if one can worship something non-personal, one is not asking whether people do in fact worship what is ordinarily taken to be non-personal (perhaps because it is conceived of in personal terms), but rather whether it is conceptually appropriate to do so. Chryssides' claim that a "It can therefore be seen that the 'object' of worship need not be a being separate from the rest of the universe or from the worshipper or devotee" (p. 371) begs the question.

Chryssides says, "The object of the practice of devotion in such a [Buddhist] context is for the recognition and attainment of oneness to take place between what are, apparently, subject and object of devotion" (p. 371).[25] Even if Chryssides is right about the object of the practice of devotion, the question remains whether this devotion is appropriately regarded as worship if nothing personal is being worshipped. The personalistic imagery involved may make it seem as if worship is taking place, or what is ordinarily regarded as non-personal may in this context be conceived of in personal terms. The issue is not whether there can be religious practices aimed at achieving such an object of devotion; but rather whether such practice is worship. Chryssides cites a Buddhist rite in which "the devotee prays ... to the bodhisattva Manjushri" for "oneness" with him (p. 371). But granted that this is a case of worship, it does not show that in Buddhism the object of devotion becomes the "recognition and attainment of oneness," or that, conceptually speaking, worship is proper in non-theistic contexts. It shows only that worship takes place in Buddhism. Buddhism is, in any case, a poor example for Chryssides to use since there is no "radical" non-personal concept of God in Buddhism. Furthermore, the example Chryssides cites is a case in which the object of devotion is personal (i.e. a bodhisattva).

In arguing that worship is appropriate for a "radical" (i.e. non-theistic concept of God) Chryssides unwittingly and interestingly adopts the theistic idea that the fundamental form religious practice must take is worship. In doing so he either equates practices such as meditation to worship, or meditation is subsumed by worship.

To a classical theist it may seem that the principal reason why pantheists should not worship has thus far been overlooked. Theists have often argued (the alleged incarnation of Christ notwithstanding) that an embodied God could not be worthy of worship.[26] Thus, according to theism, if the pantheistic Unity is embodied, then it must be unworthy of worship. But whether an embodied God is worthy of worship is really beside the point in regard to pantheism. As we have seen, the all-inclusive divine Unity may include that which is material and embodied, without itself being embodied. The Unity is not identical to the sum total of all that exists – material and non-material. Unity is not, or need not be, identified with any *body* to be predicated on the basis of a value or principle ranging over both the material and the non-material world.

If, however, the theist insists that anything worthy of worship must be totally immaterial *and not include* anything material etc., if an object must be transcendent to the world in some strong ontological sense to be worthy of worship (though this too is theistic talk), then the pantheistic Unity could not be a suitable object of worship. The reason behind the denial that anything embodied can be worthy of worship is not its materiality *per se*, but the idea that embodiment entails limitation. If "limitation" rather than materiality is the issue, then the fact that the Unity extends to the material would not by itself imply that it could not be worshipped. It would have to be shown that the Unity was, in a relevant sense, "limited."[27] But whether the theist claims the Unity cannot be worshipped because it is material, or because it is limited, it is regarded as unsuitable for worship because of its impersonal character – the very character the pantheist insists upon.[28]

I have discussed the nature of worship and found it to be inconsonant and probably incompatible with pantheism. Given the nature and principal goal of worship objects of worship must have a personal character. It might be thought that showing the pantheistic Unity should not, on conceptual grounds, be worshipped is rather uninteresting. That may be right. The implications of this result, however, are anything but insignificant. For the pantheist, the practical consequences of worship and prayer being unavailable as forms of religious practice are enormous.

In the theistic view, worship and prayer are practically synonymous with religious practice. And even in (theoretically) non-theistic religious traditions such as Buddhism and Taoism, worship and prayer are frequent if not prevalent.[29] Yet, the pantheist is faced with the difficult problem of finding a way to practise pantheism that is consistent with the finding that worship and prayer make sense only in a theistic context. As a result, one of the defining and most noticeable characteristics of pantheism will be the type of practice it takes up. The practices involved, *whatever they are*, will be different not only from those in theistic traditions, but also from those in non-theistic ones in which theistic practice is so much a part.

NOTES

1 Walt Whitman, *Leaves of Grass*, First (1885) Edition, ed. Malcom Cowley (New York: Viking Press, 1959). The selections are from "Song of Myself," the first poem in *Leaves of Grass*. See Cowley's introduction, pp. xx–xxvi, for an account of Whitman's "doctrines."

> He believed true knowledge is to be acquired not through the senses or the intellect, but through union with the Self. At such moments . . . the gum is washed from one's eyes (that is his own phrase), and one can read an infinite lesson in common things . . . This true knowledge is available to every man and woman, since each conceals a divine Self. Moreover, the divinity of all implies the perfect equality of all, the immortality of all, and the universal duty of loving one another.

> (p. xxi)

Grace Jantzen quotes part of Elizabeth Barrett Browning's poem *Aurora Leigh* in *God's World, God's Body* (Philadelphia: Westminster, 1984), p. 157,

Earth's crammed with heaven
And every common bush on fire with God;
But only those who see take off their shoes . . .
The rest sit round it and pluck blackberries,
and daub their natural faces unawares . . .

Jantzen comments: "Those who have once seen themselves, and the world about them, as the embodiment and self-manifestation of God are unlikely to continue to treat it in a cavalier way or feel it utterly alien or devoid of intrinsic significance and worth."

2 Saul Bellow, *Mr. Sammler's Planet* (New York: Viking, 1969), p. 55.

3 Alasdair MacIntyre, "Spinoza," in *Encyclopedia of Philosophy* (New York: Macmillan and Free Press, 1967), vol. 8, pp. 530–1. Cf. Abraham Wolfson, *Spinoza: A Life of Reason* (New York, 1932); Frederick Pollock, *Spinoza, his Life and Philosophy* (London, 1880), reprinted in the Reprint Library. MacIntyre's view is antithetical to that of Wolfson who says, "Of Spinoza it is probably more true than of any other philosopher that his thought cannot be divorced from his life and character without grave risks of total misapprehension." Quoted in Baruch Spinoza, *Ethics*, ed. James Gutmann (New York: Hafner, 1949), p. xii. In a letter declining the professorship at Heidelberg Spinoza says: "For, first, I think that if I want to find time for instructing youth, then I must desist from developing my philosophy. Secondly, I think that I do not know within what limits that freedom of philosophising ought to be confined in order to avoid the appearance of wishing to disturb the publicly established Religion." Quoted in Gutmann (ed.), pp. xx–xxi.

4 The letter excommunicating Spinoza is reprinted in Spinoza's *Ethics*, ed. James Gutmann. It is the only case of Jewish excommunication I know of, and it must be the thing for which the Jews of Amsterdam of the time are best known.

5 Cf. George Lindbeck, *The Nature of Doctrine: Religion and Theology in a Postliberal Age* (Philadelphia: Westminster, 1984). He argues that theological questions about doctrine are inseparable from philosophical, anthropological and sociological issues.

6 Cf. Bryan Wilson (ed.) *Rationality* (New York: Harper & Row, 1970); Martin Hollis and Steven Lukes (eds) *Rationality and Relativism* (Oxford: Blackwell, 1982).

5.1 Belief and practice

1 Pierre Bayle, *Historical and Critical Dictionary: Selections*, tr. Richard Popkin (Indianapolis: Bobbs-Merrill, 1965), p. 295.

2 Richard Swinburne, "A Theodicy of Heaven and Hell," in Alfred J. Freddoso (ed.) *The Existence and Nature of God* (Notre Dame: University of Notre Dame Press, 1983), p. 44. Swinburne thinks there is a direct correlation between belief, doctrine and practice. Contrast his view with that of George Lindbeck, *The Nature of Doctrine*. Lindbeck says, "theories of religion and of doctrine are interdependent, and

deficiencies in one area are inseparable from deficiencies in the other" (p. 7). The difference between Swinburne and Lindbeck on the relation between belief and practice indicates more fundamental differences in their understanding of religion. Swinburne, like other Christian conservatives (i.e. those who Lindbeck describes as adhering to strict "traditionalist propositional orthodoxy" (p. 10)) is dismissive of the philosophical and social-scientific approaches to religion essential to Lindbeck's "cultural-linguistic" account. Many critics of theism also neglect the kind of approach essential to Lindbeck. They too are adherents of "traditionalist propositional orthodoxy," although they deny the truth of the propositions. Propositional orthodoxy "stresses the ways in which church doctrines function as informative propositions or truth claims about objective realities" (Lindbeck, p. 16).

3 The *Tao Tê Ching* is pantheistic scripture. But the kind of philosophical Taoism it depicts is not practised and with rare exceptions never has been. Religious Taoism is practised, and it is not pantheistic – or far less so.

4 The admonition presupposes one has true or morally correct beliefs. If, in the view of the individual who is to issue the admonishment, one has morally reprehensible views, the admonition will not be issued. Instead, the admonisher might tell the person to correct their beliefs and act accordingly.

5 John Skorupski describes V. Pareto's view of the connection between belief and action, a view he rejects, as follows: "there are regular forms of behaviour, such that they, but not the reasons given for them, are invariant across societies and time. Where forms of action are constant, but 'rationalisations', 'ideologies', or 'derivations' vary ... we should conclude that explanation goes from action to the beliefs which apparently inform it, and not vice versa." John Skorupski, *Symbol and Theory: A Philosophical Study of Theories of Religion in Social Anthropology* (Cambridge: Cambridge University Press, 1976), pp. 44ff.

6 Cf. Ludwig Wittgenstein, *Lectures and Conversations on Aesthetics, Psychology and Religious Belief,* ed. Cyril Barrett (Berkeley and Los Angeles: University of California Press, 1972); D. Z. Phillips, *Death and Immortality* (London: Macmillan; New York: St Martins Press, 1970); D. Z. Phillips, *The Concept of Prayer* (London: Routledge & Kegan Paul, 1965); Peter Winch, *The Idea of a Social Science and Its Relation to Philosophy* (London: Routledge & Kegan Paul, 1958); Peter Winch, "Meaning and Religious Language," in Stuart C. Brown (ed.) *Reason and Religion* (Ithaca: Cornell University Press, 1977); Don Cupitt, *Taking Leave of God* (London: SCM, 1980).

The Wittgensteinian analysis has been out of fashion for over twenty years, but it has contemporary adherents (e.g. Winch, Phillips, Cupitt). It is difficult to explain why philosophical positions gain or lose ascendancy – especially a position like Wittgenstein's on religious discourse (or Plantinga's on "basic beliefs") which is obviously wrong. Philosophy, unlike art, has no related critical discipline (i.e. art history) that explains why some positions succeed. As expected, the reasons are often trivial – or worse.

7 John Hick, *An Interpretation of Religion* (New Haven: Yale University Press, 1989), p. 198. See pp. 198–209.

8 Hick, *An Interpretation of Religion*, p. 199. If religious discourse as ordinarily understood is meaningless, this could be a reason for claiming that believers cannot mean what they (and we) think they mean. A position like Phillips's probably rests on discredited "positivist" assumptions about what is a meaningful assertion.

9 Phillips, *Death and Immortality*, p. 49. Quoted in Hick, *An Interpretation of Religion*, p. 198. Hick also refers to Don Cupitt, *Only Human* (London: SCM, 1985), p. 54. To a considerable extent, non-realist analyses of religious discourse rely on the fideistic position that Wittgenstein is sometimes (correctly in my view) seen as arguing for in his later writings – including his *Lectures and Conversations*. For a critique of Wittgensteinian fideism see Kai Nielsen, "Wittgensteinian Fideism," *Philosophy*, 42 (1967), pp. 191–209. Cf. Alasdair MacIntyre's critique of the Wittgenstein/Winch/Phillips view in "Is Understanding Religion Compatible with Believing?," in Bryan R. Wilson (ed.) *Rationality* (New York: Harper & Row, 1970), pp. 62–77.

10 MacIntyre, "Is Understanding Religion Compatible with Believing?," p. 69. Cf. E. R. Leach, *The Political Systems of Highland Burma* (London: Bell, 1954).

11 Hick, *An Interpretation of Religion*, p. 205. Hick's view of the realist's position as "good news for all men" is optimistic. He dismisses doctrines of hell and damnation as extraneous – calling them an "aberration." But they are traditionally part of theism. Hick gives a distorted account of religion because he dismisses aspects of it he finds uncongenial. An adequate theory of religion must account for religion as it occurs, rather than as one would like it to be. Cf. Ronald Green, *Religion and Moral Reason* (Oxford: Oxford University Press, 1988), p. 228. Green also ignores the dark side of religion. See my article, "Deep Structure and The Comparative Philosophy of Religion," *Religious Studies*, 28 (1992), pp. 387–99. For an account of the significance of doctrines of heaven and hell see Swinburne, "A Theodicy of Heaven and Hell," pp. 37–54. Also see my article, "Swinburne's Heaven: One Hell of a Place," *Religious Studies*, 29 (1993).

12 Clifford Geertz, "Religion as a Cultural System," in his *The Interpretation of Cultures* (New York: Basic Books, 1973), p. 90.

13 Cf. Skorupski, *Symbol and Theory*, p. 35. "It follows from this that religious life rests at least in part on *failure* to recognise that religious ideas are symbolic representations of social reality."

14 Hick, *An Interpretation of Religion*, pp. 200–1.

15 Geertz, "Religion as a Cultural System," pp. 89–90. The religious perspective differs from the aesthetic:

> instead of effecting a disengagement from . . . factuality . . . it deepens the concern with fact and seeks to create an aura of utter

> actuality. It is this sense of the "really real" upon which the religious perspective rests and which the symbolic activities of religion as a cultural system are devoted to producing... [I]n ritual... this conviction that religious conceptions are veridical... is somehow generated.
>
> (p. 112)

This view is not compatible with a non-realist account of religion.

16 Cupitt, *Only Human*, p. 153. Skorupski explains how Cupitt's Wittgensteinian approach to the meaning of religious discourse differs from the symbolist or literalist approach. Cupitt's position is not a "symbolist" one as Skorupski defines it.

> the symbolist... [shares] with the literalist... the classical view that a unified semantic account can be given of all sentences in the traditional religious believer's language... the meaning of a sentence is determined by the meaning of its constituent expressions... The Wittgensteinian's criticism of this should... be clear. He approves the symbolist's stress on looking to the emotional and social context in which ritual performances are made, and ritual actions performed, for a grasp of what is conveyed in them; but on his view this approach should be extended to include the very meaning of what is said in such contexts; the symbolist goes wrong in recovering the ("literal") meaning of ritual statements by projecting the meaning of their constituent expressions from the function which these have in other areas of discourse.
>
> (Skorupski, pp. 15–16; cf. pp. 13–17)

17 Hick, *An Interpretation of Religion*, p. 200.

18 Skorupski, *Symbol and Theory*, p. 2. Page references in the text refer to this book. In describing the conception of religion and magic outlined below as "intellectualist," Skorupski follows established usage. According to Skorupski, I. C. Jarvie and "particularly" W. R. G. Horton "would be willing to go farthest along the intellectualist path described" (p. 244 n. 1). Earlier intellectualists include E. B. Tyler and J. G. Frazer. Intellectualism distinguishes between magic and religion in "primitive" societies, but sees them as functioning similarly. Thus, they talk about "magico-religious" beliefs. For convenience, I refer to the "religious" rather than the "magico-religious."

19 Nevertheless, Skorupski describes the "obvious economy and elegance in going on to" accept the "distinctive intellectualist thesis" once literalism is accepted. He describes intellectualism as "logically complete." "if one grants the sequence in which its questions are raised, one must all also grant that they are all the questions at this level of enquiry" (pp. 9–10).

20 Symbolists believe,

> (1) that ritual *actions* in some sense express the social order, though ritual beliefs are a posterior rationalisations, not necessarily themselves symbolic; (2) that ritual... functions in the *maintenance* of

the social order; and (3) the Durkheimian thesis, that ritual actions and beliefs belong to a system of symbolic discourse, the true *referents* of which are to be found in the social order

(Skorupski, p. 24)

21 Skorupski notes, "a metaphorically or symbolically expressed thought is a thought expressed in a form which normally *does* have a literal meaning: what makes it symbolic or metaphorical is just that (i) the literal meaning (if any) of the sentence is not the meaning to be understood, and (ii) the literal meaning of the words must be grasped if one is to 'decode' the meaning which *is* to be understood" (pp. 12–13). He describes ways in which the distinction between the "explicitly literal and the symbolic level" is made. "Religious discourse and action (a) may be unconsciously symbolic, (b) may turn out to be symbolic when its logic is properly surveyed and construed, (c) may have been originally symbolic and then become literalised, or (d) may be symbolic in the interpretation of the observer, but not in that of the actor" (p. 36).

22 Durkheim's thesis is that "the domain symbolically represented in ritual practice and belief is social reality" (p. 23). Skorupski claims "the Durkheimian thesis results from combining positivism with an anthropocentric conception of religion" (p. 31). Even if Skorupski is correct in claiming that Durkheim bases thesis involves a commitment to positivism, this is not true of the symbolist approach *per se.* Social anthropologists with no such commitment (e.g. Geertz) accept Durkheim's thesis (in some cases) on empirical grounds. I doubt Durkheim's thesis is based on positivism to the extent Skorupski claims it is, despite the support he finds in what Durkheim says about the "science of religion" and its need to analyse only what is observable. Apart from a commitment he may have to positivism, Durkheim defends his theory on empirical grounds.

23 Skorupski distinguishes between anthropocentric and cosmocentric symbolist analysis, and rejects them both. Anthropocentric symbolists claim that primitive religions' "symbolically expressed subject" is society. For cosmocentric symbolists "what was symbolised ... were natural forces and natural phenomena" (p. 66). (See pp. 53–67.) He thinks symbolist theories can be correct only if they do not conflict with literalist explanations.

> So long as the symbolist level of ritual and belief could be thought of as standing in some empirical relationship to the actions and expressed beliefs of the people studied, whether historically, unconsciously, or as an unreflectively misconstrued level of meaning, it was possible, in principle to see what kind of relevance the symbolist approach had to the project of explaining *why it is* that people have magical or religious beliefs and institutions.
>
> (pp. 51–2)

For some reason Skorupski does not think a symbolist account of the *function* of ritual can count as an explanation of "why it is" that people have religious beliefs. In Geertz's account, or Durkheim's, the function of religion does explain this. Anyway, the symbolist level of ritual *usually is* thought of as standing in an empirical relationship to the actions expressed (e.g. Freud).

24 Geertz, "Religion as a Cultural System," p. 88. Geertz accepts aspects of Durkheim's symbolist approach, but his own "cultural" approach is broader than Durkheim's and, I think, incompatible with much of it. Geertz, "following Parsons and Shils," develops "the cultural dimension of religious analysis . . . [Culture] denotes an historically transmitted pattern of meanings embodied in symbols, a system of inherited conceptions expressed in symbolic forms by means of which men communicate, perpetuate, and develop their knowledge about and attitudes toward life" (p. 89). As Geertz explains it, ritual is essential to culture. It has both symbolic-expressive and instrumental functions. His account of ritual cannot be accommodated wholly within intellectualism.

> In a ritual, the world as lived and the world as imagined, fused under the agency of a single set of symbolic forms, turn out to be the same world . . . [T]hough any religious ritual . . . involves this symbolic fusion of ethos and world view, it is mainly certain more elaborate and usually more public ones, ones in which a broad range of moods and motivations on the one hand, and metaphysical conceptions on the other are caught up, which shape the spiritual consciousness of a people . . . "cultural performances" . . . represent not only the point at which the dispositional and conceptual aspects of religious life converge for the believer, but also the point at which the interaction between them can most readily be examined by the detached observer . . . religious performances . . . for participants . . . are . . . not only models of what they believe, but also models *for* the believing of it. In these plastic dramas men attain their faith as they portray it.
>
> (pp. 112–14)

25 Cf. Geertz, "Religion as a Cultural System," pp. 87–8, 99–102.

> Even to consider people's religious beliefs as attempts to bring anomalous events . . . within the circle of the at least potentially explicable seems to smack of Tyloreanism or worse. But . . . some men . . . are unable to leave unclarified problems of analysis merely unclarified . . . Any chronic failure of one's explanatory apparatus . . . tends to lead to a deep disquiet – a tendency rather more widespread and a disquiet rather deeper than we have sometimes supposed since the pseudoscience view of religious belief was, quite rightfully, disposed . . . I was struck . . . by the degree to which my more animistically inclined informants behaved like true Tyloreans. They seem to be constantly using their beliefs to "explain" phenomena; or more accurately, to convince themselves that the phenomena were explainable . . .

26 Cf. Skorupski, p. 245 n. 15. Geertz is referred to only here.
27 Cf. Ch'en Ku-ying, *Lao Tzu, Text, Notes, and Comments*, translated and adapted by Rhett Y. W. Young and Roger T. Ames (Republic of China: Chinese Materials Center, 1981). See the introduction by Young and Ames.

5.2 Worship and prayer

1 R. G. Thwaites, *Jesuit Relations*, Cleveland, 1896–1901, vi [Quebec, 1633–34], p. 203; quoted from James Hastings (ed.) "Prayer," *Encyclopedia of Religion and Ethics* (Edinburgh: Clark 1908–26), p. 158.
2 Rudolf Otto, *The Idea of The Holy*, 2nd edn (Oxford: Oxford University Press, 1950), p. 201. Otto continues, "It is often thought that the designations of deity in impersonal, neuter terms ('It'), rather than in terms of person and masculine pronoun ('He', 'thou'), are too poor and too pale to gain a place in our Christian thought of God. But this is not always correct. Frequently such terms indicate the mysterious overplus of the non-rational and numinous, that cannot enter our 'concepts' because it is too great and too alien to them; and in this sense they are quite indispensable even in hymns and prayers" (p. 203).
3 Richard Swinburne, "A Theodicy of Heaven and Hell," p. 41. Cf. Richard Swinburne, *The Coherence of Theism* (Oxford: Oxford University Press, 1977), ch. 15. Page references to Swinburne in the text are to *The Coherence of Theism.*
  What is "adoration?" Teilhard de Chardin says, "To adore . . . That means to lose oneself in the unfathomable, to plunge into the inexhaustible, to find peace in the incorruptible . . . and to give of one's deepest to that whose depth has no end." William Temple says, "Worship is the submission of all our nature to God. It is the quickening of conscience by his holiness . . . the opening of the heart to his love; the surrender of will to his purpose – and all of this gathered up in adoration, the most selfless emotion of which our nature is capable and therefore the chief remedy of that self-centredness which is our original sin and the source of all actual evil." George Appleton (ed.) *Oxford Book of Prayer* (Oxford: Oxford University Press, 1986), p. 3. See pp. 3–18 for "Prayers of Adoration." Cf. James Hastings (ed.) "Worship," *Encyclopedia of Religion and Ethics* (Edinburgh: Clark, 1908–26).
4 Harold W. Wood, Jr, "Modern Pantheism as an Approach to Environmental Ethics," *Environmental Ethics*, 7 (1985), pp. 157–8.
5 Ninian Smart, *The Concept of Worship* (London: Macmillan, 1972), pp. 11, 26. What is the relationship between prayer and worship? Smart says, "It is hard to see that there can be a prayer which does not involve worship; but there are forms of prayer which are not necessary to worship, such as petition" (pp. 49–50). Why does Smart say that "prayer involves worship" rather than that it is a *kind* of

worship? And, granted that there are forms of prayer that are "not necessary to worship," is Smart suggesting that worship always involves prayer? Does worship always involve prayer?

Cf. George Chryssides, "Subject and Object in Worship," *Religious Studies*, 23 (1987), pp. 367–75. He says, "To worship, then, is in some sense to worship *something*, but to say this is not to imply that there must be some disembodied mind which forms the object of worship, as distinct from the worshipping subject" (p. 374).

6 Cf. H. B. Alexander, "Worship," in James Hastings (ed.) *Encyclopedia of Religion and Ethics* (Edinburgh: Clark, 1908–26), p. 754. "In order that the ritual form may be recognized as true worship, it must be accompanied by some evidence of a religious sanction, i.e., it must in some sense be directed to powers superhuman, if not supernatural... Ordinarily gods are defined as the objects of worship."

Cf. Thomas Kochumuttam, "Limits of Worship in Indian Religions," *Journal of Dharma*, 3 (1978), pp. 364–72. "For many, religion is the way one *relates* oneself to a personal creator-God, and this relation must express itself in worship... one is religious to the extent to which one worships... when I say that worship is an essential part of religions, I mean worship *proper*, which is necessarily an expression of one's dependence on a personal creator-God" (pp. 364–5). Kochumuttam goes on to argue that if religion is not understood primarily as a way of relating oneself to a personal creator-God, then rather than worship

> religion as such would mean the way one *orients oneself*... "finding out about one's position or situation"... If absolute monism is presupposed, then "orienting oneself" would mean realizing one's identity with the monistic reality... if absolute pluralism is presupposed, then "orienting oneself" would mean realizing one's absolute unrelatedness. In either case there is no place whatsoever for worship, which presupposes the dependence of the creatures on the creator-God.
>
> (p. 365)

7 Cf. Swinburne, *The Coherence of Theism*, pp. 142–3. For present purposes I have greatly oversimplified the issue here.

8 Smart, *The Concept of Worship*, p. 19. Cf. pp. 20–1.

9 "Thou art my Lord and King" is a mild expression of one's inferiority to God. Some theistic prayer is filled not just with ways in which one is inferior, but with ways in which one is insignificant, worthless, dirty etc.

10 James Rachels, "God and Human Attitudes," *Religious Studies*, 7 (1971), pp. 325–37, at 325. Rachels argues that God, conceived as a "fitting object of worship," cannot exist because "no being could ever *be* a fitting object of worship" (p. 325). He argues that worship "requires the abandonment of one's role as an autonomous moral agent" (p. 335), and that such an abandonment can never be justi-

fied. Cf. Philip Quinn, *Divine Commands and Moral Requirements* (Oxford: Clarendon Press, 1978), ch. 1.

11 Smart, *The Concept of Worship*, p. 41.

12 Swinburne says, "most theists would wish to make . . . the claim" that "men ought morally to worship God." *The Coherence of Theism*, p. 282.

13 Swinburne, "A Theodicy of Heaven and Hell," p. 41.

14 The case if complicated by the Christian view that God made a sacrifice in Christ for our salvation. This can be disregarded in the present context where the concern is why the theistic God *qua* God should be worshipped irrespective of special benefits conferred or special sacrifices made. I leave aside the obvious and fundamental questions as to why God had to make such a sacrifice to accomplish his purpose; how it can be a sacrifice etc. As Kierkegaard saw, the central claim of Christianity (i.e. the incarnation) is "absurd."

15 Swinburne asks, "Does an individual need to be eternal in order to have the lordship which deserves worship? It seems to me that he will be less in control of things, and hence less great if he is not backwardly eternal. Fully to deserve worship, he must always have existed" (cf. pp. 289–90). The suggestion is that "lordship" involves absolute control and greatness. But where is the justification for the claim that God ought to be worshipped?

16 Swinburne, *The Coherence of Theism*, pp. 283–4, n. 2. Cf. *Summa Theologiae*, 2a.2ae.80 and 81.

17 I do not mean that humans intend to literally control God through prayer. What they are trying to control is the course of their lives, and they try to do this partly by influencing God.

18 Bernard P. Dauenhauer, "Some Aspects of Language and Time in Ritual Worship," *International Journal for Philosophy of Religion*, 6 (1975), pp. 54–62, at 57. In a note Dauenhauer goes on to say,

> This characteristic explains why one who accepts a Cartesian or Scholastic natural theology which has a God who creates and conserves the world sheerly on his own, automatically so to speak, has to find some other grounds, e.g. the possibility of grace, which is not automatically bestowed, on which to make sense of ritual worship. This same characteristic allows one to make sense of certain cases where a "natural" power is praised for what it naturally does but at the same time that power is petitioned for something else.
>
> (p. 57 n. 4)

Surely Spinoza's God presents Dauenhauer with a stronger example than the God in Cartesian or Scholastic natural theology. In Scholasticism, God's efficacious presence is at least sometimes taken to occur not automatically by natural necessity, but in response to human beings.

19 Bernard Dauenhauer, "Some Aspects of Language and Time in Ritual Worship," pp. 57–8. "This object [of worship] must be capable of being . . . absent as well as present . . . of being invoked, but not coerced, into efficacious presence" (p. 58). Dauenhauer's analysis of

characteristics that an object of worship must have is useful, but his analysis of the activity of ritual worship is problematic. He says, for example, "because ritual worship *must* be repeated it is in principle impervious to adaptation and interpretation. It makes no sense to compare and contrast two performances of a ritual function as such . . . the sequence of moments within ritual worship is absolutely inflexible" (p. 60). He gives no support for these claims, and they just seem false. Ritual worship does change, but in Dauenhauer's analysis it is unclear how it can change or even that it can change.

20 Smart, *The Concept of Worship*, p. 51. While Swinburne does not regard "god is to be worshipped" as an analytic truth, it is not clear if he thinks "God is to be worshipped" (i.e. the theistic God) is true by definition. He says "the theist normally claims that God is worthy of worship both in virtue of his having such essential properties as I have discussed [i.e. omnipotence, perfect goodness, complete freedom etc.] and also in virtue of his having done of his own free will various actions" (p. 282). If God is worthy of worship because he has certain properties essentially, then it appears that God is being defined as a Being who by his very nature is to be worshipped. To recognise God as having certain properties, and to understand what having those properties entails, involves recognising that God is to be worshipped.

21 Chryssides, "Subject and Object in Worship." Page numbers in this section of the text refer to this article.

22 Chryssides says "To make use of personalistic imagery is not to pretend [that God is personal], but to symbolize . . ." (p. 373).

23 Cf., for example, "Prayer," *Encyclopedia of Religion and Ethics*, "Tao was regarded as . . . immanent in all the universe . . . [but] it cannot be said to have been an object of worship" (p. 762).

24 Cf. "Prayer (Buddhist)," *Encyclopedia of Religion and Ethics*. "To worship a deity – which is admitted by Mahayana Buddhism – means, not to adore it as a being external to oneself, but to realize the excellent qualities found in the deity. Likewise, to pray may be understood to mean asking something of a deity, but the truth is that the one who is asked and the one who asks are one in the fundamental nature, and, therefore, the prayer is in its ultimatae significance a self-inculcation, a self-committal to the moral ideals of Buddhism" (p. 168).

25 Cf. "Prayer (in Mahayana Buddhism)," *Encyclopedia of Religion and Ethics*, pp. 167–86, and p. 166. Many of Chryssides' views concerning the "goal" and purpose of worship in Buddhism are supported in this article. But it does not support his principal contention that "worship" is conceptually appropriate in cases like Buddhism where the existence of god is denied. When worship occurs in Buddhism (or religious Taoism), as it does extensively, the object of worship (e.g. the Buddha) is conceived of personalistic terms.

26 All persons are essentially non-material (i.e. incorporeal) spirits according to theism. God is also a "person," but is conceived of as non-material. If persons are necessarily embodied; if the concept of

an incorporeal being is incoherent, then theism is probably incoherent. If the concept of an incorporeal God is incoherent, and if God must be incorporeal to be worthy of worship, "we are left with the following dilemma: either God is described as embodied, and hence not worthy of worship, or else he is taken to be incorporeal, with the consequence that God-talk lapses into nonsense. In either case, Christianity becomes indefensible." Grace Jantzen, "On Worshipping as Embodied God," *Canadian Journal of Philosophy*, 8 (1978), pp. 511–19, at 512. Cf. David Wiggins, *Identity and Spatio-Temporal Continuity* (Oxford: Blackwell, 1967); Bernard Williams, "Are Persons Bodies?," in *Problems of the Self* (Cambridge: Cambridge University Press, 1973); Terence Penelhum, *Survival and Disembodied Existence* (London: Routledge & Kegan Paul, 1970); Jonathan Harrison, "The Embodiment of Mind, or What Use is Having a Body?," *Proceedings of the Aristotelian Society*, 74 (1973–4), pp. 33–55.

27 Jantzen raises important issues concerning limitation and embodiment. "Even if we grant . . . that a body is by definition finite, why should we believe, for instance, that a finite brain could not have infinite wisdom." Jantzen, "On Worshipping an Embodied God," p. 519. In general, limitation in size does not entail finiteness or limitation in respect to ability. Presumably, it is limitation with respect to ability rather than size that theists are concerned with. Yet embodiment appears to imply (at the most) only limitation in respect to size. Jantzen (like Swinburne) also criticises the idea that God would have to exist necessarily to be worthy of worship. Cf. Swinburne, *The Coherence of Theism*, pp. 290–1. For a different view see H. P. Owen, *Concepts of Deity* (London: Macmillan, 1971), p. 17.

28 Grace Jantzen argues against both the widely accepted view that an embodied God could not be religiously adequate and the view that such a God could not worthy of worship. See her discussion of "what sort of characteristics . . . are involved in *morally* justifiable worship." "On Worshipping an Embodied God," pp. 513–14. Also see her discussion of embodiment as a limitation which would undermine the possibility of appropriately worshipping anything embodied (pp. 517–19). She denies this is necessarily the case. Jantzen presupposes that only a personal being could be a morally justifiable object of worship, and she limits her discussion to the kinds of characteristics a being must have to be worthy of worship. Cf. *God's World, God's Body*.

Jantzen notes the incongruity on the part of Christian theists who claim that an embodied God would not be worthy of worship in view of the incarnation of "Jesus the Christ." Cf. "On Worshipping an Embodied God," p. 511 n. 1. For arguments against the adequacy of the notion of an embodied God see Swinburne, *The Coherence of Theism*, ch. 7; Frederick Copleston, "Man, Transcendence, and the Absence of God," *Thought*, 43 (1968), pp. 24–38; Kai Nielsen, *Scepticism* (New York: Macmillan, 1973), pp. 91–2.

29 Ninian Smart says, "Theravada does not treat the Ultimate as creator, or even as Ground of Being, nor as something to pray to or worship.

It is true that . . . there are Buddha-statues. But it would be wrong to see the Buddha in any strict sense as an object of worship." "Our Experience of the Ultimate," *Religious Studies*, 20 (1984), p. 20.

It is not very difficult to give some explanation of why a theistic practice like worship is more often than not taken up in non-theistic traditions; why, for example, contrary to the Buddha's teaching, the Buddha is often worshipped. The reasons are psychological and sociological. Cf. Thomas Kochumuttam, 'Limits of Worship in Indian Religions."

6

CONCLUSION: HOW TO
PRACTISE PANTHEISM

The religious possibilities of pantheism are strictly limited. Although it can permit reverence for, and even a quasi-mystical union with, Nature qua divine, it has no place for salvation, prayer, or any personal relationship between God and man. Stoic "Providence" is just another word for "Fate". Spinoza's "intellectual love of God" . . . is simply the mind's desire for self-identification with the determined order of things.[1]

H. P. Owen

There are two and only two systems of philosophy that can be offered. The one posits God as the transcendent cause of things; the other makes God the immanent cause. The former carefully distinguishes and separates God from the world; the latter shamefully confounds God with the universe . . . The former establishes a foundation for every religious devotion and for all piety, and this the latter fundamentally overturns and takes away.[2]

Christoph. Wittich

The final test of any theory is, of course, the practice to which it gives rise.[3]

Stephen Frosh

My claims in these concluding sections are based on the account of pantheism given thus far. However, much of what follows is speculative. It would be annoyingly coy to come this far and not be willing, for whatever reason, to make further educated guesses as to (a) what the pantheist is after (i.e. the goal of pantheism) and (b) how to get there (i.e. how to practise pantheism).

6.1 GOAL: RELATIONSHIP OR STATE?

In the woods is perpetual youth. Within these plantations a decorum and sanctity reign, a perennial festival is dressed, and the guest sees not how he should tire of them in a thousand years. In the woods we return to reason and faith. There I feel that nothing can befall me in life – no disgrace, no calamity (leaving me my eyes) which Nature cannot repair. Standing on the bare ground – my head bathed by the blithe air, and uplifted into infinite space – all mean egoism vanishes. I become a transparent eye-ball; I am nothing: I see all; the currents of the Universal Being circulate through me: I am part or particle of God.[1]

Ralph Waldo Emerson

Christoph. Wittich and H. P. Owen, both critics of Spinoza, raise the question of the religious possibilities of pantheism. In effect, they deny pantheism can be religiously useful – can function as a religion – because they claim that there is no feasible way to practise it. Both appear to equate religious practice exclusively with theistic practice such as worship, prayer and devotion.

But the pantheist has a completely different notion from the theist concerning the nature of God. Because theistic practice is intrinsically connected to the theistic conception of God and a related world-view, it is not surprising that when religious practice is conceived of theistically it appears that there is no way at all for pantheism to be practised. Pantheism rejects the theistic suppositions essential to theistic practice by denying (i) that God is a being separate from the world and (ii) that human salvation depends upon establishing a right sort of relationship with God. Thus, all that Owen and Wittich are really claiming is that theistic forms of practice are, for the most part, unavailable to the pantheist. This is no news to the pantheist, and it is a view readily concurred with in the previous chapter on worship and prayer.

Why suppose, however, that all religious practice must be theistically conceived? Since practice is conceived in terms of an idea of God, a related world-view and a conception of the goal of religion, then it is to be expected that a non-theistic (e.g. pantheistic) conception of the religious goal – along with one's beliefs about God and the world – would result in practices quite different from those "designed" to fit theism. In short, granted that pantheism "has no place for salvation, prayer, or any personal relationship between God and man," it does not follow that "the religious possibilities of pantheism are strictly limited."[2] Just as practice suitable to theism is a function of theists' conception of God and their goal in relation to that God, so pantheistic practice must fit its God and its goal.

If the goal of theism is taken to be the development of a close personal relation to God, then worship is seen as a way of developing the relation. In non-theistic religions where the goal cannot be conceived of in terms of a personal relation with God since God is not a person, much of the purpose and motivation for worship is dissipated. Worship is appropriate to theism because it is intrinsically related to, and a primary mode of achieving, the theistic goal. Worship cannot play the same role in non-theistic traditions.

In classical theism the final stage of the primary religious objective includes the "beatific vision." This involves a special intimacy with God which involves happiness, joy, peace etc. In achieving this one will have attained one's goal and purpose as a human being created by God. Worship and prayer are means by which one seeks to cultivate this relationship, and through which one comes to know the divine will as it relates to oneself and for creation as a whole. Ideally, as one comes to know these things – and in so doing knows something of the nature of God as it relates to persons – one tries to act in accordance with the will of God. In theism, to "do God's bidding" is not to relinquish one's autonomy and submit oneself to an alien will, but to do what it is that as a human being created by God one should do. One is allegedly fulfilling one's own essential purpose and goal and not someone else's.

This essentially theistic objective is inapplicable to pantheism. It refers to the divine will, and the relationship sought is with a personal God. But perhaps there is a similar or analogous religious objective for pantheists. Do pantheists seek a relationship with the impersonal Unity rather than a "state"? The choices of the religious objective for the pantheist are either a relationship with the Unity or a state of some kind. The kind of religious practice pantheism (like theism) engenders is a function of the kind of goal sought. What then is the religious objective of pantheism? If there were no such objective to pursue through practice, the question of how to practise pantheism becomes superfluous. That there is a goal to pursue is intrinsic to the nature of religion.

In his account of the distinction between meditation and worship as two fundamentally different but compatible types of religious practice, Ninian Smart explains how a religious goal relates to and partially determines the practice it engenders. In an analysis that lends support to the thesis of the previous chapter, he suggests why worship is less appropriate to a non-theistic tradition such a Theravada Buddhism than to a theistic one.[3] Smart says, "*Nirvana* [the 'central value' or goal of Theravada Buddhism] is a state accruing upon the practice of meditation rather than worship." He denies it is "sensible to say that this, *nirvana*, is a focus of worship." It is "a state of the individual, rather than an entity or being . . . it is not a personal Being with whom one could enter into transactions, as with gods."[4] Smart's reason for claiming that *nirvana* is not a focus of worship is that "it is not a personal Being." Similarly, since the pantheistic Unity is not a personal Being, it could not be a (proper) focus of worship.[5]

Smart says,

> I would not deny that people can meditate upon an object of worship and that they can regard such meditation as being a kind of worship . . . But I should want to argue that one can meditate (contemplate) . . . without worshipping. In other words, though meditation is a central part of the life of some religions and religious movements, it is not to be identified with worship *tout court* . . . What then is the difference between meditation and worship? First, no ritual need be involved in contemplation . . . Second, the practice of, for example, the stages of meditation . . . in Theravada Buddhism aims at emptying the mind of discursive thoughts, such as the thought of an object of worship . . . Thus, the state of liberation which is aimed at in some systems of yoga . . . does not involve any idea of "being close" to God or any other object of worship. Thus it is not surprising that Theravada Buddhism and Sankhya-Yoga have very weak notions of god and do not believe in a Creator of the universe. Their sights are fixed on a different type of supreme value. It may be noted that just as meditation can be seen under the guise of worship, where it occurs in a

theistic context, so God can be seen as little more than a useful device for achieving purity of consciousness: thus the Lord in the Yoga system serves as a useful model to meditate upon, but does not actually bring about the liberation of those who may mediate upon him.

(pp. 24–5)

Although pantheism and Theravada Buddhism have very different conceptions of reality which engender different goals and values, their respective goals do "not involve any idea of 'being close' to God or any other object of worship." In Theravada Buddhism the goal is a state of the individual (if Smart is right) rather than a relation. Is the goal of pantheism similarly the attainment of a "state of the individual" – albeit a different state than in Theravada Buddhism – rather than a relation? If so, then the type of practices most suitable to pantheism will not involve worship. Whether or not, and to what extent, they would involve meditation is a separate issue. This depends both on the kind of state one is trying to achieve and on the type of meditation involved.

As in other religions, the objective of pantheism is complex and has metaphysical, personal and social aspects. Religious practice is not just a way of attaining goals. It is also an affirmation of the objective, and in Geertz and Berger's account, of a world-view and ethos. Nevertheless, the general type of practice suited to pantheism can be characterised by identifying its primary goal as either "relationship" or "state."

In pantheistic systems such as Spinoza's or philosophical Taoism, the objective is best described as a state rather than a relation. Furthermore, whereas worship may play some role in traditions where there is some element of a personal god present (e.g. Theravada Buddhism), it should play no role in any type of pantheism whose rejection of a personal god is constitutive of the position. Normatively, non-personal pantheism should involve no worship.

However, just as theism correctly claims that although the principal goal of theistic practice is a relation to God this also involves a "state of the individual," so the pantheist claims that although pantheistic practice is principally concerned with a "state of an individual," a crucial and intrinsic aspect of this state is one's relation to the divine Unity. However, granted that a dichotomy between the objective as "relationship" or "state" is not firm, the principal form of practice – contemplative and meditative on the one hand, or worship on the other – follows from the objective emphasised. In theism it is on a personal relationship to God. In pantheism, the emphasis is on an individual state resulting from an understanding of, and a right relation to, the Unity. Practice will therefore be contemplative and meditative rather than devotional. As in the case of theism, pantheistic practices – like the beliefs they are related to – are meant to have practical consequences in terms of both what one does and, more generally, the way one lives.[6]

The question, of course, is how the pantheist is to arrive at "the right relation" to the Unity, thereby achieving their objective. Answering this is the principal focus of both Spinoza's *Ethics*, the *Tao Tê Ching* and most other pantheistic literature (e.g. Whitman's "Song of Myself"). What one actually does depends partly on the individual (i.e. Spinoza is no Whitman), and also on the particulars of the state sought. Since the pantheistic conception(s) of reality is ultimately very different from, for example, that of the Theravada Buddhist, there is no reason to suppose the pantheistic objective to be like *nirvana*, or liberation through identification with Brahman. The pantheist's relation to the divine Unity does not entail the obliteration of self or liberation that a Buddhist's identification with Brahman does; nor is it like the theistic mystic's union with God. There may be aspects of the state pantheists seek that are similar to Buddhist goals, and even to theistic ones – though to a far lesser extent. But, even if the pantheist's objective is as different from what the Buddhist seeks as it is from what the theist seeks, the means for achieving it remain contemplative or meditative rather than devotional.

For Spinoza, acquiring the happiness described in the *Ethics* is largely an intellectual achievement. It is difficult to see how one can attain the understanding and identification with "God" that Spinoza claims leads to peace of mind and "blessedness" (i.e. the highest achievement of the individual) without addressing the problem discursively rather than affectively by intuition and meditation – although discursive thinking and these other methods are by no means inconsistent. But even though Spinoza's approach involves little that is not discursive, it is contemplative, and the objective remains primarily a state rather than relation. Worship is not a mode of practice conducive to achieving the state Spinoza seeks.[7] Granted that Spinoza's method is intellectualistic, other approaches are possible – especially where the objective itself is conceived of differently (i.e. less intellectualistic). Spinoza of course recognises that his own method is not suited to most people and acknowledges – possibly under duress – that ordinary practice such as worship and prayer may at times engender ends he describes. Just as theists use various methods to pursue their objective – some more intellectualistic than others – so in pantheism certain kinds of practices are suited to certain kinds of people. As in other religions, the means by which pantheists pursue their objectives are generally not overtly or overly intellectualised. To do so can undermine practice by upsetting the balance between the affective and intellectual aspects of their belief system.

The pantheist is likely to view the kinds of goals that most religious traditions envision as excessive and grandiose – as neither believable nor desirable. What is more, although they are not humanists, like humanists pantheists are likely to view those objectives and related beliefs much as theistic traditions viewed those of "primitive religions" and of each other: as superstitiously anthropocentric and so capable of being naturalistically explained. The state sought by the pantheist supervenes (as in Taoism) on establishing the right relation with the Unity by means of cultivating a life suited to both the nature of the Unity and oneself. But for the pantheist this is a goal in itself, a this-worldly happiness. The pantheist eschews any notion of their being further goals; for example, the theist's beatific vision; personal immortality; *nirvana*; and even Spinoza's "blessedness," interpreted as something other-worldly.

The pantheist's happiness is nevertheless a special "state" that is difficult to achieve. Being a kind of utopian ideal it too is perhaps grandiose. Ordinary happiness is part of it but should not be conflated with the kind of thoroughgoing happiness the pantheist thinks it is possible to attain *now and again*. Much as Kierkegaard denied that "truth," "subjectivity" and even "immortality" are attainable once and for all, the pantheists deny their objective is a once and for all achievement. It is a state of well-being that involves a sustained peace of mind and the kind of happiness that comes from, or is identical with, such a state of mind. Since one's own state of mind and relation to the all-inclusive Unity are partly dependent upon other people and things, the state the pantheist seeks is not something achievable in isolation. Pantheism involves a this-worldly utopian vision based on an individual's relations to, and in a sense identification with, the Unity. Accounts of what pantheists believe should be sought after and must be given in terms of this ideal relation.

Pantheists do not create the divine Unity simply by believing in it, but they may claim to contribute to it. In bringing about the happiness and accord that are their objectives, the pantheist lessens discord that is antithetical to the Unity. Examples are found in both the Presocratics and Taoism. The manifested Tao is a standard for human behaviour, and in so far as one fails to follow the standard one fails to "comply with nature" and engender the Tao. According to Young and Ames, complying with nature through non-action (*wu-wei*) "must be taken as the very essence of the *Tao Tĕ Ching*." "Non-action" does not literally mean doing nothing, but doing nothing contrary to one's nature and the manifestations of the Tao. It "refers to an attitude of allowing a given phenomenon to develop freely in accord with its particular situation and its particular natural tendencies ... [It] means according with nature, without attempting to augment it with the artificial."[8] "Relaxed, he [the ideal ruler] prizes his words. When his accomplishments are complete and the affairs of state are in order, The common people say: 'We are naturally like this' " (*Tao Tĕ Ching*, XVII). One aspect and principal meaning of the Tao is that it is a system of self-regulating principles. In failing to understand and then comply one is interfering with that system. Unity manifests itself to the extent that the principles and values essential to it are propagated. People do not control the Unity and they are no more significant in terms of Unity than other living and non-living things. But how one lives affects the Unity just as everything else has its effect.

There is some similarity between mysticism and pantheism in that both sometimes claim that experience of a certain sort can be a source of knowledge about ultimate reality. But pantheists are not necessarily or even usually mystics. Those pantheists who are also mystics (i.e. non-theistic mystics) may have different experiences from their theistic counterparts.[9] So although some pantheists claim to intuit the nature of the Unity (e.g. Robinson Jeffers), this should not be identified with experiences associated with people like St John of the Cross. Just as the pantheist's objective is perhaps modest compared with the beatific vision or *nirvana*, so the pantheist's religious experience, even mystical experience, may be less exceptional than the "unity with the Godhead," "loss of self" and other "ineffable" experiences those in theistic mystical traditions describe. Pantheists need not claim, as some theistic mystics do, that their experience is self-authenticating. The quotation from Emerson at the beginning of this section is not a description of the quintessential mystical experience described by W. T. Stace, Evelyn Underhill, William James and others. It describes a pantheistic experience, and it is partly in terms of such experiences that the objectives of pantheism are to be elucidated.

Pantheists have certain "scriptural" resources, but pantheism is not based on revelation or scripture; nor is it founded on teachings of charismatic and prophetic figures. Pantheists do not, for example, rely on scripture as a justification for belief in the existence or nature of the divine Unity, or for telling them what to do. Natural theology is the only type acceptable to pantheists. Only in this context (i.e. investigation into the nature of God based on reason not revelation) does it make sense to ask if pantheism is true and about reasons for believing it. Claims about the divine Unity can be subject to the kind of rational inquiry theistic claims have been subject to.

However, in the context of natural theology there is reason to believe that pantheism may fare well if compared with theism (see Part II). This may be part of the reason why it has been the classic religious alternative to theism. Pantheists make no supernatural claims. Questions about miracles do not have to be asked. Sense does not have to be made out of a doctrine of the trinity, a theory of heaven and hell etc. Evil does not present the same kind of problem for pantheism as it does for theism; and most theistic arguments for the existence of God are irrelevant. In pantheism there is no question of the existence of a necessary being (i.e. the ontological argument), or a designer of the universe (i.e. the teleological argument). However, some forms of the cosmological argument might be relevant, and arguments from religious experience for the existence of God are also applicable. The latter arguments claim that such experience is indicative of a divine reality because the reality best explains the experience. The pantheist, like the theist, will try to justify belief in the Unity by arguing that its existence best explains certain experiences and certain facts about the world, experiences and facts that their objectives and practices take account of.

Anthony O'Hear has described religion as "essentially dogmatic, fetishistic and authoritarian." Like others before him, he claims "this aspect of religion is where religion derives its strength from."[10]

> social and economic conditions... have destroyed... the organically knit societies of the past and rendered unavailable the type of meaning that the genuinely common cultures... gave to their members. But the response to this cannot be to attempt, factitiously, to restore that type of meaning by invoking old symbols whose substance is now broken, or to invent new ones, for any such invention would be spurious unless, *per impossibile*, it was based in a genuinely shared life and experience.
>
> Religion, with its authoritarian, anti-critical stance, stands in stark opposition to the idea that individuals can achieve meaning from their own resources. Its hidden (or not so hidden) message is that the secret of life is to be found elsewhere, in someone else's text, dogma, or institution.
>
> (p. 248)

If a symbol system is essential to culture – if culture is itself a symbol system – it makes little sense to suppose society can get along without symbols. There is no choice whether or not to "invent" new symbols. Symbols convey meaning, and if certain meanings conveyed by certain symbols are moribund because of changes in the world, then other types of meaning, conveyed by other symbols, must propagate. While the waning of the "organically-knit" societies of the past have "rendered unavailable" the type of meaning the "genuinely common cultures of such societies gave to their members," it is possible to view the world as a whole as more "organically-knit" than ever. This is the way it is viewed by some environmentalists, politicians and even some movie producers. The notion of a "new world-order" is a symbol meant to convey this conception.

O'Hear claims that inventing new symbols "would be spurious unless, *per impossibile*, it was based in a genuinely shared life and experience." Yet, people may now share experiences more than ever; though the character of those experiences is not the kind O'Hear has in mind. If so, then the "invention" of new symbols would reflect this. At any rate, to speak of symbols as being "invented" is misleading. It is not possible to sit down and invent a cultural symbol in the way one invents a jingle. Symbols are "already there" inherent in a culture, and are neither discovered nor invented.

Pantheism does not regard itself as "essentially dogmatic, fetishistic, and authoritarian." And it denies that it "stands in stark opposition to the idea that individuals can achieve meaning from their own resources." Pantheism claims that its particular system of symbols, a system that depicts reality, helps rather than hinders people to achieve meaning from their own resources. But it recognises that one's resources, and what one does with them, are inextricably linked to others. One's resources are never simply one's own.[11] Society does not stand over and against the individual, in competition with them as a source for meaning, as O'Hear suggests. Meaning, in a sense, always comes from society and it is always conveyed by culture.

Of course, theism makes similar claims. Perhaps the fact that pantheism has never has been institutionalised; that it is not fundamentally based on revelation or scripture; and perhaps the actual claims it makes concerning the Unity, exempt it from O'Hear's charges? Both what the pantheist says, and how she says it, are important in judging if O'Hear's claims are as applicable to pantheism as they may be to theism.

6.2 WHAT TO DO

You go looking for your soul in this dramatic messianic desert mission. But of course it's everywhere, as a matter of fact. It's in everything mundane boring unworthy imperfect, as well as in everything beautiful ... a pantheist like you should know this, surely?[1]

Rain (Robyn Ferrell)

Just as traditional religions celebrate the various points of the human life cycle – birth, puberty, marriage, death –

351

pantheists can celebrate in addition to these the larger cycles in the environment... pantheists can validly celebrate the solar equinoxes and solstices as symbols for the Earth's relationship and dependence upon the Sun. Such annual events could represent pantheist "holidays"... a pantheist devotion might celebrate the hydrological... [and] other biogeochemical cycles.[2]

Harold W. Wood, Jr

[John] Muir overcame the "genteel" subjective idealist transcendentalism of Emerson to an even greater extent than did Thoreau, and arrived at the major generalisations of ecology by a combination of mystical intuition and close direct natural observation. His later religious orientation can easily be interpreted as a naturalistic pantheism.[3]

George Sessions

Pantheists like Lao Tzu or Spinoza do not see human life as "something independent and self-contained, but rather as an integral part of the cosmos."

[Lao Tzu's] metaphysical concepts are not independent of his humanism, but rather serve as a cosmic sanction for his social and political ideas. Although his primary concern is the demands of human life, he chooses to regard human life in its position in the cosmological whole... his concepts have the dual function of forming the basis for his cosmology and serving as a guide in human affairs.[4]

The pantheist tries to achieve the kind of accord with Unity, and integration with the cosmos, that results in well-being and happiness. Any activity that leads to this goal can legitimately be practised. However, as in most religions, the proper emphasis is more on a way of life adapted to one's world-view, rather than on particular religious practices.[5] How can such accord be established? What way of life is adapted to pantheism?

Looking to Spinoza's *Ethics* for practical instruction is little help. The *Tao Tê Ching* is better (although obscure in places), since it is meant to be a practical guide as much as a metaphysical treatise. The *Tao Tê Ching* is not definitive with respect to how pantheists should live, and various types of pantheism diverge from it considerably. However, it does depict a way of life consonant with pantheism generally – including Spinoza's. By examining

352

a particular account of how pantheists should live, one can also get a general idea of ways of life suited to a pantheistic world-view.

According to Young and Ames, "the very essence of the *Tao Tê Ching*" is the idea of "complying with nature through non-action" (*wu-wei*) (p. 15).[6] Non-action does not mean literally doing nothing, but rather doing nothing contrary to one's natural or original nature.

> [Non-action] refers to an attitude of allowing a given phenomenon to develop freely in accord with its particular situation and its particular natural tendencies, without imposing any form of external interference ... The concept of non-action means according with nature, without attempting to augment it with the artificial ... The dissension and contention continually apparent in the ... world are manifestations of its incompatibility with nature ... it is only when the myriad things return to their original root and preserve vacuity and tranquillity that they are consistent with nature ... The original state of the myriad things is one of "vacuity" and "tranquillity", and he [Lao Tzu] advocates a return to this state ... [Lao Tzu] seeks to guarantee the complete realisation of the individual with the qualification that this individual does not encroach upon the development of others ... By developing according to what is natural, we not only realise our full human potential, but further, we do not interfere with the cosmic harmony.
>
> (pp. 15–17, 25, 45)[7]

"Vacuity" does not mean empty and devoid of all things. As used to describe the metaphysical Tao it means that it has unlimited potential and creative power. Young and Ames, and other modern commentators, interpret non-action (*wu-wei*) as compatible with undertaking a great deal of action and instituting all sorts of policies. But this may just be a predilection on their part to interpret the *Tao Tê Ching* as consonant with their own contemporary world-views and political ideals. Lao Tzu's "non-action" may literally mean more non-action and *laissez-faire* than some interpreters grant; and it may even mean more "non-action" than makes sense.

The Tao manifests itself in the phenomenal world in the form of a system of self-regulated principles or natural laws that ensure

things develop in certain ways. "These principles can be extended
to serve as a pattern for human conduct" (p. 8). To comply with
nature through "non-action" one must discern and then emulate
these principles. There are only a few main ones. One is called
the "Principle of Circular Movement."[8] "Circularity is the movement of the Tao" (*Tao Tê Ching*, XL). Things return to their
point of origin. There is also "The Law of Antithetical Rotation."
Things can only come into being though their antitheses.
"Hence, being and non-being give birth to each other; Difficult
and easy complete each other; Long and short form each other;
High and low lean on each other; Sound and echo are harmoni-
ous with each other; And before and after follow each other"
(*Tao Tê Ching*, II). Understanding these principles is essential to
understanding how to live. Lao Tzu "encourages man to observe
a given phenomenon . . . not only in terms of its apparent aspects,
but also in terms of its seemingly latent potential as a casual
factor for an antithetical situation." When something reaches
its limit it "reverts to its original form and revolves to form its
opposite." Among the antithetical states that require understanding are masculinity and femininity; being first and being last etc.
Lao Tzu "urges man to preserve femininity rather than display
masculinity, to seek the last place rather than contend for the
first" (pp. 10–11). This is how one achieves tranquillity and overcomes those who display properties antithetical to the ones Lao
Tzu commends.

Lao Tzu's principal mode of practising pantheism is best
explained as a way of life that emulates the principles of the
manifest Tao. But this does not rule out more specific modes of
practice. Worship is not suitable, and indeed, Lao Tzu repudiates
worship and religious rites generally. But meditation remains a
possibility. The purpose of meditation is to achieve a certain state
of mind – one that has both affective and cognitive aspects. The
meditator not only aims to achieve tranquillity (peace) etc., but
also to attain knowledge about oneself and objective reality. Yet,
even the non-theistic traditions that employ meditation as a principal form of practice do not rely on it exclusively. It is not
enough to just meditate, just as in theistic traditions it is never
enough to just worship. The way a person lives, morally speaking,
is also relevant.[9] Meditation is, in part, a preparation for action
based on knowledge; and it is efficacious in different ways

depending on the moral and "spiritual" development of the individual.

This analysis of how pantheism is to be practised has thus far been focused on some of the main principles of Taoism. I turn now to a speculative consideration of a few of the more concrete issues relating to the practice of pantheism and the kind of life it involves.

In the view of both Harold Wood Jr and George Sessions, "Nature" – which appears to be equated with the "Great Outdoors" – has pride of place in a pantheistic world-view and ethos. It is assumed that pantheists are nature lovers, if not nature mystics. This view of pantheists as naturalists and rural "outdoor" people as opposed to urban city dwellers is common – even a stereotype. This is clear in Wood's "statement of faith for the adherents of modern pantheism." He says "Pantheists derive their fundamental religious experience through their personal relationship with the Universe, seeking to improve their relationship with the natural world as their fundamental religious responsibility."[10] Owen's sentiments are similar to those of Wood and Sessions. He says,

> Pantheism gives rational confirmation to the sense of unity with Nature which so many people . . . have experienced. From the most primitive vegetation rites to the most sophisticated poetry there is a vast and varied testimony to the fact that the human mind has a spontaneous tendency to feel a oneness with natural phenomena, and to see in them a manifestation of the Spirit in which they too participate. This feeling and this vision constitute a perennial strand in "natural piety".[11]

There is a rationale, however, to the "rational confirmation" of the "natural piety" Owen describes. A principal reason for the pantheist's stress on participation in Nature is that anthropocentricism is seen as incompatible with a proper recognition of Unity. It is seen as undermining the cosmocentric perspective required by pantheistic ethics, and a pantheistic way of life; as antithetical to the pantheist world-view and ethos. Involvement in nature serves to de-emphasise the anthropocentrism pantheism believes endemic to theism and seriously detrimental to well-being and Unity.[12]

This characterisation of pantheists as loving nature and as having to establish a relationship to things natural is what principally informs vague views as to how pantheism is to be practised – especially among contemporary pantheists. Practice becomes an expression of a love of nature – usually by "communing" with it. It is no wonder pantheism is often regarded as little more than a type of nature mysticism. But for the pantheist, "love" of nature is expressed primarily in ethical rather than in mystical or quasi-mystical terms. Pantheistic ethics focuses on how to live and on the individual's relation to the natural order – an order of which others are a part. One's own well-being and that of others depends on it. Since nature is taken as intrinsically valuable, and because relating appropriately to nature presupposes its preservation and protection, nature in general and environmental issues in particular are important to the pantheist. Like many others, pantheists see their well-being as intrinsically connected to the wider environment as well as to things more immediate (e.g. employment).

To think as Wood does puts the urban person at a *religiours* disadvantage. Without denying the significance Nature has for the pantheist (e.g. as a standard of behaviour, and as an object of meditation conducive to a "right" state of mind), is there reason to believe that a pantheist who prefers an urban to a pastoral setting, and who likes technology, is risking spiritual depravity? Does the pantheist have a duty to spend time in natural settings if they prefer the city? (Or is Wood simply talking about the kind of environmental concern a pantheist should have – regardless of whether they like the outdoors?) Technology is associated essentially with the urban, and the pantheist may see much of it, or too much of it, as inimical to Unity and well-being. Technology is devalued when it is taken as undermining the kinds of value pantheism seeks to promote. Technology (people using it) despoils the environment. At any rate, since the world is increasingly urban, for pantheism to be viable it will have to be possible to practise it in cities.

Yet, even if the pantheist acknowledges that "urban pantheism" is possible, that cities are (ideally) communities capable of sustaining pantheism and that technology is not intrinsically opposed to Unity, pantheism will still emphasise interaction with

Nature. The reasons for this are empirical. The idea is that if people have very little contact with Nature and little opportunity to experience the kinds of (good) things people often do experience in certain kinds of natural settings (i.e. the "natural piety" Owen describes) then they are less likely to have the kind of ethos necessary to render the pantheistic world-view intellectually acceptable. It is one thing to prefer an urban to a pastoral setting most of the time. But if you never sit in the woods, or look at the ocean or sky (i.e. if you never get out of your "own little world"), pantheism will be difficult.

Wood appears to say that attending to nature engenders a spiritual state that is just not to be had elsewhere. Yet, a person who prefers city street life may claim there is a bias towards the non-human in a pantheist's exclusive insistence on Nature. Why can't cities – themselves "natural" in a way – also be conducive to the practice of pantheism? Perhaps cities could be if they and many of their people were not as neglected and abused as much as some wilderness areas (if the comparison makes any sense). "God's country" for the pantheist denotes urban as well as pastoral settings – indeed it extends to the suburbs. Given the existence of a divine Unity one should not regard all personal preferences (e.g. for a garden) as cosmically endorsed.

If the goal of pantheism is a way of life and a kind of "state," then any locale that is generally conducive to promoting those goals is acceptable. This may have more to do with the kind of urban or rural setting one lives in than just whether the setting is urban or rural. In the quotation at the beginning of this chapter Robyn Ferrell suggests that what is crucial to attaining the relevant state of mind is itself essentially a state of mind. This is something an undue concern with setting can inhibit. But where one lives affects one's state of mind, and some cities may prove better habitats for pantheists than others. What is conducive to the practice of pantheism in one case might not be in another, and the form that practice takes may be more relative to individuals than theistic traditions allow. As in other religions, both intellectual and non-intellectual approaches are possible.

In terms of its practice, one of the striking things about pantheism is that it has not produced a church or any kind of organisation engaged in overseeing its practice. Apparently a community of pantheists is not necessary for the practice of pantheism. This is either a historical accident or it has to do with structural features of pantheism. Although it is unlikely (impossible really) that it is an accident, I am not confident that I can explain this lack of a religious organisation except in general terms. Pantheists (like many theists) tend to regard Churches and religious leaders with suspicion. The kind of orientation that the pantheist seeks *vis-à-vis* the Unity is not taken to be something a church can facilitate. The mediation churches provide is seen as superfluous or harmful – just as it has been by many mystics. Organised religions are seen as divisive and exclusivist, and churches perhaps are seen as essentially anthropocentric. It is for these kinds of reasons that there never has been a pantheistic church and probably never will be.

Returning briefly to George Lindbeck's distinction between experiential and cultural-linguistic models of religion: Lindbeck says,

> In a cultural-linguistic outlook ... it is just as hard to think of religions as it is to think of cultures or languages as having a single generic or universal experiential essence of which particular religions – or cultures or languages – are varied manifestations or modifications. One can in this outlook no more be religious in general than one can speak language in general.[13]

While it may be true (and I doubt it is) that one cannot be "religious in general" it is not the case that in the cultural-linguistic model of religion one cannot regard religions as having a common experiential basis. Where "experiential essence" is suitably interpreted this is exactly what Geertz and Berger (i.e. cultural model advocates) take to be the case. Lindbeck is right in claiming that in the cultural-linguistic model religion is not taken to be founded on, or a response to, a fundamental religious experience such as Otto's numinous. But religion does arise from common experience. People are born, they eat, sexually reproduce and die, and religion is intrinsically connected with these experiences.

What makes a religion a religion in either Geertz's or Berger's account is that it addresses fundamental human concerns. It is a commonplace in anthropology that efforts to understand alien cultures should focus on their attitudes towards these common experiential categories (i.e. birth, death etc.).[14] This is not antithetical to the cultural-linguistic model, but an ingredient of it. "The Problem of Meaning" is a complex set of issues that religious traditions address both in ways unique to themselves and in ways similar to other traditions. Pantheism is no different from any other religion in this regard. It addresses the same kinds of questions that other traditions address, and it functions in the same ways.

What is pantheism? I have avoided giving a definite account of any particular type of pantheism. My aim has not been to construct a new pantheism, or to examine any particular pantheistic system in detail. Instead, I have attempted to give a normative account of the general nature of pantheism abstracted from various pantheistic views. Pantheism has also been compared with theism, since *part* of the reason some pantheists have for adopting pantheism is their rejection of theism.

Pantheism is the belief in an all-inclusive divine Unity. It is the belief in a unifying principle or force of "goodness," or something like goodness, that is all-pervasive. Everything is, in an important sense, related to, and even part of, everything else; and this is seen as crucial to how one should live. Pantheism is not anthropocentric and it does not involve a belief in a personal deity or higher consciousness. But like theism it takes seriously the view that there is more to the world than can be accounted for, even in principle, by the natural sciences. That is one of the few places where pantheism and theism concur. Like all religions, it provides a distinctive world-view and ethos. Pantheism bases its account of how to live, in general terms, on its account of reality. From a contemporary perspective, one of the most significant things about pantheism is that it rejects the dominant secularised world-view while also rejecting theism. Pantheists believe in some higher unifying force or principle – but not in a theistic God. This world-view remains a "religious" one nonetheless.

Many interesting questions concerning the practice of pantheism remain. Some of these are less whimsical then others, and some are more important than they may at first appear. Chief among the central issues is "What are the ethics of pantheism and how are they to be practised?" To a large extent this will determine how pantheism is to be taken up.

Pantheism remains a fertile subject for natural theology. Natural theologians have hardly approached it. Pantheism should be of interest to those in the philosophy of religion who seek a way out of the constrictions (often institutional ones) put upon them by working within the confines of classical theism, especially as the issues relating to classical theism have been taken up by the contemporary christian conservative analytic philosophers of religion. There are interesting issues to be addressed in the philosophy of religion, and methods of investigating them – even in the analytic philosophy of religion – in addition to the ones currently discussed by the (mostly) contemporary christian theists and their dwindling critics.[15] Perhaps pantheism will be of most interest to those who do not believe in a theistic God, yet are concerned with many of the traditional questions that natural theologians have always asked, and that religious traditions necessarily address. Pantheism remains the classical religious alternative to theism.

Pantheism's lack of "success" in worldly terms on the religion market may have to do with the fact that it is antithetical to any power structure; the kind, for example, that is found in the Catholic church. Pantheism cannot be "used." If so, then even though pantheism may be more profoundly religious than institutionalised religions, it may be doomed to ineffectiveness because it cannot manipulate power – it cannot "play the game." Wielding various kinds of power has been a feature of religion from its most "primitive" to its most sophisticated levels – a feature churches themselves can generally not control. Pantheism negates the power struggle through its emphasis on Unity. It refuses to see religion in political and hierarchical terms. Pantheism is the religion that tries most completely to escape the limitations created by anthropocentric models of religion that create god in man's image.[16]

NOTES

1 H. P. Owen, *Concepts of Deity* (London: Macmillan, 1971), p. 73.
2 See Chapter 1, note 1.
3 Stephen Frosh, *The Politics of Psychoanalysis* (London: Macmillan, 1987), p. 13.

6.1 Goal: relationship or state?

1 Ralph Waldo Emerson, *Nature* (1836). Cf. Emerson's essay "Self Reliance."

> In what prayers do men allow themselves! That which they call a holy office is not so much as brave and manly. Prayer looks abroad and asks for some foreign addition to come through some foreign virtue, and loses itself in endless mazes of natural and supernatural, and meditorial and miraculous. Prayer that craves a particular commodity, anything less than all good, is vicious. Prayer is the contemplation of the facts of life from the highest point of view. It is the soliloquy of a beholding and jubilant soul. It is the spirit of God pronouncing his works good. But prayer as a means to effect a private end is meanness and theft. It supposes dualism and not unity in nature and consciousness. As soon as the man is at one with God, he will not beg. He will then see prayer in all action. The prayer of the farmer kneeling in his field to weed it, the prayer of the rower kneeling with the stroke of his oar, are true prayers heard throughout nature, though for cheap ends.

2 Owen says "Spinoza's 'intellectual love of God' . . . is simply the mind's desire for self-identification with the determined order of things." What does "simply" mean here? Even if this oversimplification were true, why would it undermine religious practice unless the *sina qua non* of all such practice is "the establishment of a personal relationship between God and man" – a relationship that involves prayer and salvation?

   If "Stoic 'Providence' is another word for 'Fate'," then neither term should be taken as an explanation for what is simply materially determined.

3 The only similarity between Theravada Buddhism and pantheism I draw on here is that both deny theism. Theravada Buddhism is as different from pantheism as it is from theism. Not only does it deny the existence of the divine Unity, it denies the existence of any god – whether personal or non-personal. Its conception of ultimate reality is utterly different from the theist's or pantheist's. Some forms of Buddhism may be closer to pantheism than to theism, but Theravada is not.

4 Ninian Smart, *The Concept of Worship* (London: Macmillan, 1972), pp. 23–4. He describes *nirvana* as "that state in which there is complete serenity and insight and which constitutes liberation from the otherwise unending round of rebirth" (p. 23).

5 However, "Unity," unlike *nirvana*, is not a "state of an individual" – although individuals are part of the Unity. There are problems in describing *nirvana* as a state of an individual since in attaining *nirvana* one's "self" or individuality, and everything else's, is transcended or seen as illusory.

6 Cf. Owen, *Concepts of Deity*, p. 66. "Although Spinoza's system is so speculative he intended it to have a practical effect." Spinoza says,

361

> It [his doctrine of God] teaches us to act solely according to the decree of God and to be partakers of the divine nature, the more according as our actions are more perfect and more and more understand God. This doctrine, therefore, besides bringing complete peace to the mind, has this advantage also, that it teaches us in what consists our greatest happiness or blessedness, namely, in the knowledge of God, by which we are induced to do those things which love and piety persuade us.
>
> (*Ethics*, part 2, last paragraph)

7 Spinoza denies that nature or God has any goal. "Nature has no end set before it, and ... all final causes are nothing but human fictions" (*Ethics* I, Appendix). God has no goal since "neither intellect nor will pertain to God's nature" (*Ethics* I.17, Scholium) and so "God does not produce any effect by freedom of the will" (*Ethics* I.32, Corollary I). Furthermore, since "particular things are nothing but affections of God's attributes, or modes by which God's attributes are expressed in a certain and determinate way" (*Ethics* I.25, Corollary) everything that occurs, necessarily occurs and people have no free will. "Men are deceived in that they think themselves free ... an opinion which consists only in this, that they are conscious of their actions and ignorant of the causes by which they are determined" (*Ethics* II.35, Scholium). Nevertheless, according to Spinoza, "the more we understand things ... the more we know God" (*Ethics* V.25), and happiness supervenes upon such knowledge. "The greatest virtue of the Mind is to know God ... and consequently ... the greatest Joy" (*Ethics* V.27, Demonstration). Therefore, in Spinoza's account, an individual's goal can be described as "happiness" through knowledge of God. Quotations are from *The Collected Works of Spinoza*, vol. 1, edited and translated by Edwin Curley (Princeton: Princeton University Press, 1985).

Making sense of this happiness as a goal is problematic since everything, including what one knows, comes to know and tries to know, is determined. For the Spinozistic pantheist the practice of pantheism involves the intellectual love of God through knowledge of particulars and of why things must happen the way they do. One can try to increase one's knowledge of the necessity of things, and it may seem as if one's effort is rewarded, but this just reflects an ignorance of determining causes. Both the "trying" and the results of one's effort are determined. In Spinoza's account, or one reading of it, pantheism is essentially a metaphysical belief that cannot be practised if this means doing or thinking anything other than what one is already doing and thinking. The fact that such determinism makes no practical difference *at all* to what one feels or what one does (i.e. one still tries to accomplish things and believes and feels things might be different if not for one's efforts) makes no difference. Nothing could happen any differently than it does happen.

Although Spinoza is, by far, the most prominent "pantheist" – it may be that he is not really a pantheist at all. Indeed, pantheism rejects the determinism that is an essential part of Spinoza's system. Pantheists disagree with the fundamental nature of the Unity that Spinoza describes *if* its nature is interpreted primarily in terms of substance.

8 Ch'en Ku-ying, *Lao Tzu, Text, Notes, and Comments*, translated and adapted by Rhett Y. W. Young and Roger T. Ames (Republic of China: Chinese Materials Center, 1981), pp. 15–17 of the introduction by Young and Ames.

9 Cf. Steven T. Katz (ed.) *Mysticism and Religious Traditions* (Oxford: Oxford University Press, 1983). The idea that mystical experience is univocal and can be understood out of the context of the tradition in which it occurs is disputed in some of these essays.

10 Anthony O'Hear, *Experience, Explanation and Faith* (Boston: Routledge & Kegan Paul, 1984), pp. 248–9.

11 To paraphrase the founder of The Living Theater: "I'm not free until the person who picks my bananas is free."

6.2 What to Do

1 Robyn Ferrell, *The Weather and Other Gods* (Sydney: Francis Allen, 1990), p. 156. "Rain" is the name of the character in the novel who is speaking.

2 Harold W. Wood, Jr, "Modern Pantheism as an Approach to Environmental Ethics," *Environmental Ethics*, 7 (1985), pp. 159–60.

3 George Sessions, "Spinoza and Jeffers on Man in Nature," *Inquiry*, 20 (1977), p. 517.

4 Ku-ying, *Lao Tzu, Text, Notes, and Comments*, pp. 1–2 of the introduction by Young and Ames. This, incidentally, is a good example of Geertz's analysis of religion. Page numbers in the text refer to this introduction.

5 To reiterate Geertz's view: "In religious belief and practice a group's ethos is rendered intellectually reasonable by being shown to represent a way of life ideally adapted to the actual state of affairs the world view describes, while the world view is rendered emotionally convincing by being presented as an image of an actual state of affairs peculiarly well-arranged to accommodate such a way of life." "Religion as a Cultural System," in his *The Interpretation of Cultures* (New York: Basic Books, 1973), pp. 89–90.

6 "In acting according to 'non-action', There is nothing which is not properly administered" (*Tao Tê Ching*, III). "Therefore, the Sage states: I remain non-active And the people are transformed of their own accord; I do not intervene And the people are prosperous of their own accord; I cherish tranquility And the people are rectified of their own accord; I am without desires And the people return to their natural genuineness of their own accord" (*Tao Tê Ching*, LVII). The translations are by Young and Ames.

7 Young and Ames claim that "the phrases which refer to 'complying

with nature' do not imply a natural realm with an objective existence, but rather indicate a state in which there is no imposition of forced controls and in which things are allowed to pusure their natural course of development" (p. 18). While "complying with nature" does indicate a state of non-interference, I think it does also indicate a natural realm with objective existence. The Tao informs or is constitutive of an objective natural realm. Since Young and Ames interpret the Tao as a metaphysical reality that actually exists, I do not see why they do not think "complying with nature" does not "imply a natural realm with an objective existence."

8 The names of the principles are Young and Ames's. Much of their introductory essay is devoted to explaining these principles.

9 Pursuing a moral life must be part of religious practice in pantheism, just as it is in the practice in other religions. Moral reasoning is intrinsic to religious reasoning in general. It is not, however, primarily, or even nearly, all of what religion is about – as Ronald Green claims. Green says, "religions are primarily moved by rational moral concerns and . . . ethical theory provides the single most powerful methodology for understanding religious belief." Ronald Green, *Religion and Moral Reason* (Oxford: Oxford University Press, 1988), p. 228. I discuss Green's thesis in "Deep Structure and The Comparative Philosophy of Religion," *Religious Studies*, 28 (1992), pp. 387–99.

10 Universal Pantheist Society, *Pantheism and Earthkeeping* (Big Pine, Calif.: Universal Pantheist Society, 1976), p. 3.

11 Owen, *Concepts of Deity*, p. 69.

12 Cf. Sessions, "Spinoza and Jeffers on Man in Nature," p. 521 n. 34. Sessions quotes Georges Santayana, "The Genteel Tradition in American Philosophy," in *Winds of Doctrine* (New York: Scribner's, 1926), pp. 186–215.

> A Californian whom I have recently had the pleasure of meeting observed that, if the philosophers had lived among your mountains their systems would have been different from what they are. Certainly, I should say, very different from what those systems are which the European genteel tradition has handed down since Socrates; for these systems are egotistical; directly or indirectly they are anthropocentric, and inspired by the conceited notion that man, or human reason, or the human distinction between good and evil, is the center and pivot of the universe. That is what the mountain and the woods should make you at least ashamed to assert . . . it is the yoke of this genteel tradition itself that these primeval solitudes lift from your shoulders. They suspend your forced sense of your own importance and not merely as individuals, but even as men. They allow you, in one happy moment, at once to play and to worship, to take yourselves simply, humbly, for what you are, and to salute the wild, indifferent, non-censorious infinity of nature.
>
> (p. 214)

Cf. p. 528 n. 66. Sessions quotes Robert Brophy: "Underneath their *mythoi* (the particularised, humanised plots) Jeffers stories are primarily rituals celebrating the life-pattern of a pantheistic universe which alone (constituting the *only* subject) is worthy of praise and art and life-dedication . . . Protagonists act not for themselves, but for the underlying divine rhythm of all being." Robert J. Brophy, *Robinson Jeffers: Myth, Ritual and Symbol in His Narrative Poems* (Cleveland: Case Western Reserve University Press, 1973), pp. 195–301. Jeffers is less concerned with relating to Nature in ways depicted by Owen or Wood. His pantheism is more inclusive, and more directly concerned with the metaphysical dimension of Unity and one's part in it.

13 George Lindbeck, *The Nature of Doctrine* (Philadelphia: Westminster, 1984), p. 23.

14 Cf. Peter Winch, *The Idea of a Social Science and Its Relation to Philosophy* (London: Routledge & Kegan Paul, 1958).

15 That debate now takes place almost wholly within those circles (i.e. by other believers) is cause for concern. The fact that there are few involved in contemporary analytic philosophy of religion outside the fold of contemporary christian analytic philosophy is not healthy even for the latter.

16 I have borrowed ideas in this paragraph from Kim Grant, and I thank her for valuable discussion.

BIBLIOGRAPHY

Adams, Robert M. "Must God Create the Best?" In T. V. Morris, (ed.) *The Concept of God.* Oxford: Oxford University Press, 1987, pp. 91–106.

Adams, Robert M. *The Virtue of Faith and Other Essays in Philosophical Theology.* Oxford: Oxford University Press, 1987.

Adams, Robert M. "A Modified Divine Command Theory of Ethical Wrongness." In R. M. Adams, *The Virtue of Faith and Other Essays in Philosophical Theology.* Oxford: Oxford University Press, 1987.

Adams, Robert M. "Divine Command Metaethics Modified Again." In R. M. Adams, *The Virtue of Faith and Other Essays in Philosophical Theology.* Oxford: Oxford University Press, 1987.

Adams, Marilyn McCord, and Adams, Robert M. (eds) *The Problem of Evil.* Oxford: Oxford University Press, 1990.

Alexander, H. B. "Worship." In James Hastings (ed.) *Encyclopedia of Religion and Ethics.* Edinburgh: Clark, 1980–26.

Alston, William. "Religion: Psychological Explanation of." In Paul Edwards (ed.) *Encyclopedia of Philosophy.* New York: Macmillan and Free Press, 1967, vol. 7, pp. 148–50.

Appleton, George (ed.) *Oxford Book of Prayer.* Oxford: Oxford University Press, 1986.

Armstrong, A. H. *The Architecture of the Intelligible Universe in the Philosophy of Plotinus.* Cambridge: Cambridge University Press, 1940.

Armstrong, A.H. "The Apprehension of Divinity in the Self and Cosmos in Plotinus." In R. Baine Harris (ed.) *The Significance of Neoplatonism.* Norfolk: International Society for Neoplatonic Studies, 1976, pp. 187–98.

Attfield, Robin. *The Ethics of Environmental Concern.* Oxford: Blackwell, 1983.

Audi, Robert. *Rationality, Religious Belief and Commitment.* Ithaca: Cornell University Press, 1986.

Aurelius, Marcus. *The Meditations,* translated by G. M. A. Grube. Indianapolis: Hackett, 1983.

Baier, Kurt. "The Meaning of Life." In E. D. Klemke (ed.) *The Meaning of Life.* New York: Oxford University Press, 1981, pp. 81–117.

Barnard, Frederick M. "Spinozism." In Paul Edwards (ed.) *Encyclopedia of Philosophy*. New York: Macmillan and Free Press, 1967, vol. 5, pp. 541–4.

Bayle, Pierre. *Historical and Critical Dictionary: Selections*, translated by Richard Popkin. Indianapolis: Bobbs-Merrill, 1965.

Bedell, Gary. "Bradley's Monistic Idealism." *Thomist*, 34 (1970), pp. 568–79.

Bedell, Gary. "Theistic Realism and Monistic Idealism." *Thomist*, 35 (1971), pp. 661–83.

Bellow, Saul. *Mr. Sammler's Planet*. New York: Viking, 1969.

Bennett, Jonathan. *A Study of Spinoza's Ethics*. Indianapolis: Hackett, 1984.

Berger, Peter. *The Sacred Canopy: Elements of a Sociological Theory of Religion*. New York: Doubleday, 1967.

Berman, David. *A History of Atheism in Britain: From Hobbes to Russell*. London: Croom Helm, 1988.

Bradley, F.H. *Appearance and Reality*. Oxford: Clarendon Press, 1930.

Brennan, Andrew. *Thinking About Nature: An Investigation of Nature, Value and Ecology*. London: Routledge, 1988.

Bronson, Bertrand. "Walking Stewart," *University of California Publications in English*, xiv. Berkeley and Los Angeles: University of California Press, 1943.

Brueckner, Anthony L. and Fischer, John Martin. "Why is Death Bad?" *Philosophical Studies*, 50 (1986), pp. 213–21.

Burch, George Bosworth. "Principles and Problems of Monistic Vedanta." *Philosophy East and West*, 11–12 (1961–3), pp. 231–7.

Butler, Clark. "Panpsychism: A Restatement of the Genetic Argument." *Idealistic Studies*, 8 (1978), pp. 33–9.

Byrne, P. A. "Berkeley, Scientific Realism and Creation." *Religious Studies*, 20 (1984), pp. 453–64.

Callicott, J.B. "Traditional American and Traditional Western European Attitudes Towards Nature." In R. Elliot and A. Gare (eds) *Environmental Philosophy*. Milton Keynes: Open University Press, 1983.

Carman, John. *The Theology of Ramanuja*. New Haven: Yale University Press, 1974.

Chan, Wing-tsit. *A Source Book in Chinese Philosophy*. Princeton: Princeton-University Press, 1963.

Charlton, William. "Spinoza's Monism." *Philosophical Review*, 90 (October 1981), pp. 503–29.

Cherniss, H. F. "The Characteristics and Effects of Pre-Socratic Philosophy." In D. Furley and R. Allen (eds) *Studies in Presocratic Philosophy*. London: Routledge & Kegan Paul, 1970, vol. I.

Chryssides, George D. "Subject and Object in Worship." *Religious Studies*, 23 (1987), pp. 367–75.

Coffin, Arthur B. *Robinson Jeffers: Poet of Inhumanism*. Wisconsin: University of Wisconsin Press, 1971.

Copleston, F. C. "Pantheism in Spinoza and the German Idealists." *Philosophy*, 21 (1946), pp. 42–56.

Copleston, F. C. "Man, Transcendence, and the Absence of God." *Thought*, 43 (1968), pp. 24–38.

Copleston, F.C. *Religion and The One: Philosophies East and West*. London and Tunbridge Wells: Search Press, 1982.

Crabbe, John. *Beethoven's Empire of the Mind*. Newbury: Lovell Baines, 1982.

Crombie, I.M. *An Examination of Plato's Doctrines*. London: Routledge & Kegan Paul, 1962, vol. I.

Cupitt, Don. *Taking Leave of God*. London: SCM, 1980.

Cupitt, Don. *Only Human*. London: SCM, 1985.

Dauenhauer, Bernard P. "Some Aspects of Language and Time in Ritual Worship." *International Journal for Philosophy of Religion*, 6 (1975), pp. 54–62.

Davies, Paul. *God and The New Physics*. London and New York: Penguin, 1990. First published 1983.

Demos, Raphael. "Types of Unity According to Plato and Aristotle." *Philosophy and Phenomenological Research*, 6 (1945–6), pp. 534–45.

Deutsch, Eliot. *Advaita Vedānta: A Philosophical Reconstruction*. Honolulu: East–West Center Press, 1969.

Donagan, Alan. *Spinoza*. Brighton: Harvester Wheatsheaf, 1988.

Dretske, Fred. "The Metaphysics of Freedom." *Canadian Journal of Philosophy*, 22 (1992), pp. 1–14.

Edwards, Paul. "Panpsychism." *Encyclopedia of Philosophy*. New York: Macmillan and Free Press, 1967, vol. 6, pp. 22–31.

Emerson, Ralph Waldo. *Nature*, 1836.

Evans-Pritchard, E. E. *Theories of Primitive Religion*. Oxford: Oxford University Press, 1965.

Farber, Marvin. "Types of Unity and the Problem of Monism." *Philosophy and Phenomenological Research*, 4 (1943–4), pp. 37–58.

Feldman, Fred. "Some Puzzles About the Evil of Death." *Philosophical Review*, 100 (1991), pp. 205–27.

Ferré, Nels F. S. *Living God of Nowhere and Nothing*. Philadephia: Westminster, 1966.

Ferrell, Robyn. *The Weather and Other Gods*. Sydney: Frances Allen, 1990.

Feuerbach, Ludwig. *Principles of the Philosophy of the Future*, translated by Manfred Vogel. Indianapolis: Hackett, 1986.

Fletcher, Joseph. *Situation Ethics*. Philadelphia: Westminster, 1966.

Flew, Anthony. "Are Ninian Smart's Temptations Irresistible?" *Philosophy*, 37 (1962), pp. 57–60.

Flew, Anthony (ed.) *Body, Mind and Death*. New York: Macmillan, 1964.

Flew, Anthony. *God and Philosophy*. London: Hutchinson, 1966.

Flew, Anthony. "Immortality." *Encyclopedia of Philosophy*. New York: Macmillan and Free Press, 1967, vol. 4, pp. 139–50.

Ford, Marcus P. "Pluralistic Pantheism?" *Southern Journal of Philosophy*, 17 (1979), pp. 155–61.

Ford, Marcus P. "William James: Panpsychist and Metaphysical Realist." *Transactions of the Charles Peirce Society*, 17 (1981), pp. 158–70.

Forman, M. B. (ed.) *The Letters of John Keats*. London: Oxford University Press, 4th edn, 1952.

Forrest, Peter. "Some Varieties of Monism." In R. W. Perrett (ed.) *Indian Philosophy of Religion*. Dordrecht: Kluwer, 1989, pp. 75–91.

Francks, Richard. "Omniscience, Omnipotence and Pantheism." *Philosophy*, 54 (1979), pp. 395–9.

Frankena, W. K. *Ethics*. Englewood Cliffs: Prentice Hall, 1963.

Freddoso, Alfred J. (ed.) *The Existence and Nature of God*. Notre Dame: University of Notre Dame Press, 1983.

Freud, Sigmund. *The Future of an Illusion*. New York: Norton, 1961.

Frosh, Stephen. *The Politics of Psychoanalysis*. London: Macmillan, 1987.

Funkenstein, Amos. *Theology and the Scientific Imagination from the Middle Ages to the Seventeenth Century*. Princeton: Princeton University Press, 1986.

Furley, D. and Allen, R. (eds) *Studies in Presocratic Philosophy*. London: Routledge & Kegan Paul, 1970, vol. I.

Geertz, Clifford. "Religion as a Cultural System." In his *The Interpretation of Cultures*. New York: Basic Books, 1973, ch. 4, pp. 87–125.

Geertz, Clifford. "Ethos, World View, and the Analysis of Sacred Symbols." In his *The Interpretation of Cultures*. New York: Basic Books, 1973, ch. 5, pp.126–41.

Green, Ronald, M. *Religion and Moral Reason*. Oxford: Oxford University Press, 1988.

Guthrie, W. K. C. *A History of Greek Philosophy*. Cambridge: Cambridge University Press, 1962, vol. I.

Hamlyn, D.W. *Metaphysics*. Cambridge: Cambridge University Press, 1984.

Hampshire, Stuart. *Spinoza*. London: Penguin, 1951.

Hardie, W. F. R. "Aristotle's Doctrine that Virtue is a 'Mean.' " In Jonathan Barnes, Malcolm Schofield and Richard Sorabji (eds) *Articles on Aristotle: Ethics and Politics*. London: Duckworth, 1977, pp. 33–46.

Hare, R. M. *The Language of Morals*. Oxford: Oxford University Press, 1952.

Harris, R. Baine. (ed.) *The Significance of Neoplatonism*. Norfolk: International Society for Neoplatonic Studies, 1976.

Harrison, Jonathan. "The Embodiment of Mind or What Use is Having a Body?" *Proceedings of the Aristotelian Society*, 74 (1973–4), pp. 35–55.

Hastings, James (ed.) *Encyclopedia of Religion and Ethics*. Edinburgh: Clark, 1908–26.

Hegel, G. W. F. *Lectures on the Philosophy of Religion*. Berkeley: University of California Press, 1984, vol. I.

Henderson, E. H. "Theistic Reductionism and the Practice of Worship." *International Journal for Philosophy of Religion*, 10 (1979), pp. 25–40.

Hick, John. *Evil and the God of Love*, rev. edn. New York: Harper & Row, 1978.

Hick, John. *An Interpretation of Religion*. New Haven: Yale University Press, 1989.

Hick, John. "Soul-Making and Suffering." In Marilyn McCord Adams and Robert M. Adams (eds) *The Problem of Evil*. Oxford: Oxford University Press, 1990, pp. 168–88.

Hollis, Martin and Lukes, Steven (eds) *Rationality and Relativism*. Oxford: Blackwell, 1982.

Hudson, W. Donald. "The Concept of Divine Transcendence." *Religious Studies*, 15 (1979), pp. 197–210.

Hume, David. *Enquiries Concerning Human Understanding and Concerning the Principles of Morals*, edited by L. A. Selby-Bigge. Oxford: Clarendon Press, 1975.

Hume, David. *The Natural History of Religion and Dialogues Concerning Natural Religion*, edited by A. Wayne Colver and John V. Price. Oxford: Clarendon Press, 1976.

Hume, David. *A Treatise of Human Nature*, edited by L. A. Selby-Bigge. Oxford: Clarendon Press, 1978.

Hunt, Murray W. "Some Remarks About the Embodiment of God." *Religious Studies*, 17 (1981), pp. 105–8.

Huxley, Aldous. *The Perennial Philosophy.* New York: Harper, 1945.

Inge, W. R. *The Philosophy of Plotinus.* London: Longman, 1928, vol. II.

Jaeger, Werner. *The Theology of the Early Greek Philosophers.* Oxford: Oxford University Press, 1947.

Jantzen, Grace. "On Worshipping an Embodied God." *Canadian Journal of Philosophy*, 8 (1978), pp. 511–19.

Jantzen, Grace. *God's World, God's Body.* Philadelphia: Westminster, 1984.

Jantzen, Grace. " 'Where Two are to Become One': Mysticism and Monism." In Godfrey Vesey (ed.) *The Philosophy in Christianity.* Cambridge: Cambridge University Press, 1989, pp. 147–66.

Jennings, Theodore W., Jr. *Beyond Theism: a Grammar of God Language.* Oxford: Oxford University Press, 1985.

Joad, C. E. M. "Monism in the Light of Recent Developments of Philosophy." *Proceedings of the Aristotelian Society*, 17 (1916–17), pp. 95–116.

Katz, Steven T. (ed.) *Mysticism and Religious Traditions.* Oxford: Oxford University Press, 1983.

Kenny, Anthony. "Aristotle on Happiness." In Jonathan Barnes, Malcolm Schofield and Richard Sorabji (eds) *Articles on Aristotle: Ethics and Politics.* London: Duckworth, 1977, pp. 25–32.

Kesarcodi-Watson, Ian. "Is Hinduism Pantheistic?" *Sophia*, 15 (1976), pp. 26–36.

Kierkegaard, Søren. *Concluding Unscientific Postscript*, translated by D. F. Swenson and W. Lowrie. Princeton: Princeton University Press, 1944.

Kierkegaard, Søren. *Fear and Trembling*, translated by W. Lowrie. Princeton: Princeton University Press, 1969.

Kim, Chin-Tai. "Transcendence and Immanence." *Journal of the American Academy of Religion*, 55 (1987), pp. 537–49.

Klemke, E. D. (ed.) *The Meaning of Life.* New York: Oxford University Press, 1981.

Kochumuttam, Thomas. "Limits of Worship in Indian Religions." *Journal of Dharma*, 3 (1978), pp. 364–72.

Kolakowski, Leszek. *Religion.* New York: Oxford University Press, 1982.

Ku-ying, Ch'en. *Lao Tzu, Text, Notes, and Comments*, translated and adapted by Rhett Y. W. Young and Roget T. Ames. Republic of China: Chinese Materials Center, 1981.

Kvanvig, Jonathan L. and McCann, Hugh J. "Divine Conservation and the Persistence of the World." In Thomas V. Morris (ed.) *Divine and Human Action.* Ithaca: Cornell University Press, 1988, pp. 13–49.

Kvastad, Nils Bjorn. "Pantheism and Mysticism." Part 1: *Sophia*, 14 (2) (1975), pp. 1–15. Part II: *Sophia*, 14 (3) (1975), pp.19–30.

Lang, Bernhard, and McDannell, Colleen. *Heaven: A History*. New Haven: Yale University Press, 1988.

Langer, Susan. *Philosophy in a New Key*. New York: Pelican Books, 1948.

Leach, E. R. *The Political Systens of Highland Burma*. London: Bell, 1954.

Leopold, Aldo. "The Land Ethic." In *A Sand County Almanac*. New York: Oxford University Press, 1949.

Leslie, John. *Value and Existence*. Oxford: Blackwell, 1979.

Leslie, John (ed.) *Physical Cosmology and Philosophy*. New York and London: Macmillan, 1990.

Levi, Neil, and Levine, Michael P. "Robinson on Berkeley: 'Bad Faith' or Naive Idealism?" *Idealistic Studies*, 22 (1992), p. 162–77.

Levine, Michael P. "Why Traditional Theism Does Not Entail Pantheism." *Sophia*, 23 (1984), pp. 13–20.

Levine, Michael P. " 'Can We Speak Literally of God?' " *Religious Studies*, 21 (1) (1985), pp. 53–9.

Levine, Michael P. "Cartesian Materialism and Conservation: Berkelean Immaterialism?" *Southern Journal of Philosophy*, 24 (1986), pp. 247–59.

Levine, Michael P. "More On 'Does Traditional Theism Entail Pantheism?' " *International Journal for Philosophy of Religion*, 20 (1986), pp. 31–5.

Levine, Michael P. "Berkeley's Theocentric Mentalism: Pantheism?" *Sophia*, 26 (1987), pp. 30–41.

Levine, Michael P. "Camus, Hare, and The Meaning of Life." *Sophia*, 27 (1988), pp. 13–30.

Levine, Michael P. "What Does Death Have to Do With the Meaning of Life?" *Religious Studies*, 24 (1988), pp. 457–65.

Levine, Michael P. *Hume and The Problem of Miracles: A Solution*. Dordrecht and Boston: Kluwer, 1989.

Levine, Michael P. "Divine Unity and Superfluous Synonymity." *Journal of Speculative Philosophy*, 4 (1990), pp. 211–36.

Levine, Michael P. "Deep Structure and the Comparative Philosophy of Religion." *Religious Studies*, 28 (1992), pp. 387–99.

Levine, Michael P. "Pantheism, Substance and Unity." *International Journal for Philosophy of Religion*, 32 (1992), pp.1–23.

Levine, Michael P. "Swinburne's Heaven: One Hell of a Place." *Religious Studies*, 29 (1993).

Levine, Michael P. "Adam's Modified Divine Command Theory of Ethics." *Sophia*, forthcoming.

Levy, Donald. "Macrocosm and Microcosm." *Encyclopedia of Philosophy*. New York: Macmillan and Free Press, 1967, vol. 5, pp. 121–5.

Lewis, H. D. *Our Experience of God*. New York: Macmillan, 1959.

Lindbeck, George A. *The Nature of Doctrine: Religion and Theology in a Postliberal Age*. Philadelphia: Westminster, 1984.

Lipner, J. J. "The World as God's 'Body': In Pursuit of Dialogue With Rāmānuja." *Religious Studies*, 20 (1984), pp. 145–61.

Lipner, J. J. *Rāmānuja: The Face of Truth*. London: Macmillan, 1985.

Liu, Shu-hsien. "The Confucian Approach to the Problem of Transcendence and Immanence." *Philosophy East and West*, 22 (1972), pp. 45–52.

Liu, Shu-hsien. "Commentary: Theism from a Chinese Perspective." *Philosophy East and West*, 28 (1978), pp. 413–18.

Lloyd, Genevieve. "Spinoza's Environmental Ethics." *Inquiry*, 23 (1980), pp. 293–311.

Lovejoy, Arthur. *The Great Chain of Being*. New York: Harper & Row, 1960.

MacGregor, David. *The Communist Ideal in Hegel and Marx*. Toronto: University of Toronto Press, 1984.

MacIntyre, Alasdair. "Pantheism." In Paul Edwards (ed.) *Encyclopedia of Philosophy*. New York: Macmillan and Free Press, 1967, vol. 5.

MacIntyre, Alasdair. "Spinoza." In Paul Edwards (ed.) *Encyclopedia of Philosophy*. New York: Macmillan and Free Press, 1967, vol. 8.

MacIntyre, Alasdair. "Is Understanding Religion Compatible with Believing?" In Bryan R. Wilson (ed.) *Rationality*. New York: Harper & Row, 1970, pp. 62–77.

Mackie, J. L. "Theism and Utopia." *Philosophy*, 37 (1962), pp. 153–8.

Mackie, J. L. *The Cement of the Universe*. Oxford: Oxford University Press, 1974.

Mackie, J. L. *The Miracle of Theism*. Oxford: Oxford University Press, 1982.

Macquarrie, John. *Thinking about God*. London: SCM, 1975.

Macquarrie, John. *In Search of Deity*, The Gifford Lectures 1983–4. London: SCM, 1984.

Mamo, Plato. "Is Plotinian Mysticism Monistic?" In R. Baine Harris (ed.) *The Significance of Neoplatonism*. Norfolk: International Society for Neoplatonic Studies, 1976, pp. 199–215.

Mann, William E. "Simplicity and Immutability in God." In Thomas V. Morris (ed.) *The Concept of God*. Oxford: Oxford University Press, 1987, pp. 253–67.

Mann, William E. "God's Freedom, Human Freedom, and God's Responsibility for Sin." In Thomas V. Morris (ed.) *Divine and Human Action*. Ithaca: Cornell University Press, 1988, pp. 182–210.

Mathews, Freya. *The Ecological Self*. London and New York: Routledge, 1990.

McCloskey, H. J. "God and Evil." *Philosophical Quarterly*, 10 (1960), pp. 97–114.

McFague, Sallie. *Models of God*. Philadelphia: Fortress Press, 1987.

McFarland, Thomas. *Coleridge and the Pantheist Tradition*. Oxford: Oxford University Press, 1969.

McGinn, Colin. *The Problem of Consciousness*. Oxford: Blackwell, 1991.

Melville, Herman. *Moby-Dick*. London: Penguin, 1972.

Michel, Paul Henri. *The Cosmology of Giordano Bruno*, translated by R. E. W. Maddison. Paris: Hermann; London: Methuen; Ithaca: Cornell University Press, 1973.

Mill, John Stuart. "Mr. Mansel on the Limits of Religious Thought." In Nelson Pike (ed.) *God and Evil: Readings on the Theological Problem of Evil*. Englewood Cliffs: Prentice Hall, 1964.

Min, Anselm K. "Hegel's Absolute: Transcendent or Immanent?" *Journal of Religion*, 56 (1976), pp. 61–87.

Moore, G. E. *Principia Ethica*. Cambridge: Cambridge University Press, 1965.

Morris, Thomas V. (ed.) *The Concept of God*. Oxford: Oxford University Press, 1987.

Morris, Thomas V. "Perfect Being Theology." *Noûs*, 21 (1987), pp. 19–30.

Morris, Thomas V. (ed.) *Divine and Human Action*. Ithaca: Cornell University Press, 1988.

Morris, Thomas V. (ed.) *Philosophy and the Christian Faith*. Notre Dame: University of Notre Dame Press, 1988.

Nabe, Clyde. "Transcendence and an Other World." *Sophia*, 26 (1987), pp. 2–12.

Naess, Arne. "The Shallow and the Deep, Long-range Ecology Movement." *Inquiry*, 16 (1973), pp. 95–100.

Naess, Arne. "Spinoza and Ecology." *Philosophia*, 7 (1977), pp. 45–54.

Naess, Arne. "Environmental Ethics and Spinoza's Ethics. Comments on Genevieve Lloyd's Article." *Inquiry*, 23 (1980), pp. 313–25.

Naess, Arne. "Identification as Source of Deep Ecological Attitudes." In M. Tobias (ed.) *Deep Ecology*. San Diego: Avant Books, 1983.

Naess, Arne. "The Deep Ecological Movement: Some Philosophical Aspects." *Philosophical Inquiry*, 8 (1986), pp. 10–29.

Nagel, Thomas. "Death." In his *Mortal Questions*. Cambridge: Cambridge University Press, 1979, pp. 1–10.

Nagel, Thomas. "Panpsychism." In his *Mortal Questions*. Cambridge: Cambridge University Press, 1979, ch. 3, pp. 181–95.

Nielsen, Kai. "Wittgensteinian Fideism." *Philosophy*, 42 (1967), pp. 191–209.

Nielsen, Kai. *Scepticism*. New York: Macmillan, 1973.

Nielson, Kai. *Ethics Without God*, rev. edn. Buffalo, N.Y.: Prometheus Books, 1990.

Oakes, Robert. "Classical Theism and Pantheism: A Victory for Process Theism?" *Religious Studies*, 13 (1977), pp. 167–73.

Oakes, Robert. "Does Traditional Theism Entail Pantheism?" *American Philosophical Quarterly*, 20 (1983), pp. 105–12. Reprinted in Thomas V. Morris (ed.) *The Concept of God*. Oxford: Oxford University Press, 1987, pp. 57–71.

Oakes, Robert. "Material Things: A Cartesian Conundrum." *Pacific Philosophical Quarterly*, 64 (1983), pp. 144–50.

Oakes, Robert. "Theism and Pantheism Again," *Sophia*, 24 (1985), pp. 32–7.

O'Connor, D. J. "Substance and Attribute." In Paul Edwards (ed.) *Encyclopedia of Philosophy*. New York: Macmillan and Free Press, 1967, vol. 8, pp. 36–40.

O'Hear, Anthony. *Experience, Explanation and Faith*. Boston: Routledge & Kegan Paul, 1984.

Otto, Rudolf. *Mysticism East and West*, translated by B. Bracey and R. Payne. New York: Macmillan, 1932.

Otto, Rudolf. *The Idea of the Holy*, 2nd edn. Oxford: Oxford University Press, 1950.

Outka, Gene, and Reeder, John P. Jr (eds) *Religion and Morality*. Garden City, N.Y.: Anchor, 1973.

Owen, H. P. *Concepts of Deity*. London: Macmillan, 1971.

Parkinson, G. H. R. "Hegel, Pantheism, and Spinoza." *Journal of the History of Ideas*, 38 (1977), pp. 449–59.

Passmore, John. *Man's Responsibility for Nature: Ecological Problems and Western Traditions*, 1st edn, New York: Scribner's, 1974; 2nd edn, London: Duckworth, 1980.

Peacocke, A. R. *Creation and the World of Science*. Oxford: Clarendon Press, 1979.

Penelhum, Terence. *Survival and Disembodied Existence*. London: Routledge & Kegan Paul, 1970.

Penelhum, Terence. "Divine Goodness and the Problem of Evil." In Marilyn McCord Adams and Robert M. Adams (eds) *The Problem of Evil*. Oxford: Oxford University Press, 1990.

Peterson, Michael. "Evil and Inconsistency." *Sophia*, 18 (1979), pp. 20–7.

Peterson, Michael. "Recent Work on the Problem of Evil." *American Philosophical Quarterly*, 20 (1983), pp. 321–40.

Phillips, D. Z. *The Concept of Prayer*. London: Routledge & Kegan Paul, 1965.

Phillips, D. Z. *Death and Immortality*. London: Macmillan; New York: St Martin's Press, 1970.

Pike, Nelson. *God and Evil: Readings on the Theological Problem of Evil*. Englewood Cliffs: Prentice Hall, 1964.

Pike, Nelson. *God and Timelessness*. London and New York: Routledge, 1970.

Plantinga, Alvin. "The Probabilistic Argument from Evil." *Philosophical Studies*, 35 (1979), pp. 1–53.

Plantinga, Alvin. "God, Evil and the Metaphysics of Freedom." In Marilyn McCord Adams and Robert M. Adams (eds) *The Problem of Evil*. Oxford: Oxford University Press, 1990, pp. 83–109.

Pollock, Frederick. *Spinoza, his Life and Philosophy*. London, 1880. Reprinted in the Reprint Library.

Popper, Karl. "Some Remarks on Panpsychism and Epiphenomenalism." *Dialectica*, 31 (1977), pp. 177–86.

Preus, Samuel. *Explaining Religion*. New Haven: Yale University Press, 1987.

Priestly, Joseph. *Theological and Miscellaneous Works*, John Towell Rutt. London, 1817–32; reprinted New York: Garland, 1972.

Quinn, Philip. *Divine Commands and Moral Requirements*. Oxford: Clarendon Press, 1978, ch. 1.

Quinn, Philip. "Divine Conservation and Spinozistic Pantheism." *Religious Studies*, 15 (1979), pp. 289–302.

Quinn, Philip. "Divine Conservation, Continuous Creation, and Human Action." In Alfred J. Freddoso (ed.) *The Existence and Nature of God*. Notre Dame: University of Notre Dame Press, 1983, pp. 55–79.

Quinn, Philip. "Divine Conservation, Secondary Causes, and Occasionalism." In Thomas V. Morris (ed.) *Divine and Human Action*. Cornell: Cornell University Press, 1988, pp. 50–73.

Rachels, James. "God and Human Attitudes." *Religious Studies*, 7 (1971), pp. 325–37.

Reeder, John P., Jr. *Source, Sanction and Salvation*. Englewood Cliffs: Prentice Hall, 1988.

Rees, D. A. "Greek Views of Nature and Mind." *Philosophy*, 29 (1954), pp. 99–111.

Rensch, Bernhard. "Panpsychistic Identism and its Meaning for a Universal Evolutionary Picture." *Scientia*, 112 (1977), pp. 337–47.

Rist, J. *Plotinus: The Road to Reality*. Cambridge: Cambridge University Press, 1967.

Rosenberg, Alexander. "Moral Realism and Social Science." *Midwest Studies in Philosophy*, 15 (1990), pp. 150–66.

Ross, James F. "Creation." *Journal of Philosophy*, 77 (1980), pp. 614–29.

Rotenstreich, Nathan. "Symbolism and Transcendence: On Some Philosophical Aspects of Gershom Scholem's Opus." *Review of Metaphysics*, 31 (1978), pp. 604–14.

Rowe, Christopher. "One and Many in Greek Religion." In Adolf Portman and Rudolf Ritsema (eds) *Oneness and Variety*. Leiden: E. J. Brill, 1980.

Rowe, William. "The Empirical Argument from Evil." In *Rationality, Religious Belief and Commitment*, edited by Robert Audi. Ithaca: Cornell University Press, 1986, pp. 227–47.

Rowe, William. "Evil and Theodicy." *Philosophical Topics*, 16 (1988), pp. 119–32.

Russell, Bertrand. *Why I Am Not a Christian and Other Essays*. London: George Allen & Unwin, 1975.

Russell, Bertrand. "A Free Man's Worship." In E. D. Klemke (ed.) *The Meaning of Life*. New York: Oxford University Press, 1981, pp. 55–62.

Saslaw, Shep. "Idolatry." *Sophia*, 10 (1971), pp. 14–19.

Sayre-McCord, Geoffrey (ed.) *Essays on Moral Realism*. Ithaca: Cornell University Press, 1988.

Sayre-McCord, Geoffrey. 'Introduction: The Many Faces of Moral Realism." In Geoffrey Sayre-McCord (ed.) *Essays on Moral Realism*. Ithaca: Cornell University Press, 1988.

Schlamm, Leon. "Rudolf Otto and Mystical Experience." *Religious Studies*, 27 (1991), pp. 389–98.

Schleiermacher, F. D. E. *The Christian Faith*. Edinburgh: Clark, 1928.

Schopenahuer, Arthur. "A Few Words On Pantheism." In *Essays from the Parerga and Paralipomena*, translated by T. Bailey Saunders. London: George Allen & Unwin, 1951.

Sessions, George. "Anthropocentrism and the Environmental Crisis." *Humboldt Journal of Social Relations*, 2 (Fall/Winter 1974).

Sessions, George. "Spinoza and Jeffers on Man in Nature." *Inquiry*, 20 (1977), pp. 481–528.

Siwek, Paul. "How Pantheism Resolves the Enigma of Evil." *Laval Théologique et Philosophique*, 11–12 (1955–6), pp. 213–21.

Skorupski, John. *Symbol and Theory: A Philosophical Study of Theories of*

Religion in Social Anthropology. Cambridge: Cambridge University Press, 1976.

Smart, Ninian. "Omnipotence, Evil, and Supermen." *Philosophy,* 36 (1961), pp. 188–95.

Smart, Ninian. "Probably." *Philosophy,* 37 (1962), p. 60.

Smart, Ninian. "Myth and Transcendence." *Monist,* 50 (1966), pp. 475–87.

Smart, Ninian. *The Concept of Worship.* London: Macmillan, 1972.

Smart, Ninian. "God's Body." *Union Seminary Quarterly Review,* 37 (1981–2), pp. 51–9.

Smart, Ninian. "Our Experience of the Ultimate." *Religious Studies,* 20 (1984), pp. 19–26.

Smith, Huston. "Transcendence in Traditional China." *Religious Studies,* 2 (1966), pp. 185–96.

Smith, J. A. "The Issue Between Monism and Pluralism." *Proceedings of the Aristotelian Society,* 26 (1925–6), pp. 1–24.

Smith, Quentin. "An Analysis of Holiness." *Religious Studies,* 24 (1988), pp. 511–28.

Spinoza, Baruch. *Ethics,* edited by James Gutmann. New York: Hafner, 1949.

Spinoza, Baruch. *The Collected Works of Spinoza,* translated and edited by Edwin Curley. Princeton: Princeton University Press, 1985, vol. 1.

Stokes, Michael C. *One and Many in Presocratic Philosophy.* Washington, D.C.: Center for Hellenic Studies, 1971.

Stump, Eleonore, and Kretzmann, Norman. "Eternity." In Thomas V. Morris (ed.) *The Concept of God.* Oxford: Oxford University Press, 1987, pp. 219–52.

Swinburne, Richard. *The Coherence of Theism.* Oxford: Oxford University Press, 1977.

Swinburne, Richard. *The Existence of God.* Oxford: Oxford University Press, 1979.

Swinburne, Richard. *Faith and Reason.* Oxford: Oxford University Press, 1981.

Swinburne, Richard. "A Theodicy of Heaven and Hell." In Alfred J. Freddoso (ed.) *The Existence and Nature of God.* Notre Dame: University of Notre Dame Press, 1983, pp. 37–54.

Swinburne, Richard. "Argument From the Fine-Tuning of the Universe." In John Leslie (ed.) *Physical Cosmology and Philosophy.* New York and London: Macmillan, 1990.

Tapper, Alan. *Priestley's Metaphysics.* Ph.D. Dissertation, University of Western Australia, 1987.

Taylor, Charles. *Hegel.* Cambridge: Cambridge University Press, 1975.

Taylor, Paul W. *Principles of Ethics.* Encino, Calif.: Dickenson, 1975.

Taylor, Paul W. *Respect For Nature.* Princeton: Princeton University Press, 1986.

Tillich, Paul. *Dynamics of Faith.* New York and London: Harper & Row, 1956.

Tillich, Paul. *Systematic Theology.* Chicago and London: University of Chicago Press and SCM, 1963, vols I–III.

Toland, John. *Pantheisticon.* New York and London: Garland, 1976. Reprint of 1751 edition.

Turbayne, Colin. "The Berkeley, Plato, Aristotle Connection." In Colin Turbayne (ed.) *Berkeley: Critical and Interpretative Essays.* Minnesota: University of Minnesota Press, 1982.

Van Inwagen, Peter. "The Place of Chance in a World Sustained by God." In Thomas V. Morris (ed.) *Divine and Human Action.* Ithaca: Cornell University Press, 1988, pp. 211–35.

Van Inwagen, Peter. "The Problem of Evil, the Problem of Air, and the Problem of Silence." In James Tomberlin (ed.) *Philosophical Perspectives.* California: Ridgeview, 1991, vol. 5, pp. 135–65.

Vlastos, Gregory. "Theology and Philosophy in Early Greek Thought." *Philosophical Quarterly,* 2 (1952).

Wainwright, William. "God's Body." *Journal of the American Academy of Religion,* 42 (1974), pp. 470–81.

Wainwright, William L. and Rowe, William J. (eds) *Philosophy of Religion: Selected Readings.* New York: Harcourt Brace Jovanovich, 1973. Reprinted in Thomas V. Morris (ed.) *The Concept of God.* Oxford: Oxford University Press, 1987.

Ward, Keith. "God as Creator." In Godfrey Vesey (ed.) *The Philosophy in Christianity.* Cambridge: Cambridge University Press, 1989, pp. 99–118.

Whitman, Walt. *Leaves of Grass,* First (1855) Edition, edited with an introduction by Malcolm Cowley. New York: Viking Press, 1959.

Whittaker, John H. *Matters of Faith and Matters of Principle: Religious Truth Claims and Their Logic.* Texas: Trinity University Press, 1981.

Wiggins, David. *Identity and Spatio-Temporal Continuity.* Oxford: Blackwell, 1967.

Wiggins, David. *Sameness and Substance.* Oxford: Blackwell, 1980.

Williams, Bernard. "Are Persons Bodies?" In his *Problems of the Self.* Cambridge: Cambridge University Press, 1973.

Williams, Bernard. "The Makropoulos Case." In his *Problems of the Self.* Cambridge: Cambridge University Press, 1973, ch. 6.

Wilson, Bryan R. (ed.) *Rationality.* New York: Harper & Row, 1970.

Wilson, J.G. "Transcendence and Meaning: Two Approaches." *Sophia,* 4 (1965), pp. 3–13.

Winch, Peter. *The Idea of a Social Science and Its Relation to Philosophy.* London: Routledge & Kegan Paul, 1958.

Winch, Peter. "Meaning and Religious Language." In Stuart C. Brown (ed.) *Reason and Religion.* Ithaca: Cornell University Press, 1977.

Wittgenstein, Ludwig. *Philosophical Investigations.* Oxford: Blackwell, 1958.

Wittgenstein, Ludwig. *Lectures and Conversations on Aesthetics, Psychology and Religious Belief,* edited by Cyril Barrett. Berkeley: University of California Press, 1972.

Wolfson, Abraham. *Spinoza: A Life of Reason.* New York, 1932.

Wood, Harold W., Jr. "Modern Pantheism as an Approach to Environmental Ethics." *Environmental Ethics,* 7 (1985), pp. 151–63.

NAME INDEX

SUBJECT INDEX